# irish history and culture

# irish history and culture

## aspects of a people's heritage

### edited by harold orel

THE
UNIVERSITY PRESS
OF KANSAS
Lawrence
Manhattan
Wichita

**Library of Congress Cataloging in Publication Data**
Main entry under title:

Irish history and culture.

Bibliography: p.
Includes index.
1. Ireland—Civilization—Addresses, essays,
lectures. I. Orel, Harold, 1926-
DA925.I74          941.5          75-35532
ISBN 0-7006-0136-8
ISBN 0-7006-0137-6 pbk.

# PREFACE

The sixteen essays of this volume, contributed by seven members of the faculty of the University of Kansas, are designed to explore a long, rich, and varied cultural tradition. They have been arranged chronologically, with approximately half the text concerned with events and issues significant in the nineteenth and twentieth centuries. Two contributors, Henry L. Snyder and Charles Sidman, have sketched a narrative history of Ireland from the beginnings (which are clouded by myths and tantalizingly incomplete records) to the present day. Since this history is based on a judgment that a scholarly review should avoid both apologetics and eulogy, it is deliberately noncontroversial. Moreover, the situation in Northern Ireland is a rapidly changing set of relationships. The historical chapters serve in two capacities: to explain the events that led to the emergence of Ireland as an independent nation during this century, and to provide a background essential for the understanding of the subject matter treated in the essays written by Robert Jerome Smith, Marilyn Stokstad, Kenneth C. W. Kammeyer, Norman R. Yetman, and myself.

The range of these essays is wide, for they identify major problems of concern to art historians, literary and dramatic critics, demographers, sociologists, and students of mythology and folklore. We hope that they will be judged both readable and informative, and that they will prove to be of use as readings in courses on British or Irish history, art, literature, and drama. Several of the essays are expansions and developments of ideas first tested in the classroom; all of them, taken together, will contribute to our understanding of Ireland and will encourage further reading on the subject of Irish culture.

Special thanks are due to Alexandra Mason and Georgann Eglinski of Spencer Library at the University of Kansas, who have made available to us the Special Collections of Irish materials, particularly the collection of P. S. O'Hegarty, secretary of the Irish General Post Office. These collections constitute one of the richest treasuries of Hibernian material outside of Ireland itself. In addition, Marilyn Stokstad, Henry L. Snyder, Norman R. Yetman, and Harold Orel gratefully acknowledge the assistance of the General Research Fund of the University of Kansas.

HAROLD OREL

*v*

# CONTENTS

# List of Illustrations

# IRISH MYTHOLOGY
## Robert Jerome Smith

The stories that the people of Ireland tell about themselves and their ancestors have their primary value, not in the history they may contain nor even in their literary merit (though a considerable amount of each has been found in them), but rather in their life-bestowing power, their quality of myth. The old stories—of the Fenians and the warriors of the House of Red Branch—are present realities, experiences lived, and as such must be taken into account in any assessment of the Irish world view.

Myth can be seen as a mechanism used by men to resolve contradictions that they find either in their real world or in their explanations of that world. In response to present-day exigencies some scenes from history and literature are brought to the forefront, while others are pushed back, neglected, or forgotten. How is it that even now in Ireland friend can kill friend; and men of one family can kill one another? Myth does not give answers, but rather reframes the questions in terms of archetypal events: the battle between Cúchulainn and Ferdiad; the battle between Cúchulainn and his son.

If the function of myth is to resolve such contradictions, and by such resolutions to renew vitality, it is easy to see that Ireland, not only now, but for virtually the last thousand years, has had a great need for myth. As one of the longest-colonized countries of the world, it has lost its language, a great part of its culture, and, most importantly, like a man in prison, the years of freedom needed to grow and develop. With no mechanisms for fighting the psychic consequences of such domination, self-hate is easy: "Ireland . . . has attempted nothing and achieved nothing. She has gone back in every department where other nations have advanced. She threw away her initiative and her language, and became a mean and sulky imitator of another people whom she professed to hate."[1]

The crucial question is always, Who am I? If the answer is "a vassal," or "a prisoner," or simply "a loser," the question that remains is whether one can live with this definition. If that answer is no, the life-destroying contradiction becomes apparent. The consequent reaction of people after people has been the same: they have turned to myth and folklore to revitalize and reunite themselves. Evidence of the power of these genres of thought becomes obvious as one sees in the present day one African colony after another reviving its native myths and proclaiming its independence. In the case of Ireland the process has been going on for centuries.

Who are we? The negative reply is easy: We are not English; we are not servants, nor are we imitators. But the positive statement is rather more difficult: We are what we have been and what we would have been. Ireland can only be defined in terms of what it was when free—in terms of beginnings, of the past. Luckily, Ireland still possesses sizable remnants of what has often been described as the oldest vernacular literature in Europe. The manuscripts that remain, along with, in certain areas, a sizable continuing oral tradition, furnish the material out of which the Irish are able to continually reformulate their myths. It is here that history and literature become one. Teachers in public schools make stories from early times available to their students. And while the students may be told that the stories are probably not true, they remain active in the mind, satisfying certain elemental needs of self-identification. History, on the other hand, depressing at best, furnishes scenes that show only who *they*, the oppressors, are. The product in both cases is myth, the result of a community's selection from the images available to it. This process has been going on for centuries, as taletellers, scribes, historians, and poets have copied down, changed, enlarged upon, and summarized the old stories.

From earliest times, poets in Ireland have known high position and great esteem in the society. In the early days of the Celtic domination the *filid* were a noble class. They were druids who knew the secret formulas by which one could maintain contact with other worlds; they could foretell the future and cast spells. But even more important was their function as poets who, in metered and alliterative lines, composed genealogies, festivals, histories, and stories about places, raids, and slaughters.

There was another class of poets in this society: the bards. They seem to have been more performers than poets, and were definitely of a lower social ranking than the *filid*, although the two classes existed side by side until after the Norman invasion. Then the class of *filid* seems to have disappeared, while the bards took over their old functions, singing songs of praise in the courts of the various chiefs, composing and reciting genealogies and histories at request. They continued to have a great influence in the maintenance of the language and the tradition until the Williamite War at the end of the seventeenth century, after which there was no aristocracy left to employ them.

Alongside this courtly tradition a strong oral tradition seems always to have been maintained in Ireland among the common people. Local *seanchaís*, or storytellers, boasting highly developed skills, have existed in small villages all through the country until very recent years. There are still a few left in some of the more isolated villages, although the Irish language is all but gone now, and people are turning to the schools and the mass media for their understandings of the world.

The *seanchaís* told their tales around the fire "from Samhain to Beltain" (November 1 to May 1), and were famous throughout the region. They often told tales that lasted for hours, had hundreds of tales in their repertoires, and jumped at any chance to learn new ones. There have always been traveling men on the roads of Ireland: indigents who would sing the new songs and tell tales from their own villages in return for a meal and a pallet to sleep on; minstrels; emigrants; pilgrims. The intellectual isolation even of villagers who never traveled outside their county has thus never been absolute.[2]

The *seanchaí* knew local genealogies and the origins of place-names of the region; he could tell family sagas and the local legends of meetings with the little people. And he could recite the old heroic legends of Finn and his forest warriors. As one *seanchaí* told Seamus Delargy: "Nobody knows who first composed these old stories—at least, we never got any account from anyone about them. But they are fine things to be able to tell or to listen to, so as to be able to pass the night away, especially those which are full of action, and tell of a hero's exploits."[3]

Above all, the *seanchaí* took great pride in his professionalism, in his highly perfected ability to narrate the stories with a correct style in a correct manner. At first, looking at the style of the epics told by the *filid* and bards, on the one hand, and that of the tales told by the local *seanchaís*, on the other, it would seem that there is very little relationship between them. The former are spare, severe, laconic. The latter are very developed: everything is described with care; dialogue abounds; imagery is vivid. But it must be remembered that most of the epics as we have them—the stories of the invasions, of the fairy people, and of the heroes of Red Branch—were preserved to us by scribes, who wrote at various times from about the eighth to the fifteenth centuries and were concerned with preserving the traditional histories for the sake of history rather than literature. Even when they tried to take down information from informants who knew the oral tradition, pen was not as fast as tongue, and stories became compressed into brief descriptions. It has been suggested that recent recordings of local versions of heroic legends are closer in style to the versions in oral tradition before the twelfth century than are the written versions. Gerard Murphy gives a good example of this, showing the beginning of a ninth-century story which sounds very like a rendering by a modern *seanchaí*. A fragment will suffice:

> Gartnán had his whole island gilded with red gold. On the arable land he had seven plough-teams. He had seven herds with seven score cows in each herd. He had fifty nets for deer, and out from the island were fifty nets for fishing. The fifty fish-nets had ropes from them over the windows of the kitchen. There was a bell at the end of each rope, on the rail, in front of the steward. Four men used to throw (?) the first-run salmon up to him. He himself in the meantime drank mead upon his couch.[4]

As the text goes on, however, it becomes more and more sketchy until it seems more a summary than a story. There is no indication that audiences at that time, any more than now, preferred their tales short; quite the contrary. In the opinion of Irish storytellers, says Delargy, the only tales worthy of any sensible person's attention are the long ones.[5] The shape and length of the narrative, then, were probably variable; it was re-created for every occasion in a different way by each performer. Extrapolating from present-day comparisons between taped texts and those transcribed by hand, it seems safe to conclude that most written renderings of oral tradition are shorthand summations. In this case we seem to have an amusing reflection of a scribe's attempting a complete transcription at the beginning, but falling further and further behind until all he could do was summarize.

Given this, the student of a mythology must be interested not only in the old manuscript versions but also the new tellings, however "faithless" they may be to the old. Myths vary with occasion, and occasion varies according to the needs of the people. Some needs, however, persist through centuries, along with the myths that simultaneously reflect and ameliorate them. There are a number of enduring images which, one may assume, help to form the minds of Irishmen; these may be set against the ever-novel chain of events called history.

The old *filid* classified their stories into such categories as destructions, cattle raids, battles, elopements, visions, and love tales. Since then, scribes and scholars have been inventing new classifications according to their sense of order, with the result that a great deal of shifting around has been done. Previously unconnected episodes have been joined together to fit latter-day ideas of coherence, and it is now customary to deal with the literature under such arbitrary headings as mythological tales, the Heroic cycle, the Fenian cycle, adventures, voyages, and visions. Here, since we are concerned primarily with images that still maintain their power, we will emphasize the Heroic and the Fenian cycles, presenting the major episodes and commenting on their mythical (as against their historical or philological) significance.

The main body of heroic narrative deals with Celtic tribes of central and northern Ireland, who had invaded the island in several migratory waves beginning probably around 350 B.C. Before the ninth century A.D. the Celts had divided Ireland into five provinces: Meath, Leinster, Munster, Connaught, and Ulster. Within these provinces, which were ruled by kings, there were subordinate districts, ruled by chiefs. Each leader had his retinue, which included *filid*, bards, and specialists in different crafts. The social structure was hierarchical, with many rankings. Social units included nuclear families, extended families, and lineages, outside of which individuals could not dispose of property. Well-off families lived in wooden buildings, while the less prosperous lived in *clochan*, semisubterranean oval beehivelike dwellings, a few of which can still be found in Ireland. Descent was patrilineal, as was inheritance. Property was owned by men; women came into marriage without property of their own. As we shall see, however, women were highly respected, were given high position, and had a strong influence on their husbands and sons. Indeed, one of the hallmarks of Irish heroic literature is the strong part played by women as protagonists. No Arthurian princesses these, waiting demurely for their white knights, but beautiful, sensuous, and headstrong individuals who forced the action of their often-reluctant warriors and did not hesitate to offer their "willing thighs" as reward.

Ireland itself at this time was forested; it had no ports, towns, or roads. Farming and herding were the basic subsistence strategies. The people used no money; instead, cattle were the medium of exchange, with the value of items reckoned in terms of them. The diet of the people, as is generally the case with pastoral societies, was largely derived from their livestock—milk, butter, cheese, and curds—in addition to bread and some garden crops. Beef and pork were eaten in great quantities at banquets, washed down with beer, mead, and wine.

The religion of the people was druidic; the *filid* were their priests. They presided over communal rites, divined the future, and discovered unknown facts. They were physicians, curing by both natural and supernatural means. And, as mentioned above, they were also poets and record keepers. In short, they were very talented and accomplished men who had to go through many years of apprenticeship before reaching their position.

The Celts were polytheistic. Their nature deities included Dagda, a personification of the sun, and Eiru, a goddess also associated with the sun, from whose name the Celtic names for Ireland—Eire and Erin—derive. As is the case in many religions with a hierarchy of gods, it was the gods of lowest rank that intervened most in the lives of the people. The major shrines were trees and sacred groves, as well as certain rocks, pools, and springs. The people believed also in spirits that had to be placated: fairies, pucas, water spirits, mermaids, and banshees.[6]

Between different groups there was more or less continual small-scale warfare, consisting mainly of feuding and raiding. It is with such wars that much of the heroic literature of Ireland is concerned. Many of these tales have to do with the fortunes in war of the province of Ulster under its great king Conchobar, and deal principally with the deeds of Ulster's great hero, Cúchulainn (pronounced Koo*cull*in, more or less).

Before describing the Cúchulainn stories, however, it is convenient to deal with a tale that stands outside them and yet provides one of the archetypal legends, not only of Ireland, but of much of Northern Europe —that of Deirdre and Noisiu, which is entitled "The Exile of the Sons of Uisliu." This story contains motifs that are repeated over and over again in the Ulster cycle, and that serve to emphasize some of the controlling images of the mythology.

The wife of Conchobar's storyteller is pregnant. A druid predicts that she will give birth to a beautiful girl, Deirdre, who will bring evil:

Harsh, hideous deeds done
in anger at Ulster's high king,

and little graves everywhere
—a famous tale, Derdriu [Deirdre].[7]

In metrical stanzas he foretells all that is going to happen. The warriors who are present (acting as a chorus) urge the king to kill the child, but Conchobar decides instead to raise her for himself, in a place apart, where no one will see her. So it happens, until one day she learns about Noisiu, a young man with hair like the raven, cheeks like blood, and a body like snow. (This, of course, is an interesting inversion of the standard Indo-European *Märchen*, in which it is the girl who has these attributes.) Further, Noisiu is described as having such a sweet voice that cows hearing his song give more milk, that people who hear it are filled with peace. (This motif is also widespread: it is found, most notably, in the Spanish romance about the infante Arnaldos.)[8] Noisiu is one of three valiant brothers, the sons of Uisliu. Deirdre slips out where he will see her and then challenges him. In a classic *piropo*, he comments, "A fine heifer going by." She replies: "The heifers grow big where there are no bulls." He rejects her, reminding her of the druid's prophecy, but Deirdre, heedless of the prophecy, threatens to shame him if he does not dare to take her away with him. This is the kind of threat no man can refuse, and as we shall see, time and again it leads to tragedy in the heroic epics. Noisiu and his brothers take her and go into exile. Conchobar pursues them and finally, by treachery, manages to kill the three brothers and bring Deirdre back captive.

A prisoner, and at the mercy of Conchobar, Deirdre mourns. She never smiles, eats very little, does not lift her head, and refuses to be reconciled to her fate:

> I feel his lack, wearily,
> the son of Uisliu. All I see—
> black boulders on fair flesh
> so bright once among the others.

Conchobar decides, vengefully, to share her with the other man in the world whom she hates the most, Eogan MacDurthacht, who thrust the spear into Noisiu. The three of them are in a chariot, heading for the fair of Macha. The ending occurs abruptly:

> "This is good, Derdriu," Conchobar said. Between me and Eogan you are a sheep eyeing two rams."
>
> A big block of stone was in front of her. She let her head be driven against the stone, and made a mass of fragments of it, and she was dead.

This theme, repeated in many versions, including a major one in the Fenian cycle,[9] has been shown to have been the source of the Tristan and Isolde theme.[10] In present days it reaches the minds of Irishmen through yet another major variant—*Deirdre of the Sorrows*, by J. M. Synge:

> DEIRDRE *(stands up and sees the light from Emain).* Draw a little back with the squabbling of fools when I am broken up with misery. *(She turns around.)* I see the flames of Emain starting upward in the dark night; and because of me there will be weasels and wild cats crying on a lonely wall where there were queens and armies and red gold, the way there will be a story told of a ruined city and a raving king and a woman will be young forever. *(She looks around.)* I see the trees naked and bare, and the moon shining. Little moon, little moon of Alban, it's lonesome you'll be this night, and to-morrow night, and long nights after, and you pacing the woods beyond Glen Laoi, looking every place for Deirdre and Naisi [Noisiu], the two lovers who slept so sweetly with each other.[11]

In the play, Synge has Deirdre kill herself with a knife and sink into Noisiu's grave. But of course the manner of death is not important to the mythic image; what is important is the story of the true love and irreconcilable sorrow of Deirdre.

It seems significant that in spite of the fact that Deirdre's headstrong behavior was the cause of many deaths and consequent grief and suffering in the society, just as was foretold by the druid, the emphasis of the story is not directed toward the bitter social fruits of Conchobar's failure to heed the advice of his warriors (who represent society), but rather toward the tragedy of the girl. The theme of social destiny, so often the theme of myths beginning with a prophecy, is minimized in favor of the story of the fate of one or two individuals. This would seem to be one more example, among many in European folk literature, of the disproportionately high value given to individual desire as against the social good.

However, the story of Deirdre stands alone in the literature; it is more in the tales centering around Cúchulainn and the fortunes of the House of the Red Branch of Ulster that the narrative most consistently maintains the epic tone that is characteristic of societies in the heroic stage of their development. Typically heroic descriptions, for example, are given of the richness of the king's houses and their contents, including a listing of some of the swords and shields kept there, by name:

This theme, repeated in many versions, including a major one in he Fenian cycle,[9] has been shown to have been the source of the Tristan nd Isolde theme.[10] In present days it reaches the minds of Irishmen hrough yet another major variant—*Deirdre of the Sorrows*, by J. M. ynge:

DEIRDRE (*stands up and sees the light from Emain*). Draw a little back with the squabbling of fools when I am broken up with misery. (*She turns around.*) I see the flames of Emain starting upward in the dark night; and because of me there will be weasels and wild cats crying on a lonely wall where there were queens and armies and red gold, the way there will be a story told of a ruined city and a raving king and a woman will be young forever. (*She looks around.*) I see the trees naked and bare, and the moon shining. Little moon, little moon of Alban, it's lonesome you'll be this night, and to-morrow night, and long nights fter, and you pacing the woods beyond Glen Laoi, looking very place for Deirdre and Naisi [Noisiu], the two lovers ho slept so sweetly with each other.[11]

the play, Synge has Deirdre kill herself with a knife and sink u's grave. But of course the manner of death is not important hic image; what is important is the story of the true love and le sorrow of Deirdre.

ems significant that in spite of the fact that Deirdre's head-vior was the cause of many deaths and consequent grief and the society, just as was foretold by the druid, the emphasis s not directed toward the bitter social fruits of Conchobar's d the advice of his warriors (who represent society), but the tragedy of the girl. The theme of social destiny, so often yths beginning with a prophecy, is minimized in favor of fate of one or two individuals. This would seem to be le, among many in European folk literature, of the dis-high value given to individual desire as against the so-

he story of Deirdre stands alone in the literature; it is centering around Cúchulainn and the fortunes of the Branch of Ulster that the narrative most consistently tone that is characteristic of societies in the heroic lopment. Typically heroic descriptions, for example, ness of the king's houses and their contents, including he swords and shields kept there, by name:

in the old manuscript versions but also the new tellings, however "faithless" they may be to the old. Myths vary with occasion, and occasion varies according to the needs of the people. Some needs, however, persist through centuries, along with the myths that simultaneously reflect and ameliorate them. There are a number of enduring images which, one may assume, help to form the minds of Irishmen; these may be set against the ever-novel chain of events called history.

The old *filid* classified their stories into such categories as destructions, cattle raids, battles, elopements, visions, and love tales. Since then, scribes and scholars have been inventing new classifications according to their sense of order, with the result that a great deal of shifting around has been done. Previously unconnected episodes have been joined together to fit latter-day ideas of coherence, and it is now customary to deal with the literature under such arbitrary headings as mythological tales, the Heroic cycle, the Fenian cycle, adventures, voyages, and visions. Here, since we are concerned primarily with images that still maintain their power, we will emphasize the Heroic and the Fenian cycles, presenting the major episodes and commenting on their mythical (as against their historical or philological) significance.

The main body of heroic narrative deals with Celtic tribes of central and northern Ireland, who had invaded the island in several migratory waves beginning probably around 350 B.C. Before the ninth century A.D. the Celts had divided Ireland into five provinces: Meath, Leinster, Munster, Connaught, and Ulster. Within these provinces, which were ruled by kings, there were subordinate districts, ruled by chiefs. Each leader had his retinue, which included *filid,* bards, and specialists in different crafts. The social structure was hierarchical, with many rankings. Social units included nuclear families, extended families, and lineages, outside of which individuals could not dispose of property. Well-off families lived in wooden buildings, while the less prosperous lived in *clochan,* semisubterranean oval beehivelike dwellings, a few of which can still be found in Ireland. Descent was patrilineal, as was inheritance. Property was owned by men; women came into marriage without property of their own. As we shall see, however, women were highly respected, were given high position, and had a strong influence on their husbands and sons. Indeed, one of the hallmarks of Irish heroic literature is the strong part played by women as protagonists. No Arthurian princesses these, waiting demurely for their white knights, but beautiful, sensuous, and headstrong individuals who forced the action of their often-reluctant warriors and did not hesitate to offer their "willing thighs" as reward.

Ireland itself at this time was forested; it had no ports, towns, or
Farming and herding were the basic subsistence strategies. The
used no money; instead, cattle were the medium of exchange, with
value of items reckoned in terms of them. The diet of the people, as
is generally the case with pastoral societies, was largely derived from their
livestock—milk, butter, cheese, and curds—in addition to bread and some
garden crops. Beef and pork were eaten in great quantities at banquets,
washed down with beer, mead, and wine.

The religion of the people was druidic; the *filid* were their priests.
They presided over communal rites, divined the future, and discovered
unknown facts. They were physicians, curing by both natural and supernatural means. And, as mentioned above, they were also poets and
record keepers. In short, they were very talented and accomplished men
who had to go through many years of apprenticeship before reaching
their position.

The Celts were polytheistic. Their nature deities included Dagda,
a personification of the sun, and Eiru, a goddess also associated with the
sun, from whose name the Celtic names for Ireland—Eire and Erin—derive. As is the case in many religions with a hierarchy of gods, it was
the gods of lowest rank that intervened most in the lives of the people.
The major shrines were trees and sacred groves, as well as certain rocks,
pools, and springs. The people believed also in spirits that had to be
placated: fairies, pucas, water spirits, mermaids, and banshees.[6]

Between different groups there was more or less continual small-
scale warfare, consisting mainly of feuding and raiding. It is with such
wars that much of the heroic literature of Ireland is concerned. Many
of these tales have to do with the fortunes in war of the province of Ulster
under its great king Conchobar, and deal principally with the deeds of
Ulster's great hero, Cúchulainn (pronounced Koo*cull*in, more or less).

Before describing the Cúchulainn stories, however, it is convenient
to deal with a tale that stands outside them and yet provides one of the
archetypal legends, not only of Ireland, but of much of Northern Europe
—that of Deirdre and Noisiu, which is entitled "The Exile of the Sons of
Uisliu." This story contains motifs that are repeated over and over again
in the Ulster cycle, and that serve to emphasize some of the controlling
images of the mythology.

The wife of Conchobar's storyteller is pregnant. A druid predicts
that she will give birth to a beautiful girl, Deirdre, who will bring evil:

Harsh, hideous deeds done
in anger at Ulster's high king,

and little graves everywhere
—a famous tale, Derdriu [Deirdre].[7]

In metrical stanzas he foretells all that is going t
warriors who are present (acting as a chorus) urge the
child, but Conchobar decides instead to raise her for h
apart, where no one will see her. So it happens, until
about Noisiu, a young man with hair like the raven
and a body like snow. (This, of course, is an intere
standard Indo-European *Märchen*, in which it is t
attributes.) Further, Noisiu is described as havi
that cows hearing his song give more milk, that
filled with peace. (This motif is also widesprea
bly, in the Spanish romance about the infante
of three valiant brothers, the sons of Uisliu.
will see her and then challenges him. In a
"A fine heifer going by." She replies: "The
are no bulls." He rejects her, reminding h
Deirdre, heedless of the prophecy, threat
dare to take her away with him. This
refuse, and as we shall see, time and ag
epics. Noisiu and his brothers take
pursues them and finally, by treache
and bring Deirdre back captive.

A prisoner, and at the mer
never smiles, eats very little, do
reconciled to her fate:

I feel his lack, wearily
the son of Uisliu. All
black boulders on fai
so bright once amor

Conchobar decides
the world whom she ha
the spear into Noisiu.
fair of Macha. The e

"This
me and Eog
A bi
head be d
ments of

Ochain was there, Conchobor's shield, the Ear of
Beauty—it had four gold borders around it;
Cúchulainn's black shield Dubán;
Lámthapad—the swift to hand—belonging to Conall
Cernach;
Ochnech belonging to Flidais;
Furbaide's red-gold Orderg; . . .
and other shields beyond counting.[12]

Cúchulainn is born, sired by the god Lug (apparently a Celtic
deity even before the Celts came to Ireland; the French city of Lyons
was probably named for him), to a sister of Conchobar. Very early in
life he shows his extraordinary skills. He courts a girl, Emer, who assigns
him tasks to prove himself worthy; then he is assigned further tasks by
her father, a king who does not want Cúchulainn for a son-in-law. Here
we have one of the basic plot situations of Indo-European narrative,
found from India to Ireland. In carrying out these tasks, Cúchulainn
learns the arts of war from Scáthach, a warrior-goddess, and he vanquishes Aife, another woman chieftain, by whom he conceives a son.
Cúchulainn leaves a golden ring for his son and tells Aife to name him
Connla. He then puts his unborn son under the obligation (geis) to reveal his name to no man, to make way for no man, and to refuse no man
combat. He then leaves.

What warrior skills did Cúchulainn learn from Scáthach? Another
list tells: "the apple-feat, the feats of the sword-edge and the sloped
shield; the feats of the javelin and rope; the body-feat, the feat of Cat
and the heroic salmon-leap," and some twenty others, among them a technique that Scáthach taught no one else, one that was to give him the
victory time and again: the use of the gae bolga, a lance that had to be
hurled under water from between the toes. After entering its victim, it
opened out to cause a larger number of wounds; it was always fatal.

Cúchulainn returns to his homeland, performs the other feats required of him, and marries Emer. Seven years later his son comes looking
for him. The warriors of Ulster ask him his name, and since he is under
a geis not to tell it, they are obliged to fight him. He defeats them all,
but Cúchulainn finally vanquishes him with the gae bolga. He takes the
dying boy in his arms and throws him down before his people: " 'My
son, men of Ulster,' he said. 'Here you are.' "

This, of course, is the Sohrab and Rustum tale, which is found
again in the *Hildebrandslied* and is repeated over and over in heroic literature. This tragic theme, which one sees here so transparently set up by
the apparently senseless imposition of the geis, seems to have been a re-

sponse to a very serious preoccupation of these tribal men with the precarious relationship between father and son. It is different from the theme of Jacob and his son, but perhaps the two stories are related as narrative transformations of a single universal problem.

The central plot of the Ulster cycle is that of the *Táin Bó Cuailnge* ("The Cattle Raid of Cooley"). It is the story of an attempt by the rulers of Connaught to steal away a great bull from the herd of one of the Ulster chiefs. Scenes showing motives for the raid and setting it in a metaphorical perspective exist separately from the telling of the *Táin* itself. Medb, queen of Connaught, and her husband, Ailill, are lying in bed, boasting to each other about their wealth. Upon counting it all up, they find that Ailill has one bull more than his wife has: the bull Finnbennach, which had belonged to Medb, but, refusing to be led by a woman, had gone over to Ailill's herd. Medb hears of one other bull in Ireland that is Finnbennach's equal: Donn Cuailnge, the Brown Bull of Cooley. She sets out to get it for herself, and the rest of the *Táin* is about what happens to those who allow themselves to be led by a woman.

The bulls themselves provide a metaphor for the *Táin*, in passages that can be seen as framing the adventure, before and after. The bulls were once pigkeepers for the fairy kings of Munster and Connaught. They were magicians who were able to change shape, and were the best of friends. But people tried to make trouble for them by saying that one was better than the other. They began to compete and to fight, changing themselves into birds of prey, water creatures, stags, phantoms, dragons, and maggots, always fighting each other. And finally they changed themselves into the two bulls. (This motif of changing shape later became a common one in medieval balladry; it was usually employed to dramatize a chase.) The admiration that these pastoralists felt for a great bull is well expressed in the metrical description that closes the scene:

> dark brown dire haughty with young health
> horrific overwhelming ferocious
> full of craft
> furious fiery flanks narrow
> brave brutal thick breasted
> curly browed head cocked high. . . .

So the men of Connaught, along with troops from the other three provinces of Ireland and aided by exiles from Ulster, set out on the raid. The account tells precisely how they went:

> through Muicc Cruinb,
> through Terloch Teóra Crích, the marshy lake bed

where three territories meet,
    by Tuaim Móna, the peat ridge . . . ,

and on, through more than fifty place names.

Coming unto Ulster, on the way to Cooley, they have to pass
through the land of Cúchulainn: Muirthemne. There has been no resistance to their passage, because the men of Ulster are under an old
curse: always to be incapacitated in times of their greatest need by pangs
like those of a woman giving birth. The only men excepted from the
curse are old men, young boys, and Cúchulainn, himself only seventeen
years old.

Cúchulainn recognizes the danger, but has promised a girl that he
would spend the night with her. He keeps the tryst, and then is ready
the next day to go to work. He cuts off the heads of two warriors and
their charioteers, and then sets them on the points of a tree fork he has
set in the river. When Medb sees what has happened, she asks Fergus
what manner of man has done this, and he tells her of the boyhood feats
of Cúchulainn. (This kind of embedded narrative is very unusual in oral
tradition; presumably it was inserted there by a scribe.) Before he was
five he had defeated all the other boys in sports and in fights; by the
time he was six he had killed the fierce hound of the smith Culann,
apologizing afterwards and offering to take the hound's place until he
could rear another pup for him. From this incident he was given the
name of Cúchulainn, the hound of Culann. He was given weapons and
a chariot and told that the man who armed himself on that day would
achieve fame and greatness, but his life would be short. Cúchulainn
accepted the bargain: "If I achieve fame I am content, though I had
only one day on earth." The seer also said that whoever mounted his first
chariot on that day, "his name will live forever in Ireland." And so is set
down the central value of the heroic warrior: overriding concern for his
name, which at once inspires him to heroic deeds and leaves him vulnerable to *gessa*, which anyone might impose under the threat of shame.

The army of Ailill and Medb moves on, with Cúchulainn killing
fifties and hundreds of their men daily. In spite of him, though, the raid
continues. They agree to send a man to him every day in single combat.
Though Medb tries treachery, Cúchulainn always wins.

Finally, however, Cúchulainn gets weary. His wounds are many
(although in accounts of battles he seems never to be touched), and he
has not slept from Samhain to Imbolc—from the beginning of fall to the
beginning of spring. It must be noted here that hyperbole is often a mark
of oral tradition; what obviously appears in spoken narration as only a

figure of speech to bring the action to the required level of intensity or to underline the significance of a statement (e.g., in this scene, the extent of Cúchulainn's weariness) seems, in written form, to be overdone.

At this moment Lug comes, to give Cúchulainn a chance to sleep and to heal his wounds. While he is asleep, one hundred and fifty boy warriors of Ulster come down to help Cúchulainn and are slaughtered. When Cúchulainn awakes, full of life, "fit for a festival, or for marching or mating, or for an ale-house or the mightiest assembly in Ireland," and learns of their death, he sets out to avenge them.

And here, at what was surely the climax of the *Táin* in the oral versions, we find a set of four "runs," one after another, dealing with his dressing for battle, his "warp-spasm," the battle itself, and his presentation of himself after the battle. Runs are set pieces of Irish oral narrative. Whereas the narrator generally has freedom to improvise, making scenes longer or shorter depending on his audience and the occasion, runs are memorized and of fixed form. Usually compositions of intricate and vivid description, runs are repeated in a tempo much faster than the rest of the narrative, thus emphasizing the moment being described, impressing the audience with the storyteller's craft, and giving the narrator a moment to look ahead to further actions.

First the charioteer dresses for battle; his preparations are described in detail. Then Cúchulainn prepares:

> Then the high hero Cúchulainn, Sualdam's son, builder of the Badb's fold with walls of human bodies, seized his warrior's battle-harness. This was the warlike battle-harness he wore: twenty-seven tunics of waxed skin, plated and pressed together, and fastened with strings and cords and straps against his clear skin, so that his senses or his brain wouldn't burst their bonds at the onset of his fury. Over them he put on . . . .

The description continues. He puts on his battle belt and his aprons, and he grasps his weapons: swords, spears, javelins, darts, shields, and helmet.

And then he is seized by the warp-spasm, which converts him into a monster:

> His shanks and his joints, every knuckle and angle and organ from head to foot, shook like a tree in the flood or a reed in the stream. His body made a furious twist inside his skin, so that his feet and shins and knees switched

to the rear and his heels and calves switched to the front. The balled sinews of his calves switched to the front of his shins, each big knot the size of a warrior's bunched fist. On his head the temple-sinews stretched to the nape of his neck, each mighty, immense, measureless knob as big as the head of a month-old child. . . .

The description goes on, rather ludicrously for the modern reader, but undoubtedly building an impressive image for the listener, who has no time to linger over images that race by him, piling up on one another. Consideration of this portion of the *Táin* shows perhaps more clearly than any amount of explanation that the aesthetic effect of oral literature must not be judged in terms of the effect given by its written transcription.

When the spasm has passed, Cúchulainn steps into his chariot, which is then carefully described, with all its armor and spikes and nails and sickles. The horses of the chariot are described. And then he drives out to battle.

With the sickles on the sides of his chariot, he literally mows down the enemy. He kills a hundred, then two hundred, then three hundred, then four hundred, then five hundred—all this in the first attack of his first real battle with the enemy. They fall "sole to sole and neck to headless neck." He leaves a bed of them, six bodies deep. Finally a list is given of all the chiefs killed: "two called Cruaid, two named Calad, two named Cír, two named Cíar, two named Ecell . . . ," for a total of one hundred and thirty kings, "as well as an unaccountable horde of dogs and horses, women and boys and children and rabble of all kinds."

Cúchulainn comes out of the battle without a scratch, and the next morning, fearing that the image that the enemy had gotten of him did not do him justice, he comes out to display himself in all his beauty. Another long run describes him as having shining golden curly hair with gems scattered through it, four dimples in each cheek, and seven pupils in each eye. His festive clothing includes a purple mantle, a gold-and-silver brooch, a silk tunic, a crimson shield with a gold rim, and a gold-hilted sword. He holds in his hands nineteen heads, "the crop of one night's warfare on the four provinces of Ireland." (This, of course, rather than being a contradiction to the passage about the slaying of the hundred and thirty kings, simply confirms the formulaic nature of the earlier passage.) All the women of Connaught and Munster climb on the backs of their men to gaze at Cúchulainn. Medb herself does so.

And the action then declines in intensity to further episodes of single combat. Medb finds herself hard put to find any champions to meet with Cúchulainn. Finally she sends for Ferdiad, Cúchulainn's beloved foster brother. Together Cúchulainn and Ferdiad had learned the arts of war from Scáthach, and they were bound to each other in a blood pact of friendship. Medb first makes a reluctant Ferdiad come to her camp by sending bards to satirize and mock him "so there would be nowhere in the world for him to lay his head in peace." Again, we see here the vulnerability of a man in a society in which Name is so important and in which women and poets can consequently wield power. Medb tries to get him to fight Cúchulainn by offering him land, riches, her daughter, and "my own friendly thighs," and finally, when all else fails, she persuades him by mentioning that Cúchulainn had said he could beat Ferdiad easily.

And so the battle of the two heroes, individuals standing for Ulster and Connaught, is set up. This is a very different battle from those that preceded, which simply showed the invincibility of Cúchulainn and the utter impotence of the rest of Ireland. This is a fight between brothers and equals.

They begin, in true epic style, by boasting and taunting. And then the four-day battle begins, with each fighting fairly and scrupulously, each alternately allowing the other his choice of weapons. The first day they fight with darts, then spears; and at the end of the day they embrace and kiss. The second day they fight with stabbing spears, and at the end of the day embrace again. On the third day they use broadswords. And on the last day, it is Cúchulainn's turn to choose, and he suggests that they fight in the ford. Ferdiad realizes that he will probably lose there, but nevertheless he agrees. Another run occurs, reproducing the frenzy of the battle. Ferdiad almost wins, but at the last moment Cúchulainn calls for the *gae bolga*, against which there is no defense, and kills Ferdiad with it.

> Hound of the bright deeds,
> you have killed me unfairly.
> Your guilt clings to me
> as my blood sticks to you.

Before this, both Cúchulainn and Ferdiad have realized the extent of Medb's treachery. Cúchulainn says, "Now I know it was your doom/ when a woman sent you here/to fight against your foster-brother." And

> Yours is the blame for what must come,
> son of Damán mac Dáiri
> —coming, at a woman's word,
> to cross swords with your foster-brother.

And Ferdiad replies: "Cúchulainn, tide of bravery,/I know that Medb
has ruined us."

It is treachery piled on treachery, then; and much like Deirdre
mourning for Noisiu, Cúchulainn mourns the death of Ferdiad in a tre-
mendously touching scene. For some thirty-five stanzas Cúchulainn laments, describing the beauty of his friend—

> I loved the noble way you blushed,
> and loved your fine, perfect form.
> I loved your blue clear eye,
> your way of speech, your skillfulness—

and describing the adventures they had gone on together, the forts they
had leveled, and the men they had killed. And finally there is the famous
section in which this phrase is repeated over and over: "All play, all
sport, until Ferdia came to the ford."

> All play, all sport,
> until Ferdia came to the ford.
> I thought beloved Ferdia
> would live forever after me
> —yesterday, a mountain-side;
> today, nothing but a shade.

It is one of the great tragic scenes; it completes a trio of nuclear family
tragedies of the Ulster cycle: of husband and wife, of father and son,
and of brothers. Each of the tragedies is significant both on the social
and the individual levels; all can be taken literally (as particular occurrences) or metaphorically (as statements about Ireland and its provinces).

Cúchulainn lies incapacitated with his wounds, but soon the men
of Ulster will be rising from their "pangs." Meanwhile a series of other
heroes engages the enemy. These encounters gradually prepare the scene
for the last battle and the shifting of the focus of the action from representatives of societies to the societies themselves.

Finally Conchobar rises and calls up his armies; again there is the
listing of names, which both defines the people and conveys the impres-
sion of a great force:

> Rise up now, Finnchad, and summon Deda to me, from his
> bay, and Leamain and Fallach and Fergus's son Illann
> from Gabar; Dorlunsa from Imchlár, Derg Imderg the Red,
> Fedilmid Cilair Chetaig, Faeladán and Rochad mac Faithe-
> main from Rígdonn; Lugaid and Lugda; Cathbad from his
> bay . . . ;

and so on, through the naming of some one hundred and twenty Ulster-men (including Cúchulainn).

There are divination chants, predicting the great slaughter, and then the scene shifts to the camp of Medb and Ailill, where the scout MacRoth is describing the armies of Ulster as they come. Company by company he describes them, along with their leaders. And one by one, in answer to the question, Who is that? Fergus, exiled former king of Ulster, identifies the leader and tells what a great warrior he is.

And as many men as are there, concludes MacRoth (at approximately three thousand men to the company, the figure would come to some sixty thousand), there are more on their way.

Ailill calls up his armies, three men of each name to make some ninety leaders, all that are left after the work done by Cúchulainn. And the battle begins. Fergus sets out to do battle, but he is turned away from fighting Conchobar, and finally Cúchulainn forces him to give way, because of an agreement they had made. Fergus withdraws his troop. Others of Medb's allies withdraw as well.

Medb leaves the battle to urinate: "The place is called Fual Medba, Medb's Foul Place, ever since." Cúchulainn came upon her as she squatted, but did not kill her, "not being a killer of women":

> The battle was over.
> Medb said to Fergus:
> "We have had shame and shambles here today,
> Fergus."
> "We followed the rump of a misguiding woman,"
> Fergus said. "It is the usual thing for a herd led by a mare
> to be strayed and destroyed."

There is no doubt but that on one level at least this a statement of the theme of the *Táin*: the tragic results of the overvaluing of the desires of a woman, for whatever reason. The theme is stated again and again, by one after another of the heroes of Medb's army, not excluding Fergus. Even when he is fighting in the last battle, an Ulsterman reproaches him: "You rage very hard at your kith and kin for the sake of a whore's backside."

Medb, defeated, makes off with the bull; and in the final scene of the *Táin*, the two bulls meet and fight, circling the whole of Ireland. When morning comes, the Donn Cuailnge appears with the remains of Finnbennach on his horns. It heads back toward Ulster, leaving parts of the other bull's body in one place after another and thus establishing the place name of each site: "He drank again at Ath Luain, and left Finn-bennach's loins there—that is how the place was named Ath Luain, the

Ford of the Loins." Then the Donn Cuailnge itself drops dead between Ulster and Uí Echach at Druim Tairb: "So Druim Tairb, the Ridge of the Bull, is the name of that place." All through the *Táin*, a striking aspect of the narration of battles and fights is the way in which they inspire the naming of places. It is through events of men that places become significant, then, and through place names that events of the past become memorialized.

The significance of the *Táin* thus seems to be expressed through two metaphorical and one social rendering of the same conflict: (1) that of the friendly pigkeepers; (2) that between Cúchulainn and his foster brother; and (3) that of the armies of Ulster and Connaught. On each of the levels the same things happen. In terms of social stratification the conflicts are repeated on the levels of social totem, hero, and king. The *Táin* is a perfect example of the use of redundancy to reinforce an urgent social message having to do with treachery, honor, and the slaughter of friends by friends.

In addition to the heroic message of the *Táin*, in the Ulster cycle two other aspects stand out, which will only be mentioned here: first, the powerfully drawn women characters, often protagonists, who are perhaps more alive than the women of any other literature; and second, the tragic sense of fate, often shown through the imposition of *gessa*. One dark story from the cycle shows the feeling in an exceptional scene in which Conaire, who is made king of Ireland provided he observes nine enigmatic *gessa*, helplessly sees himself violating one *geis* after another. He exclaims to himself, shortly before his inevitable death, in what may be taken as an epitaph for the men of Ulster, past and present: "All my *gessa* have overtaken me tonight!"[13]

Alongside the images of the world evoked by the Ulster cycle, another and very different world of narratives exists, with its own heroes, its own setting, and its own reflection in the very landscape through which one moves in Ireland. This world is the one of Finn MacCumail and his *fian*, a standing army of warriors. The stories of Finn evoke a world that is in many ways contradictory to that of Cúchulainn. They represent a society of about the second or third century A.D., the world of subject peoples rather than ruling peoples (which latter did not require standing armies), primarily of another part of Ireland (Munster and Leinster).

While the compositions about the House of Red Branch can be dated to the Early Middle Irish period (c. 900 to c. 1200 A.D.) and even before, the Fenian stories date in the main from the Late Middle Irish period on, with the majority of them having been composed after the Norman invasion in 1170. And while the Ulster tales are in the form of historical records, the Fenian tales are largely in ballad form. They constitute some of our earliest ballad documentation.

Perhaps the major contradiction between these two sets of images, though, lies in the attitudes they express toward society and culture. Cúchulainn is every bit the hero and representative of his society; Finn is a hero of a group that stands outside the ordinary social world. His group does not herd cattle; instead it hunts to get its food. It lies completely outside the ordinary hierarchical system of obligations that governs the rest of society; the Fenians of the texts owe no necessary allegiance to any king. That this was not historically the case is, of course, beside the point. The values of the Fenians and their chronicler-creators are romantic. Nature is to be preferred to culture. An illustration: The two sons of King Feradach Fechtnach divide Ireland between them. "Tuathat took the treasures and the cattle and the forts and villages; Fiacha took the rocks and estuaries, the fruits and fish and game." When the noblemen protest that the slaves are not equal, Cailte, a Fenian, replies, "The share which you think the worse is the one that we should prefer."[14] The image of forest life is made vivid by extraordinary lays, such as a description of Arran:

> Skittish deer are on her peaks,
> Delicious berries on her manes,
> Cool waters in her rivers,
> Mast upon her dun oaks.[15]

Also opposed to the cultural in the Fenian cycle is the supernatural. Whereas in the Ulster cycle the supernatural occasionally intrudes itself upon the cultural actions of tribal wars and preparations for wars, in the Fenian cycle men actually go into the other world and do battle with and obtain favors from the supernatural Tuatha de Danaan and other fairy peoples.

The cultural value of acquisition, which is so prominent in the Ulster cycle and is well exemplified in the scene in which Medb and Ailill boast to each other of their possessions, is negated in the Fenian cycle. The greatest virtue here is generosity, and Finn is such a good lord that "were but the brown leaf which the wood sheds from it gold—were but the white billows silver—Finn would have given it all away." Oisin had the same character:

> In the matter of gold, of silver, or concerning meat, Oisin
> never denied any man; nor, though another's generosity

were such as might fit a chief, did Oisin ever seek ought of him.[16]

Indeed austerity was a virtue required of all the Fenians. When they came into the group they had to undergo an initiation ceremony which tested their merit (they had to be prime poets and excellent warriors) and formally cut off their kinship ties, so that no one outside the Fenians could claim recompense if one of them were killed, or could be subject to reprisals for anything he did.[17]

One final contrast must be noted, though it has been implied in the above: that whereas the Ulster sagas were recited by professional poets, the Fenian ballads were sung by the people. Indeed, it is striking that whereas the Ulster cycle seems to have become entirely extinct in the oral tradition, the Fenian cycle, both in the form of ballads and elaborate prose stories, flourishes in that tradition to the present day.

Now, while all the above contrasts have frequently been noted, it has generally been in a historical rather than a synchronic context. The question remains as to how two such apparently contradictory definitions of the world can coexist in the mind of the Irishman without a strain of contradiction being felt. One obvious explanation could be that the stories simply represent two different historical epochs and are therefore not contradictory. This sort of explanation is built on the false assumption that the tales are remembered for their historical value. There is perhaps a more satisfactory explanation. First, though, a bit about the content of the Finn mythology.

Though the ballads and stories are, in general, complete in themselves and are not arranged in fixed sequence, attempts have been made to fix them inside frame stories. In these stories Oisin, son of Finn, has survived for several hundred years after the death of his father and the last of the Fenians. He meets St. Patrick and is baptized by him. The stories are those he told the saint. Oisin refuses the consolation of Christianity for his loss of the Fenians and their way of life:

> I would sooner at rising time hear grouse on mountain peaks than the voice of the cleric indoors bleating like a sheep or a goat.[18]

By using negatives and by listing the deficiencies of the present, he recreates the old way of life:

> No gatherings, no music, no harps, no bestowal of wealth,
> no deeds of horsemanship, no rewarding of the learned with
> gold, no art, no festive drinking.

No courting or hunting, the two crafts we looked forward
to, no fighting, no raiding, no learning of athletic feats.

Never any equipment of war, nor playing of games as was
our wont, no swimming with blameless warriors—Time
passes wearily in Elphin tonight.[19]

At the request of Patrick, he tells the stories of the Fenians.
Throughout the work, then, there is an Ishmael theme operating: all
these men are dead, and there is no hope for them. The tales are about
Finn, "the Fair One," who can foretell the future by sucking on his thumb,
and his warrior band (*fian*), which is composed of two clans: Finn's own
Clann Baiscne, and Clann Morna, whose head is Goll MacMorna.

The praises of Finn are sung often in the ballads, but most of the
heroic actions described in the Fenian cycle are not his but rather those
of other members of his group. In a seventeenth-century poem they fight
with phantoms:

Nine bodies rise out of the corner from the side next to us:
nine heads from the other side of the iron couch.

They set up nine horrid screeches: though matched in
loudness, they were not matched in harmony: the churl
answered in turn, and the headless body answered.

Though each rough strain of theirs was bad, the headless
body's strain was worse: there was no strain but was tolerable compared to the shriek of the one-eyed man.[20]

They fight in the dark. Morning comes, and house and phantoms
are gone.

In a folktale collected in this century, one finds equivalent motifs
that tend to remove the stories from any semblance of historical coherence: Finn and some of his men get lost on their way home from hunting
and stop in at a house they see behind them. A dinner is prepared for
them, but a sheep upsets the table and scatters the food. None of Finn's
men can tie up the sheep. But the old man does it easily. It later turns
out that the old man is Death, the sheep is Strength, and the young
woman in the house is Youth. Then she grants them each a wish. Others
wish for grace, for a love spot, for invulnerability. Finn asks that he
might lose the smell of clay, "which he had had ever since he sinned with
a woman who was dead."[21]

Indeed, Finn does have "a smell of clay." He is often treacherous,
contriving the deaths of people he dislikes or distrusts. At the end of the
story of Diarmaid and Gráinne, an important variant of the Deirdre

story, Diarmaid is mortally wounded by a boar, and Finn comes upon him thus. Diarmaid asks Finn to heal him with a drink from his magic hands. Finn refuses; but after a plea from his own grandson, Finn goes to fetch water. Myles Dillon summarizes the rest of the scene: "But as he came from the well, he let the water flow through his fingers when he remembered Gráinne. Twice he did this, and the third time, when he came with the water, Diarmaid was dead."[22] Finally, he kills his own daughter's son, who is also the grandson of Goll MacMorna, and thus precipitates the fight that leads to the death of Goll.

Finn, who is crafty, full of equanimity, and highly praised by all, is the chief of the Fenians, and he is the one whose name tends to be attached to random folktales; but it is Goll, the one-eyed slayer of Finn's father, who is presented as the heroic warrior. In contrast to Finn, he is straightforward and chivalrous. In Connaught and Donegal it is Goll, not Finn, who is the hero of the Fenian oral tradition.[23]

The clans of Baiscne and Morna are enemies. Finn's father, Cumhall, has driven the clan of Morna out of Ireland and has implacably pursued them even overseas. Finally Goll kills Cumhall, and not long afterward the two clans are reconciled. The king groups them into one *fian*, and gives leadership of it to Finn. A number of times Goll saves Finn's life, but finally Finn turns against him and forces him alone up onto a high crag, the setting of a number of the most heroic poems of the cycle. Goll has been there for thirty days, constantly fighting and without food. He curses Finn's clan. He recognizes his position: "Lone am I on this crag, though I am overcome with hunger, since to-night there is with me but one poor woe-begone woman."[24] He boasts of his past deeds, listing men he has killed, telling the story of the rivalry between his clan and that of Finn's, and always coming back to an awareness of his present position:

> We gave battle gloriously to the fearless battalions; many were in evil plight through me, and we ourselves were full of wounds.
>
> Fifteen hundred dexterously I slew of this host: I left them in a heap of bones, though to-night I am lonely.[25]

In another poem, one of the great ones of the Fenian cycle, Goll's wife leaves him. He encourages her to go to the camp of Finn and wed someone there. She suggests that he should eat of the dead men around him and drink milk from her breasts, but he will not do it. She pities his condition, but he turns his mind to his victories, and thus the poem ends:

I brought the Munstermen to grief on the Tuesday in Magh Léana: I delivered battle bravely on the morn in Magh Eanaigh.

Eochaidh Red-spot son of Mál, of Ulster's proud-faced overking, I plunged into that hero my spear: I brought them to sorrow, woman.[26]

In a final ballad, Oisin tells Patrick the story of the death of Goll. How many fell in the battle? "One man, four men, and thirty hundred, fell by Goll of mighty deed." He then proceeds to list them.

But finally Goll is killed:

The brave tower of battles fell, haughty Goll, son of Morna, head of the heroes, king of the lords, the race of Morna of the broad shields.

Though many a fight was fought before by Goll Mac Morna of the companies, it was by hunger the man perished, though he had taken the spoils of hardy men.[27]

These stories of Goll, as well as their development and propagation throughout the North, mark the acceptance of the Fenian cycle throughout Ireland. Their having been virtually monopolized by folk storytellers all through history points to the conclusion that the tales of the Fenians appealed principally to subject peoples, not only in terms of dominated tribes or clans but even of the lower classes in the complex hierarchical organization of dominant groups. In short, the Fenian tales achieved their popularity because through the centuries more and more of the Irish people became vassals, until finally almost everyone was in that state.

The tales serve another purpose, necessary if any memory of the past should be preserved: they reconcile pagan values with churchly virtues. St. Patrick asks his guardian angels if it is all right with God if he listens to the pagan stories; they tell him that it is. From then on he is insatiable in his desire for stories: "Set this down, O Brogan, in writing." So one need not worry about the propriety of telling the tales: God through his angels and his saint has endorsed them. Oisin, for all his doubts, was baptized before he died. And what lingers is not the frame tales themselves, but a simple statement giving sanction to the story, to the effect that this is the story as Oisin told it to St. Patrick.

If the hypothesis is correct that the Fenian stories have remained in oral tradition during the last thousand years while the Ulster cycle has dropped out because during most of that time the Irish have been a vassal people, one would expect that with its new nationhood Ireland would reembrace the Ulster cycle, so that Cúchulainn would tend to replace Finn in the popular consciousness, possibly as the result of his stories being taught in the public schools. And to the extent that the worldwide tendency toward secularization is making itself felt in Ireland, one would expect that tendency to reinforce the pagan replacement.

On the other hand, Ulster is still an English colony, not part of the state of Ireland at all. Is this political fact enough to deprive the nation of its hero in spite of the above-mentioned conditions? One would expect that the contradiction between the myth and reality would force a change in the one or the other—and myths are notoriously resistant to change.

There are many other archetypal images in the Irish imagination: the fairy people who once ruled and still live in Ireland; the mythical races that successively invaded Ireland, then ruled, and finally were defeated; St. Patrick himself, with his miracles and curses on the land, and his fellow saints—Columcille, Brendan, and Brigit; historical figures like O'Connell and the tragic Parnell; and the IRA, along with its early heroics and its present terrorism. But the images that are most active in defining the people as they would be—in giving them the charter of worth without which a person or a people cannot go on—would seem to be the two warriors and their peoples: Cúchulainn and the Red Branch; Finn and the Fenians.

# NOTES

1. D. P. Moran, "The Battle of Civilizations," in *Ideals in Ireland*, ed. Lady Gregory (London, 1901), pp. 36–37.
2. Information on the storytelling tradition of Ireland has been principally derived from James H. Delargy's classic study "The Gaelic Story-Teller, with Some Notes on Gaelic Folk-Tales," *Proceedings of the British Academy* 31:177–221 (1945).
3. Ibid., pp. 185–86.
4. Gerard Murphy, *Saga and Myth in Ancient Ireland* (Dublin, 1961; reprinted in Eleanor Knott and Gerard Murphy, *Early Irish Literature* [New York: Barnes & Noble, 1966]), p. 100, quoting from K. Meyer, *Anecdota from Irish Manuscripts*.
5. Delargy, "The Gaelic Story-Teller," p. 208.
6. For a brief overview of the ethnology of the Celts, John Messenger's *Inis Beag: Isle of Ireland* (New York: Holt, Rinehart & Winston, 1969) is highly recommended. Much of the above description was based on this source.
7. References and citations to the Ulster cycle are to Thomas Kinsella's translation of *The Táin* (London: Oxford University Press, 1970) except where otherwise noted. There are a number of other renderings, each excellent in its own way, but the Kinsella version was selected as being at once one of the most carefully done and the most available for supplementary use by students. However, where

Kinsella's spelling of proper names is different from more established spellings, the established forms are used. Many readers will recognize the name Deirdre, while few will recognize Derdriu.

8. "Romance del infante Arnaldos," in Ramón Menéndez Pidal, *Flor Nueva de romances viejos* (13th ed.; Buenos Aires, 1962), p. 185.
9. See below.
10. Gertrude Schoepperle [Loomis], *Tristan and Isolt* (London, 1913).
11. *Deirdre of the Sorrows*, Act 3, in David Greene, ed., *An Anthology of Irish Literature* (New York: Modern Library, 1954), p. 465. This play was first produced in 1910.
12. The giving of proper names to weapons goes back to the epic of Gilgamesh, at least a thousand years before Christ.
13. Myles Dillon, *Early Irish Literature* (Chicago: University of Chicago Press, 1948), p. 29.
14. Ibid., p. 33.
15. Ibid., p. 37.
16. "Colloquy of the Old Men," in Greene, *Anthology of Irish Literature*, p. 88.
17. "The Fianna," in Greene, *Anthology of Irish Literature*, p. 96.
18. Gerard Murphy, ed. and trans., *Duanaire Finn*, Part 2 (London: Simpkin Marshall, for Irish Texts Society, 1933), p. 181.
19. Ibid., p. 195.
20. Eoin (John) MacNeil, ed. and trans., *Duanaire Finn*, Part 1 (London: David Nutt, for Irish Texts Society, 1908), p. 129.
21. Sean O'Sullivan, ed. and trans., *Folktales of Ireland* (Chicago: University of Chicago Press, 1966), pp. 57–60. My summary.
22. Dillon, *Early Irish Literature*, p. 48.
23. MacNeill, *Duanaire Finn*, Part 1, p. xxxvii.
24. Ibid., p. 200.
25. Ibid., p. 203.
26. Ibid.; p. 122.
27. Ibid., p. 166.

# 2

# FROM THE BEGINNINGS TO THE END
# OF THE MIDDLE AGES

## *Henry L. Snyder*

$T$he early history of Ireland, at least
up until the fifth century A.D., is known to us only in the most fragmentary
fashion. A rich literature, which takes its origin from a period beginning
several centuries later, commemorates this so-called heroic age and re-
counts tales of valor and martial prowess. These tales describe warlike
people who are easily identified with the Celts. The Celts not only dominated western Europe for several centuries before the beginning of the
Christian Era, they even extended their sway to Rome, which they sacked
in 390 B.C., and to Greece. The names, the deeds, and the "history" these
tales purport to describe, however, must now be recognized as pure fiction. The *Labor Gabala*, with its strict genealogy and succession of Irish
kings, and the *Ulidian Tales*, especially the famous *Táin*, are creations of
fertile imaginations, of scribes who aimed at glorifying their race and
dignifying their past. Some features of the mode of life that is described
may ring true, but the events that are described have no historical foundation. For one whose earliest recollection of Irish history was through
the acquisition of a late-nineteenth-century edition of *Whitaker's Alma-
nac*, with its long and precise chronological table of Irish kings, all of

25

whom seemed to have died a violent death, some of the glamour of the Irish past is lost by this mundane revelation. Still, impressive accomplishments remain to be told, and the flowering of Irish Christianity in the succeeding period brings a glory and a distinction to Ireland that represent no magnification. Before turning to that period, however, we must summarize what historians have been able to glean about the history of Ireland before the coming of Christianity, when the historical period begins.

Ireland became an island about fifty thousand years ago, when it was separated from the European mainland, leaving Britain as the westernmost portion of the Continent. Britain, in turn, did not follow Ireland's example until a much more recent period, a mere ten thousand years ago. As a consequence, Ireland has a much more limited range of flora and fauna, and contains some rare species found elsewhere on the European littoral only in Spain. The island is ringed by mountains, which form a bowl-shaped area in the center—a large central plain. This central plain is composed primarily of carboniferous limestone, which explains the richness of its soil and the quality of its pastures. Some 75 percent of the land is waste; the rest, arable. Blessed with an abundant rainfall, Ireland is a country of many rivers.

The first inhabitants of the island came over from Scotland and settled in the north of Ireland about 6,000 B.C. They have left little trace of their existence, but through the implements they left behind we can identify them with the Middle Stone Age, or Mesolithic, people who inhabited western Europe about this time. They were followed in Europe and then in Ireland by the Neolithic, or New Stone Age, men, who originated in the Near East and were the first to learn the art of cultivating the soil. Spreading across southern Europe, some of them migrated to Ireland from Brittany, while others went on to Britain and northern Europe. These small, dark-skinned people must have arrived in Ireland about 5,000 B.C. In addition to their stone axes, examples of their pottery have been found, as well as the burial places where they raised great stone monuments to their dead. The mounds or cairns that covered their burial places are impressive in size, and a number of them have been discovered. These people had also learned to extract metals from the land, and they worked with copper and gold. Their bronze workings into jewelry and vessels of various kinds were of fine quality, and were among Ireland's earliest exports. But the successors of these early inhabitants possessed far-greater artistic skills. Our principal concern, then, must be with these successors—the Celts—who first made their appearance in Ireland several centuries later, about 1200 B.C.

Several waves of these Celtic invaders or settlers have been iden-

KINGDOM of the NORTH

KINGDOM of ULIDIA

SUBKINGDOM of BREFNI

KINGDOM of ORIEL

KINGDOM of CONNAUGHT

KINGDOM of MEATH

KINGDOM of LEINSTER

THOMOND

KINGDOM of MUNSTER

Cooley
Ballycastle
Somerset
Derry
AILEACH
R. Bann
Donegal
LOUGH NEAGH
Bangor
INISHMURRAY
KILLADEAS
EMAIN MACHA
R. Quoile
LOUGH ERNE
(Armagh)
UPPER LOUGH ERNE
BOYLE ABBEY
Clogher
MONASTERBOICE
Kells
NEW GRANGE
CRUACHAN
Elphin
Roscommon
Trim
TARA
CONG
Tuam
ATHENRY
Clonard
Clontarf
ST. MACDARA'S ISLAND
CLONFERT
Clonmacnois
Durrow
Dublin
R. Shannon
Kildare
WICKLOW MTNS.
GLENDALOUGH
DYSERT O'DEA
Carlow
Limerick
Kilkenny
SCATTERY ISLAND
Cashel
JERPOINT
KILMALKEDAR GALLERUS
AHENNY
Wexford
DINGLE PENINSULA
Waterford
REASK
Lismore
Cork
GREAT SKELLIG

IRELAND BEFORE THE NORMANS

tified, perhaps as many as four, although their identification and their origin can be postulated but not defined with complete certainty. The common bond that links these peoples together is a linguistic one, though we also ascribe to them the introduction of new skills and techniques— iron metallurgy, wheeled vehicles or chariots, and fortified hilltop settlements. The first Celts intermingled with the existing inhabitants. Speaking a dialect identified as P-Celtic, they preserved their identity only in North Britain as the Picts. The Welsh and Bretons are a closely related group; their speech, also derived from P-Celtic, was probably very similar to that of the British. The second wave, the Builg or Erainn, also came over from Britain. They ultimately gave their name to the island. Another group of tribes, the Larginian, who settled in Ireland, notably in Leinster and Connaught, claimed to come from Gaul. The wave of Celts that we designate Q-Celts brought the dialect from which modern Irish or Gaelic is derived. They came to Ireland directly from the Continent, perhaps from Gaul, or possibly from Spain. The Celtic culture that we identify as La Tène, from its origin in Switzerland, was the contribution of one of the later groups of Celtic invaders, although the contributions of each group of immigrants will probably always rest in part upon conjecture because of the paucity of the evidence. What we can ascertain is that by the end of the heroic age (the age immortalized in the great Gaelic epics, sometime around the close of the fourth century after Christ) all these peoples—pre-Celts, P-Celts, and Q-Celts alike—had merged into one culture and spoke a common language. By the beginning of the historical period, for which written records survive, they were a common people.

The consolidation and victory of Celtic culture and language was followed by a reversal of the invasion pattern. Beginning in the fourth century A.D., the Irish began to raid the British coast, gradually extending their control over the western portions of Britain, notably Scotland and Wales. These raiding parties or invaders were called Scotti by the Romans. We owe the name of Scotland to their establishment of a kingdom in the north of Britain. The Welsh called these invaders by a different name—Gwyddyl—and the Irish adopted this name as Goidil or Gael. These pagan warriors ultimately occupied portions of the western and northern regions of Britain. Their attacks hastened the demise of the crumbling Roman outpost in Britain. Vortigern—the native ruler of the British, who took over the mantle of Roman authority—was prompted to seek outside assistance in order to repel these inroads upon his territories. He turned eastward for succor, importing Saxon mercenaries to reinforce his troops and to combat the invaders from the west. This action had far-reaching consequences upon Britain, but that story must be sought elsewhere.

The Celts took over the existing political divisions of the country that they found on their arrival—the organization of the island into five kingdoms. These were further subdivided into smaller units called *tuatha*. The Celts also took over the sacred places of their predecessors, but adapted them to their own religion. The two chief centers were Tara and Emain Macha. Others followed—Aileach in Ulster, Cruachan in Connaught—but Tara was always preeminent. This low hill, overlooking the river Boyne, was the focal point of the Celtic inhabitants of the island. There they built a wooden hall for their meetings; it was some 700 feet in length—a considerable edifice for the time. All that remain today are some trenches and circular depressions which suggest certain functions, but no more. Nevertheless, a visitor to Tara will quickly discover why this unprepossessing site was selected, for it commands a sweeping view for at least ten miles in every direction. The person honored as high king of Tara was the closest the Irish came to having a chief of state, but he had little authority. Chosen by the Celtic ruling class, customarily from the relatives of the ruling king while he was still alive, the successor to the kingship *(ardri)* eventually had to be a descendant of a great chief who ruled at the dawn of the historical period. This chief was Niall of the Nine Hostages, a member of the ruling family of the Connachta. A warrior-prince who was one of the leaders in the expeditions across the Irish Sea, he and his brothers and sons established kingdoms in Ulster and Connaught. Niall's descendants took the name of Ui Neill, and they ruled as high kings of Tara until 1022. Niall (also called Conn Niall) ruled at Tara from 380 to 405, presiding over the great festivals that were held every three years, to which the other kings came to pay him homage. It was he who was reputed to have built the five great roads of Ireland that connect Tara with the rest of the island. He was also the founder of the *fianna*, the great military hosts of the Celts that were created to protect the country against enemies from beyond the seas.

The reign of Niall, one of the few Celtic lords who could claim suzerainty over the whole of the country in fact as well as in name, also gave rise indirectly to another unique Irish leader, who created an alternative unifying force that was more powerful and endured for longer than the lay authority established by Niall. About the year 405 one of the raiding parties sent by Niall into Britain brought back a group of slaves which included a young Christian boy named Patrick. Six years later, Patrick escaped, went back to Britain, took priestly vows, and determined to return to Ireland and to carry the message of Christianity to the Irish. His dream became a reality in 432, when he was made a bishop by the Church of Gaul and was sent on his Christianizing mission to Ireland.

Patrick eventually established his base in Ulster, and after a period of slow progress he was given land at Armagh on which to build a church. Through the generosity of a local prince, Armagh thus had the honor of becoming the headquarters of the Church in Ireland. With the aid of other priests who were sent over from Gaul to assist him in his labors, Patrick set up other missions around Ireland and established bishoprics and diocesan centers. The highly individual character of Celtic culture and the lack of even the most rudimentary urban developments resulted in an organization that contrasted markedly with that of the Church on the Continent. There were no large, well-defined political units on which to base the diocesan structure. Patrick was forced to appoint a bishop to each of the small kingdoms, or *tuatha*, with the result that more than three hundred were created before the organization of the Church was completed. Moreover, the lack of towns or large concentrations of any kind—Ireland had no more than five hundred thousand inhabitants in all —precluded the establishment of the usual sort of parish organization. Rather than the lay structure giving rise to diocesan organization, the reverse was true. Patrick created, and his followers built, essentially a monastic church; and the monasteries established around the country were the only centers or major settlements that the country was to know until the arrival of the Scandinavians four centuries later. For even the fragile unity given to the country by Niall and his immediate successors gradually faded, and the country once more broke up into a series of small kingdoms, composed primarily of self-contained agrarian communities. The heroic age of conquest—when Celtic tribes from Ireland terrorized Britain and established dependencies in Scotland, England, and Wales—was succeeded by an age in which the Irish were if anything more influential but spread their influence through the Cross rather than the sword.

Under the monastic form of Church government organized by Patrick's successors, the Church in the sixth century took on the characteristic form by which we know it. As the Anglo-Saxons invaded England and gradually conquered a major part of Britain, which lies to the east of Ireland, the Irish Church was cut off from the most regular form of communication with Rome. For more than a century it was isolated from the Continental Church, which was undergoing important new reforms. The rites of the Irish Church slowly grew more and more independent of those of the Roman Church. The monasteries and their orders, rather than the cathedral chapters and the parish clergy, directed the life of the Church and provided leadership to the laity. The abbots, rather than the bishops, were the real governors of the Church. But this emphasis upon the development of the monasteries at the expense of the parish clergy, as well as the wealth that accrued to the monasteries, had its compensations. From the beginning, the monasteries had been centers of learning—schools, purveyors of Latin culture. Clonard (in Meath), Lismore, Derry, Kildare, became the centers not only for the Church but also for Irish social, intellectual, and commercial life. The fine arts were cultivated; and Irish craftsmen, scribes, illuminators, and artisans became famous throughout western Europe for the quality and richness of their products, which were all the more valued as the traditional centers of European culture and learning were ravaged and laid waste by the barbarians from northern Europe. They became indeed outposts of learning, refuges, and conservators of Latin-Christian culture.

The successors of Patrick and his priests saw that their mission, in order to repay the blessings that the Church had bestowed on the country, was to rekindle the flame of Christianity in Britain and on the Continent, where the Church had given way to pagan faiths brought by the latest conquerors. One of the first of the great missionaries who set out from Ireland was Columba, a descendant of the family of Niall. He followed his countrymen to the west coast of Scotland, where they had already carved out an independent kingdom in the land of the Picts; and in 563 he established a colony on the island of Iona, off the west coast of Britain. From this base he proceeded to Christianize Scotland, bringing new luster and fame to the Church of Ireland. Some seventy years later another Irish monk, Aidan, was brought to Northumbria by its king, Oswald, and established an Irish outpost on the island of Lindisfarne, off the east coast of Britain. Other Irish monks fanned out over the rest of northern England, even descending as far as the Thames, carrying their religion to territories where trace of it had disappeared with the retreat of the Romans. But their isolation from developments at Rome now began to tell. A counter effort to reconvert England had been launched from the south of England in 597 by Augustine, who had been sent there by the pope himself. Establishing himself at Canterbury, as Patrick had at Armagh, he slowly made converts throughout England, establishing diocesan centers at York, Winchester, and St. Albans. One of his followers, Wilfrid, abbot of Ripon, challenged the Irish clergy at a great synod held at Whitby in 664, where he upbraided his rival missionaries for their archaic rites and antiquated or heretical customs. Wilfrid persuaded the local ruler to the propriety and orthodoxy of the Roman

Church, and the Irish were forced to give way. Though the Irish, too, adopted the customs of the Roman Church and adapted themselves to the changes that had been taking place on the Continent, their influence slowly waned, and the Church in England began to take its lead from Canterbury rather than from Lindisfarne or Armagh. The missionary activities of the Irish monks did not cease, but the scene of their activities shifted from Britain to the Continent. The Irish Church, now reconciled to Rome, came into its full flower. During the next two centuries its representatives wandered over all of western Europe, carrying the gospel and Latin culture from the Baltic to the Mediterranean. Some made their mark as teachers; others, as scholars. They were especially admired for their skill as artists and illuminators. Irish scribes—in Ireland, at Lindisfarne, and at monasteries throughout Europe—created illuminated manuscripts that remain among the great treasures produced by the Church during its first millenium. Among the first of these missionaries were those who Christianized the Franks. Then they spread farther afield as Columbanus converted Lombardy and Burgundy. From there they passed over into Switzerland, establishing monasteries and schools. The most famous scholar-teacher among the Irish who settled in central Europe was John Scotus. He gained as his patron the emperor himself, who appointed him director of the school that enjoyed his patronage at Laon.

Since the last wave of Celtic immigrants at the beginning of the Christian Era, Ireland had not sustained any further invasion. With the end of the heroic age she had settled into a relatively peaceful state. An open, bountiful land, Ireland was sparsely inhabited and was marked by small agrarian settlements. More important centers were to be found only around the monastic establishments, for the Irish were not town dwellers. Even the many kings and princes who abounded after the brief and fragile unity achieved by Ui Niall were presumed to have lived in humble dwellings, which were often situated on an island in one of Ireland's many lakes for protection. A nominal suzerainty was exercised by one of Niall's descendants in the north, based upon Connaught; there was another in the south, based on Meath. But these kings had only titular authority over the many lesser chiefs whom they were supposed to rule. This lack of a central authority and of an efficient national host (the Fianna Fail notwithstanding), as well as a general lack of military sophistication, made the Irish an easy prey to a new invasion. The topography of Ireland, with its many navigable rivers, which laid open the whole island to attack from the sea, encouraged buccaneers to come and seize the wealth that had accumulated in the great monastic centers.

They were also attracted by the natural bounty which the land provided. The people who responded to this challenge were the Vikings.

Turgesius was the first of his people to make his way to Ireland, landing there in 831. He took his ships upon the Shannon and the Bann rivers, and took possession of Armagh, the home of the Irish Church. The Irish were prompt to defend themselves, and they enjoyed success for some time under the then high king Malachy, who defeated the Vikings in 848. But another wave of invaders soon followed, for in 852 more Vikings came over to make a landing at Dublin Bay, where they established a fortress and their headquarters. As the Vikings intensified their attacks on England in the latter part of the century, a period of relative calm ensued, and they intermingled with the native Celtic population, even taking one of them for their chief.

The Norse invasion was renewed at the beginning of the tenth century. During the next half-century the Vikings established a series of fortresses around the southern half of the island at the mouths of the major rivers. It is to them that Ireland owes the foundation of what still remain its major cities—Dublin, Wexford, Cork, Limerick, and Waterford. Once again the Irish put up a stiff resistance, and the king of Dublin, Olaf, was defeated, with his warriors, in 977. Domnall, the high king and the victor, gradually brought most of southern Ireland under his control. Indeed, resistance to the Viking invaders, which resulted in the uniting of the English people under Alfred at roughly the same period, had a similar effect in Ireland. Brian Boru, son of a ruling chief in northern Munster, wrested the crown of Munster from the Viking murderers of his brother in 976. Once in possession of Munster, he used it as a base to bring the rest of the country under his rule. Adding Leinster to the territories under his rule, he had control of all of southern Ireland by 984. He now singled out as his great rival, Malachy, king of Meath, who occupied a similar position to the north. After defeating opponents who tried to dispossess him in Leinster, Brian marched to Dublin, which he occupied in 999. Three years later he demanded and received homage as high king from Malachy, who was powerless to resist him. Two years later Brian made a grand circuit of the country as high king, a feat unrivaled until then in Irish history. For the first time a king could legitimately claim to be leader of all the Irish. In return for support for his rule, he reinforced the primacy of Armagh in the Irish Church, thus bringing unity to both Church and state. The remaining years of his life he devoted to restoring the Church both in fabric and in spirit, and he enjoyed the support of Malachy in his endeavors.

His end came when he was impelled to take the field of battle once more, because of the treachery of relatives of his wife, whom he had married late in life. His stepson Sitric, who controlled Dublin, challenged his rule, and Brian laid siege to Dublin in 1013 in an effort to bring him into submission. Sitric, the beleagured commander, called for aid from the Vikings; and after giving up the siege, Brian met the Viking host at Clontarf on Good Friday in 1014. The Celts were victorious over the Vikings. But their king was a casualty of the battle, and Ireland once more broke up into a series of petty states, each quarreling with the others for supremacy. The unity achieved by Brian proved to be fragile and transitory. The opportunity to establish a true Irish national state was lost at his death, not because of foreign conquest—the Vikings had been defeated—but because of dissension and competition among the Celts themselves.

The Vikings indeed remained in the country, but they became an asset rather than a threat or liability. Though they maintained their independence from the Irish chieftains, they collaborated with the Celtic inhabitants of Ireland, complementing rather than competing with the people with whom they shared the island. The fortresses they had established became towns, which acted as commercial centers and entrepôts for all the inhabitants of the country. Viking ships and Viking seafaring skills also provided Ireland with a fishing fleet and with vessels to transport Irish products to foreign markets. The Ostmen, for so they were called, accepted Christianity, and bishoprics were created in their main centers. This was a parish-oriented, urban organization rather than the monastic-centered Church of the Irish, and the Ostmen looked across the sea to England and Rome for leadership, rather than to Armagh. The decline of a central authority in the state was paralleled by a similar division in the Church.

After the death of his rival and then coadjutor, Malachy resumed the high kingship, but only for a few years, since he died in 1022. It was another century before a man of equal stature could enforce his claims for the high kingship and for the submission of the other kings to him. The last great native ruler of the country hailed from Connaught, where he ruled as king. Turlough O'Connor secured the allegiance of the other Irish kings, and held the high kingship for thirty-seven years, from 1119 to 1156. His son and successor lacked the ability and fortitude to succeed him in power as well as estate. Other claimants were no more successful, and any chance for the eventual restoration of a unified Irish state was lost by the arrival of the Normans in 1168.

The invasion of the Normans was made possible by, and resulted from, the disunity and decay that were prevalent in both Church and state in Ireland. Complaints against the evils and abuses in the Irish Church had reached Rome more than twenty-five years earlier; and though reforms were attempted, including the reorganization of the Church and the addition of two new archbishops (Tuam and Leinster), the lack of a centralized government to support a national church compromised the strength and integrity of the Church. As a result of the complaints that had reached his ears, Pope Adrian IV (the only English pope) gave his blessing to Henry II as early as 1159 to take possession of Ireland, but Henry II abandoned the idea of conquest for the time being, at the behest of his mother, Matilda. The immediate impetus for the invasion in 1168 came from an appeal by Dermot, king of Leinster, who was beset by a coalition of petty Irish princes who held grievances against him. After Dermot was expelled from his territories by his feudatories, who had the sanction of the high king, he sailed to England for assistance. After receiving the approval of Henry II of England, he solicited assistance from the Anglo-Norman nobility, and he offered his daughter's hand and the succession of his kingdom in Leinster to Richard, earl of Pembroke, in return for an expedition to drive out Dermot's evictors.

The invasion was undertaken in 1168, and continued through the next year. At first the English king simply gave his blessing, leaving the actual conduct of his affairs to his nobles. But as the progress and success of the invaders became evident, the king decided that he should take control in order to prevent his nobles from carving out independent states over which he would have no jurisdiction. He ordered the adventurers to return, and then he persuaded their leader to hand over to him as king the port towns established by the Vikings. In 1171 Henry II himself sailed for Ireland, and he enlarged the conquests that had already been made by adding Waterford and Wexford to the territories under his control. After a successful campaign, Henry proceeded to Dublin, which opened its gates to him; and he spent the winter there. Forced to return to England to attend to domestic matters in the spring of 1172, he put this new addition to his realm in the hands of one of his trusted subordinates, Hugo de Lacy, who thus became the first English viceroy in the country. De Lacy was also granted the province of Meath, to counter the claims of the organizer of the first Norman invaders, Strongbow, who asserted his authority successfully over Leinster. Elsewhere the king's suzerainty was nominal at best, though the clergy were marshalled strongly behind the new ruler because of the support of the pope, Alexander III.

From the beginning, Norman rule was constantly being challenged by the Irish leaders who were still in free possession of their domains.

This pattern persisted for some four hundred years, until the whole of the island was finally brought under English control at the end of Elizabeth's reign. After a variety of disputes, in which Strongbow was not above suspicion himself, a treaty was reached in 1175 which granted Roderick O'Connor, king of Connaught, the right to retain his territories in return both for paying tribute to Henry II and for requiring the other Irish kings to pay tribute through him. A later adventurer, John de Courcy, reduced a major part of Ulster to his rule in 1177. In that year Henry II, with the consent of the pope, made his son John lord of Ireland. Then John inherited the crown of England, and his Irish title was taken over by his successors as part of their inheritance, but the title and authority thus possessed were personal. John's accession to the English throne brought an end to the separate status of Ireland. Nevertheless, Ireland was a fief of the English king, not a dependency of England herself. This distinction, which did not end until the advent of Henry VIII, was to cause difficulties in later centuries; ultimately it led to the Act of Union of 1800. John sailed to Ireland in 1185, at the age of nineteen, to take formal possession of his domains. He treated his new subjects with rudeness and derision, and turned their willingness to accept his rule into rebellion. John and his subordinates were not competent to deal with the situation, so that by the time the young prince left eight months later, the power of the Normans had diminished—the opposite of what he had set out to accomplish. At the death of John's father in 1189, Norman control was limited to sections of the coast, land along the Shannon and in Leinster, and portions of Meath and Ulster. Elsewhere, especially in the mountains, the native population remained free of Norman control. John, now king of England, returned to Ireland, planning to force the submission of his rebel subjects, which now included some of the Norman families. The chief accomplishment of his visit was the introduction of English machinery of government and the establishment of English law in Ireland. At this time he divided the kingdoms under his control into twelve counties, with names that they bear down to this day. Although he did not subdue the Irish kings, he was able at least to force them to pay him homage. But the main legacy of his work was the pattern of government in the feudal mold that he left behind. However, it extended no further than Norman soldiers could impose it; thus, the challenge of total conquest was left to his successors.

There followed now a bewildering succession of viceroys who left little mark upon the country during their tenure. The extent of English rule in Ireland, never imposing, slowly declined during this period. Henry III, often beleagured and always preoccupied with problems nearer at home, gave his lordship of Ireland scant attention. His son Edward I, though far more able, was equally taken up with the problems of Wales and Scotland, as well as with domestic concerns. Ireland was primarily of use to him as a source of supplies and troops. In spite of his successful efforts to strengthen the control of the central government in England, he not only allowed the government in Ireland to decay, he also contributed to the acceleration of the process. He continued the practice of his predecessors in granting liberties or exemptions in Ireland, to the detriment of royal authority and the income that should have appertained to it. Besides these exempt jurisdictions, which included four of the counties created by his grandfather—Meath, Wexford, Carlow, and Kilkenny— other parts of Ireland were granted similar status. The Fitzgeralds in Desmond and the De Clares in Thomond achieved a degree of autonomy, which they passed on to their descendants. They formed the nucleus of the third party in Ireland—that of the Anglo-Irish, or old English, who were to play such a prominent part in modern Irish history. These nobles passed out honors to their inferiors, dispensed justice, and appointed the sheriffs for their counties. The royal authority declined to such an extent that the king's writ ran only in lands held by the Church. The lack of a strong central authority and the independence of much of the nobility gave rise to continual strife and dissension in the country.

The reputation and prowess of Edward I as ruler and military leader were such as to command the support of even his errant Irish subjects, and the lordship of Ireland was an important source of troops and funds for the warrior-king's aggressive policies. His son Edward II was sadly unfit to succeed such a sovereign, and he fell a victim to his own lack of military ability. In 1315, the same year that Edward II was defeated in Scotland by Robert the Bruce, the Scottish hero's brother Edward invaded Ireland. For two years he raged through the country, and although he was finally ejected, the cost to Ireland was heavy. The native chieftains took advantage of this embarrassment to the English crown to join forces against their common enemy. Under the leadership of the O'Connors, descendants of the last king of all Ireland, they met the Anglo-Normans at Athenry and went down to defeat. The De Burghs, earls of Ulster, now reigned supreme in Ulster and Connaught. But though the Irish leaders lost in their effort to eject the Norman settlers, the conquerors approached their objective at a much slower rate during the course of the next two centuries. The attention of the kings of England was focused on the Continent, and the military resources were squandered in France rather than being conserved to complete the conquest of Ireland. While English rule was slowly eroded, Irish tribal leaders regained their untrammeled authority. Edward II's reign saw the ennobling of three great Anglo-Irish families who came to occupy a commanding position in Irish affairs, dominating the government of the country until the second part of the seventeenth century. The first to be created was the greatest until the time of the Tudors, the earls of Kildare, whose territories lay close by Dublin, the center of and at times the only remaining place of English influence in Ireland. The head of a related family was created earl of Desmond in 1329; this line also grew to great power, gaining virtual independence as English authority gradually receded. The third of this trio is the one likely to be most familiar to students of the early modern period. This was the earl of Ormonde. The title was granted to the descendants of a man who had come over to Ireland with Henry III and had been made hereditary butler to the king. Hence he took his family name from the office he held. The Butlers maintained considerable influence in Ireland down into the Hanoverian period. They gradually acquired a unique reputation for their loyalty and service to the English crown.

The very use of the term "Anglo-Irish" introduces a perennial problem that plagued English kings for centuries as they saw with frustration how ultimate control over Ireland continually eluded them. It was a problem that first came to a head during the reign of Edward III. Under his rule the number of Englishmen resident in Ireland slowly declined. The colonists or settlers were not regularly afforced with new arrivals, and the longer they remained in Ireland, the more completely they adopted the habits and customs of the native Irish. Beginning in 1338 the king sought to combat this practice. Englishmen were given a monopoly of legal offices, but the monopoly was often violated. Each successive wave of new arrivals, sent over by England to control the natives, was soon assimilated into the native population. Moreover, as English authority declined and the country was exposed to endless feuds and struggles, a number of the landowners returned to England, leaving their estates in the hands of agents. The phenomenon of absenteeism, so prevalent in modern times in Ireland, has a long if hardly distinguished ancestry. In 1361 Edward III ordered some sixty-three absentee lords to return to their country, and to support the government of his son Clarence, who had obtained the earldom of Ulster by marriage and the viceroyship by the appointment of his father. In that same year, Clarence summoned a meeting of the Irish Parliament at Kilkenny, where he sought to make the best of the bad state of affairs in which he found himself. He gave legal recognition to the fact that there were two, if not three, Irelands—that part within the range of English control from Dublin, which was called the Pale, and that without. It was a desperate measure to preserve the last vestige of English rule in Ireland. Within the Pale both Englishmen and Irishmen were to speak English and follow English customs. The Statute of Kilkenny (1366), which adumbrated these charges, went further: it barred Irish games, Irish storytellers, and other pernicious influences. Even the Church was to be preserved exclusively for bona fide Englishmen, and Irishmen were barred from receiving preferment. To no avail. What the statute gave testimony to was the effectiveness with which the natives and their customs had successfully withstood the wave of English invaders and the considerable progress that they had made in freeing themselves of alien rule.

Rather than reverse the trend by this means, Edward III contributed to the further decline of English influence in Ireland by drawing upon the dwindling English population for soldiers to man his armies. His successor, Richard II, was no more successful. Even loyal Anglo-Irish leaders objected by refusing to serve the king as viceroy. When the centers of English influence—the coastal towns—came under attack and succumbed to rebel Irish leaders, the king himself came over in person in 1394 to suppress them. The trip was his undoing, as his enemies in England conspired against him while he was away. His loss at home was paralleled by similar losses in Ireland. Though he brought over a large army, it was not competent to deal with the guerrilla tactics of the natives. In the fifteenth century, only Henry V managed to find an effective subaltern for his obstreperous colony to the west. In the person of John Talbot, who was viceroy from 1414 to 1419, he found a man able at least to restore some stability to the Pale, but the insatiable demands of the army in France caused many Irish troops to be sent to the Continent; and this again weakened the government in Ireland. English authority reached its nadir under Edward IV (1560–1582), when the Pale was reduced to little more than the lands lying immediately around Dublin. The siren call of Irish customs was so great, and Englishmen still succumbed so regularly, that Parliament was forced to stiffen the prohibitions against Irish ways in 1465. As this did not check the decline, Parliament went to the last extremity in 1480, forbidding all trade between the Pale and the rest of Ireland. A beleagured outpost in a hostile country, Dublin did little more than keep the flame of English rule fitfully alive during the fifteenth century. The result of the prohibitions was to cut the English off from all commerce with the natives, and consequently to prevent the Irish from being exposed to those English customs that the kings were so anxious to establish.

The existence of the Pale in the later Middle Ages did guarantee one important aspect of English rule in Ireland—it ensured the perpetuation of English law and English institutions. Having survived the later Middle Ages, they were still functioning when Henry Tudor came to the throne and laid the basis for their revival in the sixteenth century. Even though this influence was limited to the Pale, Ireland developed an elaborate system of government which was closely related to similar developments in England. It included a council and a parliament, together with the usual staff of senior ministers or administrators. To some extent this process was retarded by the constantly changing flow of deputies or justiciars that characterized the Irish government at that time. Still, Ireland already had a functioning council and a parliament by the end of the thirteenth century. The Common Council, the equivalent of the contemporary English Great Council, played an active role. From this Council grew the Parliament, which first received deputations of commoners in 1324, almost the same time that they began attending in England. The thirteenth century also saw the creation of the office of treasurer and of justiciar. The Parliament treated the same categories of business as did its English counterpart—judicial, legislative, administrative—but its authority was limited, and it met infrequently. The key body was the Council, which gradually lost the portion of its membership that was drawn from the baronage and clergy to the House of Lords and then evolved into an efficient body composed primarily of ministers. It became the principal instrument of and enforcement agency for executive policy, and it ranged over the whole gamut of subjects requiring the attention and action of the viceroy. But we speak of forms almost without substance. The actual responsibilities of these bodies and officers were severely restricted because of the limited extent of English rule. It was not until the accession of Henry Tudor that the government began to extend once more its base of power—the beginning of the final and successful phase of English attempts to reduce Ireland to submission.

## SUGGESTIONS FOR FURTHER READING

GENERAL WORKS:

Beckett, James C. *The Making of Modern Ireland, 1603–1923.* New York: Knopf, 1966.

———. *A Short History of Ireland.* London and New York: Hutchinson's University Library, 1952.

Cullen, Louis M. *Life in Ireland.* London: Batsford, and New York: G. P. Putnam's Sons, 1968.

Curtis, Edmund. *A History of Ireland.* 6th ed., rev. London: Methuen, 1951.

Lyons, Francis S. L. *Ireland since the Famine.* London: Weidenfeld & Nicolson, 1971.

Moody, Theodore W., and Martin, F. X. *The Course of Irish History.* New York: Weybright & Talley, 1967.

Norman, Edward R. *A History of Modern Ireland.* Coral Gables, Fla.: University of Miami Press, 1971.

**FOR THIS CHAPTER:**

Chadwick, Nora K. *The Age of the Saints in the Early Celtic Church.* London and New York: Oxford University Press, 1961.

De Paor, Máire, and de Paor, Liam. *Early Christian Ireland.* London: Thames & Hudson, and New York: Praeger, 1958.

Flower, Robin. *The Irish Tradition.* Oxford: Clarendon Press, 1947.

Hanson, Richard P. C. *Saint Patrick: His Origins and Career.* London and New York: Oxford University Press, 1968.

Hughes, Kathleen. *The Church in Early Irish Society.* London: Methuen, 1966.

Norman, Edward R., and St. Joseph, J. K. S. *The Early Development of Irish Society.* London: Cambridge University Press, 1969.

Orpen, Goddard H. *Ireland under the Normans, 1169–1333.* 4 vols. Oxford: Clarendon Press, 1968.

Raftery, Joseph. *Prehistoric Ireland.* London and New York: Batsford, 1951.

Richardson, Henry G., and Sayles, G. O. *The Irish Parliament in the Middle Ages.* Philadelphia: University of Pennsylvania Press, 1952.

Ruthven, Annette J. Otway. *A History of Medieval Ireland.* London: Ernest Benn, and New York: Barnes & Noble, 1968.

Thomas, Charles. *Britain and Ireland in Early Christian Times:* A.D. *400–800.* London: Thames & Hudson, 1971.

# 3

# THE ART OF PREHISTORIC AND EARLY CHRISTIAN IRELAND

## Marilyn Stokstad

In Ireland, rival groups of people have struggled for supremacy since the second millenium B.C. Metal work, carving, and building styles and techniques show the superimposition of one culture over another, and myths suggest clashes such as that between worshippers of an earth-mother goddess and followers of a cult of sky gods. The Celts, who are so closely identified with the Irish today, were themselves invaders from the Continent. The Celts introduced the so-called Iron Age into Ireland in the fifth century B.C.

With the advent of recorded history, the conflicts are documented. In the Early Christian period, Irish religious practices did not conform to those of the Church of Rome, and the antagonism became so great that a church synod was held at Whitby, England, in the seventh century in an unsuccessful (from the Irish point of view) attempt to mediate differences. In the ninth century, Christian Irish and pagan Vikings battled for the island; in the twelfth century, Anglo-Normans—a people who had moved from Scandinavia to northern France (Normandy), then to

England—invaded Ireland.[1] In short, century after century, new people —and new art forms—arrived in Ireland. They enriched but never entirely supplanted the Celtic culture, so that Irish art maintained its Celtic character in spite of political disasters.

The arts of Ireland reflect a special kind of magic—not the "misty Celtic twilight" imagined by modern Romantics, but rather the brilliant magic of the smith and the poet, of the master of metal and the master of words. The smith, working with the very essence of power—fire and light, caught in matter as gold or glass—forged the weapons and tools that had the power to extend and enhance a warrior's strength or a woman's skill. The smith also created the treasure hoard—precious metals,

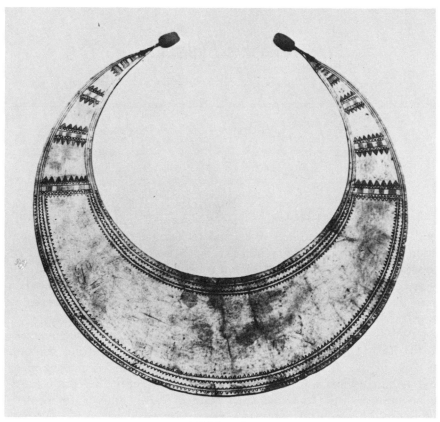

Gold Lunula
c. 1800 B.C.; found in Ross, county Westmeath
National Museum of Ireland, Dublin

*Irish History and Culture*
44

jewels, and enamels—the objects that sparkled, glittered, and gleamed. He fashioned the jewelry that denoted wealth and power. Later, for the Christian Church, he created the chalices, the bells, and the shrines for relics—the utensils needed to reenact and celebrate the Last Supper and the sacrifice of Christ. In short, the smith made wonderfully functional objects which he enriched with decoration that encompassed all the prehistoric symbols of energy and life.

Eagle
Evangelist, *Book of Durrow* f. 84v.
Seventh century
Vellum, 9½″ x 6½″
Trinity College Library, Dublin, MS. 57
Photo by permission of the Board of Trinity College, Dublin

The scribe, on his part, transformed the epic oral tradition into written words and books, and thus gave visual life and permanence to the word itself. Inspired by the patterns of the metal worker, the artist began to decorate his letters almost beyond recognition. The Word of God, preserved and enriched by the scribe and encased in gold and jewels by the smith, stood on the altar of each simple church as the chief treasure of the Celtic Christian world.

The hoard of gold and the hoard of words, both enriched with their supernatural symbols, were treasured and augmented by each succeeding wave of invader-settlers. The Celtic artist saw all life in terms of creative energy, not in terms of simple visual experience; thus the constantly moving and regenerating spiral became the pictorial symbol of the endless cycle of death and rebirth.[2] The literal symbol came late, and then was elaborated until it reached the new level of reality found in the *Táin* or the *Book of Kells*. The exuberance and exaggeration of such Irish masterpieces demonstrate the quality of the Irish imagination—flowing freely but within the clear bounds of intellectual control—which could create a fantastically real dream world as precise and as brilliant in line and color as gold filigree or millefiore enamel, and as plausible as any visual image of the sensate world.

Geometric figures decorate one of the most impressive prehistoric structures in Ireland, the tumulus at New Grange near the river Boyne.[3] This giant mound, with its carved entrance and inner chamber, is part of a Stone Age necropolis, built perhaps as early as 2,000 B.C. The New Grange tumulus is actually a mound, 280 feet in diameter and still nearly 45 feet high, built up of river pebbles and faced at the base with huge standing stones. A passage, 62 feet long and lined with megaliths, leads to a tripartite chamber, 20 feet high and covered with a corbeled vault. Eighteenth-century antiquaries, such as Thomas Wright of Durham (see chapter 8), thought that the Danes built the mound as a sanctuary for Woden, Thor, and Freya. Describing his exploration of the tumulus in 1745, Wright wrote:

> It appears that Ground of the Gallery or way in, has with the Hill itself shrunk very much, so that at A [on his drawing], I was forced to creep upon my Hands to get into it, and not without some apprehension of danger, for fear some of the incumbent Stones might give way, but the Central Cave being an arched Dome, has very well kept its place, & seems not to have shrunk at all, probably there the foundation might be stone.[4]

Chi Rho, *Book of Kells* f. 34r.
Early ninth century; vellum; 13″ x 9½″ (originally 15″ x 11″)
Trinity College Library, Dublin, MS. 58
Photo by permission of the Board of Trinity College, Dublin

*Prehistoric and Early Christian Ireland*
47

New Grange Tumulus in 1746
"Section of the artificial mount at Grange in East Meath"
Thomas Wright, *Observations on . . . Remains of Antiquity in Ireland*
Book II, plate 10 (Irish copy, 1791)
University of Kansas Libraries, MS. D115
Photo by permission of University of Kansas Libraries

Engraved Stones
Tumulus near New Grange, c. 2500 B.C., county Meath
Photo by Marilyn Stokstad

The large stones around the entrance, as well as those in the interior of the New Grange tumulus, are elaborately decorated with engraved cups, rings, spirals, and lozenges. Joseph Raftery sees the paired spirals and lozenges as the eyes and nose of a face and suggests that the tumulus and its decoration are tangible expressions of an earth-mother cult. The epics of pagan Ireland suggest that the worship of the goddess was supplanted by a new religion, the sky cult of a male god, whose devotees subdued the population but never wholly erased the native beliefs.

Gold "sun discs," surviving from the second millenium B.C., suggest that long before the Celts arrived in Ireland some people worshiped solar as well as earth deities; however, the use and significance of the "sun discs" are not clear. The discs are usually found in pairs, and each disc has two small holes near the center so that it could have been fastened to a garment or another object. The discs are thin sheets of gold with a raised design on one side which divides the circle into quadrants, thus forming an equal-armed cross. Parallel lines, triangles, dots, or zigzags form a border. Gold lunulae, also thin sheets of beaten gold with exquisite geometric engraved decoration, are contemporary with the discs. The delicacy and precision of the engraving of both the discs and the lunulae indicate that their makers were skilled metal workers with a high level of aesthetic sensitivity.

The most famous of these prehistoric gold ornaments are the twisted gold neck rings, or torcs (ornaments associated with the "barbarians" even by the Greeks and Romans). Although gold is a relatively soft and malleable metal, it is also brittle and will snap when twisted. Thus the smiths had to invent methods to produce the effects they wanted. To make a torc, they bound a thin strip of gold between two base metal bars, twisted the three together, and then "unscrewed" the gold strip from the supports. They made more elaborate torcs by bending two strips of gold at right angles, joining them at the fold to form a cruciform rod, and then handling this rod like a simple torc to achieve a brilliant effect of multiple spiraling flanges. Sometimes they made simple spiral neck rings by twisting five or six strands of gold wire around a plain gold rod. This brilliant Bronze Age civilization ended about 1200 B.C.

Sometime, probably during the fifth century B.C., the La Tène Celts arrived in Ireland from the Continent.[5] Their style and techniques of metal working continued to be practiced into the Early Christian period (fifth century A.D.). Celtic smiths made implements of bronze (copper, iron, and tin) or iron, and they continued to use gold and silver for ornaments. Their techniques can be studied, since foundries have been discovered where the ore was crushed with heavy hammers and

Box Containing a Bronze-and-Gold Torc
Second or first century B.C.; found in Somerset, county Galway
National Museum of Ireland, Dublin
Photo by permission of the National Museum of Ireland

smelted in circular clay-lined pits in the ground. The workers placed alternating layers of charcoal and ore in the pit, and then built the clay liner up to form a dome above ground level, through which they inserted two bellows, pumped alternately, to maintain the uniform high heat required for smelting. As the ore became molten metal, it trickled to the bottom of the pit, where it collected and could be removed after it cooled. The raw product could be kept in the rounded pit form and/or melted and poured into bars of smaller, more convenient sizes. The Roman unit of weight for iron (the pig of 112 pounds), plus any excess weight, was marked on the top of the ingot.

By the first centuries of the Christian Era, not only were all the metal-working techniques (engraving, casting, repoussé, even filigree) being used in Ireland, but also champlevé and millefiore enameling were perfected. In champlevé enamel the colored glass paste was laid in metal cells and then fused by heating the piece in small clay heating trays, using a blow pipe. Elaborate plaques of yellow or white and blue millefiore were made by arranging colored glass rods in patterns. The bundles were then heated, fused, and drawn out to produce a single thin rod which would thus retain the miniaturized pattern. Thin sections could be cut from the rod and cemented into cells (recesses in the metal), or they could be mounted like jewels. Celtic artists often combined red and yellow champlevé enamel with three-dimensional swelling spiral and trumpet patterns and triskeles in repoussé. Instead of merely working patterns on the surface of the metal, the smith also made separate casts or enameled plaques to attach to the object.

One of the most beautiful examples of this metal work is a bronze box (which has been variously dated) containing a gold torc, which was found beside a *rath* ("fort") at Somerset, county Galway. The box is round, flat, and only about an inch high. Easy to overlook in its case among the gold treasures of the National Museum in Dublin, it is an impressive work of art because of the perfection of the proportions of its ornament and the sophisticated geometry of its asymmetrical swelling curves.

The smiths made many objects whose purpose is not now known —large discs, a complex combination of scalloped plaques with attached cones and discs (known as the Petrie Crown), and ornaments known as latchets—as well as weapons and great trumpets similar to the trumpets found in Danish bogs. All these objects are decorated with spirals and triskeles, running spirals and whirligigs, and trumpet and tendril-like forms. These decorative forms—associated as they are with solar symbols; with the movement of heavenly bodies and seasons; with life, death, and rebirth—may have a religious or magical significance. The Turoe Stone in county Galway, for example, is a great granite boulder nearly four feet high (a survival of the megalithic cults) which has been shaped into a domed pillar—a phallic form—and carved with curvilinear interlocking ornament typical of the La Tène Celts. The Turoe Stone, like the Irish epics, represents the clash and union of cultures—earth and sky cults, native and invader.

In contrast to the splendid metal work, building techniques were not highly developed in early Ireland. Dwellings in both pagan and Early Christian Ireland consisted of the so-called ring forts, or *raths*. The ring fort was probably not a fortress but rather a farmstead 60 to 110 feet across. A bank of earth with a ditch, often on the inside and thus affording little protection, was built around a slightly higher piece of land. Two, three, or even four concentric rings may have been built, probably to indicate the importance and prestige of the chief. These walls served as enclosures for livestock and as some protection against the national occupation of cattle raiding. (So common was cattle raiding that in the Early Christian period even abbots augmented the resources of their monasteries in this way. The great Ulster epic of Cúchulainn is entitled the *Cattle Raid of Cooley*.) Within the enclosure, timber or wattle-and-daub (crude wicker work and mud) structures were erected

Turoe Stone
Third to second century B.C.(?); county Galway
Granite, four feet high
Photo by permission of the Commissioners of Public Works in Ireland

as dwellings and shelters for animals. In literature the house (*tech*), which was "made," was distinguished from the outer wall (*rath*), which was "dug." For greater security these dwellings might be erected on artificially constructed mounds in bogs (*crannogs*). Since central Ireland was filled with bogs and swamps, such a system provided a logical means of security. Houses had one or two rooms, with one or two doors, although they had no hearth or chimney. Floors might be paved, and some attention was paid to proper drainage. An occasional stone house has survived; and, of course, later monastic settlements provide evidence for the appearance of early architecture.

The Celts, though unified racially and culturally, had little political unity. Ireland under their domination was divided into more than one hundred fifty small kingdoms which were based on a tribal organization. The political center, such as it was, was at Tara, where a high king held court. The Celts had no cities, no organized trade, no coinage. Although they used the ogham script for inscriptions, they had no written literature.

Their religion was druidism. The druids, the poets, and the artists (especially the smiths) were the powerful carriers of the history and traditions of the people.

In the first century A.D., Roman commanders of the legions in Britain looked across the turbulent Irish Sea at Ireland and decided that the island was not worth the trouble of conquest. The island developed without the interference, or advantages, of Roman rule. Petty warfare, cattle raiding, and trade in slaves and metal remained the sources of wealth.

One of these slaves, a captured British Roman, was Patrick, who escaped and later returned as the Apostle to the Celts in A.D. 432. He founded Armagh in Ulster as the first episcopal see.[6] An eighth-century "Catalogue of the Saints of Ireland" describes the early missionaries:

> The first order of Catholic saints, was in the time of Patrick; and then they were all bishops, distinguished and holy, and full of the Holy Ghost, 350 in number, founders of churches, they had one head, Christ, and one chief, Patrick. They had one Mass, one liturgy, one tonsure from ear to ear. They celebrated one Easter, on the fourteenth moon after the vernal equinox, and what was excommunicated by one church all excommunicated. They did not reject the service and society of women because founded on the rock, Christ, they feared not the blast of temptation.[7]

The Celts were no more ready to submit to a centralized church government than to a unified political system. Semiautonomous monasteries rather than a tightly organized system of parishes and bishoprics characterized church organization in Early Christian Ireland. The ecclesiastical community easily adapted itself to the Irish political and social structure of clans and small kingdoms. Secular and religious rulers had a patriarchal responsibility for the welfare of the clan, including the fertility of fields and animals and success in war. Although St. Patrick did not found monasteries as such, the Christian organization was monastic, and by the end of the fifth century, monasticism was widespread in Ireland.

In the sixth century, St. Columba (521–597) established an Irish monastic order, and the Columban Rule was followed in Ireland until the eleventh century. In spite of the fact that the early missionaries brought with them the literary tradition of Christian Rome, only scanty records survive from the fifth and sixth centuries. Nevertheless, we know that by the sixth century, important monasteries had been founded in Clonmacnois, Durrow, Bangor, and Glendalough, and even St. Patrick's primatial see of Armagh became monastic. The Church in Ireland developed along different lines than it did in England, where Roman Catholicism had been accepted. The conflict between the Roman and Celtic churches came to a head at the Synod of Whitby in 664, when the Roman Church was declared the official church in England. The Irish retired in high dudgeon to their island. Cut off later from contact with England and the Continent by the Viking invasions, the Irish Church developed in semi-isolation until the Norman invasions of the twelfth century.

Ecclesiastical communities at the time of St. Columba were similar to secular ones—that is, the oratory, cells, and kitchen were surrounded by circular earthworks. Such an establishment was called a city, and was ruled by a bishop. Monasteries were large and powerful, but since, like the secular communities, they were built of impermanent materials—earth ramparts, wattle-and-daub shelters, timber guest houses, schools, oratories —almost nothing survives from the earliest period.

On the Dingle Peninsula, where the scarcity of timber made building in stone necessary, oratories that were built in the eighth or ninth century still stand. The most perfect of these structures, the oratory at Gallerus, is 10 by 15 feet internally, with walls 3½ feet thick. The walls,

Oratory at Gallarus
Eighth or ninth century; Dingle Peninsula, county Kerry
Photo by Harold Orel

the high ridged roof, and the corbeled vault were built as a single form. The building was lit by a small, round-headed east window and a trabeated west door. Two holes at the sides of the door indicate that there were posts for wooden door valves. The oratory may date from the eighth century and was certainly in use in the ninth century. So conservative was the Irish Church that the architecture undoubtedly reflects early tradition, whatever the dates of the surviving building.

One of the most dramatic early Irish monastic sites is the Great Skellig, a jagged peak of stone rising 715 feet out of the sea off the west coast of the Dingle Peninsula. Six hundred feet above the sea a rock shelf provides a space for human habitation. (A medieval church dedicated to St. Michael gave the name Skellig Michael to the site). Three flights of stairs lead to the monastery. The monks had two wells; they tended garden plots on shelves on the west face of the rock. Six beehivelike cells (*clochans*)—10 feet square inside and 17 feet high to the roof, with walls as much as 6 feet thick—and two oratories, all of dry-stone con-

Monastic Site, Skellig Rock
Known as Skellig Michael, county Kerry
Photo by permission of the Commissioners of Public Works in Ireland

struction, survive on the ledge. The walls and roof of these simple buildings form a continuous mass, corbeled inward to form a covering. The floor plan is roughly rectangular, so that the walls, as they slope inward, gradually assume a rounded shape, and the building resembles an upturned boat. Each cell has a single entrance. The cells are carefully built. They even have wall niches and paved floors, and they are completely weatherproof even today.

Verses from the mid-seventh-century poem on the *Rule of Bangor* seem equally appropriate to Skellig Michael:

> House full of delicious things
> and built upon a rock;
> and no less the true vine
> brought out of Egypt's land.
>
> Surely an enduring city,
> strong and unified,
> worthy and glorious,
> set upon a hill.[8]

Few monasteries had the dramatic and romantic setting of Skellig Michael. Glendalough, in the Wicklow Mountains, and Clonmacnois, on the Shannon River, were protected by earthen ramparts; as they grew in prosperity or fame, the individual cells and the churches or oratories were multiplied in number rather than increased in size. Seven churches still stand at Clonmacnois. The monastic community thus took on the appearance of a city; in fact, it substituted for one, for the concept of the secular city built for commerce and war was only introduced into Ireland by the Vikings in the ninth century.

More churches were built of wood than of stone; but since none have survived, their appearance is recorded only in reliquaries, which might be house-shaped to form a home and tomb for the saint (the Lough Erne shrine), in stone sculpture (the cap stone of the cross at Monasterboice), in manuscript illuminations (the *Book of Kells* f. 202v.), and in later stone buildings such as "St. Columba's House" at Kells or "St. Kevin's Kitchen" at Glendalough. The churches were evidently small, rectangular aisleless structures with vertical proportions enhanced by a steeply pitched roof. The timbers of the sides form the gable wall, continue up the slope of the gable like barge boards, and end in finials at the peak of the gable. These finials could be elaborately carved, as the examples in stone at St. Mac Dara's Island, the temple in the *Book of Kells*, or the metal reliquaries suggest. The roofs were covered with tiles or shingles.

Temptation of Christ, *Book of Kells* f. 202v.
Early ninth century; vellum
Trinity College Library, Dublin
Photo by permission of the Board of Trinity College, Dublin

*Prehistoric and Early Christian Ireland*

St. Kevin's Kitchen: Round Tower
Monastic site, founded sixth century, Glendalough, county Wicklow
Photo by Marilyn Stokstad

The beautiful but mysterious plaque in the museum at St. Germain-en-Laye, France, may be the gilt bronze gable end or finial of a large eighth-century reliquary.[9] A small, gilt bronze gable end with similar finials is now in the National Museum of Ireland. (It has an openwork animal interlace, and probably dates from the eleventh or twelfth century.) The west façade of the Romanesque church at Kilmalkedar, county Kerry, also has a gable finial like the plaque at St. Germain-en-Laye. The beast-head finials on the Temple in the *Book of Kells* curl around in toward each other, but the idea is similar. The St. Germain "object" is a complex spiral of serpents with red studs for eyes. Its design illustrates the combination of Celtic spiral with the animal style which spread from central Asia across northern Europe and eastward into China, reaching its height in Mongolia, Scandinavia, and Celtic Ireland.

The monasteries were surrounded not only with material protection in the form of walls but also with spiritual guardians in the form of crosses erected at the cardinal points. Such a use of monumental stone crosses may derive from memorial stones. The earliest stone memorials were upright slabs with a simple inscription in ogham script. The ogham

Plaque with Animal Ornament
Eighth century; gilt bronze
St. Germain-en-Laye

alphabet, which was used from the second to the seventh centuries, may
have been introduced from Scotland. In the ogham alphabet, each letter
is indicated by from one to five lines (perhaps inspired by fingers?) engraved across or beside the edge of a stone, a stick, or a line, and reading
from bottom to top.[10] Inscriptions found on memorial stones follow a
standard formula in which the word "monument" is understood; that is,
"(monument) of the son of ———."

The Christian equivalent of the ogham stone is the memorial stone
with the inscription "Pray for ———" and the Chi-Rho (monogram of
Christ). The Chi-Rho was elaborated with spirals, knots, and a cross
formed by swinging arcs with a compass, such as the Reask cross pillar,
with its ornament so reminiscent of pagan Celtic decoration.

The tradition of erecting memorial stones and cross slabs continued
in the seventh and eighth centuries. No longer was the cross simply engraved on a slab: the entire stone was cut into a cross shape. These
crosses were set up to mark the center and the boundaries of the monastic
settlement, also to mark sites for prayers. The cross stands on a base of
truncated pyramidal shape, and the arms are surrounded by a pierced
ring of stone cut as one with shaft and transom. The figure of Christ is
not represented in the early examples; instead, for example at Ahenny,
the crosses are carved in imitation of metal work, with plaques of interlace and spiral, bosses at the points of attachment, and heavy moldings

Reask Pillar
Sixth to seventh century A.D.
County Kerry
Photo by permission of the Commis-
sioners of Public Works in Ireland

South Cross (east face)
Eighth century
Ahenny, county Tipperary
Photo by permission of the Commis-
sioners of Public Works in Ireland

where the plates would join—in short, a processional cross of metal and wood has been translated into a stone monument.

The origin and meaning of the distinctive ring on Irish high crosses are still debated. Does it refer to Christ's halo, or to the cruciform sun disc, or, as ingeniously suggested by Professor O'Riordan, does it add a brace to relieve the strain at the juncture of staff and cross piece?[11]

The Irish high crosses were also influenced by the crosses of Northumbria, which were erected as monuments to people or events and were intended to take the place of churches. Northumbrian crosses were carved with figures whose three-dimensionality was inspired by Roman art. The Irish began to use elaborate scenes with figures on their crosses in the ninth century. The most famous and elaborate Irish cross is the Cross of Muiredach at Monasterboice.[12]

The masterpieces of Irish art are not monumental sculpture and architecture, but rather metal work and manuscript illumination, such as the Ardagh chalice, the Tara brooch, and the *Book of Kells*. Manuscripts became particularly important. One of the principal duties of the monastic community, along with prayer, was to preserve and transmit scriptures and scriptural exegesis. The Irish schools led western Christendom in the study of classical language and learning, and students flocked to them from England and the Continent.

Students learning to read and write, and scholars making notes, used wax tablets, two sets of which have been preserved. Six wooden tablets with indented panels filled with wax, on which were written Psalms 30, 31, and 32 in Latin, were found in the Springmount Bog in county Antrim (see note 13). The tablets were strung together and fastened with leather straps. They date from the second half of the sixth century, and are the oldest examples of writing in Ireland. Another set of tablets from a bog in county Derry are clearly student work. They record rules of Latin grammar.

Only skilled scribes and illuminators worked on parchment, copying the texts available to them in the monastic library. The importance of book production cannot be overestimated. The monks copied not only the books of the Bible but the Lives of saints and the secular history and literature written in both Irish and Latin. Even some of the oral tradition of pagan Ireland, such as the great Ulster saga of Cúchulainn—the *Táin Bó Cuailnge*—was recorded and preserved by monastic scribes. In the twelfth-century copy of the *Táin* the scribe wrote: "But I, who have written this history, or rather fable, am doubtful about many things in this history or fable. For some of them are the figments of demons, some of them poetic imaginings, some true, some not, some for the delight of fools!"[14] At least he did his work and preserved for posterity a great piece of literature.

Scribes, in their notes in margins or at the end of a work, provide reminders that they were human beings, not heroes. Wrote one: "Pleasant is the glint of the sun today upon these margins, because it flickers so."[15] And another complained:

My hand is weary with writing; my sharp great point is not thick; my slender-beaked pen juts forth a beetle-hued draught of bright blue ink.

A steady stream of wisdom springs from my well-coloured neat fair hand; on the page it pours its draught of ink of the green-skinned holly.

I send my little dripping pen unceasingly over an assemblage of books of great beauty, to enrich the possessions of men of art—whence my hand is weary with writing.[16]

The earliest surviving manuscript is a Psalter known as the *Cathach of St. Columba*.[17] It may date from the sixth century. This manuscript already shows a distinctive style of writing and ornament. The initials are larger than the text, and ornaments with spirals, pothook-like scrolls, and figures are outlined by red dots. The letters following the initial are also larger, gradually decreasing in size to form a transition to the script of the text. Thus the ornamentation of enlarged initials and the transition of initial to text are already established features of manuscript decoration in the sixth—or at least in the seventh—century.

Many legends surround the *Cathach*. According to Adamnan of Iona, who wrote the Life of St. Columba (in 680–690), the saint secretly made a copy of a Psalter belonging to Finnian. Finnian demanded both his book and the copy. St. Columba argued that the book was not hurt or reduced in value by the copy and that, in fact, Finnian had no right to keep a sacred text to himself. Finally, King Dermot judged in favor of Finnian, saying: "As the calf follows the cow, so the copy follows the original." St. Columba was so angry that he cursed the king; whereupon they went to war, and by means of his prayers and fasting (naturally), St. Columba won. Nevertheless, as a penance the saint left Ireland and went to Iona (in 563 or 565), where he began Celtic missionary activity in Scotland and England. The importance of the written word and, of course, the Word of God to an illiterate people is underscored by this story, in which the possession of a book was cause for war. The *Cathach* became a battle talisman which insured victory to its hereditary keepers, the O'Donnells.

The *Book of Durrow*,[18] the earliest copy of St. Jerome's edition of the four Gospels to have elaborate full-page decorations, has been dated in the middle or the second half of the seventh century. The book was preserved at St. Columba's monastery of Durrow, although it was not necessarily produced there. (It was presented to Trinity College in 1661 by the Protestant bishop of Meath, vice-chancellor of the college.) The date, provenance, sources, and the artistic and textual relationships of the *Book of Durrow* are a continuing source of study and controversy. The style has been related to Anglo-Saxon, Coptic, Pictish, and other sources. Regardless of its scholarly interest, the manuscript is an imposing monument in the history of Christian art.

The scheme of decoration that came to be followed in most Irish manuscripts can be seen in the *Book of Durrow*. The *Book* opens with a

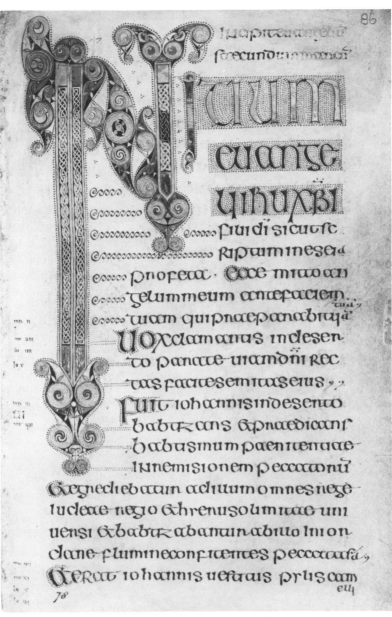

Text Page, *Book of Durrow* f. 86r.
Seventh century; vellum
Trinity College Library, Dublin
Photo by permission of the Board of Trinity College, Dublin

carpet page (allover decoration), which is followed by a cruciform page, with the symbols of the four Evangelists, and then by canon tables. (The canon tables are an early form of concordance of the Gospels.) At the beginning of each Gospel is the symbol of the appropriate Evangelist, another carpet page, and finally the large ornamental initial and opening words of that Gospel. The artist draws confidently and never falters over his elaborate spirals, braids, and interlaces.

Many trial pieces have been found in which the draftsman has worked out an interlace on a piece of bone, either by simple scratching or by more finished engraving. Somewhat reassuring to a twentieth-century person, confronted with demonstrations of the skill of the medieval craftsman, are the large bones found in excavations in Dublin and elsewhere on which the artist has tried again and again to draw a logical geometric interlace. He makes many attempts at interlaces and animals: some are awkward, unsuccessful trials; sometimes he gives up entirely.

The Evangelist symbols in the *Book of Durrow* are brilliantly abstract—truly evocations, not representations, of beings. The colors are limited to black, yellow, rusty red, and green. The sense of movement in several planes is stronger in the *Book of Durrow* than in the later manuscripts, such as the *Book of Kells*. The colored animals and ribbon are set against a dark background; and the changing color of beasts and scroll causes them to seem to move back and forth, in and out, slightly. The light tonality of the colors is given an added vividness by the dark ink and the precisely reserved parchment. Furthermore, the artist does not permit the ornament to grow freely over the page; rather, he keeps it

Trial Piece
Eighth century; bone; from Lagore, county Meath
National Museum of Ireland, Dublin
Photo by permission of the National Museum of Ireland

contained within panels, almost like the plaques of interlace used by the metalworkers on reliquaries. The artist used all the motifs found in seventh-century metal work, especially the spiral, dotting, and ribbon interlace. To this he added a carpet page like a mosaic pavement or a textile pattern, in which he surrounded the cross with three geometric bosses, perhaps a symbol of the Trinity, and a border of animal interlace. He turned the fat, biting serpents and quadrupeds, typical of Norse and Saxon ornament, into a rhythmic and graceful Irish variation of the motif.

The insignia of the Irish ecclesiastic in literature and art was not his Gospel or Psalter but his staff (*bachall*, from Latin *baculus*) and his bell. A profile figure carrying a staff and a bell is pictured trudging across the stone slab from Killadeas, county Femanagh. Most Irish bells were hand bells that resembled Roman dinner bells; however, the largest

Killadeas Pillar
Figure with bell and crosier (*bachal*); eighth century; county Femanagh
Photo by permission of Historic Monument Branch,
Department of Finance, Archaeological Survey, Belfast

*Prehistoric and Early Christian Ireland*

bells (14 inches high) may have been hung permanently. The majority of surviving bells were of folded sheet iron, riveted along the side seams; a few bells were cast in bronze, and only occasionally were they decorated. Early Irish bells are rectangular, with rounded corners, and decrease in size toward the handle. The handle may be formed by a loop at the top, or the narrow top may be extended up into the handle, as in the bell inscribed *Patrici*. The clapper was suspended from an inner loop below the handle. Bells associated with early saints became objects of veneration and were kept in elaborately decorated shrines, the most famous of which is the shrine of St. Patrick's bell.

The most beautiful of the bells is the Lough Lene bell from county Westmeath, which is dated in the eighth or ninth century. It is cast in

Bell of Lough Lene
Eighth or ninth century; bronze; found in Lough Lene, county Westmeath
National Museum of Ireland, Dublin
Photo by permission of the National Museum of Ireland

bronze and is lightly engraved with a ring cross the full height of the front of the bell. Both the handle and the rim are decorated with delicate linear geometric patterns; the rim has a series of seven rectangular panels filled with a diagonal fret set against a hatched ground.

A very tall, slender cast bronze bell (inscribed in the seventeenth century "*Patrici*, 1272") might possibly come from St. Patrick's time, the fifth century. The bell comes from Donaghmore Church, county Tyrone. Its hereditary keepers were the O'Mellans, who in the fourteenth century alternated with the Mulhollands as keepers of St. Patrick's bell and its shrine. The bell *Patrici* is said to have been presented by St. Patrick to St. MacCartan, bishop of Clogher.

The masterpiece of Celtic metal work and one of the finest examples of this art from any time or place is the Ardagh chalice, a two-handled, silver chalice found at Ardagh, county Limerick. Every

Ardagh Chalice
Eighth century; silver, bronze, gold, enamel
Found at Ardagh, county Limerick
National Museum of Ireland, Dublin
Photo by permission of the National Museum of Ireland

*Prehistoric and Early Christian Ireland*

Ardagh Chalice, Detail of Handle
Photo by permission of the National Museum of Ireland

technique of metalwork used in Early Christian Ireland may be studied in this piece at the highest level of perfection. The chalice consists of a massive round cup and a broad, equally massive foot, both of silver, joined by a short cast gilt bronze stem, which is enriched with spiral and interlace patterns. Below the rim of the bowl and around the edge of the foot are panels of decoration. On the bowl, panels of gold filigree with alternating animal and geometric interlace are separated by studs of red and blue glass enamel in silver stepped patterns. Below this ornamental band the names of eleven Apostles and St. Paul (replacing Judas) are engraved very delicately in reserve letters against a stippled background. The engraving and stippling continues as an interlace around the handles and the central ornamental discs; it ends in confronted dragon heads. Panels of gold filigree, glass beads, and enamel studs (raised on filigree mounts) adorn the handles. The handles and their escutcheons repeat the circular patterns of the chalice and the decoration of the upper rim. The remaining decorative panels on the foot are gilt bronze frets. Under the flange of the foot there are additional patterns of silver interlace and woven silver and copper wires. Both sides are set with studs either of blue glass backed with patterned foil or of red and yellow enamel. Hidden under the base is a large cone-shaped crystal, which is surrounded by concentric rings of exceptionally intricate interlace and spiral patterns similar to those on the stem. Inside, the bowl is plain except for the neat round rivets attaching the handles, the roundels, and the stem. This magnificent chalice was made in the early eighth century. The designs developed by the metalworkers over the centuries were adopted for Christian use, and inspired the scribes to readapt them in the painting of the great books for display on the altar.

Comparable in date, in refinement of technique, and in artistic vocabulary is a piece of secular jewelry, the Tara brooch, which was found on the seashore near Drogheda, county Louth. (The name is pure fantasy; the brooch has nothing to do with Tara.) The heavily gilt silver brooch was richly decorated on both sides of the ring and pin. On the front are inset panels of gold filigree interlace, glass studs, and amber beads, some of which have additional granulation and gold filigree decoration. The back is different in style from the front. Patterns of spirals, scrolls, and triskeles, some of which are really three serpents, are either cast in the metal of the ring or are cut out of a sheet of silver which has been laid over a copper base to produce a spiral pattern in silhouette. At the top of the ring a panel in the same pierced technique is worked in gold over copper. A silver mesh chain is attached to the brooch by a silver gilt hinge, which is formed by two biting animals. Two tiny human faces of purple glass are set opposite each other on the hinge. The artist used serpents with heads turned back on themselves and tails twisted together as a border for the brooch. The painters adopted the motif as a frame for their most elaborate pages—for example, as often seen in the *Book of Kells.*

The *Book of Kells*[19] is the most exuberant, complex, and sophisticated work of manuscript illumination and ornament ever produced. Giraldus Cambrensis must have been describing the *Book of Kells*, or a remarkably similar manuscript, when he described the wonderful *Book of Kildare* in his *Topography of Ireland* (1185). Giraldus's excellent analysis of the style is still one of the best descriptions of early Irish painting:

> Among all the miracles of Kildare nothing seems to me more miraculous than that wonderful book which they say was written at the dictation of an angel during the lifetime of the virgin [St. Brigit]. This book contains the four Gospels according to the concordance of St. Jerome, with almost as many drawings as pages, and all of them in marvellous colours. Here you can look upon the face of the divine majesty drawn in a miraculous way; here too upon

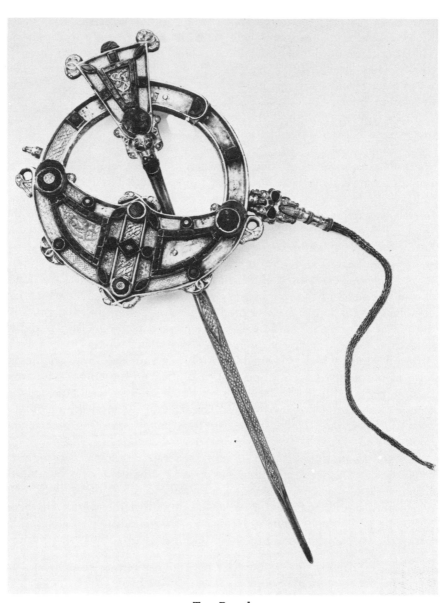

Tara Brooch
Eighth century; silver, gold, amber, glass; found near mouth of river Boyne
National Museum of Ireland, Dublin
Photo by permission of the National Museum of Ireland

the mystical representations of the Evangelists, now having six, now four, and now two, wings. Here you will see the eagle; there the calf. Here the face of a man; there that of a lion. And there are almost innumerable other drawings. If you look at them carelessly and casually and not too closely, you may judge them to be mere daubs rather than careful compositions. You will see nothing subtle where everything is subtle. But if you take the trouble to look very closely, and penetrate with your eyes to the secrets of the artistry, you will notice such intricacies, so delicate and subtle, so close together and well-knitted, so involved and bound together, and so fresh still in their colourings that you will not hesitate to declare that all these things must have been the result of the work, not of men, but of angels.[20]

It seems not too far-fetched to attribute supernatural powers and divine inspiration to the scribes and painters of the *Book of Kells*. Giraldus Cambrensis wrote:

> On the night before the day on which the scribe was to begin the book, an angel stood beside him in his sleep and showed him a drawing made on a tablet which he carried in his hand, and said to him: "Do you think that you can make this drawing on the first page of the book that you are about to begin?" The scribe, not feeling that he was capable of an art so subtle, and trusting little in his knowledge of something almost unknown and very unusual, replied: "No." The angel said to him: "To-morrow tell your lady [St. Brigit], so that she may pour forth prayers for you to the Lord, that he may open both your bodily and mental eyes so as to see the more keenly and understand the more subtly, and may direct you in the guiding of your hand." All this was done, and on the following night the angel came again and held before him the same and many other drawings. By the help of the divine grace, the scribe, taking particular notice of them all, and faithfully committing them to his memory, was able to reproduce them exactly in the suitable places in the book. And so with the angel indicating the designs, Brigid praying, and the scribe imitating, that book was composed.[21]

The manuscript was almost surely begun, and perhaps completed, in Iona just before the Viking invasion, and was brought to Kells when the monks were forced to flee their home. The book led a precarious

Animal Interlace
*Book of Kells* f. 250v.
Early ninth century; vellum
Trinity College Library, Dublin
Photo by permission of the Board of Trinity College, Dublin

existence. In 1007 its theft from the church at Kells was recorded in the *Annals of Ulster*, and although the book was recovered, the golden cover was lost forever. At the dissolution of the monastery, the manuscript evidently remained in the care of the abbot, Richard Plunket. By 1568 it had passed into the possession of Gerald Plunket of Dublin. In the seventeenth century it belonged, successively, to James Ussher, his daughter, Cromwell's army, and the crown; it finally was given to Trinity College, Dublin, by Charles II. The *Book of Kells* still may be seen in the college library, along with its distinguished companion, the *Book of Durrow*.

The makers of the *Book of Kells* follow and elaborate on the arrangement of the decoration of the *Book of Durrow*. To the Durrow scheme the painters have added portraits as well as symbols of the Evangelists, elaborate opening text pages, and full-page paintings, including the Virgin and Child, the Temptation of Christ, and the Arrest of Christ. A painting of the Last Judgment may also have been planned. Throughout the manuscript there are decorated initials and a marvelous variety of animals, birds, and even people. Several artists worked on the book. One specialized in intricate ornamental patterns executed with all the precision of a metalworker; another painted the full page figures; yet another, the genre scenes.[22] All of them had an incredible facility for draftsmanship and a brilliant sense of color—purple, blue, green, yellow, rust. The artists were inspired by the art of the classical world as interpreted by the Byzantines when they drew figures, but their ornament is Irish. The union of spiral, geometric interlace, and animal ornament with witty realistic representations of animals and men produces a style that gives the manuscript a special magic and presents a challenge to those who will study it with care and in detail.

The illustrations in the *Book of Kells*—more than any other Irish painting—seem to evoke the spirit, and sometimes even images, from the epic battles of Cúchulainn.[23] The description of Cúchulainn's battle fury by the poets of the *Táin* could apply to the struggling men and beasts of the *Book of Kells* (f. 250v.):

> The first warp-spasm seized Cúchulainn, and made him into a monstrous thing, hideous and shapeless, unheard of. . . . His body made a furious twist inside his skin, so that his feet and shins and knees switched to the rear and his heels and calves switched to the front. . . . His face and features became a red bowl: he sucked one eye so deep into his head that a wild crane couldn't probe it onto his cheek out of the depths of his skull; the other eye fell out along his cheek. His mouth weirdly distorted: his cheek peeled back from his jaws until the gullet appeared, his lungs and liver flapped in his mouth and throat, his lower jaw struck the upper a lion-killing blow, and fiery flakes large as a ram's fleece reached his mouth from his throat.[24]

Or again:

> The hair of his head twisted like the tangle of a red thornbush stuck in a gap; if a royal apple tree with all its kingly fruit were shaken above him, scarce an apple would

reach the ground but each would be spiked on a bristle of his hair as it stood up on his scalp with rage. The hero-halo rose out of his brow, long and broad as a warrior's whetstone, long as a snout, and he went mad rattling his shields, urging on his charioteer and harassing the hosts. Then, tall and thick, steady and strong, high as the mast of a noble ship, rose up from the dead centre of his skull a straight spout of black blood darkly and magically smoking like the smoke from a royal hostel when a king is coming to be cared for at the close of a winter day.[25]

The use of repetition and exaggeration to build up emotional and aesthetic effects is also common to both the spoken/written account and the written/painted word:

> Your enemy shook you then as easily as a loving mother slaps her son! He tossed you aside as if he was rinsing a cup in a tub! He crushed you like a mill crushing fine malt! He went through you like a drill through an oak! He bound you in knots like a creeper entangling a tree! He pounced on you like a hawk on a little bird![26]

The poet's fantasizing on color and surface details in his description of the hero resembles the painter's portraits of his hero, Christ (f. 32v.):

> And certainly the youth Cúchulainn mac Sualdaim was handsome as he came to show his form to the armies. You would think he had three distinct heads of hair—brown at the base, blood-red in the middle, and a crown of golden yellow. This hair was settled strikingly into three coils on the cleft at the back of his head. Each long loose-flowing strand hung down in shining splendour over his shoulders, deep-gold and beautiful and fine as a thread of gold. A hundred neat red-gold curls shone darkly on his neck, and his head was covered with a hundred crimson threads matted with gems. He had four dimples in each cheek— yellow, green, crimson and blue—and seven bright pupils, eye-jewels, in each kingly eye. Each foot had seven toes and each hand seven fingers, the nails with the grip of a hawk's claw or a gryphon's clench. He wore his festive raiment that day. This is what he wore: a fitted purple mantle, fringed and fine, folded five times and held at his white clear breast by a brooch of light-gold and silver decorated with gold inlays—a shining source of light too bright in its blinding brilliance for men to look at. A fretted silk tunic covered him down to the top of his warrior's apron of dark-

red royal silk. He carried a dark deep-red crimson shield—
five disks within a light-gold rim—and a gold-hilted sword
in a high clasp on his belt, its ivory guard decorated with
gold.[27]

Christ, *Book of Kells* f. 32v.
Early ninth century; vellum
Trinity College Library, Dublin
Photo by permission of the Board of Trinity College, Dublin

The minds that could create and appreciate the *Book of Kells* could also produce that fantastic and beautiful epic *The Táin* and call it history. Perhaps in the twentieth century the labyrinthine work of James Joyce best reflects the same imagination.

Irish art, then, at its height in the seventh, eighth, and ninth centuries, is characterized by elaborate ambiguities and almost unresolved tensions which are nevertheless always controlled by a highly disciplined and organized mentality—a mind that may prefer riddles to statements and elaboration seemingly for its own sake, but always with an underlying purpose. The richness of ornament never completely engulfs the object. The most fanciful animal interlace is still subject to the geometrician's structure. The pen of the scribe and the brush of the painter re-create the brilliant filigree of the metalworker; the goldsmith enriches his precise and dazzling engraving with the glow of color in enamel. Through the ages the goldsmith's precision and sense of craft dominate Irish art, whether in the Christian period or in the prehistoric or pagan Celtic periods. The gold lunulae and torcs, the bronze boxes and bells, the Ardagh chalice and the *Book of Kells*—all demonstrate the same respect for material and form, the impeccable craftsmanship, and the refined sense of ornament which are prized by Irish artists.

## NOTES

1. *A Concise History of Ireland*, by Máire and Conor Cruise O'Brien (London: Thames & Hudson, 1972), and *A Concise History of Irish Art*, by Bruce Arnold (London: Thames & Hudson, 1969, and New York: Praeger, 1968), provide convenient outlines into which more detailed studies may be set. For a closer examination of monuments and documents see Françoise Henry, *Irish Art* (3 vols.; Ithaca, N.Y.: Cornell University Press, 1965–1970); Ludwig Bieler, *Ireland: Harbinger of the Middle Ages* (London: Oxford University Press, 1963); Estyn Evans, *Prehistoric and Early Christian Ireland: A Guide* (London: Batsford, 1966); Peter Harbison, *Guide to the National Monuments in the Republic of Ireland* (Dublin: Gill & Macmillan, 1970).
2. Marvin Chauncey Ross and Phillipe Verdier, *Arts of the Migration Period in the Walters Art Gallery* (Baltimore: Walters Art Gallery, 1961); Emma C. Bunker, C. Bruce Chatwin, and Ann R. Farkas, *"Animal Style" Art from East to West* (New York: Asia Society, 1970).
3. For Prehistoric art in Ireland see Nancy K. Sandars, *Prehistoric Art in Europe* (Harmondsworth, Eng.: Penguin, 1968); Joseph Raftery, *Prehistoric Ireland* (London and New York: Batsford, 1951); Seán P. O'Ríordáin, *Antiquities of the Irish Countryside* (Cork, Ire., 1942, and London: Methuen, 1953).
4. Thomas Wright of Durham, *Observations on . . . Remains of Antiquity in Ireland,* bk. 1, pl. 10, notes. See chapter 8 of this book.

5. For a brief introduction to Celtic culture see Proinsias Mac Cana, *Celtic Mythology* (London and New York: Hamlyn, 1970); and Joseph Raftery, *The Celts* (Cork, Ire.: Mercier Press, 1967), which contains a series of excellent essays on language, archeology, and religion, first given as radio lectures in 1960. Additional studies of Celtic culture and artistic style include Nils Åberg, *The Occident and the Orient in the Art of the Seventh Century* (3 vols.; Stockholm: Wahlström & Widstrand, 1943–1947), vol. 2: *British Isles*; Myles Dillon and Nora K. Chadwick, *The Celtic Realms* (London: Weidenfeld & Nicolson, 1967); Cyril Fox, *Pattern and Purpose* (Cardiff: National Museum of Wales, 1958); Paul Jacobsthal, *Early Celtic Art* (2 vols.; Oxford: Clarendon Press, 1944); Thomas F. O'Rahilly, *Early Irish History and Mythology* (Dublin: Dublin Institute for Advanced Studies, 1946); Anne Ross, *Pagan Celtic Britain* (London: Routledge & K. Paul, 1967); also note Henry, *Irish Art*, 1:203–24.

6. For the Early Christian period in Ireland see Beiler, *Ireland: Harbinger of the Middle Ages*; Henry, *Irish Art*, vols. 1 and 2; Evans, *Prehistoric and Early Christian Ireland*; Harold G. Leask, *Irish Churches and Monastic Buildings* (Dundalk, Ire.: Dundalgan Press, 1955), and *Glendalough, Co. Wicklow* (Dublin: Stationery Office, 1951); Máire and Liam de Paor, *Early Christian Ireland* (London: Thames & Hudson, and New York: Praeger, 1958); Joseph Raftery, ed., *Christian Art in Ancient Ireland* (vol. 2; Dublin: Stationery Office of Ireland, 1941); John Ryan, *Irish Monasticism: Origins and Early Development* (Dublin: Talbot Press, 1931).

7. De Paor, *Early Christian Ireland*, pp. 47–48.

8. Bieler, *Ireland: Harbinger of the Middle Ages*, p. 64.

9. See comparative exhibition in the National Museum of Ireland; Bunker, Chatwin, and Farkas, *"Animal Style" Art from East to West*, entry no. 145 (Chatwin); Henry, *Irish Art*, vol. 1, pl. 66 and fig. 28, pp. 215 and 100; J. Hunt, "On Two 'D' Shaped Objects in the Saint-Germain Museum," *Proceedings of the Royal Irish Academy*, pt. C, 1956, pp. 153 ff.

10. Evans, *Prehistoric and Early Christian Ireland*; de Paor, *Early Christian Ireland*.

11. O'Ríordáin, *Antiquities of the Irish Countryside*.

12. See chapter 4 of this book.

13. E. C. R. Armstrong and R. A. S. Macalister, "Wooden Box with Leaves Indented and Waxed, . . .," *Journal of the Royal Society of Antiquaries of Ireland* 50:160–66 (1920).

14. David Green, "Early Irish Society," in *Early Irish Society*, ed. Myles Dillon (Dublin: Colm O'Lochlainn for the Cultural Relations Committee of Ireland, 1954), p. 88.

15. De Paor, *Early Christian Ireland*, p. 66; Robin Flower, *The Irish Tradition* (Oxford: Clarendon Press, 1947), p. 42.

16. Gerard Murphy, *Early Irish Lyrics* (Oxford: Clarendon Press, 1956), p. 71.

17. The manuscript is now in the Royal Irish Academy. H. Lawlor, "The Cathach of Saint Columba," *Proceedings of the Royal Irish Academy*, vol. 23, sect. 102 (1911); Henry, *Irish Art*, 1:58–61; Carl Nordenfalk, "Before the Book of Durrow," *Acta Archaeologica* 18:141–74 (1947); Saint Adamnan, *Adomman's Life of Columba*, with translation and notes by A. O. and M. O. Anderson (London and New York: T. Nelson, 1961).

18. Trinity College, Dublin, Library, no. 57 (A.IV.5); facsimile edition of *Evangeliorum Quattuor Codex Durmachensis* ([Olten]: Urs Graf, 1960), vol. 1, facsimile, vol. 2, text by A. A. Luce, G. O. Simms, P. Meyer, and L. Bieler; Henry, *Irish Art*, 1:166–75; Joseph Raftery, "Ex Oriente . . .," *Journal of the Royal Society of Antiquaries of Ireland* 95:193–204 (1965); Carl Nordenfalk, "An Illustrated Diatessaron," *Art Bulletin*, vol. 50, no. 2, pp. 119–40 (June 1968).

Readily available books with color reproductions of Irish painting include André Grabar and C. Nordenfalk, trans. Stuart Gilbert, *Early Medieval Painting* (New York: Skira, 1957), and James Johnson Sweeney, *Irish Illuminated Manuscripts of the Early Christian Period* (New York: New American Library, by arrangement with UNESCO, 1965).

19. Trinity College, Dublin, Library, no. 58 (A.I.6); facsimile edition of *Evangeliorum Quattuor Codex Cenannensis* (Berne: Urs Graf, 1950–1951), vols. 1 and 2, facsimile, vol. 3, text by E. H. Alton, P. Meyer, and G. O. Simms; Henry, *Irish Art*, 2:68–95; Grabar and Nordenfalk, *Early Medieval Painting*; A. M. Friend, "The Canon Tables of the Book of Kells," *Medieval Studies in Memory of A. Kingsley Porter* (Cambridge, Mass.: Harvard University Press, 1939), pp. 611 ff.; *Evangeliorum Quattuor Codex Lindisfarnensis* (Olten and Lausanne: Urs Graf, 1956–1960), vol. 1, facsimile, vol. 2, text, by T. J. Brown et al.

20. Giraldus Cambrensis, *The First Version of* The Topography of Ireland *by Giraldus Cambrensis* [1185], trans. John J. O'Meara (Dundalk, Ire.: Dundalgan Press, 1951), p. 67.

21. Ibid., p. 68.

22. Henry, *Irish Art*, 2:73 ff. Henry's distinction of the various hands is not universally accepted.

23. *The Táin* (from the Irish epic *Táin Bó Cuailnge*), trans. Thomas Kinsella (Dublin: Dolmen Press, 1969, London and New York: Oxford University Press, 1970).

24. Ibid., p. 150.

25. Ibid., p. 153.

26. Ibid., p. 195.

27. Ibid., pp. 156, 158.

# SUGGESTIONS FOR FURTHER READING

Arnold, Bruce. *A Concise History of Irish Art.* New York: Praeger, 1968.

Bieler, Ludwig. *Ireland: Harbinger of the Middle Ages.* London: Oxford University Press, 1963.

*Book of Durrow*, facsimile edition. [Olten, Switz.]: Urs Graf, 1960.

*Book of Kells*, facsimile edition. Berne: Urs Graf, 1950–1951.

De Paor, Máire, and de Paor, Liam. *Early Christian Ireland.* London: Thames & Hudson, 1958.

Dillon, Myles, and Chadwick, Nora K. *The Celtic Realms.* London: Weidenfeld & Nicolson, 1967.

Fox, Cyril. *Pattern and Purpose.* Cardiff: National Museum of Wales, 1958.

Henry, Françoise. *Irish Art.* 3 vols. London: Methuen, and Ithaca, N.Y.: Cornell University Press, 1965–1970.

Jacobsthal, Paul. *Early Celtic Art.* 2 vols. Oxford: Clarendon Press, 1944.

Leask, Harold G. *Irish Churches and Monastic Buildings.* Dundalk, Ire.: Dundalgan Press, 1955.

Raftery, Joseph, ed. *Christian Art in Ancient Ireland.* Vol. 2. Dublin: Stationery Office of Ireland, 1941.

Ross, Anne. *Pagan Celtic Britain.* London: Routledge & K. Paul, 1967.

Sandars, Nancy K. *Prehistoric Art in Europe.* Harmondsworth, Eng.: Penguin, 1968.

# 4

# MEDIEVAL ART

## Marilyn Stokstad

In A.D. 793 the Vikings raided the Northumbrian monastery of Lindesfarne, and two years later, in 795, they sailed around the British Isles to attack Ireland. The people of the Isles, like those on the Continent, were to live in fear of the Norsemen for the next two hundred years. A poem in praise of the stormy sea survives as a reminder of those grim centuries:

> Bitter is the wind tonight,
> It tosses the ocean's white hair:
> Tonight I fear not the fierce warriors of Norway
> Coursing on the Irish Sea.[1]

The Viking invasions had a profound impact on Ireland.[2] Monastic communities were destroyed, and with them much of the learning and many of the treasures of Early Christian Ireland. On the other hand, the Vikings contributed to art and architecture in Ireland; for example, Irish artists added Scandinavian serpents and dragons to their repertoire of decoration. More importantly, the Vikings established real cities for the first time in Ireland; seaports such as Dublin, Wexford, and Waterford were all Viking trading centers and military and naval bases. The Vikings also forced the natives to build in stone for defense.

79

Among the most beautiful and distinctive buildings surviving from the Middle Ages are the round towers standing near the Irish churches, such as those erected at Clonmacnois. They, too, are examples of Viking influence on the country, since these towers could be used as refuges and watchtowers for both the religious and the secular communities. The towers have walls of very thick rubble and ashlar masonry which are surmounted by cone-shaped masonry capstones. Originally the floors were of wood, and movable interior ladders provided access to upper chambers. The only other interior fittings were hooks, fixed in the walls of the upper room or bell chamber, on which to hang book bags. The walls are broken by an occasional window and a door placed high up on the wall. The entrance was closed by a heavy door, and loopholes were provided, through which the defenders could fire missiles or push off scaling ladders. If the door was forced and a fire started in the lower floor, the chimneylike shape of the tower and the placement of windows only at

Monastic Site
Founded in 548–549; churches, two round towers, High Crosses, graveyard
Clonmacnois, county Offaly
Photo by Marilyn Stokstad

the top created an excellent draft, which turned the interior into a fiery furnace. Monks fleeing with their treasures to the tower during a siege had to trust in the strength of the walls and in the intervention of the saints to save them.

Monumental stone crosses continued to be erected during intervals of peace between Viking raids. Artists inspired by Continental art attempted more elaborate iconographical programs and more complex figure compositions.[3] The Cross of Muiredach at Monasterboice is the most famous of these large Irish crosses. An abbot, Muiredach, is mentioned in the inscription; however, there were two abbots of that name —one died in 844, and one in 922. The cross was probably erected under the abbacy of the tenth-century Muiredach, since he was one of the leaders of the Irish Church, a scribe and the "high stewart," that is, a secular statesman. Further evidence of a tenth-century date for the cross is offered by the related Cross of the Scriptures at Clonmacnois, erected by Bishop Colman (904–910), and the cross of Abbot Dubtach (927–938) at Durrow. These crosses are also outstanding for their elaborate iconographical programs and for the high quality of their carving.

Muiredach's cross is decorated with the Crucifixion on the west face, the Last Judgment on the east, and bands of ornament on the narrow north and south sides. In the scene of the Crucifixion the sequence of events of Good Friday is ignored by the artist in the interests of a symmetrical composition. Longinus with the lance, symbolizing the Church, and the sponge bearer, symbolizing the Synagogue, are represented at each side of Christ, whose head is supported by a pair of angels. On the east side, where the Last Judgment fills the entire head of the cross, Christ stands in the center, holding a cross and a flowering staff, the symbol of Resurrection, looking almost like a Christian Osiris. The weighing of the souls, another Egyptian theme, is represented directly below Christ. The blessed and the damned, at His right and left, fill the arms of the cross. On the side of the blessed, both a trumpeter and a harpist (a very Irish addition) sound the call to Judgment; on the side of the damned, energetic demons—one armed with a fork—kick the souls into Hell. Thus, on the Cross of Muiredach we have the earliest representation of a complete Last Judgment in sculpture.

The stem of the cross is also elaborately carved. On the eastern side of the stem there are scenes from the Old Testament—Adam and Eve, the murder of Abel, David and Goliath, Moses striking the rock and bringing water to the Israelites—and finally the New Testament adoration of the kings. On the west side of the stem are the arrest of Christ, Doubting Thomas, and the *Traditio Legis* (the giving of the keys to St.

Crucifixion, West Face of Muiredach's Cross
923 A.D.; Monasterboice, county Louth
Photo by Henry Snyder

Peter). Pilate is shown washing his hands at the end of the arm of the
cross. The choice of subjects must have been influenced by the illustrated
cycles from the Old Testament or the life of Christ which were introduced into Ireland by means of Carolingian ivories and manuscripts.
Early iconographical programs emphasized the symbolic value of the
subjects rather than their historical sequence. The scenes are related
vertically in historical sequence, and horizontally they are equated symbolically. Thus the arrest of Christ is juxtaposed with the fall of man and

Last Judgment, East Face of Muiredach's Cross
923 A.D.; Monasterboice, county Louth
Photo by permission of the Commissioners of Public Works in Ireland

the murder of Abel; Doubting Thomas, with Moses striking the rock; and finally the universal power and dominion of the established Church are emphasized, with the *Traditio Legis*, on the one side, corresponding to the Epiphany, on the other. St. Peter and Moses are equated with the Synagogue; St. Paul and the Magi with the Church of the Gentiles. But the giving of the Keys to St. Peter and the Book of Law to St. Paul are represented as being of equal importance.

Although the narrative panels have great iconographical interest, the significance of the scenes far outweighs their aesthetic quality. The sculpture remains rather unsophisticated in detail and composition, with figures symmetrically arranged and closely packed into rectangular panels. On the other hand, the narrower sides and the wheel joining the arms of the cross are filled with fine ornament, based on metal work and manuscripts—running animal interlaces, geometric patterns, and elaborate knotted ribbon interlaces. The carver of the Cross of Muiredach also used a symmetrical vine scroll, which is inhabited by leaping, clasping paired animals, which are reminiscent of Anglo-Saxon sculpture. The large scale and the complexity of the iconography of the Irish crosses make them imposing and intellectually challenging monuments which may provide a link between East and West and between Early Christian and Romanesque art. The sculpture on the high crosses played a didactic and decorative role similar to the carving on Continental church portals in the twelfth and thirteenth centuries.

In spite of the scarcity of surviving material, the ornament on the Cross of Muiredach reminds us that the art of both the metalworker and the scribe remained important in Ireland throughout the tenth and eleventh centuries. Because the Vikings were finally converted to Christianity, the scarcity of objects can no longer be accounted for by their raids. Unfortunately for the art historian, Christians are not buried with their finest possessions; thus we are deprived of the valuable grave treasures found in pagan burials. One of the few large objects surviving from this period is the shrine—or reliquary case—for the Gospels of St. Molaise, which was reworked at the beginning of the eleventh century. The new shrine, made by Gilla Biathin for Abbot Cenfaelad (1001–1025) is typical of the coarser metalwork of the eleventh century. The cover has a cross and the symbols of the four Evangelists, each inscribed with his name. The cross is decorated with panels of heavy gold filigree, and the four Evangelists are modeled in low relief. They are extremely stylized and almost hidden by the strange interlocked-zigzag pattern of their wings. The greatest sculptural quality is achieved in the modeling of Luke's symbol, in which sturdy legs are marked by spiral joints; and the full-face representation of the head has a robust three-dimensionality in spite of the decorative hatching.

An Irish Psalter in the British Museum illustrates the painting style of the early tenth century.[4] Although badly damaged by fire, and thus deformed and discolored, two illustrations—David killing Goliath, and David the Musician—have survived. The fight between David and Goliath is reminiscent of the same scene on the Cross of Muiredach: massive figures fill the rectangular panel, and Goliath's superhuman size is indi-

Shrine for the Gospels of St. Molaise
Early eleventh century; silver, gold filigree
National Museum of Ireland, Dublin
Photo by permission of the National Museum of Ireland

cated by bending the legs of the giant into the available space. Similar details, such as David's small crook and Goliath's pointed helmet, add to the evidence that the two works are connected. The high degree of stylization of the figures, the lack of any indication of setting or spatial relationship, and finally what Henry calls the "violence" of the style[5] are characteristics common to both the sculpture and the painting. David and Goliath are reduced to blocks of purple and red; their heads are squares with an eye in the center; David's sling and the ribbon border of his garment become confused in space. However, the very crudeness of

David and Goliath Psalter
Tenth century; British Museum, London, Cotton MS. Vitellius f. xi
Photo by permission of the British Museum, London

the stylization produces a powerful impact; the fatal stone is caught in midair; it travels toward the head of Goliath, whose demise is already indicated by a closed eye, seemingly "stitched" shut. The detail with which the sling is represented and the fact that it takes on a magical serpentlike life of its own, yet is lightly held by a loop around David's little finger, both add to the disturbing quality of suspended doom achieved by the artists. The artist encloses his scene in a decorative frame, which is made up of symmetrical panels of coarse interlace and fret patterns.

That manuscripts survived at all in the Irish monasteries during the period of the Viking invasions is remarkable. After Brian Boru defeated the Vikings in 1014, men were sent abroad to buy books, in order to replace the libraries that had been destroyed, and thus to revive learning in the country.[6]

Metalwork, rather than manuscript illumination, led the revival of the arts in the Romanesque period.[7] Bells, crosiers (*bachalls*), and crosses—the characteristic attributes of Irish saints—again were made with consummate skill. St. Patrick's bell and shrine are among the most famous treasures of Ireland; they are mentioned repeatedly in records through the centuries. The bell is supposed to have been taken from St. Patrick's grave in 552, at which time it was placed in a shrine. The bell is of thin sheet iron coated with bronze, and it has an iron clapper. The bell is known as the Bell of the Will. Nothing remains of the original shrine; the present shrine was ordered by the archbishop of Armagh sometime between 1091 and 1105. The shrine can be dated this precisely because the name of the archbishop and of the high king of Tara are given in an inscription in Irish on the back panel:

> A prayer for Domnall O'Lachlaind [King of Ireland 1083–1121] under whose auspices this bell was made. And for Domnall, successor of Patrick [Abbot of Armagh 1091–1105] in whose house it was made. And for Cathalan O'Mael-Challand, Steward of the bell. And for Cu Deulig O'Inmainen and his sons who covered it.[8]

The shrine is built up of a series of bronze plates overlaid with panels of filigree or pierced silver. A cross formed of filigree panels around a central circle set with a crystal divides the front of the shrine into four panels, which are filled with geometric and zoomorphic interlace of gold or gold-plated bronze wire. (This crystal, a second crystal, and studs of red glass are all later additions.) A very complex open animal interlace of silver in circles surrounds cubical knobs with rings, which

St. Patrick's Bell and Shrine
Bell: reputed to be sixth century; iron and bronze
Shrine: 1091–1105; bronze with silver, gold, crystal, glass, about 10″ high
National Museum of Ireland, Dublin
Photo by permission of the National Museum of Ireland

are used in carrying the shrine. The back panel is a geometric design in silver openwork with equal armed crosses over a gilt bronze panel (a type of back plate pierced with crosses that is commonly used in reliquaries). The handle of the bell is covered with an exceptionally elegant interlace, derived from northern animal ornament, in gold and silver filigree. On the back of the handle a pair of birds in a treelike spiral face each other under entwined pairs of dragons and serpents.

Curiously enough, imitation bells were also made. One of these, a late-eleventh-century bell called the Bell of St. Senan or the Little Bell of Gold, was supposed to have belonged to St. Senan, a sixth-century saint, who founded the monastery on Inis Cathaigh (Scattery Island) on the county Clare side of the Shannon River. The relic was in the care of

Shrine for Bell of St. Senan
Eleventh century
Gilt bronze and nielloed silver
National Museum of Ireland, Dublin
Photo by permission of the National Museum of Ireland

the Keane family until the early twentieth century. In Ireland the great relics had hereditary keepers—in some cases families still performed this function in the nineteenth century; thus medieval treasuries are often better documented in Ireland than is the case on the Continent.

St. Senan's bell was not actually gold but cast bronze, decorated with panels in gilt bronze framed by strips of nielloed silver set with light-green-glass studs. This eleventh-century "forgery" was enshrined in the fourteenth century by being covered with silver-gilt plates ornamented in niello with paired and intertwined wyverns, vine scrolls, a harpy, and quadrupeds. A comparison between this fourteenth-century animal style and the ornament on the shrine of St. Patrick's bell is especially instructive. This bell, in fact, illustrates imitations or revivals of two different periods. The coarseness of the eleventh-century work and the angularity of the fourteenth-century work, as well as the general decline in sheer craftsmanship and technical virtuosity in both, are dramatically apparent when St. Senan's bell is compared with metalwork of the sixth to ninth centuries.

Bells, books, and *bachalls* of the Irish saints were the most popular and powerful miracle-working relics. Since the saints could charm and curse with their canes and crosiers, the sticks were considered to have supernatural powers even after the death of their owners. Monasteries or churches preserved *bachalls* as relics in magnificent shrines. The most famous *bachall* of all was the staff of Jesus, given by an angel to St. Patrick and kept in Armagh. It was burned in Dublin in the sixteenth century, when the Reformation clergy tried to stamp out the old beliefs.

Irish crosiers have a distinctive form: the crook ends in a flat, clipped-off drop rather than the long, curling loop preferred on the Continent. The crook has an animallike appearance, and is often given a crest of openwork cast animals. The shaft of the staff is made up of alternating cylinders and knops (swelling ornamental bands used to cover a join line in metal objects); and the staff ends in a pointed ferrule, which must be strong enough to support the weight of the entire relic. The surfaces of the crook and of the knops and ferrule were richly decorated—in later examples by a rectilinear pattern of bands joined by bosses, the interstices of which were filled with interlace in the style of Viking jewelry and wood carving. The shrines were of bronze or silver and were often gilt. They were further decorated with filigree, niello, silver inlay, glass studs, and red, white, and blue millefiore plaques.

The earliest known staff shrine, dated about A.D. 700, was found in Stavanger, where it was probably carried by Vikings. Most examples date from the twelfth century, however. These twelfth-century shrines probably replaced earlier ones which had simply worn out, since the staves within the metal shrines could be of an earlier date. Because of the supernatural power of the staff of a saint, the staff was subject to hard use through the centuries, and thus acquired a military, legal, political, and social, as well as a religious, function. The *bachall* became the battle standard carried by an army. It was used for oaths to solemnify and sanctify the law and to ratify treaties. It could cure diseases. Like a pagan idol, the *bachall* provided protection for its people.

The well-preserved Lismore crosier consists of a complete crook and crest, three knops separating long tubes of sheet bronze, and a very heavy ferrule. The crosier was found in Lismore Castle in 1814, where it had been built into a wall, probably in order to hide and protect it during the Reformation. The wooden staff purportedly belonged to St. Carthach (Mo Chuda), founder of the monastery of Lismore, county Waterford, who died in 637. The shrine is dated by an inscription in Irish on the base, which asks that six prayers be said for Niall, son of Mac Aeducain, bishop of Lismore from 1090 to 1113. The crook is decorated with red,

Lismore Crosier
Twelfth century; bronze, silver, filigree, enamel
Lismore, county Waterford
National Museum of Ireland, Dublin
Photo by permission of the National Museum of Ireland

white, and blue millefiori discs at intersections of rectangular panels which once must have been filled with gold filigree interlaces. A few small filigree panels survive on the drop. The knops also have glass studs and millefiori plaques, and the center knop has geometric and animal interlace divided by silver bands. The crest is composed of three magnificent crouching, biting beasts, whose jaws, legs, and tails form an openwork interlace.

The massive ferrule of the *bachall*, which is strong enough to support the considerable weight of metal and wood, is decorated with animal and human interlaces in panels separated by wide silver bands, and is joined to the staff by four human heads, of Celtic appearance in spite of their long hair. Four human figures are ingeniously worked into an equal-armed cross; each grasps the neck of a companion with his legs, and the four straight, armless bodies cross at the center of the design.

The most magnificent example of Irish metalwork of the period is neither a bell nor a *bachall*, but rather the Cross of Cong, a processional

**Maelisu**
Cross of Cong, front; 1119–1123
Oak encased in silver, gilt bronze, crystal
Fragment of the True Cross, enshrined at Roscommon in 1119
National Museum of Ireland, Dublin
Photo by permission of the National Museum of Ireland

cross of oak encased in gilt bronze plates and silver strips over bronze. In the center of the cross there is a large, domical rock-crystal disc, which once must have covered a piece of the True Cross. The *Annals of Inisfallen* for the Year 1123 record that a piece of the True Cross was brought to Ireland in 1119 from Rome, and was enshrined at Roscommon at the order of Turlough O'Connor, high king of Ireland.[9] The subsequent travels of the relic to Cong are not recorded.

Inscriptions in Irish and Latin run along the silver panels on the sides of the cross. "In this cross is preserved the Cross on which the founder of the world suffered" is written in Latin, and the following passage is written in Irish:

Pray for Muredach U Dubthaig, the Senior of Erin
[Muireacach O'Duffy, Archbishop of Connaught, d. 1150].

Maelisu
Cross of Cong, back
1119–1123
Oak encased in silver and gilt bronze
National Museum of Ireland, Dublin
Photo by permission of the National Museum of Ireland

*Medieval Art*
93

Pray for Therdel(luch) U Concho(bair) for the king of
Erin for whom this shrine was made [King Turlough
O'Connor]. Pray for Domnall Mac Flannacan U Dub(thaig),
bishop of Connacht and comarb of Chomman and Ciaran,
under whose superintendence the shrine was made [Bishop
Donel O'Duffy, c. 1136]. Pray for Maelisu MacBratdan U
Echan, who made this shrine.[10]

The Cross of Cong is among the finest works of Romanesque art
in Ireland. The cross is decorated with gilt bronze plaques of animal
interlace, framed by silver bands and punctuated at the angles by studs
of red, green, and blue-and-white glass on the front and by discs of red
and yellow enamel at the back. Spiral filigree and silver niello spirals
frame the crystal on the front. The back had four panels (one is missing)
of openwork animal interlace on gilt bronze panels, framed in silver. The
animal interlace resembles the decoration associated with the Urnes style
in Norway and England—a tangle of large quadrupeds, delicate bipeds,
and serpents. The cross is held in the jaws of a magnificent double-
headed beast, and additional beasts join the base to the staff. The animals
have small round heads, round ears, striated muzzles, curling lower jaws,
curling hair as long as their spines, striped bodies, outlined spiral joints,
and inset bead eyes. The occurrence of such animals in England and
Ireland illustrates the continuance of relations between Scandinavia and
the British Isles throughout the Romanesque period.

The victories of Brian Boru and others over the Vikings did not
result in a consolidated kingdom and a long period of stability and prosperity. Instead, warfare among the petty kingdoms continued throughout
the island until 1169, when the Anglo-Normans under the earl of Pembroke—Strongbow—conquered the country. Strongbow claimed that he
came to the aid of the king of Leinster, but he married the princess, Eva,
and was recognized as the successor to the king.[11] Sensing political and
economic advantages in the subjugation of Ireland and fearing the
strength of Strongbow, King Henry II went to Dublin himself, where he
held court in a huge wooden hall built for the purpose. Henry claimed
Ireland; and he ruled the land through viceroys, awarding Leinster to
Strongbow, who died a year later, before he could fully consolidate his
territory; Meath to Hugh de Lacy, who established himself at Trim Castle in 1172, and was assassinated in 1186; Ulster to John de Courcy; and
Dublin to the citizens of Bristol. The Irish king O'Connor retained Connaught. In a church synod held at Lismore, the Roman Church of the
Normans was declared to be the Church of Ireland.

Ireland remained an independent fief of the crown; thus, when John came to the throne of England, Ireland was his personal fief, not a part of the English nation; and the Irish barons continued their semi-autonomous local rule. Thus, in Ireland the long history of struggle between absentee rulers and local magnates began.

The most impressive Anglo-Norman architectural monuments in Ireland are the great castles, rather than churches. The castles demonstrate the practical organizational ability and martial prowess of the invaders; the churches, the aesthetic level and the breadth of culture of both foreign churchmen and native ecclesiastics.

The Normans introduced into Ireland the *motte*-and-bailey castle, which had served them so well on the Continent and in England. Easily and quickly constructed by untrained workmen, the *motte*-and-bailey castle was essentially a circular earthwork and palisade (already used in Ireland) with a high artificial mound in the center, on which were erected a wooden tower and additional walls. Such a building was useful in securing newly occupied territory; but its vulnerability to fire made it, of necessity, a temporary structure. As soon as possible, the wooden palisade had to be replaced by stone walls, and the tower by a stone keep.

Such a development must have occurred at Trim, which is the most impressive Norman castle to be seen in Ireland today. The first castle on the site was built in 1172, only three years after the Conquest, by Hugh de Lacy. It was composed of a house, a ditch, and a palisade. Since the *Song of Dermot* tells of the flight of the garrison and the burning of the castle by the Irish, the building must have been of timber. Trim was rebuilt at once, first in wood and then in stone—the stone keep perhaps just before 1200 and certainly before 1220, when the castle is mentioned in the *Annals of Innisfallen*. Walter de Lacy was lord of Meath from about 1194 to 1240, with Trim as a headquarters, except for a brief period (1210–1215) when Meath was invaded by King John.[12]

The keep at Trim is an imposing example of the Norman square stone keep, with massive walls 11 feet thick and 70 feet high. Two rooms occupy each of the three stories, which are joined by staircases within the thickness of the wall. The keep has an unusually old-fashioned design for the thirteenth century. The square keep had fallen out of favor because of the vulnerability of its corners to mining, battering rams, and missiles, a problem that was solved by the erection of round towers. At Trim not only is the keep square, but in the center of each side a square room has been constructed with even thinner walls, thus increasing the number of vulnerable corners from four to twelve. These four chambers served to enlarge the size of the keep at each floor. One such projection,

Castle at Trim
Norman keep, c. 1200; curtain walls, mid-thirteenth century; county Meath
Photo by Marilyn Stokstad

Cashel
Tower and chapel, twelfth century; cathedral, thirteenth; hall, fifteenth;
St. Dominick's Abbey, thirteenth-fifteenth; county Tipperary
Photo by permission of the Commissioners of Public Works in Ireland

a combination entrance tower and chapel, was usual in the twelfth-century keeps, and may have inspired the building of rooms on the other three sides. Since defensive strength has been sacrificed for additional internal space, the castle may have been designed when siege machinery and tactics were relatively simple in Ireland. By the time the weakness of the design had become a real military hazard, the curtain walls with "modern" round towers had been added, and these provided sufficient protection.

For military purposes, keeps were gradually abandoned in favor of the curtain wall in the thirteenth century. As the administrative center of Meath, the keep of Trim was a court as well as a fortress, and served as a symbol of Norman power. Walter de Lacy and his successors undoubtedly needed more space than was provided even in the expanded keep. The castle yard, or bailey, covered about three acres, and was defended by a curtain wall, which was 486 yards long, with five semicircular towers, two fortified gateways, sally ports, and (originally) a moat and the river Boyne. These defenses were begun about 1220. Walter's daughter Matilda married Geoffrey de Geneville, a crusader who was lord justice of Ireland in 1273 and was the brother of Jean de Joinville, the companion and biographer of St. Louis of France. This family connection suggests that the lords of Trim must have known the latest developments in military architecture in France and the Crusader States, and that the conservatism of their own stronghold was perhaps at least in part due to the recognition of the castle as a *symbol* of power and authority.

The gateways at Trim are still very impressive. The west gate is a relatively conservative rectangular gatehouse with portcullis. The gate on the south is a round tower which still preserves its barbican, or outer defensive courtyard, and gate. The barbican extended over the moat and enclosed a drawbridge within its walls. The barbican turret has arrow slits for the convenience of the defenders in harassing and eliminating the attackers. In short, by the time the excellent outer defenses were built at Trim, the strange but impressive keep would be effectively defended and devoted essentially to civilian uses. The civil architecture within the walls of Trim Castle was of wood—stables and garrison quarters, kitchens, storerooms—as was usual in the larger medieval castles.

A town rose outside the castle, and by the fourteenth century the wall of the town joined the castle on the southwest corner. During the wars of the sixteenth and seventeenth centuries the castle, though in a ruinous state, was still used; but it was finally destroyed by Cromwell's

Bishop Cormac MacCarthy's Chapel
1127–1134; Rock of Cashel, county Tipperary
Photo by permission of the Commissioners of Public Works in Ireland

troops and was abandoned. The city remained. (Swift's "Stella" lived in Trim; and her house, dated 1717, still stands.)

Brian Boru's stronghold at Cashel is a more romantic ruin than Trim Castle, and the ecclesiastical and civil buildings on and around the Rock of Cashel provide a complete resume of the art of the Romanesque and Gothic periods. The dramatic site—a rock outcrop supposedly cast on the plain by magic—was fortified as early as the fourth century A.D. St. Patrick established a bishopric at Cashel; Brian Boru was crowned there in 977, and made the place his capital. In 1101 the Rock was given to the Church; and Bishop Cormac MacCarthy built a chapel, which was begun in 1127 and consecrated in 1134. The bishop may also have built the round tower. Between the tower and the chapel stood the cathedral, a building that was rebuilt in the thirteenth century. Cashel became the seat of an archbishop in 1152. The site remained important strategically as well as ecclesiastically; therefore the buildings suffered considerable damage, especially in the fifteenth and seventeenth centuries. By the eighteenth century the cathedral lay in ruins.

Cormac's Chapel is the finest Romanesque church in Ireland. Towers flank the rectangular choir in a manner that is reminiscent of the Norman towers of Exeter cathedral or of German Romanesque churches. A connection with Germany may not be far-fetched, since the presence in Ireland in the early twelfth century of two masons from Ratisbon is recorded. On the other hand, the verticality of the building, the arcaded walls, the decoration of the chancel arch, and the elaborate carving of the doorways—all reflect Norman architecture. The ribbed barrel vault of the nave resembles vaults in southwestern France, especially Saintonge, which had close relations with the British Isles during the Middle Ages. The normal pilgrimage route from the British Isles to Santiago de Compostela lay by sea to the ports of Santiago, and then overland along the route described in the twelfth-century *Pilgrim's Guide*.[13] The groin vault on round arches in the choir is closer to Norman innovations found at the cathedrals of Durham and Peterborough. The plan—with rectangular nave and square choir, the upper rooms and stone roof, and the use of an upper vaulted chamber under the steep roof and over the barrel-vaulted nave—are characteristic of Irish architecture. The independent, slender round tower, 92 feet high, is also a distinctive Irish form.

The decoration of the chapel is influenced by both Norman and Scandinavian art. A tomb covered with interlacing serpents and monsters in Urnes style still stands at the west end of the chapel.[14] The tympanum of the main door, however, has a centaur shooting a lion with a bow and arrow—a typically Eastern motif found in Norman Sicily. Solemn human faces are carved in each voussoir, together with a profusion of geometric motifs, as in England.

Few Irish Romanesque churches have the variety and truly international eclecticism of Cormac's chapel. Other centers of Romanesque art, such as the monasteries in the valley of the Shannon and the Boyne rivers, seem simple and conservative. Irish builders of the eleventh and twelfth centuries remained faithful to tradition; they seem to have looked back to the proportions, plans, and structure of early oratories. Thus, masons built aisleless rectangular or square naves and choirs; laid stone roofs directly on vaults; eliminated transepts or arcades; and evidenced little desire to experiment with vaults or decoration. Churches at Glendalough, Clonmacnois, and Kells (for example, St. Kevin's Kitchen and St. Columba's House) are all part of this conservative Irish Romanesque building tradition. (According to Françoise Henry, St. Kevin's Kitchen and St. Columba's House are both eleventh-century buildings.)[15] Ecclesiastical buildings continued to be very small. St. Kevin's Kitchen, for example, is only 22 feet, 8 inches by 14 feet, 7 inches.

The Norman churches, although small in scale and conservative architecturally, often have sculpture that demonstrates a knowledge of widely scattered Continental building. Most churches had a single portal at the west and a chancel arch, both of which might be carved with Anglo-Norman, Scandinavian, or southwestern French motifs.[16] Portals such as those at the Nun's Church in Clonmacnois (consecrated 1167) or the twelfth-century portal at Clonfert have voussoirs, with chevrons, zigzags, and lozenges, as well as decorative columns that are typical of Anglo-Norman work; they also have dragons and serpents from Scandinavia, and rows of human and animal heads—not the English beak-head monsters, but rather the relatively natural human and horse heads of southwestern France.

The portal of the church founded by St. Brendan the Navigator at Clonfert in Galway is one of the most remarkable creations of the Irish Romanesque. The wide, round-arched, deeply recessed portal is capped by a steeply pitched false gable, twenty-six feet high. The low, almost engraved, relief decoration on the jambs and colonettes contrasts with the voussoirs, which are covered with a full repertoire of Norman ornament—including animal and geometric interlace, discs, bosses, lozenges, ropes, four-leaf flowers, and, in very high relief, a row of animal heads chewing on a torus molding. The ornamentation—both the heads and the interlaces—resembles the decoration of the Cross of Cong.

The gable above the door is filled with the human heads, which are carved in vigorous relief. One row is set under an arcade of richly

West Façade and Doorway of Clonfert Cathedral
Twelfth century (1130?); Confert, county Galway
Photo by permission of the Commissioners of Public Works in Ireland

decorated, stumpy engaged columns; and the rest alternate with triangular daisylike flowers in low relief. Folklorists have speculated that the design relates to the Celtic Cult of the Head, in which the heads of enemies were displayed in niches and over entrances.[17] The Clonfert heads could just as well be related to Christian usage elsewhere, for example, in Spain, where the College of Apostles was often represented in an arcade over the door and the combination of three-dimensional sculptured heads and painted bodies was used, for example, at Oviedo; or they could relate to the example of enamel workers in both France and Spain, where cast heads were applied to two-dimensional, champlevé enamel bodies, and to haloes of saints standing under enamel or three-dimensional arcades. The rows of heads that fill the triangular gable resemble the

Mozarabic representations of crowds of witnesses, which were often arranged in just such a compact fashion in manuscript illustrations.

No documents exist to date the portal. Henry dates it about 1125 to 1135 on the basis of its resemblance to the Cross of Cong.[18] Other authorities, including Leask,[19] would make it later, about 1160, because of its extremely rich decoration. The earlier date of around 1130 seems reasonable. The bishop for whom the Cross of Cong was made, Donel O'Duffy, died in 1136 at Clonfert. On the other hand, the bishop of Clonfert in the 1160s was a Cistercian from Boyle Abbey; he certainly would not have condoned such an elaborate sculptural program as that on the west façade. Incidentally, the related portal at Dysert O'Dea is decorated not only with animal and human heads and interlaces but also with scalloped voussoirs of the type found in Romanesque portals under Moorish influence in twelfth-century Spain. Dysert O'Dea has also been related to the Cross of Cong and to French sculpture of the first half of the twelfth century.

The study of the art of the succeeding century—the Gothic style —can be a frustrating experience in Ireland.[20] The cathedrals in Dublin, for example, are heavily restored and rebuilt, although close study of them is repaid by the discovery of sections of excellent thirteenth-century work. At Cashel a new building program began about 1230 with the construction of the choir of the cathedral. The new building had a single aisle, which is lit by tall lancet windows, with additional tiny windows in the spandrels. By mid century, transepts, which had wide passages in the walls and stair turrets on the west side, were added; and the foundations of a crossing tower were laid. By 1260 the nave had been begun, but it was never finished because the bishop ran deeply into debt. The architect evidently based his design on western English buildings such as Wells cathedral. Finally, in the fifteenth century, a fortified residential tower was erected at Cashel in the space that had been reserved to complete the nave of the cathedral. The tower and the battlements along the nave walls add to the military character of the site.

Gothic sculpture is even rarer than architecture. An oak figure of St. Molaise, carved about 1300, which was found in Inishmurray, county Sligo, is one of the most monumental late medieval figures. This over-life-size standing saint seems to have been based on western English work, such as that found at Wells. The provincial simplicity of its style, however, suggests the rude strength of folk art. The body adheres to the rectangular form of the log from which it was hewn. The drapery falls in regular parallel vertical folds; and the chasuble, as it is lifted by the upraised arms (the hands and forearms are missing), breaks into a reg-

**St. Molaise**
C. 1300; oak, more than life size
Inishmurray, county Sligo
National Museum of Ireland, Dublin
Photo by permission of the National Museum of Ireland

ular pattern of intersecting folds. The long face, which is extended with a short full beard, indicated by parallel striations; the bulging forehead; the slit mouth; and the long narrow nose, cut almost as one with the large bulging eyes, are all reminiscent of early Celtic heads.

By the fifteenth century, Ireland had become a cultural backwater. In the cloister at the twelfth-century Cistercian abbey of Jerpoint,[21] saints, apostles, an abbot, a bishop, six knights, three ladies, and one nondescript man were added to the columns. In contrast to the sophisticated international Cistercian architecture, the sculpture is so simple that it approaches folk art.

The sculpture has been analyzed by E. C. Rae,[22] who has identified one knight and lady tentatively as Sir Piers Butler and Margaret Fitzgerald, daughter of the eighth earl of Kildare, who were married in 1485. The costume is consistent with such a date; the armor of the knight was commonly used from the late fourteenth to the sixteenth century. The

Knight of Jerpoint
Knight with shield of the Butler family, fifteenth century
Twelfth-century cloister of Cistercian Abbey of Jerpoint, county Kilkenny
Photo by permission of the Commissioners of Public Works in Ireland

elaboration of the sculptural program suggests that the work may have been intended as a memorial to the donors' deceased ancestors, whose souls, it was hoped, rested with the saints in heaven as their sculptured portraits did on earth. The Butlers (Fitzwalter, butler of Ireland) had come to Ireland with the Normans, and had remained as nominal vassals of the English king. By 1329 the head of the family had become earl of Ormonde, one of the most powerful lords of Ireland. Centuries later, James Butler (1610–1685) became lord lieutenant of Ireland for King Charles I and then was made duke of Ormonde by Charles II at the Restoration. The continuing importance of the Butler family adds interest to the solemn knight of Jerpoint.

Harp of Brian Boru
Fourteenth or fifteenth century
Slightly more than two feet high
Trinity College Library, Dublin
Photo by permission of the Board of Trinity College, Dublin

*Medieval Art*

The music and poetry of the bards, rather than architecture and sculpture, are more representative of Irish culture in the later Middle Ages. In this culture, which was often more attuned to the word (spoken or sung) than to the visual image, the harp stands as the symbol of Ireland. In the eighteenth century, just as scholars began to delve into Ireland's ancient history, a beautiful harp was found. Although it is called the Harp of Brian Boru, it cannot be more than five—or, at most, six—hundred years old. Still, it is the oldest and finest harp in Ireland, and the one that is copied by modern instrument makers. The decoration in geometric patterns, animal interlaces, and animal heads has its source in Viking ornament. The harp—now a prized possession of Trinity College Library, along with the *Book of Kells*—exerts its romantic attraction for those who still visualize it as the harp that once sounded in that other romantic fiction—"Tara's halls." For those absorbed by romanticized history and casual antiquarianism, it is well to remember the words of William Butler Yeats:

> Romantic Ireland's dead and gone,
> It's with O'Leary in the grave.[23]

# NOTES

1. Kathleen Hughes, *The Church in Early Irish Society* (London: Methuen, 1966), p. 201.
2. For the impact of the Vikings and their art on Ireland see Françoise Henry, *Irish Art during the Viking Invasions, 800–1020 A.D.* (vol. 2 of the three-volume series *Irish Art*; London: Methuen, 1967), as well as other general reference works mentioned in the notes to chap. 3 of this book. Works by the nineteenth-century scholars G. Petrie and Margaret Stokes are still useful. See also the catalogue for the exhibition *Rosc '71: Scandinavian Art of the Viking Age* (Dublin, 1971), introduction by David Wilson; Thomas D. Kendrick, *Late Saxon and Viking Art* (London: Methuen, 1949); David M. Wilson and Ole Klindt-Jensen, *Viking Art* (London: Allen & Unwin, 1966). Viking art has been studied by other scholars, including Haakon Shetelig, Bjørn Hougen, and Nils Åberg.
3. Françoise Henry, *Irish High Crosses* (Dublin: Published for the Cultural Relations Committee of Ireland at the Three Candles, 1964). Henry S. Crawford, "A Descriptive List of the Early Irish Crosses," *Journal of the Royal Society of Antiquaries of Ireland* 37:187–239 (1907), "Some Crosses Not Mentioned in the List of Irish Crosses," *Journal of the Royal Society of Antiquaries of Ireland* 38:181–82 (1908), "Supplementary List of Early Irish Crosses," *Journal of the Royal Society of Antiquaries of Ireland* 48:174–79 (1918), and *Handbook of Carved Ornament from Irish Monuments of the Christian Period* (Dublin: Royal Society of Antiquaries of Ireland, 1926); Arthur Kingsley Porter, *The Crosses and Culture of Ireland* (New Haven, Conn.: Yale University Press, 1931).

4. London, British Museum, Cotton Ms. Vitellius F. XI.
5. Henry, *Irish Art during the Viking Invasions*, p. 107.
6. *The War of the Gaedhil with the Gaill, or the Invasions by the Danes and Other Norsemen*, trans. J. H. Todd (London, 1867).
7. For Irish Romanesque art see Françoise Henry, *Irish Art in the Romanesque Period, 1020–1170 A.D.* (vol. 3 of *Irish Art*; London: Methuen, 1970); Kenneth John Conant, *Carolingian and Romanesque Architecture, 800 to 1200* (Harmondsworth, Eng.: Penguin, 1959); R. A. Stalley, *Architecture and Sculpture in Ireland, 1150–1350* (Dublin: Gill & Macmillan, 1971); Harold G. Leask, *Irish Castles and Castellated Houses* (Dundalk, Ire.: Dundalgan Press, 1941), and *Irish Churches and Monastic Buildings* (3 vols.; Dundalk, Ire.: Dundalgan Press, 1955–1960).
8. Translation by David Wilson.
9. Margaret Stokes, *Notes on the Cross of Cong* (Dublin, 1895), pp. 4–5.
10. Ibid., p. 2.
11. See the painting by Daniel Maclise (1806–1870), *The Marriage of Princess Eva and Strongbow*, the National Gallery, Dublin; and James White, "Irish Romantic Painting," *Apollo*, October 1966, pp. 268–75.
12. Joseph P. Kelly, *Trim Castle* (Trim, Ire., 1965); Leask, *Irish Castles and Castellated Houses*; Stalley, *Architecture and Sculpture in Ireland*, pp. 32–39.
13. Marilyn Stokstad, *Santiago de Compostela in the Age of the Pilgrimages* (Norman: University of Oklahoma Press, forthcoming).
14. Compare wood carvings at Urnes, Norway.
15. Henry, *Irish Art in the Romanesque Period*, pp. 146–51.
16. Françoise Henry and George Zarnecki, "Romanesque Arches with Human and Animal Heads," *Journal of the British Archeological Association*, 3d ser., 20/21: 1–19 (1957–1958).
17. Proinsias Mac Cana, *Celtic Mythology* (London and New York: Hamlyn, 1970), p. 104.
18. Henry, *Irish Art in the Romanesque Period*, p. 160.
19. Leask, *Irish Churches*, 1:137–42.
20. Stalley, *Architecture and Sculpture in Ireland*; Leask, *Irish Churches*, vol. 2: *Gothic Architecture to 1400*.
21. Françoise Henry, "Irish Cistercian Monasteries and Their Carved Decoration," *Apollo*, October 1966, pp. 260–67; Stalley, *Architecture and Sculpture in Ireland*, pp. 97–100.
22. E. C. Rae, "The Sculpture of the Cloister of Jerpoint Abbey," *Journal of the Royal Society of Antiquaries of Ireland* 96:59–91 (1966).
23. William Butler Yeats, "September, 1913."

# SUGGESTIONS FOR FURTHER READING

Henry, Françoise. *Irish Art*. Vols. 2 and 3 especially. London: Methuen, and Ithaca, N.Y.: Cornell University Press, 1965-1970.
———. *Irish High Crosses*. Dublin: Published for the Cultural Relations Committee of Ireland at the Three Candles, 1964.
Kendrick, Thomas D. *Late Saxon and Viking Art*. London: Methuen, 1949.
Leask, Harold G. *Irish Castles and Castellated Houses*. Dundalk, Ire.: Dundalgan Press, 1941.
———. *Irish Churches and Monastic Buildings*. 3 vols. Dundalk, Ire.: Dundalgan Press, 1955–1960.

Stalley, R. A. *Architecture and Sculpture in Ireland, 1150–1350*. Dublin: Gill & Macmillan, 1971.

Wilson, David. *Rosc '71: Scandinavian Art of the Viking Age*. Dublin, 1971.

———, and Klindt-Jensen, Ole. *Viking Art*. London: Allen & Unwin, 1966.

# FROM THE ACCESSION
# OF THE TUDORS TO THE TREATY
# OF LIMERICK
## *Henry L. Snyder*

When Henry VII came to the throne of England, Ireland was only nominally part of his crown. For nearly half a century the country had been Yorkist in its allegiance. But civil strife in England was so endemic for the greater part of the century that no king had been able to devote any attention to Ireland. It was virtually independent for all practical purposes. After 1460 the Irish Parliament ratified only those English laws that it found acceptable, and in the next decade it went so far as to elect its own governor, declaring Thomas, earl of Kildare, as justiciar. Kildare and his son Gerald, the eighth earl, were de facto rulers of the country. This was not to say that their rule was effective throughout Ireland. Their jurisdiction was most effective in and around the Pale, where their estates were centered. Besides Kildare, this included portions of Meath, Carlow, and Dublin, and areas adjacent to it. Though intermarried into the Irish, the Kildares were still the most English in style of the great Irish lords. The major part of the south and southwest was controlled by two other great Anglo-Irish families, the earls of Desmond and Ormonde. The Ormondes were Lancastrians who had fallen out of favor under the Yorkist kings; this had enabled the Desmonds and the Kildares to aggrandize their power and wealth. All three earls held sway in their own territories, like the Irish kings of yore, the Desmonds being closest in spirit and custom to their subjects. Controlling lands in Kerry, Cork, Limerick, Waterford, and Tipperary, the Desmonds appointed their own sheriffs and administered the law independent of royal intervention.

During the first part of his reign, Henry VII often had reason to rue the presence of this unruly and rebellious island. Kildare went so far as to accept Lambert Simnel—one of the challengers to Henry's throne —as Edward VI, crown him king of Ireland, and then support his invasion of England. Perkin Warbeck, the next contestant for the English crown, also found a ready welcome in Ireland in 1491 from those who were eager to make common cause against the Tudors. Henry, not daring to depose Kildare, restored the Butlers to the earldom of Ormonde, which had been forfeited since 1461, and tried to use Ormonde as a counterweight to Kildare. However, the feuding of the two nobles and their families kept the country in constant turmoil. By providing a ready haven for Henry's enemies, Ireland was a continual threat to the king's security.

In 1494, once England was under control, Henry turned to one of his loyal English lieutenants in an effort to restore effective rule in Ireland. After naming his infant son Henry as lord lieutenant of Ireland, Henry made Sir Edward Poynings deputy and sent Poynings to Dublin to take charge. Poynings faced a herculean task, but in his administration, which lasted little more than a year, he made significant progress. He put down rebels in Ulster, and in 1495, when Perkin returned to Ireland, Poynings defeated Perkin's forces, which had laid siege to Waterford. More importantly, he overhauled the administration, bringing to the Irish government the same efficiency and new professionalism that Henry had introduced in England. The financial departments were reorganized, and the collection of taxes was improved, so that Ireland ceased to be such a heavy drain on the royal revenues. Poynings is best remembered for the Parliament he held at Drogheda in December 1494, which enacted an important series of statutes designed to restore English authority in the country. Some forty-nine acts were passed in all. Their scope reflects the ills to which the country had been subjected insofar as England was concerned. Revenue officers were put under the treasurer, who in turn was made directly responsible to the king; and the powers of the sheriffs, which were controlled by the nobility, were drastically curtailed. The reforms were broad and wide-ranging, but the most famous act was the

## Scale

0 — 25 — 50
**Miles**

0 — 25 — 50
**Kilometers**

Aran Island
Isle of Innisfree

Ballycastle

THE ROUTE

ANTRIM

DeBOY

TYRCONNEL

Derry

O'NEILL

U L S T E R

O'DONNELL

Dungannon

Lisburn

Bangor

FERMANAGH

TYRONE

IVEAGH

O'ROURKE

Dundalk

O'REILLY

Drogheda

IAR
CONNACHT
Clifden

C O N N A U G H T

Tuam

LOUGH LENE

OFFALY

Mullingar

TRIM

Trim

THE

ENGLISH

CONNEMARA

HYMANY

AUGHRIM

L E I N S T E R

Liffey R.

PALE

Galway

BURKE

Kildare

Kiltartan

LEIX

THOMOND

(O'BRIEN)

ORMOND

Limerick

Kilkenny

MACMURROUGH

Cashel

M
U
N
S
T
E
R

Clonmel

Wexford

WEXFORD

Waterford

DESMOND

Cork

Kinsale

**IRELAND AT THE ACCESSION OF HENRY VII**

one that came to bear the deputy's name. It provided that no parliament could be held until it was specifically authorized by the king. When it met, it could consider only bills that were approved for its consideration by the crown, and the final approval of all legislation was subject to the review of both the Irish and the English Privy Councils. In effect, the legislature was emasculated and made wholly subservient to the English crown. Although the implementation of this act was gradually relaxed, it remained in force until 1782, and was one of the most potent means by which the kings of England brought Ireland under their sway. Public legislation that was passed by the English Parliament was automatically extended to Ireland. Another act provided for the construction of ditches all around the English Pale, to safeguard the loyal inhabitants from hostile raids by the native Irish.

Poynings's success was hardly complete. The Anglo-Irish nobility still controlled a major portion of the country, and the north and northeast were in the hands of native chieftains, who were completely outside of English control. The only loyal supporters the king could rely upon were to be found in the towns. The old English settlers in the four counties, both lay and clerical, put their faith in the king. They formed the basis of Poynings's support; they also constituted the majority in the Parliament. The contest with the Anglo-Irish families for control of the state went on for another generation. The earls of Kildare reigned supreme until 1534, and Dublin was as much their capital—and the center of Anglo-Irish power—as it was the crown's. Because of the legislation passed under Poynings, the king regained some control over the executive, and he began to replace the officers of state with loyal Englishmen —a pattern that was to remain the norm until the nineteenth century. But until the power of the Anglo-Irish families was broken or made subservient to the wishes of the king, Ireland remained a feudal, semi-independent state. Many decades of patient and unceasing effort were required to develop a body of loyal administrators who could manage the government, collect the revenues, and extend the king's authority in accordance with the new pattern that was emerging in England. The civil wars in England had had a devastating effect upon the royal revenues there, but the decline in income to the crown was as nothing compared to the loss from the state of Ireland. But the first step had been taken: the erosion of royal authority had been arrested, and its restoration had begun.

The eighth earl of Kildare remained in effective control of the country until his death in 1513, respected by both the Anglo-Irish and the native population. His son and successor inherited the government of Ireland as well as the personal titles and estates of his father, but the days of his family's rule were numbered. His chief rival in Ireland, the head of the Butlers, had the confidence of the new king; and the Lancastrian loyalties of the Butlers weighted the balance in their favor. The king's principal minister, Wolsey, also resented Kildare's independence and worked for his downfall. A suspicion that Kildare was in league with France against Henry VIII caused him to be imprisoned in the Tower in 1527. Kildare never recovered his position. Though allowed to return to Ireland in 1532, he left Ireland for the last time in 1534. His son and heir, Lord Offaly, rebelled against the crown in that year; and by the end of the decade they and many of their family were dead, and the power of the family had been broken.

Henry VIII embarked upon a new policy—of rule by loyal English deputies; at the same time he sought to pacify the Anglo-Irish lords and Irish chiefs and to reconcile them to the crown. Three able deputies— William Skeffington (1530–1535), Lord Grey (1536–1540), and Anthony St. Leger (1540–1548)—were the instruments of this new policy. Skeffington put down Offaly's rebellion, thus breaking the power of the Kildares. Grey presided over the Reformation Parliament in Ireland, which restored the lands of absentee landlords to the crown, thereby making the crown a great landlord. Grey also persuaded a number of the native chiefs to make their submission to the king at the Parliament. He extended the area under English control by employing small but well-disciplined English forces, which proved superior to their more numerous but untrained native opponents. St. Leger was originally sent over as a member of a commission to investigate complaints made against Grey, and he stayed on to head the government. He continued the policy of pacification and Anglicization that had been initiated by his predecessors, and he proved to be a particularly effective administrator. Henry's policy of persuasion might eventually have won over his Irish subjects to his rule but for the coincidence of the Reformation, which proved to be the undoing of the English in Ireland.

The Irish Church was in a deplorable state at the time of the Reformation. The general state of laxity and corruption within the Church that was endemic throughout western Europe was exacerbated in Ireland. Violence, extortion, and excessive fees were common charges against the clergy. Immorality in the Church was rife, and clerical marriage was not uncommon. The king's influence in appointments was limited outside the Pale. Many sees were left vacant for long periods of time, and the fabric of the Church, both physical and spiritual, was in a state of decrepitude. The poverty of the Church and the still-prevailing scarcity of urban concentrations of population were partially responsible for this state. The venality of the parish clergy and their indifference to their charges created an atmosphere of resentment that could have been as favorable in Ireland to the Reformation as it was in England. The Irish Parliament passed legislation similar to that enacted in England; but the heresy laws were not replicated, and the dissolution of the monasteries took far longer to carry out—some even survived into the next century. The native chiefs accepted the Reformation, as it coincided with the pacification policy through which they acquired their new titles; they were accepted at court, and were incorporated into the English ruling structure. But the Reformation failed, because the common people were neglected.

Though the Church was in a bad state, the monasteries, always the stronghold of the Church in Ireland, fared better than their English counterparts. Education was largely in the hands of the monks, which gave them a greater sense of purpose and also won them the respect and gratitude of the people. A zealous reformer was appointed to the see of Dublin, but the reform-minded clergy whom he brought with him from England to remodel the Church spoke no Irish, and therefore could not reach the common people. Indeed, the Reformation was not officially promulgated in Ireland until the next reign, that of Edward VI, in 1551. The new liturgy, in English, was introduced over the strenuous objections of the primate, but even this was not intelligible to the mass of the population. In an attempt to reconcile the primate and the clergy, the liturgy was even translated into Irish. But it was too late. The steadfast conduct of the friars, which was reinforced by the Jesuits and a growing new Catholic hierarchy appointed by the pope for Ireland, kept the faith of the people loyal to Rome. The real strength of the clergy in Ireland was among the friars; they kept the Catholic faith alive. They fanned the resentment of the native population against the Anglicization program of the king, and thus Church and Celt were linked in a popular national opposition to the crown and gave strength to each other. In 1542 the Jesuits came to Ireland and stiffened the resistance of the clergy. The result was the failure of the Reformation in Ireland. For the English the greatest loss was the failure of the program of reconciliation and assimilation which would have bound Ireland to England. Many of the seeds of the nationalist movement, which was to bring independence in the twentieth century, were laid in the fourth decade of the sixteenth century.

Although Mary restored the old religion, in other aspects she was as determined as her predecessors to carry through the program of Anglicization. Indeed, she ordered her deputy, the earl of Sussex, to initiate a plantation scheme in the districts of Leix and Offaly, replacing the

O'Connors and the O'Mores, who had rebelled in Edward's reign. His efforts provoked a second and a third rebellion in the disputed territories (which were renamed Queen's County and King's County). Sussex had no sooner restored order there than he was called to Ulster to act against another outbreak, but his expedition had little effect.

The conquest of Ireland was finally realized in the reign of the last of the Tudors. The prospect that had so often eluded Elizabeth's predecessors was now within her grasp, and she had the time, the will, and ultimately the resources to realize it. Her conduct was neither precipitous nor dramatic. Though she restored the official church to Protestantism, she took no punitive action against the Roman Catholics as long as they remained loyal to her. Like her father and grandfather, she lacked the money to undertake a major military conquest of the rest of Ireland, but at the same time, fear of Spanish intervention prompted her to embark upon a more measured but nevertheless consistent policy of extending her authority to the parts of the island that were still under native control. The whole of the country was gradually divided into shires, and an English administration was introduced successively into Leinster, Munster, and Connaught, so that by 1585 these areas were incorporated into the government of the Pale. Ireland was not simply a local problem for Elizabeth, but rather a problem that had international dimensions. Ireland became a pawn in the struggle between England and Spain, and a center for activities against England. Ireland played a key role in the Counter Reformation, and was a center of Jesuit activity. The bitterness of the ideological struggle that engulfed Europe spilled over into Ireland. When the chiefs of Munster rebelled against the crown in 1579, resisting the Anglicization of their lands, they received support from Spain and Italy. In turn, this foreign intervention strengthened Elizabeth's determination to stamp out the revolt. By 1583 the English were in complete control of Ireland, but the years of war had devastated the country, and the price of victory was the destruction of crops, farmlands, and dwellings, as well as the deaths of more than thirty thousand people in the last year alone. Elizabeth revived the idea of a plantation by putting loyal Englishmen in possession of the lands forfeited by the rebels. The plantation did not succeed, but Munster ceased to be a source of trouble, and the queen could concentrate her energies and forces on other trouble spots in the country.

The last stronghold of the native chiefs was Ulster. Ulster had been the scene of Sussex's activities at the end of Mary's reign, when the deputy first had gone north to eject Scottish settlers in Antrim, and then had returned to fight them a second time when they had leagued with

Shane O'Neill, the claimant to the title and lands of the greatest Irish family in the north. Shane went over to England in 1562 to plead his inheritance before Elizabeth, and he won her reluctant consent to his claim. On his return to Ireland, Shane, who was trying to extend his authority, defeated the Scots in a battle near Ballycastle in 1565. His victory gave him control of almost the whole of Ulster. His aggression was more than Elizabeth could tolerate, and she ordered her deputy, Sir Henry Sidney, to proceed against him. But it was another party of the Scots who were responsible for Shane's death in 1569, thus avenging the earlier defeat of their countrymen at Shane's hands.

The O'Neill inheritance was now divided between Shane's cousin, Turlough, and his nephew Hugh, whom the English installed in the area of Armagh as Turlough's rival. This policy of divide and conquer worked for a time—until 1593, when Hugh joined up with the Scots to defeat Turlough—and then the three parties joined in an alliance against the English. Hugh—who had succeeded to the English title of Tyrone and to the O'Neill chieftainship, which had been surrendered by Turlough—now became the leader of the native opposition to the English rulers. He took the offensive against Elizabeth in 1595, when he attacked the Pale, while his allies raided Connaught.

The final effort to subdue Ireland was at hand, and the struggle lasted until the very end of Elizabeth's reign. A succession of viceroys tackled the Irish rebels: William Russell, Lord Burgh, and Elizabeth's favorite, the earl of Essex, who was at the head of the largest English army ever sent to Ireland up until that time. All three tried their skill against Tyrone; each in turn was unsuccessful. It was left to the last of the Tudor deputies, Lord Mountjoy, to secure the victory that had eluded all those who had gone before him. Dispatched to Ireland in 1600, Mountjoy methodically set out to encircle Tyrone and his forces, gradually tightening the ring and holding him in check by establishing a series of forts. Tyrone was in league with the Spanish, who sent an expedition to aid him in 1601. They landed, however, in the south at Kinsale, and it was six months before Tyrone and his allies could make their way down from Ulster to join them. Mountjoy, who had laid siege to the Spanish forces, ran the risk of entrapment between the Spanish and Irish forces, but his disciplined troops were more than a match for the poorly organized Irish forces. The Irish attacked and were repulsed. Following the capitulation of the Spanish, Mountjoy followed Tyrone north to Ulster, and O'Neill, without any hope of holding out, submitted to Mountjoy in 1603. The conquest of Ireland was complete.

The completion of the Tudor conquest of Ireland marked a new stage in Irish history. Until the mid sixteenth century, Irish culture, customs, and language had existed alongside their English counterparts, which prevailed inside the Pale. Ireland was a prosperous country, and the people enjoyed their religion and their traditional way of life without any serious limitations. The second half of the sixteenth century saw the destruction of this culture and much of the prosperity of the native population. The country was divided into shires, and the English system of government was extended to all parts of the country. The Irish lordships were forfeited or broken up, and many of the inhabitants were dispossessed in order to make room for English colonists. The Reformation was imposed on the Irish Church; but alongside the Irish Church there developed a new Roman Catholic hierarchy which commanded the loyalties of the great majority of the population, though it did so without official sanction and support. A religious schism developed in the country which paralleled and reinforced the cultural and national differences. Half a century of warfare had ruined much of the agriculture. Orchards, farmlands, animals, and dwellings were destroyed. Tens of thousands of people were dislocated and reduced to the poverty level; many died of privation or disease. The old system of landholding was broken up, and a new profiteering class of landowners, often absentee, began to take the place of the native Irish ruling families. An alien ruling class, which was separated by culture, religion, and national origin, took over the country. Irish commerce also suffered heavily. Ireland had long enjoyed a brisk trade with Spain. The Spanish Netherlands was a principal market for Irish linen and wool. This trade was systematically reduced, and in many instances destroyed. The weaving trade became the major casualty, as the export of cloth from Ireland was forbidden. But even the native market declined, as the yarn was exported to England to be woven into cloth and then resold to the Irish for domestic consumption. The debasement of the currency—a serious problem throughout Europe and in England—was particularly bad in Ireland, as it was a tool used by the English to increase their profits in the trade between the two countries at the expense of the Irish. The value of the Irish pound was kept below the English pound until the nineteenth century. The attacks on Irish trade, as well as the wars of conquest, told heavily on the towns, which did not recover for nearly two hundred years. The efforts to eradicate Irish culture, coupled with the Reformation and the dissolution of the monasteries, had a disastrous effect on Irish learning. Irish laws, Irish books, and itinerant bards and poets—the carriers of Irish culture—were systematically rooted out. Because the monks had been the traditional teachers and schoolmasters, the educational system was decimated. The press became a tool of the English conquerors; therefore the native culture survived precariously through oral tradition and through the work of scribes. Trinity College (founded in 1593, and for more than two centuries the only university in Ireland), although it was a noble and respected institution, was founded by Englishmen for the dissemination of English culture; it was an alien foundation in a subjugated land. The established church had become a mere shell. It lost so much of its income that few parishes could support a clergyman, and church attendance practically ceased. The clandestine Roman Catholic Church alone was active, in the hands of the Jesuits and the friars. The Jesuits maintained schools in the towns, but the Roman Catholic clergy, like their English brethren, were trained abroad at establishments in Spain, the Spanish Netherlands, and France.

The accession of James I gave new hope to the native population. Toleration for the Catholics was expected; therefore they began to worship openly in public. They were soon disabused. Mountjoy, who remained in office, put an end to their hopes. His successor, Sir Arthur Chichester, who was appointed the next year, defined the policy more strictly. At first he directed his main efforts toward enforcing the oath of supremacy—a loyalty oath to the English crown which had to be taken by all priests and officials. Those who refused to comply were severely penalized. This policy was followed by instructions from the king to enforce the Elizabethan Act of Uniformity, which had virtually become a dead letter. All the Roman Catholic priests were ordered to leave the country by the end of 1605; however, no effort was made to carry out the order. The pattern was disquieting, nevertheless.

After the submission of Tyrone in 1603, Tyrone and other Irish nobles were restored to the government of the Ulster counties. Disputes broke out among them, fostered by the English deputy, who saw an opportunity to reduce further the heritable jurisdictions of the Irish chiefs. The voluntary exile of several chiefs in 1607, followed by the rebellion of several more, resulted in the forfeiture of almost the whole of Ulster to the crown. This action gave the impetus to implementing a large-scale scheme to ensure the loyalty of that area to the crown—the creation of a vast plantation in Ulster. The consequences are visible to this day.

Ulster was the last part of Ireland to be brought under English rule. Until the end of the sixteenth century, Irish law still prevailed there. This was especially true in regard to landholding; and much of the land was in the hands of the chiefs, who held them for their tribes. The members of the tribes were permitted to cultivate the land at will, but without receiving formal tenure. The freeholders or swordsmen had held arms under the rebel chieftains. Applying the principles of English rather than Irish law, the lawyers found that the landholdings belonged to the chiefs rather than to the tribes, and consequently title to them passed to the crown. This provided the legal basis for redistribution of land to new settlers. Chichester wanted to give priority to the loyal Irish who wanted land, and then grant the balance to colonists. Instead, the king ruled that the Irish were not to be permitted leases, but rather that all the land was to go to undertakers, which would reduce the natives to an inferior tenant status. The land was systematically divided up into parcels of prescribed sizes, which were granted to individual undertakers, English and Scots, who were only allowed to have British tenants; Irish officials, who might have Irish or British tenants; and a limited number of native freeholders. The result was a qualified success. The English proved to be poor managers; only the area later called Londonderry, which was contracted for by the city of London, proved to be a commercial success. The Scots proved to be much more interested and industrious. As a consequence, Ulster gradually assumed the character of a predominantly Scottish development. Both the ease of communication with Scotland and the greater proximity of Scotland favored the Scots. Another factor that soon gave the settlement its distinctive character was the religious policy followed by James I in Scotland. A firm supporter of an episcopal form of church government, because of the support it provided for the civil government, he instituted an episcopacy in Scotland. Many staunch Presbyterian ministers voluntarily withdrew rather than submit to the king's edict, and they emigrated to the new plantation. The Ulster Scots were therefore markedly Presbyterian and homogeneous in their religion, thus providing a stark contrast to the overwhelmingly Catholic population of the rest of the country. Initially, this was not a major point of dissension.

The Scots provided a new prosperity and a settled quality to the region. Their industry and productivity confirmed the English government in the wisdom of its decision to establish the plantation. The rapid growth and development of the plantation soon had repercussions on the rest of Ireland. Initially the old English population of the Pale—which had remained Roman Catholic, at the same time retaining its loyalty to England—had shown little concern for the dispossession of the native Irish in the north. They themselves, as loyal subjects, were unaffected by the confiscations. But the government now saw an opportunity to build up an enlarged Protestant majority in the Parliament, and so it created enough new boroughs in the north to meet this objective. The resistance of the old English to this scheme, and their appeal to the king, brought a temporary suspension of the plan; but the threat of harsher laws against the Catholics caused great concern to those of that persuasion. Within three decades the realization of these fears was to cement an alliance of the old English with their coreligionists among the native Irish, and the religious division which has underlain so many of the problems of Ireland since that time was fixed.

From the appointment of Chichester in 1606 until the coming of Wentworth in 1633, no progress was made towards a solution of the outstanding problems, but rather a slow but steady intensification of points at issue between the king and his Irish subjects. A rise in Catholicism was observed by all the deputies, in spite of their efforts to enforce uniformity. The Spanish courtship of Charles brightened the hopes of the Catholics; it also emboldened the priests. When Charles returned from Spain without a bride in 1623, there was an immediate reaction. All the priests were banished from the kingdom, but to no avail. A full-fledged, illegal hierarchy was now in existence, and the king failed to enforce the ban. Waterford, a Catholic center, had its charter revoked by Charles I upon his accession, but the king was unable to find Protestants who were willing to undertake responsibility for the corporation. After the success of the Ulster plantation, new plantations were undertaken in Wexford, Longford, and King's County. None was successful, and the experiments only served to embitter still further the king's Catholic subjects. The series of forfeitures and confiscations had created a large population of dispossessed landholders and idlers, thus creating a law-enforcement problem. One solution was to permit emigration. The influx of new colonists was matched by a steady flow of Catholics into exile. The swordsmen—freeholders who had furnished Tyrone with his army—were actively recruited by foreign sovereigns. For the next two centuries this process of attrition continued, and the exodus reached flood stage after the major rebellions during the civil wars and the Revolution. During the exodus, which was known later as "the flight of the wild geese," generations of the most promising young men of Ireland bade farewell to their country and entered the service of Spain, France, Poland, and virtually every other European country, staffing their armies and their civil administrations. As hope dwindled and despair prevailed, the Catholic majority slowly settled into a sullen acquiescence to the English presence.

When Charles came to the throne in 1625, he found himself seriously in want of money. Ireland had to be made self-supporting, since the English treasury could not afford to maintain the Irish establishment; therefore the king convened an assembly of the leading men of the country to work out an arrangement. As a conciliatory gesture, the king restored the charter to Waterford. The assembled Catholic laity responded by offering to grant the king the money he required if a limited toleration was instituted. The terms requested—known as "the Graces" —included protection of Catholic landholdings, freedom of worship, and the right of Catholics to hold office. These concessions were opposed by the Protestants, but a number of them were made by the king. The Catholics did not obtain the parliamentary guarantees of the concessions, which was one of their initial conditions. They were satisfied that the power of the purse would hold the king to their terms. But the interests of the Roman Catholics—Irish and old English alike—were increasingly challenged by the new settlers, both English and Scottish. Although the Catholics still controlled the greater part of the land, the new English played an increasingly important role in the Irish government and sought to limit the concessions made to their opponents. The quarreling between the two parties was carried on both within and without the council, and a strong hand was needed to settle the disputes. The king had such a man at hand—Thomas Wentworth, the president of the Council of the North, who was sent to Ireland in 1533 to bring order to the realm, stability to the government, and prosperity to the king's finances.

Wentworth was an efficient and determined governor. His policies, which provoked strong reactions among the Irish, have been the subject of some debate throughout the centuries since his deputyship. A devout Protestant, he was determined to civilize the wild, nomadic Irish and to teach them the virtues of good husbandry and a settled existence. His attention was directed first to the overhaul of the government: the treasury, the army, and the navy each received his scrutiny. When found wanting, they received the benefit of his reforms. All the agencies of government were exposed to his policies of "thorough." Pleased by his success, he obtained the permission of the king to call the Parliament in 1634. His purpose was twofold: to obtain both parliamentary assent to a plan for establishing the revenue on a more solid basis (it was dependent then on the voluntary cooperation of the Catholic nobility) and legislative support for an expanded program of Anglicization. The first required the support of the Catholics; the second the denial of their desire for parliamentary confirmation of the "Graces." The first session of the Parliament met all his expectations: six subsidies were granted unanimously, with Wentworth's assurance that they would not be sent outside Ireland. When he refused to allow the majority of the "Graces" to be enacted into law in the second session, reserving the majority for discretionary executive action, the Catholics opposed his legislative program. Wentworth's rejection of the two Graces affecting land tenure were particularly alarming, because it made clear his intention to support and extend the plantation system and to put Catholic landholdings in jeopardy. Protestant supporters were quickly marshaled, and his legislation was passed. The new acts were all in conformity with his policy of enlarging and fixing the administrative responsibilities of the government and with his policy of forcing the Irish to abandon their old customs. Their backward farming practices were dealt with severely. But it was beyond the power of the deputy to erase, by legislative means alone, the primitive methods of animal husbandry and land cultivation that had been ingrained by centuries of practice. Plucking of sheep instead of shearing them for their wool, ploughing by the tail (fastening the plough directly to the horse's tail), and burning the harvest to divide the grain from the straw persisted for decades and even centuries yet to come. Pious exhortations and legal prohibitions were not enough.

Wentworth's ministrations extended to the Church, which was in a sad state of neglect. Much of the land and many of the livings had been appropriated for private purposes, and Wentworth's insistence upon their restitution made powerful enemies for him, most notably the earl of Cork (one of the most influential of the new English), whose estate had been swelled to the tune of more than £30,000 by illegal Church acquisitions. The Puritan-leaning clergy also resented his reforms, and opposition to the deputy was reinforced by his expropriation of Catholic landholdings in Connaught and Galway to make room for his new plantations. Due to his personal interest and supervision, Irish trade revived, the customs were considerably increased (with the profits shared by the king and the deputy), and the worst abuses in the administration were corrected. But all depended upon the presence of Wentworth himself, and his achievements were made at the cost of creating a strong personal opposition, which was only too willing to undo his reforms once the deputy's presence was required elsewhere.

The outbreak of the Bishops' War in Scotland in 1637 and the rapid deterioration of the king's affairs in England required all possible assistance. Wentworth was recalled to England in 1640, where he finally won the great prizes he had so long desired, the earldom of Strafford and the management of the king's government. But the prize came too late, and within a year he went to his martyrdom, executed by the king's enemies, who found him too formidable an obstacle to their plans.

The impact on Ireland of the disturbances in England which culminated in the civil wars and the Commonwealth are what concern us here. Wentworth's opponents in Ireland took advantage of his absence, and subsequent death, to dismantle much of his system. The old English, the settlers in the north, and Protestants from all over Ireland joined together in the Irish Parliament to revenge themselves upon their harsh taskmaster. They also cooperated with the English Parliament in preparing charges against Wentworth for use in his impeachment. The old English took further advantage of the king's weakness to secure confirmation of the Graces, but their Catholic Irish brethren were less sanguine about the effect of events in England. They saw the power of the Puritan militants in the English and Scottish parliaments as a direct threat to their own existence, so they determined to seize control of the Irish government and thus secure their independence. An uprising was planned by the discontented Irish in Ulster who had been dispossessed by the plantation. The scheme also involved the taking of Dublin Castle, the seat of the Irish administration. The plot to take Dublin Castle was betrayed, and therefore failed, but the uprisings in Ulster were carried out. The Catholic Irish rebels were soon joined by the old English, who made common cause with their coreligionists; and the alliance thus welded was to endure permanently.

Though unsuccessful in the Pale, the rebellion gathered momentum in the north because the Dublin government lacked the resources to put it down. There were sympathetic uprisings all over the island. The principal objective in Ulster had been to expel the Protestants, and this objective was shared by the Catholics elsewhere, who saw their main purpose as ridding the country of the English. During the course of the next two years, thousands of Protestants were murdered, and their properties were taken over. Estimates of those killed vary: the number is generally reckoned to have been less than twenty-five thousand, but the effect was that of the large-scale massacre which was rumored to have taken place. It set the Catholics sharply against the Protestants, and put a fear into the latter that could only be satisfied by the total suppression of the Catholic inhabitants of the island. The stage was set for the harsh years of the penal period which were to follow. The English Parliament voted support for putting down the rebellion, though few troops were sent over. The Protestant inhabitants of the Pale organized under the young earl of Ormonde, scion of the house of Butler, who had been raised as a Protestant in England under Wentworth's patronage. The Catholics responded by holding a meeting at Kilkenny in May 1642, where a supreme council was organized. This was followed by a meeting of a general assembly in October and by the organization of county councils and armed forces to administer the country. The Catholics pledged their loyalty to the king and the laws of the realm, but only insofar as their religion was preserved. After the outbreak of the civil war in England, Charles I came to terms with the Irish rebels in order to gain their support against his enemies at home. Ormonde, who was conciliatory and sympathetic to the Catholics, was granted the lord lieutenancy. Ireland was in a confused state for some years, with English, Protestant Irish, Catholic Irish, and Scottish troops all at large in the country. The central government was reduced to near impotency until the arrival of Cromwell.

After the execution of the king in January 1649, Cromwell first established his authority in England; then he embarked for Ireland, where he landed in August. Ormonde made common cause with the Catholics against the invader, but the Irish were unable to resist the disciplined forces of the New Model Army. After taking Drogheda and putting the garrison to the sword, Cromwell repressed Wexford with equal ferocity. His progress slowed down thereafter, and after defeating an Irish army at Clonmel in March 1650, Cromwell returned to England, leaving the reduction of the country to be completed by his son-in-law Henry Ireton. By the end of the year, Ireton's task was almost finished, though some pockets of resistance were not eliminated until 1652. Offered the right to go into exile, more than thirty thousand Irish soldiers left the country after the final treaty, leaving their countrymen at the merciless hands of their Protestant conquerors.

Short of capital, Parliament had financed the conquest by promises of land to be confiscated from the rebels. The cost of the war had exceeded Parliament's expectations, thereby increasing the amount of land needed to satisfy the adventurers. By the Act of Settlement, passed in 1652, the whole of the country was regarded as forfeit to the government. Only those Irish who could prove their loyalty to the Commonwealth were allowed to retain land, and then not their own holdings. Ireland was divided into two parts. Connaught and Clare were reserved for the loyalists, who were transplanted there and given new lands. The balance of the twenty-six counties were reserved for the creditors of the government—the adventurers who had financed the conquest, and the officers and soldiers who had manned the army. Nearly seven years passed before the transfer of land was completed. By the next year the king was once more back on the throne; and his supporters, back from exile, pressed for restitution of their lands. The king owed his restoration to Monck and Broghill, who were determined that the Cromwellian land settlement should remain undisturbed. The Act of Settlement provided for a court of claims to hear pleas by dispossessed Irishmen of their innocence of complicity in the late rebellion, and some restorations were admitted. Ultimately a third of the land that was in the hands of the Cromwellians at the time of the Restoration was turned back to the Irish landholders, but the net result of the settlement was still of major dimensions. The Catholics were reduced from holding 59 percent of the land to 22 percent once all claims were settled. Worse was yet to follow.

Ormonde was raised to a duke and was restored to his government of Ireland. The land compromise was his solution to the conflicting claims of the Irish and the Cromwellians. Though he was armed with good intentions and was loyal to his country, he found himself in an impossible situation, attacked from both sides. Faithful to the royalist cause throughout the civil wars and interregnum, he was yet a strong Protestant and was faithful to the constitution. The Catholics worked for his removal; they found a leader in Richard Talbot, a Catholic convert who was a close friend and supporter of the king's brother and heir, James, duke of York. Charges of misusing the revenue were brought against Ormonde in 1669, and he was replaced in rapid succession by Ossory, Robartes, and, finally, Lord Berkeley, who was more amenable to Catholic desires. Talbot, the real manager of Irish affairs, obtained official recognition for Roman Catholics, but at the cost of his own banishment because of protests from the English Parliament. Berkeley was replaced by the earl of Essex, who was pressured by the king to make further concessions to the Catholics, but Essex would go no further than to permit Catholics to take local offices, thus paving the way for them to assume control of the parliamentary boroughs. Resisting further concessions to the Catholics, Essex was replaced in 1677 by Ormonde. Ormonde was welcomed back by the Irish Protestants as their leader, and he remained in office until the death of Charles II. Toleration for the Catholics remained in effect, but Ormonde was unwilling to make a formal agreement without equal concessions by the Catholics, requiring them not only to recognize the authority of the crown but also to deny the right of the pope to depose the sovereign. Since they refused his terms, the status quo prevailed until the new reign.

The Restoration period saw a gradual return of prosperity to the kingdom, as the disruption and dislocation of the previous score of years was slowly accommodated. This was the more remarkable because, in the 1660s, the English imposed a series of acts upon Ireland that were designed to restrict Ireland's trade to suit English interests. The Navigation Acts passed by the Commonwealth were renewed after the Restoration, and by the terms of an act of 1663 Ireland was barred from trade with the colonies, an English monopoly. In the same year the importation of Irish cattle into England was barred for the second half of each year, and the prohibition was made complete in 1667. Ireland therefore turned to the Continent to find markets for its cattle, developing an important trade with the Dutch Republic. With the ban on exporting cattle to

England, farmers increased their flocks of sheep; they also looked to the Continent for a market for their wool, because of restrictions on trading with England in that commodity as well.

Even before the death of Charles II, Talbot, who had returned from exile, was scheming once again to overturn the Act of Settlement. The earl of Clarendon, James II's brother-in-law, was appointed viceroy; but the manager of Irish affairs was again Talbot, now raised to the peerage as earl of Tyrconnel. He now engineered the introduction of Roman Catholics into the army, using Monmouth's rebellion in England as an excuse for enlarging the forces, and he pressed to introduce Catholics into the civil establishment. When Clarendon protested, the king removed him and appointed Tyrconnel as Claredon's successor in early 1687. With the government in the hands of the leader of the Roman Catholics, the Protestant inhabitants of Ireland feared for their lives and fortunes, and a mass exodus followed. Tyrconnel pressed forward with his program, remodeling the magistracy and the judiciary, and went so far as to send over a bill for repealing the Act of Settlement to the king for his approval in 1688. The revolution in that year removed James II from power in England, but left Tyrconnel in complete control in Ireland. However, the revolution proved the undoing of the Catholics. After taking refuge in France, James II made his way to Ireland, where he landed at Kinsale in March 1689 with French support. His interests really lay across the Irish Sea, and he intended to use Ireland as a base for recovering his throne in Britain. The Irish were primarily concerned with their own future, so they forced the king to call a parliament in order to satisfy their demands. This Parliament, which was under the complete control of the Catholics, quickly declared its independence of its sister legislature in England. The long-sought repeal of the Act of Settlement was enacted, and the lands of William III's supporters were confiscated. Revenging themselves for the harsh usage by the Cromwellians, the Catholics ordered the death of more than two thousand Protestants by a legislative act of attainder. An official policy of religious toleration was instituted, and the payment of tithes was limited to the support of the tithepayer's own church. The impositions placed on Irish trade by the English were lifted, and the importation of English coal was prohibited. But the triumph of the Catholics was short-lived. Protestant troops remained in control of Derry, holding out for fifteen weeks until they were relieved by English forces. In August 1689 William's commander, Schomberg, landed with fourteen thousand troops at Bangor and advanced towards Dublin. His army was met by a Catholic army under James II, and the two armies remained on the defensive throughout the summer near Dundalk. The following year William III landed to conduct the campaign in person. Confronting James's army at the Boyne on 30 June, he defeated the Catholics and put James to flight. Tyrconnel withdrew to Limerick, where William's army was defeated by reinforcements brought up by Sarsfield. The Protestant forces had some recompense when Marlborough captured Cork and Kinsale in October. The following spring, fresh supplies and reinforcements arrived for the Catholics from France, but the English under Ginkel mounted a new offensive. The opposing armies met near the Shannon at Aughrim, and the fate of Ireland was decided by a Protestant victory. Ginkel pushed on to Galway and then Limerick, where a treaty was signed on 30 October 1691. The fortunes of the Catholics had reached their nadir.

## SUGGESTIONS FOR FURTHER READING

Bagwell, Richard. *Ireland under the Stuarts and during the Interregnum.* London: Holland Press, 1963.
————. *Ireland under the Tudors.* London: Holland Press, 1963.
Bottigheimer, Karl S. *English Money and Irish Land.* Oxford: Clarendon Press, 1971.
Clarke, Aidan. *The Old English in Ireland, 1625–42.* Ithaca, N.Y.: Cornell University Press, 1966.
Conway, Agnes E. *Henry VII's Relations with Scotland and Ireland, 1485–1498.* Cambridge, Eng.: The University Press, 1932.
Edie, Carolyn A. *The Irish Cattle Bills.* Philadelphia: American Philosophical Society, 1970.
Edwards, Robert Dudley. *Church and State in Tudor Ireland.* Dublin and Cork: Talbot Press, 1935.
Falls, Cyril B. *Elizabeth's Irish Wars.* London: Methuen, 1950.
Jones, Frederick M. *Mountjoy, 1563-1606: The Last Elizabethan Deputy.* Dublin: Clonmore & Reynolds, 1958.
Kearney, Hugh F. *Strafford in Ireland.* Manchester, Eng.: Manchester University Press, 1959.
MacLysaght, Edward. *Irish Life in the Seventeenth Century: After Cromwell.* 2d ed., rev. & enl. Cork, Ire.: Cork University Press, 1950.
Quinn, David B. *The Elizabethans and the Irish.* Ithaca, N.Y.: Cornell University Press, for the Folger Shakespeare Library, 1966.
Simms, John G. *Jacobite Ireland, 1685–91.* London: Routledge & K. Paul, 1969.
For a list of general works on the history of Ireland see chapter 2.

# FESTIVALS
# AND CALENDAR CUSTOMS

## Robert Jerome Smith

hile history tends to deal with events—with given moments that have changed a people's way of life— folklore tends to emphasize what may be referred to as the statics of culture. Whereas history records novelties, folklore chronicles the persistent, the enduring. As important to the knowledge of a people as an understanding of the string of events by which linear time is chronicled is a vision of their yearly round of life, the cycle of daily and seasonal activity that provides man with his sustenance.

Thus, the focus here is on ideal types, as it must always be when limitations of space and time compel one to abstract to such a level as "the Irishman does thus," or "the Irish believe so." By the same token, the present tense employed in such statements is meant to convey the "ethnographic present" rather than to suggest that they reflect today's situation in Ireland. As such, they refer less to an empirical state of affairs than to a mental construct—an idea in the minds of Irishmen (and of scholars)—of the nature of things; an idea from which today's occurrences inevitably vary, and are seen as variants.

The Irish, like the other peoples of the world, have developed through the centuries a manner of dividing up the perpetual sequence of night and day (and night does come *before* day; hence the significance of Christmas Eve and Hallowe'en), which allows them to organize and anticipate their activities. And they have set aside particular occasions, especially first and last days, for special observances and celebrations. With the dividing up of the year, different activities may become attached to certain times, either loosely or, when their significance is magical, very closely. Thus, you *should* get your potatoes in by St. Patrick's Day, but you *must not* visit wells before sunrise on May Day. Also, people need times for gatherings. And these times have to be spaced out to appear with regularity, so that when one is working, he can anticipate diversion not too far away: for example, in July, when food may be scarce and spirits low, one thinks forward to Garland Sunday or the Assumption (or, very long ago, to Lughnasa), to the time of harvest and the accompanying celebration. These set occasions supply for the individual, in the words of Clyde Kluckhohn, fixed points in a world of bewildering change and disappointment.[1]

The old Irish calendar, which has been brought to present times, divided the year into four quarters, each of which began with a festival: Samhain, November 1; Imbolc, February 1; Beltane, May 1; and Lughnasa, August 1. Each of the quarters had its own typical activity; there is an early myth which justifies and gives charter to the arrangement. The Tuatha de Danaan (a race that later went underground and became the Little People) fought a great battle with the Fomorians, whose leader was Bres, a godlike figure. The Tuatha de Danaan had been subject to Bres, but Bres had become oppressive and had failed to provide enough feasts. Vanquished by the Tuatha, he asked what he could do for them, and then offered to provide them with the munificent blessing of a harvest in every quarter of the year. They refused, saying:

> This has suited us:
> Spring for plowing and sowing,
> Summer for strengthening the corn,
> Autumn for the ripeness of corn and reaping,
> Winter for consuming it.[2]

This agricultural scheme for calculating the yearly round is clearly superimposed on the herding cycle of the country. The Irish have always been more herdsmen than farmers, and the routine succession of taking the cattle to the high pastures at Beltane and bringing them back to the lowlands at Samhain gives these two holidays rather more significance than the others. Even until recent times these were the semiannual rent days. The telling of tales has also traditionally been restricted to the period between Samhain and Beltane.

The solstices do not seem to ever have had as much significance attached to them in Ireland as in other European countries. The year began and ended with Samhain, which means the end of summer (as night precedes day, so, it seems, winter precedes summer). With later invasions—of priests, Vikings, Normans, and Englishmen—other calendars were imposed. The winter solstice festivals of Christmas and St. Stephen's Day were brought in, and the summer solstice festival of St. John's was taken up, along with a system of reckoning that put the beginning of the year at no psychologically significant time. New Year's? It never became a festival, though being thought of (after a time) as the first day of the year, it acquired the significance that we tend to attach to first and last things, seeing them as portentous. Thus, if a dark-haired man were the first to enter your house in the new year, the year would be a good one.

After New Year's, the first noteworthy festival day is February first, the feast of St. Brigid.[3] This good woman, with Patrick and Columcille (Columba) one of the three great saints of Ireland, was born in bondage. Sold by her father, she was later freed and then returned voluntarily to him as a serving girl. As a cowherd, she milked the cows and made the butter. Extremely warmhearted, she gave things away with a prodigality that was often the despair of her associates. She wove the first piece of cloth in Ireland, and so became the patron of weavers and spinners. Even when she became the head of a monastery, she remained devoted to rural occupations—reaping, and making butter and ale. Wild ducks came to her when she called; she was also able to tame a wild boar. A common woman, then, and an Irish woman, she was warm, compassionate, generous, and with a delightful vision of paradise: "A great lake of ale for the King of Kings; . . . the family of heaven to be drinking it through all time; . . . cheerfulness to be in their drinking; . . . Jesus to be here among them; . . . vessels full of alms to be giving away."[4]

St. Brigid is closely linked with the Virgin Mary, whose festival of Candlemas falls on February second. It is said that when Mary was giving birth to Jesus, Brigid averted the eyes of the onlookers, so a grateful Mary let Brigid have her festival first.[5] Brigid has become associated with fire, and the fire that is blessed at Candlemas is thought to be hers. Indeed, St. Brigid has a number of attributes that may be carried over from pre-Christian times: On her day, people can do no work that involves spinning, digging, or turning a wheel: "St. Brigid's Day is free from twistings." St. Brigid's crosses are made from rushes on this day, then stuck in the roof thatching to protect the house. The first good weather comes with her day, because (variant 1) she placed her foot in water on her feast day or because (variant 2) she dipped her finger in the brook, and off went the hen that hatches the cold.

The months of February and March are the most menacing to the health of man and animal: "February kills the sheep," they say, "March the people." Of a man whose health is failing, it may be said that "he'll never go up the March hill." Halfway up that hill, on the seventeenth, comes St. Patrick's day. On that day, St. Patrick removed the cold stone from the stream (or turned the worn side of the stone up), so, while every other day after St. Brigid's Day has been fine, *every* day is fine after his own day. This is the end of the cold weather, and farmers can start to work in the fields. They should begin planting their potatoes and sowing their grain.

While very little is known about St. Patrick in terms of trustworthy documentary evidence that will satisfy modern historians, certainly there is a rich amount of mythical lore which both reflects and helps mold the minds of his people. For the folklorist, what is interesting is not so much what really happened as what people think has happened; what they decide has happened. From this point of view, the most significant aspect of St. Patrick's life is not so much the dogmas and rites or the monasteries that he introduced, but what the Irish people did to these novelties, how they transformed them to accord with their view of the world.

Hagiography comes to us, as does mythology, from two sources: learned written accounts and the oral tradition. Written testimonies both draw on and are taken up by oral tradition. Where the one tends to stereotype saints in a way that has come to be known as sanctimonious, the folk tend to make them more human. Writers of the lives of saints emphasize their miracles; the folk talk also about their curses.

The skeleton of the story of St. Patrick is about a boy in Roman England. Patrick, son of a prosperous father, was sold into captivity in Ireland, worked for some years as a shepherd, and then was told by God that there was a boat awaiting him. He escaped, took the boat, and came to shore in a wilderness. He finally reached home, joined the Church, gave up his inherited position, and returned to Ireland, a land at the edge of the known world, to convert the heathen. He did convert them, and so after his death he was made the patron saint of the land. Upon this skeleton of "facts," from very early times we find a fleshing-out of the story. For example, while Patrick and the sailors, starving, were wandering in the devastated land (Gaul? Scotland?), the sea captain, a pagan, suggested that Patrick should pray to his god for food. He did so, and immediately a herd of pigs appeared. From then on, they had all the food they needed. The pagans were convinced and were converted. At about the time that they finally came to an inhabited land, a heavy rock pinned the saint to the ground; he called on St. Elias for help, "and was delivered from the danger." To this legend, folklorists have contributed a variant themselves. Sabine Baring-Gould, writing under the influence of a school that tended to interpret all traditional stories as corruptions of ancient accounts of sun worship, suggested in his *Lives of the Saints* that the still half-pagan Patrick must have really called "Helios, Helios," and been misinterpreted.[6] One understands Baring-Gould's stretching for an explanation, however. There seems to be no good explanation for why, of all people, he should have called on his contemporary St. Elias, who was patriarch of Jerusalem and was later exiled for his opposition to Monophysism.

An angel named Victor called Patrick back to Ireland, causing Patrick to hear Irish voices begging him to come. One version says that he was very moved by the experience, because he recognized the voices; another version presents a vivid image: "He thought he saw all the children of that country from the wombs of their mothers stretching out their hands and piteously crying to him for relief" (which is no mean trick).

Most of the legends about Patrick deal with the time that he spent in Ireland after his return. The most persistent one, of course, is the one that represents him as having driven the snakes out of Ireland. "Yet in Ierland is stupendyous thynges," says Dr. Andrew Boorde in his *The Fyrst Boke of the Introduction of Knowledge*, written in the first half of the sixteenth century (by which time it was already an old story); "for there is neyther Pyes [magpies] nor venymus wormes. There is no Adder, nor Snake, no Toode, nor Lyzerd, nor no Euyt, nor none such lyke. I haue sene stones the whiche haue had the forme and shap of a snake and other venimous wormes. And the people of the countre sayth that suche stones were wormes, and they were turned into stones by the power of God and the prayers of saynt Patryk. And Englysh marchauntes of England do fetch of the erth of Irlonde to caste in their gardens, to kepe out and to kyll venimous wormes."[7] Edward Tylor points out that both the legend about poisonous soil and the one about ridding the island of serpents have antecedents from Crete and the Lerin Islands. He goes on: "What is left . . . is a philosophic myth accounting for the existence of fossil ammonites as being petrified snakes, to which myth a historical position is given by claiming it as a miracle, and ascribing it to St. Patrick."[8] The legends, then, he suggests, exist to satisfy man's natural intellectual appetite to know why things are as they are.

However, another explanation (which illustrates how alternative explanations themselves can become legendary) is that Norman invaders heard about St. Patrick and, since the Norse word for "toad" is *"paud,"* thought that his name meant "toad-expeller"; so they originated the story and began spreading it around. The origin of the legend, then, lies in someone's mistaken etymologizing. Take your choice. One virtue of the second explanation (however unsatisfactory it may otherwise be) is that it tends to support the opinion of some modern scholars that the legend, which is found over and over again in English travel books but only very rarely in the oral tradition of Gaelic-speaking country people, has always appealed more to non-Gaelic than to Gaelic tradition. The nearest such Irish legend is that Patrick, when he went onto a mountain to pray, was encircled by a great number of demon-birds. He threw a bell at them, and they disappeared, not to return again for seven years, seven months, seven days, and seven nights. The bell that Patrick threw at the birds can still be seen, in a Dublin museum, with a piece chipped out of its side.

Hardly had Patrick gotten his mission of conversion of the heathen under way, according to an early *Life*, when he found himself in a contest with a druid to see whose religion was the more powerful. The druid, to show the power of his religion, "rose in the air, as though ascending to the skies. Then Patrick prayed, and angelic hands flung a snowball at him out of heaven, which knocked him [the druid] down on a sharp stone at Patrick's feet, and that was the end of him."[9] The oral tradition confirms that it was dangerous to slight the saint.

In another contest, Patrick's followers were put in a house made of dry wood, while a Protestant's (*sic*) followers were put in a house of green wood, and both houses were then put to the torch. The protestants were burned to a crisp, while Patrick's followers emerged unscathed (and ever since, goes one version, people have worn green on St. Patrick's Day).[10]

It was dangerous to displease the saint or to refuse to become converted. A man who tried to deceive him by pretending to be dead, died. A pagan who refused to be converted though he should be buried under seven feet of clay was so buried, and beetles ate him (his soul was saved, however). An uncharitable family refused Patrick hospitality when he appeared at their door one evening, and then sent him to sleep in the stable. The next morning all that was left of the house and its occupants was a hole in the ground. Angered by a tinker and a cowherd, Patrick pronounced that tinkers would for ever wander through the world, while "the weariness of the smiths will descend on the cowherds." Indeed, Ireland itself was not safe from its ostensible savior. He turned his curses on it three times in his sleep, and each time the country was saved only by the quick thinking of his servant, who deflected the force of the curses onto the tops of the rushes, the lowing of the kine, and the top of the furze. These three things are, as a result, as useless as Ireland would have been, had it not been for the alert servant.[11]

A legend that exists in many versions in Catholic countries has attached itself to the death of St. Patrick. His followers, not sure about where to bury him in the face of many claimants on his body, attached his bier to four white oxen, and allowed them their heads. They took him to a slope above the Quoile River in county Down, and thence they would not move.[12] So they buried him there, and on the night of his funeral the sun stayed in the sky to light the observances.[13] In return for their devotion to the saint, the Irish will be judged by Patrick himself on the last day (another version has it that he will rather be the advocate of the Irish, with special permission to bring them all into the presence of God, even the sinners among them).

Given Ireland's strong identification with the saint, it is perhaps surprising that local observances of his day are not more pronounced. An important pilgrimage to his mountain comes later in the year, but his day is celebrated much more in New York than in Ireland. Nevertheless, however fragile the connection between myth and ritual in this case, the image of Patrick is a major one, localizing and concretizing the attributes of God—powerful, stern, subject to rage, dangerous, though also protective of those who obey him—and identifying these attributes with Ireland itself.

As in most Catholic countries, Shrove Tuesday, the last day before the beginning of Lent, used to be celebrated with feasting, since it was a last day to fatten up before the Lenten austerities. There were also parties, and a goodly number of people were married on that day, however odd a time it might seem for marriage on the face of it.

Good Friday is the best day for sowing corn; it was also a day for visiting holy wells and the graves of the dead. In some parts of the country there were games and horse racing. Easter seems to be not very distinguishable from what it is in England or America. May Day, on the other hand, was in ancient times a very important festival, perhaps the most important of the Celtic calendar. Named after the fires of the god Bel, it was the beginning of the summer and the time to take the cattle off to their summer pasture. First, though, they had to be freed from and strengthened against disease by being passed between two "neat fires." At this time of the year the semiannual rent was due to the landlord. Hearth fires were put out and then relit from the May fire. Witches and fairies were active on that evening, and many protective charms were employed. Wells were guarded, as were fields, since if someone were to skim the water off the one or the dew off the other, the farm would lose its fertile power to produce crops, the power having been concentrated on the surface on that night. A goodly amount of rain in May is always desired: "a wild and rainy May fills the haggard with corn and hay" (the "haggard" being not the "worn out" but the "farmyard").

Whitsuntide, beginning fifty days after Easter, on Pentecost, is a threatening time, a "kinkish" time, a dangerous time. One has to be careful not to take trips away from home during this period, for fear of never returning. The weather is characterized as heavy and close (though the dates can vary, of course, by more than a month, from May 11 to June 14), and people are supposed to be irritable and depressed.[14] Ideas about the fate of babies born on Whitsunday vary. They may grow up with the evil eye, or they may have special curative powers. There seems to be general agreement, though, that whether for good or ill, they will be exceptional.

On St. John's Day, the twenty-fourth of June, midsummer fires are lit throughout the countryside, and are accompanied by merrymaking. It can hardly be overemphasized that festivals, both great and small, provide structured occasions for people to interact outside the contexts of work; we need not assume that the games and sports associated with such evenings as May Day were ever necessarily part of a ritual sacrifice, or a belief in the sickness of the sun, or whatever.[15]

July used to be considered a month of want, coming just before the potato harvest (before new, earlier-ripening varieties were introduced), and so one often finds bleak references to "Hungry July," "July of the Cabbage," and so forth. The time between St. John's Day and harvest was called the bitter six weeks. This period ended, in past centuries, with the festival that marked the beginning of harvest, the festival of Lughnasa, on about the first of August. The festival itself disappeared long ago, but apparently practices and beliefs anciently associated with it survive in other festivals of about this time, especially Garland Sunday (the last Sunday in July) and the feast of the Assumption, on August 15. In many places, people still climb to high places on these dates for picnicking, games, and dancing. The grain harvest proceeds during this time also, until by St. Bartholomew's Day (August 24), threshing has begun.

By Hallowe'en (the old Celtic Samhain) all the crops should be in. Fruit can no longer be picked, because the Puca—a maleficent spirit that often appears as a dog or a horse—befouls all that remains on that evening. In Celtic times this was the first of the two great festivals of the year, and many of its elements have remained, syncretized into Christian interpretations and imagery. The beginning of the year, Samhain was the occasion for bringing back the cattle from the high pastures, and so it was a time of homecoming: just as absent relatives came back for the celebration, so did dead ones. The Church, following its well-tested practice of superimposing more-or-less equivalent Christian festivals on the pagan ones, moved its feasts of All Saints and All Souls to this date.[16] If, in the past, the Celts had remembered their dead at this time, let them continue to do so, but in a Christian context. Of course, beliefs and practices that did not directly impinge on church dogma continued in the new context. The dead were both welcome and feared, for a spirit, whether it wants to or not, can do harm to a man. Food was put out, and the door was left ajar, so that the dead could partake of it; but people stayed in, believing that, with the air full of spirits, terrible things could happen to one. This was also a time for performing protective acts against witches and evil spirits, and like all special days, it was an especially propitious time for divining the future.

At Hallowe'en "the cold stone is returned to the water," or "the cold side of the stone is turned up," and the weather progressively begins to get worse; this is the beginning of winter. Rent is paid, and the time for the slaughtering of animals has begun. The feast of St. Martin's (November 11) is the occasion for the sacrificial killing of an animal. On the eve of the feast an animal is killed by the head of the house, and its blood is sprinkled on the four inside corners of the house, on the doorposts, and on the threshold. This protects the house against misfortune for the year. The animal is then eaten. Obviously the practice has nothing to do with St. Martin of Tours, with whose day the festival is associated. Irish legend identifies St. Martin as a miller who was crushed by a mill wheel (for this reason no wheel should work on his day). A manuscript dating from about A.D. 1500 identifies Martin as the one who gave St. Patrick his monk's tonsure, and Patrick in return established the practice of feasting on that day. The story does give evidence for the existence of the feast at least from this time, and probably from a much earlier time.[17]

Christmas is at present the most important of the yearly holidays, with preparations going on for weeks before the festive occasion: new clothes are made, houses readied, and presents bought. Then on the festive days themselves there are drinking and feasting, visiting and homecomings, candle-lighting, gift-giving, and the arranging of marriages. The last of the decorations are taken down only on Epiphany (January 6), after which there are only twenty-four more days before St. Brigit dips her foot in the water, and we have returned to a new beginning.

# PATRONAL FESTIVALS

In the course of the Christianization of Europe, the Church utilized the device of identifying its own saints with the holy places and with the occasions of the old religion. The purpose of the Church was to take the feelings of veneration and awe that the people already possessed and then turn them toward the Christian god. The old festivals thus became Christian patronal festivals. In Ireland these festivals, which are known as "patterns," survived very strongly (as indeed they still survive in most other Catholic countries) until the last century. Sites of the old festivals and pilgrimages are on high places or, most usually, at holy wells. Most of these sites are in the north-central part of the island, in Connaught and Leinster, but others are distributed throughout all the island.

Patronal festivals, or patterns, are quite different from the special days of the calendar. While the latter involve only observance of certain customs, either by individuals or families, patterns are community celebrations. In paying their respects to the saint who represents them and protects them, the participants are paying their respects to themselves as a community; and in their celebrations they are reaffirming the benefits of living together. Through the saint the people of a community salute one another in a double context of formality and festivity. The festival, indeed, seems dialectical by nature, evoking the intense and antithetical feelings of devotion and joy; and by balancing these feelings, the festival leaves the participants in a renewed state of emotional equilibrium.

The goal of all too many studies of patronal festivals has been to determine the origin of the festival. Real origins do not matter in tradition (though ostensible ones do); the key question with regard to the mind of the people is not what was offered but what was accepted. The fact is that the patronal festivals endured in Ireland for centuries (and perhaps it is still too early to say that they are finally done for) without the participants in them taking the slightest interest in their Celtic origins. This would lead one to believe that the question of origins is not a significant one, except, of course, for archaeologists.

For centuries, many festivals in Ireland have been visited by pilgrims: some bring together people from the whole of Ireland and even from abroad; others are more regional; while still others are limited to small localities. Let us look first at the aspect of devotion. In going to a festival, one of the first things to be done is to pay one's respects to the saint. If one has made promises or has special favors to ask, the devotions may be rather rigorous. Thackeray relays to us a Protestant account of the devotional aspect of the Croagh Patrick pattern, which was held on a mountain top. One of his informants described the ascent, a very steep and difficult one, which he made in the company of thousands of people who were making their way barefoot to the several "stations" upon the hill:

"The first station consists of one heap of stones, round which they must walk seven times, casting a stone on the heap each time, and before and after every stone's throw saying a prayer.

"The second station is on the top of the mountain. Here there is a great altar—a shapeless heap of stones. The poor wretches crawl *on their knees* into this place, say fifteen prayers, and after going round the entire top of the mountain fifteen times, say fifteen prayers again.

"The third station is near the bottom of the mountain at the further side from Westport. It consists of three heaps. The penitents must go seven times round these collectively, and seven times afterwards round each individually, saying a prayer before and after each progress."

My informant describes the people as coming away from this "frightful exhibition, suffering severe pain, wounded and bleeding in the knees and feet, and some of the women shrieking with the pain of their wounds. Fancy thousands of these bent upon their work, and priests standing by to encourage them!"[18]

The penances are, of course, a part of the contract entered into with the patron: "Do this for me, and I will do that in return." They express the seriousness of the matter and the urgency of emotion felt by the pilgrim. In their function of purging unhealthy emotions, they are very efficacious. Nevertheless, most pilgrimages for most people do not incorporate such painful practices. At the well of Uarán, for example, the pilgrim makes three rounds of the well, each round consisting of seven circuits of the well, and ends by kneeling on a stone bearing St. Patrick's knee print. Another popular devotion is the vigil—sitting, kneeling, or standing for a given length of time at a holy place. For most participants most of the time, the devotional aspects of the festival, rather than corresponding to a crisis in their lives, maintain and preserve the favorable relationship between the people and their gods.

And devotion is only half of this maintenance pattern; for the saint, once and well saluted, then gives his aegis to the festivities. Thus the nineteenth-century observer was wrong when he suggested that "whatever atoning penalties they may go through, it is hinted that the purified spirit of the abbot of Kells does not preside over all the proceedings of the day, but that sins are committed sufficiently to qualify parties for a new pilgrimage the following year."[19] Although witty and graphic, the account misses the point: that this is one day of the year that does not have to be atoned for. It is a time out of time, a necessary relief from the necessary inhibitions of the other 364 days of the year. Another observer, while feeling obliged to make the same joke, elaborates on the festive behavior of another pattern:

> Their devotions performed, they return merry and shod, no longer concerned for those sins that were the cause of this so severe a penance; but as if, having now paid off the old score, they longed to go on in the new again, they return in all haste to a green spot of ground on the east side of the hill towards the land, and here men and women fall a dancing and carousing the rest of the day; for alesellers in great numbers on these days have their booths here as in a fair, and to be sure the merry bagpipers fail not to pay their attendance. Thus in lewd and obscene dancing, and in excess of drinking, the remainder of the day is spent, as if they celebrated the Bacchanalia, rather than the memory of a pious saint, or their own penitentials; and oftentimes it falls out that more blood is shed on the grass from broken pates and drunken quarrels, when the pilgrimages are ended, than was before on the stones from their bare feet and knees during their devotions.[20]

The general picture is of a time when, in the minds of the people, the overriding Principle of Limited Good is suspended, and they are cast into the incredible situation in which there is plenty for everyone, and what one wants to do can be done. "The pipers struck up their merry tunes in the tents," says the Reverend Henry MacManus of another festival, "and the dancing began. Nor was there any lack of 'creature comforts.' Bread and cakes were abundantly supplied by pedlars, and whiskey flowed on all sides. Under such circumstances, we may conceive the uproarious hilarity of an excitable people. Nor did it cease till the Sabbath sun 'sought the western wave.' "[21]

As indicated by the above reports, a common characteristic of the festive aspect of patterns, and indeed of patronal festivals in many countries, is that they are often considered licentious. Licentious behavior is not the same as criminal or illegal behavior; rather it must be considered as at the dividing line between proper and improper behavior, where the devotional aspect (the most proper behavior possible) lies at the other end of the continuum.

Licentiousness is generally defined in terms of drunkenness, sexual freedom, and fighting. All three seem to have been richly present in the Irish patterns. Heavy drinking of the poteen is always commented on by observers; sexual promiscuity is often indicated but not described in detail (this is a difficult aspect of festival behavior to document). We do have a number of good accounts of fights between factions, though, which perhaps more than anything else were responsible for the decline of the patterns as an Irish institution. Factions were simply gangs, sometimes organized along family lines or community lines, but often in other ways as well. And where you have gangs, you have the problem of honor and pride and the challenge of insult. A man drags his coat on the ground and dares any goddamned O'Leary to step on it, and the battle has begun. A good account of such a battle in 1834 was given by H. D. Inglis. The place was Maumeen, in county Galway, and the groups involved were the Joyces and the boys from Connemara:

> All was quiet when I reached the ground; and I was warmly welcomed as a stranger, by many, who invited me into their tents. Of course I accepted the invitation; and the pure potheen circulated freely. By and by, however, some boastful expression of a Joyce appeared to give offence to several at the far end of the tent; and something loud and contemptuous was spoken of by two or three in a breath. The language which, in compliment to me, had been English, suddenly changed to Irish. Two or three glasses of potheen were quickly gulped by most of the boys; and the innkeeper who had accompanied me, and who sat by me, whispered that there would soon be some fighting. I had seen abundance of fighting on a small scale, in Ireland; but, I confess, I had been barbarous enough to wish I might see a regular faction fight; and now I was likely to be gratified. Taking the hint of the innkeeper, I shook hands with the new "boys" nearest to me, right and left; and taking advantage of a sudden burst of voices, I stepped over my bench, and, retiring from my tent, took up a safe position on some neighbouring rocks.
>
> I had not long to wait: out sallied the Joyces and a score of other "boys," from several tents at once, as if there had been some pre-concerted signal; and the flourishing of shillelahs did not long precede the using of them. Any one to see an Irish fight, for the first time, would conclude that a score or two must inevitably be put *hors de combat*. The very flourish of a regular shillelah, and the shout that ac-

companies it, seem to be the immediate precursors of a fractured skull; but the affair, though bad enough, is not so fatal as it appears to be: the shillelahs, no doubt, do sometimes descend on a head, which is forthwith a broken head; but they oftener descend upon each other: and the fight soon becomes one of personal strength. The parties close and grapple; and the most powerful man throws his adversary: fair play is but little attended to: two or three often attack a single man; nor is there a cessation of blows, even when a man is on the ground. On the present occasion, five or six were disabled: but there was no homicide; and after a *scrimmage*, which lasted perhaps ten minutes, the Joyces remained masters of the field. The women took no part in the fight; . . .

When the fight ended, there were not many remaining, excepting those who were still in the tents, and who chanced to be of neither faction. Most of the women had left the place when the quarrel began, and some of the men too. I noticed, after the fight, that some, who had been opposed to each other, shook hands and kissed; and appeared as good friends as before.[22]

Danaher, in another context, mentions that bystanders could join in if they wanted to; he cites the case of the polite little girl "who pulled the coat tails of a gentleman busily occupied in beating the lard out of another gentleman, with the question, 'Excuse me, sir, but me da wants to know is it private or can he join in?'" He also says that women did join in when their men were losing. Their weapon was not a stick but rather "a stout woolen stocking with a stone weighing a pound or so in the toe of it."[23]

In a symbiotic relationship to the festival stood the fair, which was celebrated on the same days, the fair doing most of its business in the morning, after which the action moved to the festival grounds. The fair one thinks of immediately in the context of fighting was the Donnybrook fair. What was it like? Opinions are divided. It was outside the city of Dublin, and already by the middle of the nineteenth century had a terrible reputation among decent people. Thus, in the Irish *Parliamentary Gazeteer* of 1845 we find:

Donnybrook Fair, professedly for the sale of horses and black cattle, but really for vulgar dissipation, and formerly for criminal outrage and the most revolting debauchery. It was for generations a perfect prodigy of moral horrors—a concentration of disgrace upon, not Ireland alone, but civilized Europe. It far surpassed all other fairs in the multitude and grossness of its disgusting incidents of vice; and, in general, it exhibited such continuous scenes of riot, bloodshed, debauchery and brutality, as only the coarsest taste and the most hardened heart could witness without painful emotion.[24]

Yet the German visitor Prince Puckler-Muskau, visiting the fair in 1828, gives a very different picture: "They were more like French people, though their gaiety was mingled with more humour and more genuine good nature; both of which are national traits of the Irish and are always doubled by poteen (the best sort of whiskey, illicitly distilled)." But he finds no trace of violence at all, though he takes note of the poverty he sees, as well as the love-making and drunkenness.[25]

What we see exposed through these two quotations is the development of Victorian respectable outrage, so typical of the nineteenth century. Indeed, though, we must not be overly harsh on that century, since we also find that members of the clergy, as far back as the fifth and sixth centuries in other countries, expressed such indignation toward behavior at folk festivals and made resolutions and orders to do away with such irreligious practices. However, in most places through the centuries the people gaily ignored these directives, and the Church did not try too hard to enforce them. In most Catholic countries the enlightened priests, realizing that the folk did not understand the nature of things as well as they themselves did, "tolerated," and still tolerate, the licentious aspects of the patronal festival.

In Ireland, however, the case was different. Danaher protests that Victorian respectability killed the patterns: "It wasn't respectable to make the rounds at the holy well, so laity and clergy alike combined to suppress most of the patterns."[26]

It is a sad story. Account after account ends on the same note: "There used to be a patron at the place, and there used to be dancing and sport at it. There were tents for drink there too, but in the end there used to be fighting and quarrelling at it. Then the priests went against the drink. There is no gathering there now, but anyone who has a pilgrimage to make goes there and makes his rounds and then sets his face towards home again."[27]

John Messenger reports that on "Inis Beag" there used to be three days of revelry. "It was the prevalence of factional fighting and promiscuous behavior engendered by drunkenness which prompted the church to restrict the traditional practices of pattern day." Messenger observed the vigil of 1960. Only eleven people were present at the old church.

There was no work done on that day, and the dance usually held on the evening was canceled.[28]

It is sad, because this would seem to be another case of a tradition being killed by "enlightened" people who have been very logical and have thus lost something that is very valuable to the individual and the community because their logic was based on wrong or inadequate premises. If the only value of a pattern were in the devotional aspect, the pattern of course needed purifying. The trouble is that the festival's value, even to the Church, lies perhaps quite as much in the festive as in the devotional aspects, if religion is not to be seen as a grim and solemn thing. America has never had the good fortune to have these annual festivals which tie a people together and provide them with a catharsis of the frustrations of the year; Ireland, no more fortunate, had them, but let them get away.

## NOTES

1. Clyde Kluckhohn, "Myths and Rituals: A General Theory," *Harvard Theological Review* 35:45–79 (January 1942).
2. Translated by Máire MacNeill in her *The Festival of Lughnasa* (London: Oxford University Press, 1962), p. 5.
3. Most of the data on calendar customs was derived from the following works, themselves composite visions of the folkways of Ireland: Kevin Danaher, *In Ireland Long Ago* (Cork, Ire., 1962); Emyr Estyn Evans, *Irish Folk Ways* (London: Routledge & Paul, 1961), and *Irish Heritage* (Dundalk, Ire., 1967; 1st ed., 1942); Seán Ó'Súilleabháin, *A Handbook of Irish Folklore* ([Dublin]: The Educational Co. of Ireland, for the Folklore of Ireland Society, 1942), and *Irish Folk Custom and Belief* (Dublin: Published for the Cultural Relations Committee of Ireland at the Three Candles, 1967). For contemporary practices I relied on John C. Messenger, *Inis Beag: Isle of Ireland* (New York: Holt, Rinehart & Winston, 1969).
4. Cited by Roger Loomis in *Funk and Wagnalls Standard Dictionary of Folklore, Mythology and Legend* (2 vols.; New York: Funk & Wagnalls, 1949–1950), 2:966, s.v. "Saint Brigit."
5. Seán Ó'Súilleabháin, *Scéalta Cráibteaca*, vol. 21 of *Béaloideas* (Dublin: Published for the Educational Co. of Ireland, 1952), p. 304.
6. Sabine Baring-Gould, *The Lives of the Saints* (Edinburgh: J. Grant, 1914), 3:294.
7. Andrew Boorde, *The Fyrst Boke of the Introduction of Knowledge*, ed. F. J. Furnivall (London: N. Trübner, for the Early English Text Society, 1870), p. 133.
8. Edward Tylor, *The Origins of Culture* (New York: Harper & Brothers, 1958), p. 372. Originally published as chapters 1–9 of *Primitive Culture* (London: John Murray, 1871).
9. Baring-Gould, *Lives of the Saints*, 3:297.

10. Ó'Súilleabháin, *Scéalta Cráibteaca*, p. 326.
11. Ibid., pp. 325–27.
12. Padraic Colum, ed., *A Treasury of Irish Folklore* (New York: Crown Publishers, 1954), p. 123.
13. Baring-Gould, *Lives of the Saints*, 3:305.
14. Messenger, *Inis Beag*, p. 104. I can find no good explanation for this conception of Whitsuntide as being a dangerous time. It would not seem to be a reflection of a general weather pattern, since the dates vary so; in other countries it is seen as a pleasant time, when the weather is good and is conducive to picnics and excursions.
15. For a more extended discussion of this point, see my "Licentious Behavior in Hispanic Festivals," *Western Folklore* 31:290–98 (October 1972).
16. Though at different times, see Edwin O. James, *Seasonal Feasts and Festivals* (New York: Barnes & Noble, 1961), pp. 316–19.
17. See Messenger, *Inis Beag*, pp. 104–5; also Henry Morris, "St. Martin's Eve," *Béaloideas* 9:230–35 (1939).
18. William Makepeace Thackeray (under the pseudonym M. A. Titmarsh), *The Irish Sketch-Book* (London: Chapman & Hall, 1843), 2:100–101.
19. *From Angling Excursions of Gregory Greendrake* (4th ed., 1832), cited in Mac-Neill, *The Festival of Lughnasa*, p. 134. MacNeill's work is a veritable treasury of documentation of Irish festivals.
20. Sir Henry Piers, *Description of Westmeath*, in Charles Vallancey's *Collectanea de Rebus Hibernicus* (2d ed.; Dublin, 1786), cited by MacNeill, *The Festival of Lughnasa*, pp. 132–33.
21. The Reverend Henry MacManus, *Sketches of the Irish Highlands* (Dublin, 1863), cited by MacNeill, *The Festival of Lughnasa*, p. 126.
22. Henry D. Inglis, *Ireland in 1834* (3d ed.; London, 1835), cited in MacNeill, *The Festival of Lughnasa*, pp. 125-26.
23. Danaher, *In Ireland Long Ago*, p. 151.
24. Cited in Evans, *Irish Folk Ways*, p. 256.
25. Cited in Colum, *A Treasury of Irish Folklore*, p. 403.
26. Danaher, *In Ireland Long Ago*, p. 148.
27. Cited by MacNeill, *The Festival of Lughnasa*, p. 127.
28. Messenger, *Inis Beag*, p. 92.

# 7

# FROM THE TREATY OF LIMERICK TO THE UNION WITH GREAT BRITAIN

*Henry L. Snyder*

Wiliam III had been anxious to speed the recovery of Ireland so that he could devote his full energies and resources to the war with Louis XIV that he was engaged in on the Continent. He was prepared to offer moderate terms to the rebels, and instructed Ginkel to do so. The Treaty of Limerick (1691) reflected this attitude. Officers and soldiers in James's army, accompanied by their families and belongings, were permitted to emigrate to the Continent. Ginkel promised to provide them with transportation, and more than twelve thousand persons took advantage of this offer, joining the many thousands of Irish who were already in exile. The civil articles of the treaty guaranteed to the Catholics the same rights they had enjoyed in the reign of Charles II, though the Act of Settlement was to be maintained. These conditions, which required parliamentary sanction, were repudiated by the English Parliament after a long delay. The Protestants had the upper hand, and they were determined to eliminate any possibility of further rebellion. Parliament also passed a series of acts that effectively barred Catholics from any power in the government. All proceedings of the Revolutionary Parliament were annulled. The Irish corporations were restored to their status as of 1689. New oaths were imposed, including those against transubstantiation and the invocation of saints, as required by the Test Acts in England. Catholics were effectively and completely excluded from public life in Ireland, as in England, which was a direct violation of the Treaty of Limerick. A series of statutes, which were collectively called the penal code, was enacted. These laws placed still more severe restrictions upon the Catholics. At first the Irish Parliament was sympathetic to the Catholics, but this sense of justice and toleration gradually vanished. Initially, only the religious orders were expelled, but all regular Roman Catholic clergy were banished by an act passed in 1697. Intermarriage between Protestants and Catholics was forbidden. A Protestant woman who violated the act forfeited her estate. Catholics were excluded from the legal profession. Children who were sent abroad to attend Catholic schools were not permitted to reenter the country. Catholics were not permitted to teach school or to bear firearms. The list of prohibitions and penalties seems endless. The old Irish custom of gavelkind, the division of a person's estates equally among all his heirs, was made obligatory for Roman Catholics, the intent being to break up the few remaining large Catholic landholdings after a few generations. Catholics were not allowed to buy real property or to lease it for more than thirteen years. If the eldest son of a Catholic landowner became a convert to Protestantism, title to all his father's estates was vested in him. The result was that all long leases were in the hands of Protestant farmers who bought up the leases at low prices, and then sublet the lands to Catholics at high rents.

The harshness of the laws against Catholics was paralleled by the land settlement, which completed the redistribution that had begun with the Elizabethan confiscations and had been continued by the Cromwellian settlement. There were no more wholesale confiscations after 1703. The pattern of landholding remained stable after this point, but this stability was achieved only by a further diminution of the number of Catholic landowners. After the Restoration the Catholics had partially recovered from the deprivations that they had suffered under the Commonwealth. At the time of the Glorious Revolution, Protestants held virtually all the land in Ulster and a majority of the land east of the Shannon. Catholic landholdings were concentrated west of the Shannon, especially in Galway and in Connaught, where the Catholics had been transplanted in the 1650s. As a result of the outlawry of the rebels, Catholic holdings were further reduced from approximately 22 percent to 14 percent of the arable land. In no county did Catholic landowners remain in the majority. The number of major landowners—thirteen hundred in 1688—was reduced by more than a third, to fewer than nine hundred. The major outcry came, not at the confiscation, but with the grants that William III made from the confiscations. Most of the lands went to his favorites. Nine-tenths of the more than 600,000 acres went to only forty-four people. More than one-fifth went to the earl of Portland, and a sixth went to Portland's successor in the king's affections—Keppel. The king's mistress received the personal estate of the duke of York, another 100,000 acres, which produced some £26,000 a year in income.

At the end of the Nine Years' War (1688–1697), the Tories regained control of the English Parliament, and then made an inquiry into William's land grants. The result was the Act of Resumption—a deliberate insult to the king—which vested the confiscated lands in trustees. The trustees were charged with selling the lands, but they found a dearth of ready buyers. Ultimately, almost half of the property went to a corporation of promoters—the Hollow Sword Blade Company, which was notorious for its role in the creation of the South Sea Company at the end of the War of the Spanish Succession.

The Protestant Ascendancy, which was later to be so well remembered for its share in the breakup of the Liberal party under Gladstone and the formation of the Unionist party with the Conservatives (at the end of the nineteenth century), was confirmed in its control of the country by the revolution settlement. The Jacobite Parliament had made English ownership of the land and control of the government the central issues in dispute, and the Williamite conquest decided those issues. After the revolution the power of the Irish government was seriously compromised. Its freedom of action was much curtailed; it was held strictly accountable to the ministry at London. The days of the great viceroys who fixed their residence at Dublin for the whole of their tenure of office were no more. No viceroy possessing the stature and respect of the first duke of Ormonde held the lord lieutenancy after the revolution. The lord lieutenants from 1689 until the reign of George III (1760) were nonresidents who came over to Dublin only to convene the biennial meeting of Parliament. The post was usually given to a politician of some prominence or social standing, but more often than not the assignment was looked on as a form of honorable exile. The earl of Rochester, who was lord lieutenant from 1700 to 1703 and a principal leader of the High Church party in England, was ordered to his post by the queen in early 1703, as a means of ridding the cabinet and Parliament of a troublemaker; but Rochester resigned his post rather than accept this polite form of political banishment. The queen was forced to use similar tactics with his successor, the second earl of Ormonde, who lingered too long in England for the taste of her chief ministers. The earl of Pembroke, who succeeded him in 1707, was a stop-gap candidate. He was replaced in turn by the earl of Wharton, who was keenly interested in the post mainly for the emoluments of the office. He needed them in order to repair his fortune, which had been greatly reduced by his electioneering expenses in England. When George I acceded to the throne in 1714, the office was reputed to be worth £6,000 a year in salary and another £6,000 in gratuities, making it easily the most valuable office in the queen's gift.[1] But Wharton only went to Ireland for the parliamentary sessions. He preferred to spend his time at home in England, taking an active role in the queen's councils and occupying the seat at the cabinet table to which his place entitled him. For the most part the office was exercised by deputies—called lord justices—who managed the routine of government in the absence of the lord lieutenant. Appointed in combinations of two and three, they consisted usually of the commander in chief, the primate, and the chancellor, though other prominent officials were sometimes appointed. They were invariably English by birth; their most important qualifications were loyalty to the sovereign and subservience to the English ministry.

Although members of the Protestant ruling class were gratified by the victory over the Catholics, their happiness was not unalloyed. They formed a small minority in an overwhelmingly Catholic country. Their own prosperity depended ultimately upon the success of all classes. The penal laws and, even more, the commercial laws, which intensified the restrictions imposed upon Irish trade at the time of the Restoration in 1660, had the inevitable effect of depressing the value both of their own estates and of the products of their lands. Moreover, the Irish rulers chafed at the political restrictions imposed by the English Parliament and at the continuing irritation of the provisions of Poynings's Law. When they saw the scandals that marked the disposal of the forfeited estates after the revolution, and found that they reaped no benefit (the lands went primarily to foreign favorites of the king), they expressed their resentment at the king's policy; furthermore, the Irish Parliament opposed further confiscations. There was a reversion of sympathy for the Catholic population, especially in the House of Lords, where the bishops dominated. The sympathy that was expressed for the Catholics found no parallel in the attitude of the Anglican ruling class towards the Presbyterians of the north. The punitive legislation directed against the Catholics also operated in many cases against the Dissenters, who had no greater share in the government than did the deprived Catholics, although they were permitted to hold local offices. The Dissenters suffered similar treatment in England, but in Ireland they had even less choice. Since their fortunes ultimately depended upon the maintenance of the Protestant Ascendancy, they had no choice but to submit.

Ulster was so overwhelmingly Presbyterian in religion that Presbyterianism enjoyed many of the advantages held by the established Church elsewhere in the country. The Presbyterians had their own synods and churches, as well as a well-educated and ordained clergy. They only lacked official sanction. Elsewhere in Ireland, as in England, Protestant sects were tolerated by the Anglican Church and were allowed to worship in peace.

The Parliament that met in 1692 was the first Parliament to meet since 1666 (the records of the Jacobite Parliament of 1689 do not appear in the journals). The Irish Parliament had never been particularly active. The work resulting from the revolution prompted the Parliament to meet more frequently after it was once convened; beginning in 1703, it settled down to a regular pattern of sessions every two years. Under the terms of Poynings's Law, it still could consider only bills that were directed to it by the Privy Council. Actually, Parliament initiated "heads of bills," which were bills in all but name. Nevertheless, their legislation still had to be submitted to the king in Council both in Ireland and in England, and the English Privy Council was not above severely modifying bills sent over to it, or even rejecting them entirely. The bills thus modified were returned to Dublin, where Parliament could only accept or reject them. In England the bills were reviewed first by the attorney general and the solicitor general. The Privy Council had almost ceased to function, its duties having been taken over by the cabinet. A subcommittee of the Privy Council—which included not only such members of the cabinet as the chancellor, the lord president, the secretaries of state, and Irish members of the Privy Council, but also the chief justices—sat to review the bills. The subcommittee then recommended to the sovereign the appropriate action, which was then taken in a formal meeting of the Council. The Test Act of 1704 was one such addition made to a bill during the course of its review in London. Another example of English modification was the action of the Council in 1709, when it reduced from four to one the number of arsenals proposed for the storage of arms, because it feared that stores of arms maintained outside Dublin were too easy a temptation to potential rebels.

After the Nine Years' War the standing army in England was reduced to seven thousand men after a bitter controversy in the press and in Parliament. The main intent of the Tories who instigated this measure was to deprive William III of his Dutch guards; but lurking in the back of everyone's mind was the memory of the rule of the major generals in England. Parliament would not tolerate a large permanent military force which could be used by the crown in peacetime as an instrument of oppression. The consequence of this action was that the government had no substantial reserves to draw on in wartime, since the forces provided were barely adequate for peacetime needs. The crown was under no such restraint in Ireland, so a large force was maintained on the Irish establishment, ostensibly to ensure domestic tranquility, but also to be drawn on in wartime for service on whatever battlefields the British saw action.

The mercantile system which became official policy in England in the mid-seventeenth century, as well as the accompanying commercial acts which ensured the subordination of Irish commerce to English interests, received further elaboration after the revolution. The Cattle Acts of 1663 had forced the Irish to develop a market for their commodities on the Continent. Ireland also began to serve as an important provisioning point for foreign ships sailing to the Americas. Ireland had been allowed to export its raw wool only to England; thus the price of Irish wool had to bear the costs of freight and import duties. Nevertheless, it still undersold the native English product, so the wool trade prospered. After the Revolution of 1688, low prices in England made the trade unprofitable, and the Irish turned to Continental markets, though such trade was illegal. Ormonde had fought to protect Irish commerce from English restrictions after the Restoration; but the administrators of Ireland after the revolution were committed to English interests, so they ignored the needs of their Irish charges. In 1698 a 20 percent export duty was imposed on all Irish cloth. The next year, England passed legislation prohibiting the export of Irish cloth to any market other than England, while still retaining the heavy duties imposed in 1660. The result was the destruction of the cloth trade, as well as the cloth industry, in Ireland. Some illegal trade was still carried on with France, and all sorts of subterfuges were devised for smuggling cloth out; but this was not enough to maintain the industry. Irish workers migrated to the Continent, where new factories were set up for weaving Irish wool. The effect upon the Irish economy was serious, as there was no other industry to replace it.

The linen trade, which had been encouraged since the time of Wentworth, did not fare much better. The cloth could not be exported to England, which was supplied with a superior French product. Ormonde brought in French weavers to improve the quality of the Irish cloth, and a new group of French refugees settled in Ireland after the revolution, setting up a linen industry near Lisburn. The bulk of the yarn was exported to England, so that the mother country could profit from the manufacture of the cloth; but the prohibition of exports to England of linen cloth was lifted, and the Irish were even permitted to compete in the colonial trade with their coarse cloth after 1705. Other industries also suffered discouragement from the English—cotton, glass, and so forth. Because Irish manufacturers were forced to employ English bottoms, the small Irish shipping industry was ruined. The decay of Irish industry caused by these measures threw many skilled workers out of employment, forcing them back on the land for subsistence. Yet the ban on exporting foodstuffs had an equally debilitating effect, so that the Irish economy languished for decades until external factors caused a gradual improvement in the middle of the eighteenth century. The impoverished condition of the people meant that every bad harvest invariably resulted in a famine, and the population slowly declined under the burden of its many misfortunes.

Until the turn of the century the hereditary revenues of the crown, which had been established at the Restoration, were adequate for maintaining the government. Thereafter they fell short, and new taxes were required in order to make up the deficit. This was the basis for the biennial meeting of Parliament. The Parliament was not given much scope to represent the interests of the country. To begin with, it was drawn solely from the small Anglican minority. Until the passage of the Octennial Act in 1768, new elections were mandatory only at the beginning of a new reign. Only two elections were held between 1714 and 1760, and thus whatever influence the electors cared to exercise could only be brought to bear at by-elections. But of the 300 members of the Commons, at least 176 were nominated by patrons. Circumscribed in its legislative function by Poynings's Law, the upper house suffered the additional indignity of having its appellate jurisdiction transferred to the British Parliament in 1719. In the Declaratory Act of that same year the British Parliament affirmed its full authority to legislate for Ireland. The independence of the English judiciary had been guaranteed by the Act of Succession of 1701; but Irish judges continued to hold office only at the pleasure of the crown until the reign of George III. The Irish establishment was a lucrative source of sinecures for English politicians, and the pension list supported many dependents of the English crown. Most of the judges, every chancellor, the primate, and most of the bishops—that is, the overwhelming majority of senior officers in the establishment—were Englishmen. Since many of the peers were absentees, the bishops formed a substantial share of the working majority in the House of Lords; they also controlled many of the seats in the lower house. The political influence of the Anglican hierarchy was most notable in the executive department, where the primates acted as the chief ministers or lord justices from 1724 until 1764.

Though the Ascendancy class was notoriously unrepresentative and self-interested, its members still protested measures that were inimical to the country when their own interests suffered as well. Even before the parliamentary union of England and Scotland in 1707 there were advocates of a parliamentary union between Ireland and England that would bring Ireland and Irishmen into an equal footing with England and would promote their mutual advantage. But there was no benefit to England from such an agreement. Far better to have Ireland completely subservient, and to have its resources placed at the disposal of the crown. The wonder is that Ireland accepted the situation so docilely. Though Scotland was the destination of the Pretender's invasion in 1708 and served as the base of a Jacobite invasion of England in 1715 and again in 1745, throughout the century Catholic Ireland remained loyal to its foreign, Protestant king.

After the excitement of the Jacobite period, Ireland gradually became a backwater and succumbed to economic stagnation. Some Jacobites had a little influence in the government during the last Tory ministry of Anne's reign, but George I installed staunch Hanoverian Whigs in their places, and political stagnation set in to match that of the economy. Many of the English owners of Irish estates were absentees. It was calculated that more than a third of the rents were sent across the Irish Sea to England, which had adverse effects upon the economy. This absenteeism was the result of the countless grants of confiscated land to English speculators. Catholics were not allowed to buy land, but were only suffered to lease it for short terms. They, in turn, sublet to poor tenant farmers, and the chain was sometimes extended further. The great mass of the people ground out a bare subsistence living off the land. The pittance they received for their labors was reduced still further by tithes to the Church, rents to the landlords, and dues to their own priests. Absentee landlords had no incentive to make improvements on their holdings, and the poor tenants possessed no capital with which to do so. If the tenants did manage to improve the yield to more than one-third of the rent, their leases could be canceled. No mechanism existed to recompense the tenants for improvements made to the property. They were completely at the mercy of the ruling class. Some Catholics turned their croplands to pasture in order to avoid tithes. Others kept their lands as waste. The cultivation of grain declined. The number of paupers increased, but there was no system of poor relief on the English model to provide them with assistance.

Occasionally the English ministry acted so callously and so injuriously to Irish interests that those who were in a position to protest did so. Such was the case in 1724, when the king's mistress was granted the right to mint copper coins for Ireland, and then sold the patent for a handsome profit. The protests were made most effectively by the greatest Irishman of the age, Jonathan Swift, himself a member of the privileged minority; his *Drapier Letters* provoked such a reaction that the ministry in England itself was threatened. But this was exceptional, and for several decades after the Hanoverian succession the somnolence of the Irish state was seldom stirred. Several of the lord lieutenants, notably Carteret (1724–1730) and Chesterfield (1745), were men of outstanding ability who took their duties seriously; but the interests ranged against them were too powerful, and their attempts to ameliorate the lot of their subjects proved futile.

There were two societies in eighteenth-century Ireland. The garrison society of the Protestant Ascendancy had its focus in Dublin. As the century advanced and prosperity returned to the country, Dublin became the center of a flourishing provincial society. The biennial visit of the lord lieutenant was the high point of the social season. The presence of the Irish courts and bureaucracy gave the town a sense of importance; it was responsible for a steady stream of visitors. Members of the aristocracy and leading gentry maintained second homes in Dublin, and the town possessed a kind of attraction and a role in the country that were not unlike what London enjoyed in England, though on a much smaller scale. In this respect Ireland was more fortunate than Scotland, for Edinburgh suffered a major decline after its Parliament was ended and many of the major departments of state were consolidated with those at London. The wealth of the great landowners was also displayed in magnificent country houses, again on the English model. Set against this society was the society of the native Gaelic population, which was at or below the subsistence level and had been deprived of all but the most rudimentary educational opportunities. Though the native Irish had abandoned the nomadic habits of their ancestors, their living conditions were hardly better. They lived in squalid huts with thatched roofs, which were nearly bare of furnishings; even so, the people managed to retain their sense of humor, their love of music, and their gift for poetry. Forced to rely on oral tradition and transmission, they preserved their Gaelic tongue, passed on the stories and epics of their forefathers, and even spawned new poets to carry on the native literary tradition.

Ireland, principally Dublin, was celebrated for its cultural advances in the eighteenth century. Many of Ireland's brightest sons migrated to England to establish their reputations and seek their fortunes, but any nation that could produce a Swift, a Berkeley, or a Burke was to be admired, if not envied. Booksellers were numerous, and lack of a copyright law made Dublin reprints of English publications a good bargain. Dublin enjoyed fine newspapers, excellent theater, and a good reputation as a musical town. The richness and variety of Dublin society gradually extended to the provinces. By 1750 Dublin was the second largest city in the empire, with a population in excess of one hundred thousand. Cork was the next largest city, with a population of about sixty thousand, which placed it on a par with the largest provincial centers in Britain. Cork owed its prosperity to its fine harbor and the beef trade. Waterford, another important commercial center, had a large fishery. Kilkenny, which was connected to Dublin by a good turnpike, had the finest provincial society outside Dublin.

The turning point in the political history of the country came in the middle of the eighteenth century, when the conduct of the primate Archbishop Stone, coupled with a dispute between the crown and the Parliament over the disposition of a surplus in the revenue, resulted in the organization of a formal opposition in the Parliament. This return of factionalism is known as "the revolt of the undertakers." The contest that dominated the political arena lay between the great Irish families of the Ascendancy—the undertakers, who had managed the government for the crown since early in the century—and the English ministers, who sought to control it directly. The undertakers now turned patriots; they based their opposition on the misapplication of public monies—a charge that could as easily have been laid against them during their own management of the public revenues. They now sought to reassert parliamentary control over the executive, and they appropriated funds for local projects, in order to eliminate any revenue surplus that could be used to satisfy the obligations of the English government. The rivalry of the newly developed parties increased the excitement and stakes in politics, and it awakened a new interest in the activities of Parliament. The price of borough seats rose rapidly, and corruption—that is, the use of patronage and government funds to support the government interest in the legislature—was also on the increase. Hartington, who was sent over as viceroy in 1755, temporarily restored calm to the political scene by buying off the opposition and restoring the undertakers to a share in the patronage of the crown in return for their accepting once more the responsibility for managing the Parliament in the king's interest.

The first years of George III's reign were relatively uneventful. The new Irish Parliament elected at the time of his accession in 1760 proved to be of high quality. The parties in the Parliament were evenly balanced, and party leaders looked outside Parliament for the additional support that would give them a preponderance of influence. The most obvious source was the Catholics, for the Catholic gentry began to agitate for the removal of the disabilities under which they suffered. Religious differences were no longer so great an issue, and the penal laws primarily affected property. The Nationalist party began to press for the same advantages for Irish Protestants as English Protestants enjoyed in their own country; it set as its first two goals the limitation of the term of Parliament and the restriction of pensions, which had grown at an alarming rate for a decade. A septennial bill was introduced on several occasions in Parliament, and support for the bill came from all over the country. The Irish government could not afford to reject the bill; therefore it sent the bill over to England for the *coup de grâce*. The members of the Commons were instructed by their constituents to refuse to pass any money bill until the septennial bill was passed, and therefore the legislative process stopped for three months in 1764. Other reform measures were introduced, though none succeeded at this time. When the two leading Irish ministers died in 1764, the English government decided to send over a lieutenant, who would reside permanently in Dublin during his tenure in office, to wrest control of the government from the undertakers. It was not easy to find a suitable candidate for this charge, but finally in 1767 Lord Townshend accepted the challenge and took up his station.

Townshend began his viceroyship under favorable auspices, and in his opening address to Parliament he announced that the judges would henceforth be appointed for life. When the Nationalists introduced a bill to enact this promise into law, the English government added qualifications, giving to itself the right of removal. The ire of the Nationalists was provoked, and they caused the altered bill to be rejected. Townshend introduced a measure to increase the size of the army, but the Commons tied it to a septennial act. The Irish army was maintained out of the hereditary revenue, and thus was beyond the reach of the legislature; but the increase was looked upon as too expensive for the government to support. The English ministry was so anxious to obtain the augmentation that it approved an octennial act in early 1768, a measure which may be regarded as the first step towards legislative independence for Ireland. The undertakers now laid down new conditions for favorable treatment of the augmentation, and when they were refused, they went into opposition. The bill was defeated, and Townshend, who was determined to break the power of the undertakers, dissolved the Parliament. Though Townshend was successful in pushing the augmentation through the new Parliament, his method of managing the Parliament and his protest against the limitations placed by Parliament on the use of the troops heightened his unpopularity; it also drove the undertakers into the arms of the Patriot party. The recall of Townshend in 1772 reconciled some of the opposition leaders to the government; the two most eminent ones— Hely Hutchinson and Henry Flood—were bought off with lucrative places.

The problems of the crown in America soon embroiled the Irish government in new difficulties with the parties. The Patriots used the government's discomfiture to press for new concessions, especially in the commercial sphere, since the rebellion of the American colonies deprived Ireland of its main market for linen and also affected its provision trade. In response to the demands of the Patriots, a bill was introduced in the British Parliament in 1778 which would have replaced the commercial laws, but it was defeated because of the opposition of English manu-facturing interests. The Irish retaliated with a boycott of British products, which produced a few concessions. The year 1778 was even more notable for the first break in the penal code, because the demand for additional soldiers that was caused by the American war forced the government to permit Catholics to enlist in the army and in the marines. The fear that Catholics would support France also prompted the government to intro-duce legislation enabling Catholics to take leases for periods up to 999 years (a tacit admission of their right to buy property) and to inherit property; this did away with gavelkind.

The greatest years of the Irish Parliament were at hand. England was at war with France, as well as with the colonies, and Ireland had been stripped of its troops. The problem of providing protection for the country was deemed a serious one, for the English fleet was engaged elsewhere, and the coast was vulnerable to invasion. The Protestant gen-try and nobility resolved to raise a militia at their own expense, and some forty-two thousand men were recruited, who came to be known as the Volunteers. When the Parliament met in 1779, there was widespread discontent over the limited nature of the commercial concessions made the previous year. Lord North, the English prime minister, could not face a hostile Ireland, in view of the other dangers confronting his country; therefore he enacted a series of measures during 1779 and 1780 that put Irish trade on nearly the same footing as that of England, in domestic, colonial, and foreign markets. At the same time Irish Dissenters were restored to full participation in the government, a half-century before the same right was extended to Dissenters in England.

The Volunteers now commanded a strong following throughout the country; they included in their number the most prominent and important families of the Protestant Ascendancy. Now choosing to extend their activities to the political arena, they were responsible for the introduction of a whole series of reform measures in Parliament in 1780. At first they enjoyed only a limited success. The principal measure enacted in 1781 was a habeas corpus act, but other reform measures were defeated. It was only after major changes took place in England that the climate became favorable for reintroduction of these measures. On 15 February 1782 a great meeting of the Ulster Volunteers was held at Dungannon. One hundred forty-three units representing twenty-five thousand men were present. A series of resolutions, prepared by Henry Flood, Henry Grattan—the greatest of the Patriot leaders—and others, called for the independence of the Irish legislature and other reforms. A few days later the same questions were moved in the House of Commons after Parliament had convened. The government postponed a response, and sought guidance from England. While Parliament was adjourned for its Easter recess, Lord North resigned his premiership, and a new Whig ministry, headed by Lord Rockingham and dedicated to reform, was installed in England. The duke of Portland was sent over as viceroy, arriving a bare two days before Parliament was due to reconvene. Grattan refused the viceroy's request for a further adjournment, and when Parliament met on the sixteenth of April, Dublin was jammed with Volunteers, who paraded in the streets and packed the galleries of the House of Commons. In one of the great moments of Irish history, Grattan delivered a stirring speech, in which he moved that an address be sent to the king requesting that the impositions on the powers of the Irish Parliament be removed, while at the same time the link between the crowns would remain indissoluble. The House then adjourned to await the king's reply. Portland urged the English ministry to make the desired concessions, while Grattan refused to enter into any negotiations with the English until his principal demands were met. The English government—which was weak and inexperienced, and basically well-disposed towards Ireland—was in no position to refuse; therefore the British Parliament gave its assent in a series of resolutions on 17 May. Enabling legislation was quickly introduced. It repealed the Declaratory Act, which had given the British legislature the right to legislate for Ireland; the appellate jurisdiction of the British House of Lords over the Irish courts was abandoned; and Poynings's Law was repealed. The Mutiny Act, which was essential to the discipline of the army, was changed from being perpetual legislation to being term legislation. When the Irish Parliament met, Portland announced these and other concessions. Then another round of bills was introduced, which relieved the Catholics of further disabilities and removed the restrictions upon the Catholic clergy. The independence of the Irish legislature was finally secured.

Anglo-Irish relations now entered a new phase. Though legislative independence had been achieved, the executive was still in the hands of the king, and hence of the English ministry. By the skillful employment of patronage, the crown could still manage the Irish Parliament through the borough proprietors. Grattan believed that Parliament would be the agent for its own reform. Flood, who was more realistic, thought that further pressure would be needed in order to force the borough proprietors to relinquish their control. He called a national convention of the Volunteers, at which he passed a program for electoral reform and an enlargement of the franchise. Unfortunately, Grattan resented Flood's leadership, therefore he opposed Flood's measures in Parliament, supporting the government against his fellow Patriots. Consequently the bills failed, and the chance to reform Parliament was irretrievably lost.

The removal of the restrictions upon Irish trade did not give the impetus to it that everyone had expected. The next few years were periods of serious commercial distress. Grattan attributed the crisis to a shortage of foodstuffs, and a law was enacted that provided for bounties to be paid on the production of grain. It soon had the desired effect, and Ireland changed from a grain-importing to a grain-exporting country. New land was brought under cultivation, rents were increased, and more people found employment on the land. Because England was reduced to importing grain to feed its population, Ireland became a principal supplier of grain to her sister country. The long-range consequences of the bounty were not so favorable: it increased the number of small holdings, encouraged an increase in population, and resulted in a new depression when the price of grain fell after the Napoleonic Wars. The new prime minister, William Pitt the Younger, had expressed concern over the newly won independence of Ireland; he saw the commercial crisis as a means to bind Ireland firmly to England once again. He offered to remove the remaining restrictions on Irish trade if Ireland would agree to contribute funds to the support of the empire. Although this scheme was accepted in Ireland, it had to be abandoned because of the opposition of the English merchants.

The rest of the decade proved relatively uneventful, especially in light of the momentous chain of events that transformed the nature of the

Irish government and the situation of the Catholics during the Volunteer phase. But the outbreak of the French Revolution unleashed a new series of forces that had far-reaching repercussions in Ireland as well as England. In 1791 the Belfast Volunteers demonstrated for the abolition of all religious qualifications, instead supporting a union of Protestants and Catholics to accomplish this objective. In October the Society of United Irishmen was founded to promote a thoroughgoing reform of the legislature. The Patriot party had promoted its own reform platform in the 1790 session of the legislature, thus prompting the government to dissolve the Parliament and call for new elections. The elections resulted in fresh gains for the reformers, but their reform bill, introduced in 1794, was more conservative either than Flood's of 1782 or the radical measures advocated by the United Irishmen. The Whig party envisaged a reform that would place political power safely in its own hands; it showed no propensity to surrender its supremacy to the masses.

[Still another group came forward with a program of reform, but its goals were not those of the parliamentary reformers. The Catholic Committee, which had been revitalized by the withdrawal of the conservatives and reinforced by the growing commercial importance of the Catholics, sent representatives to England early in 1792, demanding the repeal of the remaining parts of the penal code. The opposition to their demands were stronger in Ireland than in England. Pitt was much more favorably disposed toward Catholic Emancipation than he was toward parliamentary reform, but the Irish government was dominated by conservatives, the Lord Chancellor Fitzgibbon having the greatest influence. A limited measure of relief was passed later in the year, but the opposition of the Irish government restricted its terms. The Catholics recognized that without parliamentary representation they lacked the strength to achieve their full program, and they joined forces with the Ulster reformers. The result was that Catholic Emancipation now became linked with parliamentary reform. Grattan endorsed the conjunction of the two movements in a speech at the opening of Parliament in February 1793, and a Catholic relief bill was introduced in the Commons soon thereafter. [The bill provided for the removal of all remaining personal-property disabilities, admitted Catholics to the franchise in towns and counties, and opened the magistracy, corporations, and services to them. In the final form of the bill, which was passed into law in April, most of the principal places in the government and the judiciary were still denied to Catholics, and they were not allowed to sit in either house of Parliament.

Moderate reform measures gave way to radical agitation and conservative repression when Earl Camden was sent over as viceroy. In close league with the Chancellor, now earl of Clare, the government was determined to permit no further concessions to the Catholics. The Catholics, whose strength steadily increased at the same time that widespread support for their relief gave hope for achieving it, were doomed to disappointment. The reaction of the Irish government had fatal consequences for the country, because it reawakened the religious animosities that had been slowly disappearing, and it impelled the Catholics to radical action and even revolution in order to secure their rights now that legal channels to secure their aims had been closed to them. The situation rapidly disintegrated. The Parliament passed a series of measures that was designed to suppress radical agitation and the peaceful assembly of the reformers. In September 1795 the Orange Society was founded to maintain the Protestant supremacy, and the persecution of the Catholics was eagerly pursued. In 1796 Grattan introduced a Catholic Emancipation bill for the last time in Parliament, but his bill was once again defeated.

The radical element now saw insurrection as the only means to achieve its aims. Wolfe Tone, the republican founder of the United Irishmen, traveled to America and thence to France, where he arranged for an invasion force. The expedition, which sailed at the end of 1796, was turned back by storms, and the English were saved, even though they had no defenses prepared for repelling the invaders. Ulster was put under martial law, and the harsh repression carried out by the army in the north added fuel to the fire of the radicals and provoked the disgust of many of the Protestants. Grattan condemned the government and withdrew from Parliament with his followers in protest. The United Irishmen determined to try again, planning an uprising for early 1798. Their plans were betrayed to the government, and their leaders were apprehended; but other members of the organization planned afresh, scheduling another insurrection. Once more the rebels were betrayed and apprehended, but the peasantry met as directed, and furnished armed resistance to the government. The rebels were compromised by their lack of leadership. Nevertheless they enjoyed a series of small victories over the militia before they were put down by the newly arrived commander in chief and viceroy, Cornwallis (of American fame).

The constant fear of rebellion, as well as the spread of violence and anarchy, convinced the more conservative Protestants that their salvation lay only through a parliamentary union with England, and they found their champion in the chancellor, Clare. The majority of the Irish were opposed to Union, because it would mean subordination once more to an English legislature, a raise in taxes, and a loss of income and prestige to Dublin with the removal of the Parliament. Pitt, who had been concerned about the possibility of Irish independence ever since the passage of the legislation that had removed the restraints upon the Irish Parliament, welcomed a plan that would bind Ireland permanently to England. Pitt was even willing to concede Catholic Emancipation in return for Catholic support of a Union, and the Catholics were persuaded to support the Union on this basis. If the Irish Parliament had been allowed to act freely, and if a true sampling of public opinion had been taken and followed, the Union would never have taken place. That it did was the result of the most thorough-going and unprincipled use of patronage and corruption that Ireland or England had ever experienced. The borough patrons, who lost their rights of nomination, were bought out at a cost of £15,000 a seat, which resulted in the addition of £1,250,000 to the Irish national debt. Every possible bit of pressure was applied. When Parliament met in January 1800, the government had a safe majority, and the Union was accepted within the month. Once it passed, the Union measure was introduced in the British Parliament, where it received the royal assent on August first. The Catholics now looked for fulfillment of their emancipation, which had been promised in return for their support. They were cruelly disappointed, for Pitt and his allies had acted without consulting the king, and George III refused to countenance Catholic Emancipation as being a violation of his coronation oath. Once more the chance for the amicable and voluntary reconciliation of the two countries was lost. The Union began on an ominous note. Charges of treachery and betrayal were laid to those who promoted it, and Ireland entered its forced partnership at a disadvantage, under conditions that doomed the Union to ultimate failure from its very foundation.

## NOTE

1. The civil establishment of Ireland, Blenheim MSS. G1–19. I wish to express my gratitude to the duke of Marlborough for granting me access to the manuscripts in his custody.

## SUGGESTIONS FOR FURTHER READING

Beckett, James C. *Protestant Dissent in Ireland, 1689–1780*. London: Faber & Faber, 1948.

Bolton, Geoffrey C. *The Passing of the Irish Act of Union*. London: Oxford University Press, 1966.

Corkery, Daniel. *The Hidden Ireland*. Dublin: M. H. Gill & Son, 1925.

Cullen, Louis M. *Anglo-Irish Trade, 1660–1800.* Manchester, Eng.: Manchester University Press, and New York: A. M. Kelley, 1968.

James, Francis G. *Ireland in the Empire, 1688–1770.* Harvard Historical Monographs, no. 68. Cambridge, Mass.: Harvard University Press, 1973.

Johnston, Edith M. *Great Britain and Ireland, 1760–1800.* Edinburgh: Oliver & Boyd, for the University Court of the University of St. Andrews, 1963.

Lecky, William E. H. *A History of Ireland in the Eighteenth Century.* London: Longmans Green, 1892.

McDowell, Robert B. *Irish Public Opinion, 1750–1800.* London: Faber & Faber, 1944.

Munter, Robert L. *The History of the Irish Newspaper, 1685–1760.* London: Cambridge University Press, 1967.

O'Connell, Maurice R. *Irish Politics and Social Conflict in the Age of the American Revolution.* Philadelphia: University of Pennsylvania Press, 1965.

Simms, John G. *The Williamite Confiscation in Ireland, 1690–1703.* London: Faber & Faber, 1956.

For a list of general works on the history of Ireland see chapter 2.

# ANTIQUARIANISM AND ARCHITECTURE IN EIGHTEENTH-CENTURY IRELAND

*Marilyn Stokstad and Linda Gill*

One important aspect of the cultural revival of Ireland in the eighteenth century was the rise of interest in Irish history and antiquities. The rediscovery and appreciation of a glorious national past became an essential ingredient in the revival both of a national spirit and of the arts in Ireland. English antiquaries played an important role. The earliest scientific study of Irish antiquities was made in 1698, when Edward Lhuyd, keeper of the Ashmolean Museum in Oxford, made a tour of the British Isles to study the Celtic language, and, while in Ireland, examined the New Grange tumulus. The first Irishman to study his country's past was a doctor in Dublin, William Molyneux, who in 1725 published "A Discourse concerning Danish Mounts in Ireland." Thomas Wright of Durham (1711–1786), the astronomer and mathematician whose work as an architect, landscape gardener, and antiquarian is just now beginning to attract attention, went to Ireland in 1746 to study prehistoric and historic antiquities.[1] His biographer, Ralph Allan of Darlington, wrote in the *Gentleman's Magazine* (February 1793, pp. 126–27):

> In 1746, Mr. Wright made a voyage to Ireland, where we find him under the patronage of Lord Limerick and the Bishop of Raphoe. He continued the winter at Dundalk, and returned to England the 16th of June, 1747. During his stay in Ireland, he was engaged in visiting places of antiquity, and collecting drawings and materials for his Louthiana, the first volume of which, with a multitude of curious plates, he published in the year 1748.*
>
> *The second volume, with the drawings yet remaining unpublished, together with a volume of antiquities collected in England, are both now in Mr. Allan's possession.[2]

Wright's work on Ireland began with a study of "Plans, Views &c. of some of the Chief Castles, Keeps, and Ancient Dwellings, as they are now standing in Ireland. Formerly Places of great Strength, but Now in Ruins."[3] Typical of his reports are the views and description of "Castle Doe in the County of Donnygall, and ancient seat of the Mac Swines." Wright's account of a visit is far more entertaining and informative than a modern guide book:

> This Fortress was the Habitation of the Rebellious Veres Earls of Oxford, who in ye Reign of Richard the IId were banished England, & fixing here took the name of Mac-Swine.
> It is a very old & odd Building, but in much better Repair, than most of the Castles remaining in that part of the Kingdom.
> It stands upon a plain & near ye Sea, & commands all that Coast.
> Not far from it on the west, is a very extraordinary marine Chimney, if I may so call it; the Rock being perforated to a Cave below, to which when a Spring tide sets in & the Wind strongly blows from ye North against it a Column of Waters is thrown up out of it 300 feet high & with so great a force as to shake all the Ground round for a considerable Distance like an Earthquake.
> It is called Mac-Swyne's Gun & in it's Reaction by the power of Suction, it draws every thing near it into its Vortex, so that if Birds go too near it, they are sure to be drawn into the Funnell, & torn to pieces, & their feathers thrown up again.

The Rock is all bare for 500 feet round it, & a Gentleman in ye Neighbourhood has a noted Rabit-Warren, that produces him several Hundreds a year in the value of the Skins.

This great natural fountain did not play when I was there, it being near low Water. Too curious & inadvertent people I have been informed, have been drawn so near it as to have had their Hats and Wigs taken off their Heads into it, & sent up again all torn to pieces.

A little way from this are two other smaller Chimneys called Mac-Swyne's pistols, probably before the Sea approached so near them, they might have been the Habitation of some of the Natives— The Country here is all very wild & sandy, where little other Shelter could be found, & probably Rabbits, Sea Fowl & Fish was all the Food the Natives could formerly procure.[4]

"View of Castle Doe in the County of Donnygall, the ancient
Seat of the Mac-Swines."
Thomas Wright, *Observations on . . . Remains of Antiquity in Ireland*, 1746,
Book I, plate IV (Irish copy, 1791), University of Kansas Libraries, MS. D115
Photo by permission of the University of Kansas Libraries

Wright loves picturesque ruins; he describes a castle on the Shannon between Limerick and Killaloe as a "very ornamental ruin to ye Country." A growing romanticism and moralism intrude in his notes on a castle near Mullingar in Westmeath:

> It stands by the side of a large & deep Morass, formerly most of it Water, & from its insolent title *Pass if you Can*, It may be surmised to have once kept much of that Country in some sort of Subjection. There were many such in Ireland, during the Heptarchy of that Nation, & afforded Spencer a fine & large field for his fables in the Fairy Queen, many of which had something like a real foundation to build upon. Tho' I believe the corrupt Morals of Mankind in that age was his principal motive for undertaking so long & laborious a Work.[5]

Wright's archeological interests appear in the second part of his study.[6] Book 2 concerns "Plans, Views &c. &c. Of Some of the most remarkable Forts, and Mounts, as they now appear in Ireland. Formerly choice Stations and strong Holds of the Danes." For example, he devotes seven plates to a study of New Grange tumulus, which he had thoroughly explored (see chap. 3). In Book 3—"Plans, Views, &c. of Several Remarkable Remains of Antiquity in Ireland. Originally Attributed to The Danes & Druids"—he included views of the "Danish Towers" at Antrim and Kells, which he thought had been built as beacons to lead roving bands of hunters to their homes. At the end of this book he included the tower houses in Westmeath, which are similar to Scottish border towers, remarking on their rude simplicity and probable Elizabethan origin.

Wright was led through his scientific interests into a study of ancient and medieval architecture, which, although he did not fully understand it, he at least recorded. He wrote in the preface to his book, "As Opportunity fell in my way I made the Collections of those Remains upon the Spot where I found them, & judging them well worthy of drawing I here present them to ye Publick, & not without Hope they will not prove unpleasing to ye Curious."[7] Such were the beginnings of archeological studies in Ireland. When Wright died in 1789, his library and collection were dispersed. His *Observations on Some of the most Remarkable Remains of Antiquity in Ireland* was acquired by Ralph Allen, and a copy of this manuscript, made in Ireland, eventually came to the University of Kansas. On the flyleaf of the Kansas manuscript is written:

> The late Francis Grose Esq<sup>r</sup>. on his Arrival in this Kingdom (1791) brought over the Original of this Work in

the Handwriting of M[r]. Wright & kindly allowed me the use of it. His Death happening soon after, it lay with me a few months during which time with the help of friends I took an exact Copy especially as to the Drawings, as it will shew that M[r]. Wright was not so neat at the pencil as has been generally supposed— On the Cover of the Book was a Memorandum stating it to be the property of M[r]. Allan of Darlington who purchased it at Mr. Wright's sale— I returned it to M[r]. Gandon.

 M[r]. Gough in his Topography p. 811 says— "M[r]. Wright now settled at Briar's Green near Brancepeth, Durham has in M.S. ready for the press a 'Journey thro' Ireland with Drawings of the Antiquities' & a second Volume of the Louthiana both ready for publishing on proper encouragement. His Collections of his own drawings are innumerable & fine." —Austin Cooper 1791—N.B.—The Drawings of the first Book were made by myself, all the others by Jos[h]. Turner & the Text written by Jos[h] Cooper.— A.C.[8]

The people mentioned in this note were all enthusiastic antiquaries who held responsible positions in government and commerce. Austin Cooper is typical of the dedicated scholar of the time.[9] At age fifteen, in 1774, he began work for the treasury. He was able to study and record ruins throughout the country, because his post as paymaster to civil and military pensioners required that he travel extensively. Through family connections he became deputy constable of Dublin Castle in 1786, and when his uncle retired in 1793, he was promoted to chief clerk of the Treasury Office. He assembled a large collection of books, coins, and drawings, including the library of William Conyngham (president of the Antiquarian Society and treasurer of the Royal Irish Academy), which he purchased at Conyngham's death, as well as his own extensive collection of notebooks and diaries. Cooper's wife, Sarah Turner, was the daughter of Joseph Turner, one of the builders of Merrion Square, where the couple lived. Joseph Turner and Austin's cousin Joseph Cooper must have been fellow enthusiasts, for the three men copied Wright's unpublished volume on Ireland. The effort involved in preserving and circulating books even at the end of the eighteenth century in Dublin reminds us of how determined scholars—whether medieval scribes, eighteenth-century antiquaries, or modern bibliophiles—are to enhance their libraries.

 Appropriately enough, considering the traditional literary distinction of Ireland and the efforts of the antiquaries, libraries were among the first important buildings to be erected in Dublin in the eighteenth century.[10] The library of Archbishop Narcissus Marsh, which was de-

*Marsh's Library in the Nineteenth Century*
Painting by Walter Osborne (1859–1903)
National Gallery of Ireland, Dublin
Photo by courtesy of the National Gallery of Ireland

*Irish History and Culture*

Old Library of Trinity College (lower story enclosed in 1892)
By Thomas Burgh; in foreground: campanile of 1853; flanking the square,
the chapel (1789) and examination hall or theater (1777–1791)
by Sir William Chambers
Photo by Marilyn Stokstad

signed by Sir William Robinson (surveyor general for Ireland from 1661 to 1700), is the oldest public library in Ireland. Marsh built it in the early years of the eighteenth century, beginning about 1702. Although the exterior of the building was refaced in the nineteenth century, the interior, with its locked cubicles for readers and its books arranged in bays by each window, still survives. Today the library typifies the cultural and scholarly aspirations as well as the excellent taste of the eighteenth-century leaders.

Another library—one that is now even more famous—was built for Trinity College in the period 1712–1732 by the second surveyor general, Col. Thomas Burgh, who held that office from 1700 to 1730. Trinity College had been founded by Elizabeth I in 1592 as a center for Protestant education. The library was a severe two-story rectangular building raised over an open arcade, with a central wall to support the great weight of books above. The idea of raising the library up on piers was eminently practical (as recent tragic floods in Italy and the United States have demonstrated), for the books were thus kept free of the damp. The loggia also provided scholars with a sheltered promenade in the wet Irish climate. (Unfortunately, in 1892 the arcade was walled and windowed in.)

The rectangular solidity of the building, which is twenty-seven bays in length, was emphasized by two horizontal bands of windows and a balustraded cornice, but the feeling of mass was relieved by five very slightly projecting bays in the center and three at each end.

The main reading room, which has a double range of tall bookcases alternating with standing desk-bookcases in each window bay, provides an ample and dignified setting for some of the most precious documents of early Christianity in the North: the *Book of Durrow*, the *Book of Kells*, and the *Book of Armagh*. The interior is divided into three parts —staircase hall, long room (200 feet long), and Fagel Library—making Trinity College Library one of the largest single-room libraries still in use. The staircase, by Richard Cassel, with plaster work by Edward Simple, was inserted in 1750.

The two-dimensionality and restraint of early Georgian architecture, as seen in the libraries, continued in Dublin's domestic architecture throughout the century, although in civic architecture new influences became apparent. The Palladianism of Lord Burlington; the influence of Abbé Marc-Antoine Laugier and Piranesi; the travels abroad by Englishmen such as Robert Wood, James Stuart, Nicholas Revett, and Robert Adam (and their resulting publications)—all have been cited as the source of the English Neoclassic style, which was introduced into Ireland by William Chambers and other architects.

William Chambers (1723–1796) specialized in town and country houses for the nobility, but he also designed gateways, stables, and monuments.[11] He preferred a simple Palladian style for houses, which he then decorated on the interior with a restrained, elegant combination of classical motifs—lyres, sphinxes, garlands, and flowing acanthus—in the style of the architects of Louis XV. Chambers went to Ireland at the request of James Caulfeild, first earl of Charlemont in 1759. He designed important buildings in Dublin, including the theater and the chapel for Trinity College, the casino at Marino, and Charlemont House (now the Municipal Gallery of Modern Art).

Meanwhile, the more complex and varied style of Robert Adam (1728–1792) and his brother James (1730–1794) became popular in England.[12] The Adam brothers worked within the Neoclassical tradition, but they created original designs based on motifs drawn from different periods and places. Elements of the "Adam Style," as it became known, were spread throughout the British Isles by means of their books on architecture and decoration.

By 1775 a new generation of architects, less classical than Sir William Chambers and less fanciful than Robert Adam, began to produce a British version of French Neoclassicism. James Gandon (1743–1823) introduced this new style into Ireland.[13] Gandon was an English Huguenot who had studied with Chambers in London. He and a young Irish architect, John Woolfe, captured the attention of the public by continuing Colin Campbell's monumental architectural study, *Vitruvius Britannicus.* They published two more volumes (4 and 5) in 1767 and 1771. In 1769 Gandon was awarded a gold medal for architecture—the first such award made by the Royal Society in London. John Beresford, commissioner for Irish Revenue, convinced him to leave England for Ireland in 1781 to design the new Custom House in Dublin. Working with him as an assistant and draftsman was James Malton (d. 1803), to whom we are indebted for a series of views of the buildings of Dublin at the end of the eighteenth century.

The building of the Custom House produced a wave of ill will and protest among merchants who did not want to leave the old site, which was up the river. The protestors even organized a mob to destroy the work as it progressed, so that for a year Gandon had to live in virtual imprisonment, for security, in order to supervise the work. (A vivid account of building in Dublin and Gandon's difficulties may be found in Maurice Craig's lively and scholarly *Dublin, 1660–1860.*)[14] The building was completed in ten years at a cost of £300,000. Built around two courtyards, the Custom House has façades that are slightly reminiscent of Chambers's work and a dome that is similar to those at Greenwich, outside London.

In 1785 Gandon received another important commission, to incorporate the Public Offices and the courts into a single building. The resulting Four Courts balances the Custom House as a unified and powerful architectural composition farther up the Liffey River. Gandon placed the four courtrooms on the diagonal axes of a square block, and put a circular domed hall in the center. Above this hall he raised a colonnaded drum, sufficiently reminiscent of St. Paul's Cathedral in London for one to expect a dome and lantern; however he crowned the composition with a relatively shallow dome. Gandon's admiration for Sir Christopher Wren is further demonstrated in his principal façade, facing on the river, which is based on the lower part of the west front of St. Paul's.

Gandon, through his later contemporaries and pupils and in his buildings in Dublin and other Irish towns, provided models of good classical design which established a style that lasted into the nineteenth century. The Four Courts and the Custom House were nearly destroyed during the fighting in Dublin in 1921. After considerable debate, in which the buildings were belittled and decried as symbols of the British Ascend-

*Custom House, Dublin*
1781–1791, by James Malton (d. 1803)
Water color
National Gallery of Ireland, Dublin
Photo by courtesy of the National Gallery of Ireland

Custom House, Dublin
1781–1791 (rebuilt after 1921), by James Gandon (1743–1824)
Photo by Marilyn Stokstad

*Irish History and Culture*

Four Courts, Dublin
1785–1796 (rebuilt after 1921), by James Gandon (1743–1824)
Photo by Henry Snyder

ancy, Gandon's masterpieces were rebuilt and restored (perhaps not only because of their excellence but because their critics could neither define "Irish" architecture nor design an "Irish" building).

Gandon became the most important architect in Dublin during the period of independence of the Irish Parliament. His buildings have become synonymous with Dublin, since their domes dominated the waterfront of the Liffey: the Four Courts (built 1786–96, burned in 1921, and then rebuilt), the Custom House (designed and built 1781–1791, burned in 1921, and rebuilt), the Rotunda Hospital (finished by Gandon), the eastern façade of the Parliament (designed in 1785, built later), and Old Carlisle Bridge (destroyed, but copied in O'Connell Bridge). While one hesitates to overemphasize political or social explanations for a style, Gandon's exceptionally fine designs, which were enlivened with excellent sculpture by Smyth, seem to provide a visual equivalent for the aspirations of the Irish political leaders. Through his use of domes and porticoes, excellent proportions, restrained moldings, pediments and balustraded cornices, and through his balance of rustication and refinement, he gave the civic architecture of Dublin a mature grace and grandeur which were also being sought in the United States and France to express similar ideals of political freedom and human dignity.[15]

In a portrait by Tilly Kettle, Gandon is represented seated beside a balustrade behind which is a sweeping view of Dublin with great buildings: the Four Courts, the Rotunda Hospital, and the Custom House. He holds a sheaf of plans, the uppermost of which is a version of the Four Courts. Gandon appears in the painting as the genial, attractive man described by his biographers. In the portrait, only the head and composition are by Kettle, who was in Dublin briefly about 1783, two years before the Four Courts was commissioned. The architectural background (and on the basis of style one may say the rest of the painting) are by a second, an inferior, artist, probably William Cuming (1769–1852), who was a friend of Gandon's. The painting demonstrates the level of competence to be expected in a provincial capital, where itinerant painters were common. The collaboration of a professional artist and an amateur in the portrait of Gandon produced better than average results.[16] Such works, which are largely overlooked in the study of the history of art, often illustrate the general level of sophistication of a society better than do the acknowledged masterpieces of the period.

Dublin's appearance as a graceful and gracious Georgian city was determined not only by public buildings, such as those designed by James Gandon, but also by careful city planning and by the high quality of private building. A Wide Streets Commission was appointed in 1757, and for the rest of the century the commissioners devoted themselves to the systematic development of the city. The commissioners laid out avenues (the first was Parliament Street) and squares which survive today. Advised by Gandon, they developed an ideal of spaciousness and logical design which makes the center of Dublin a showcase for eighteenth-century city planning.

Many young sculptors were employed as craftsmen in the extensive building and rebuilding of Dublin and other Irish cities during the prosperous eighteenth century. The Royal Dublin Society, which was founded in 1731 and incorporated in 1750 "for improving Husbandry, Manufactures and other Useful Arts," offered free classes in art to students of both sexes in order to prepare them to enter the craft guilds or, since the guilds were open only to Protestants, to enable them to work for master craftsmen. Instruction in ornament, figure, and architectural drawing began in 1742; and since then over ten thousand students have attended the school.[17] With both training and employment available, many Irish art students became sculptors, although most of them worked as draftsmen and carvers of woodwork and plaster for the elaborate interior finishes preferred in Ireland. The Irish contribution to the design and production of fine furniture, silver, and glass is also well known; however, less attention has been paid to individual sculptors.

*James Gandon*, 1783
By Tilly Kettle and William Cuming
49″ x 38½″
National Gallery of Ireland, Dublin
Photo by courtesy of the National Gallery of Ireland

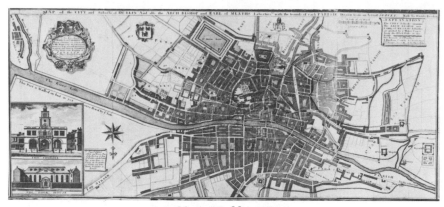

*Map of Dublin,* 1728
J. Bowles after Charles Brooking, 23¼″ x 56⅓″
National Gallery of Ireland, Dublin
Photo by courtesy of the National Gallery of Ireland

*Trinity College, Dublin*
1790–1791
Water color by James Malton (d. 1803)
National Gallery of Ireland, Dublin
Photo by courtesy of the National Gallery of Ireland

Edward Smyth (1749–1812) may well be Ireland's finest eighteenth-century sculptor; his best work is equal to the finest sculpture in the British Isles. Smyth began his career as a simple carver of architectural ornaments for the builder Henry Darley, who in turn worked for James Gandon. As an architectural sculptor, who was responsible for the sculpture on most of Gandon's buildings, Smyth suffers from both overexposure and anonymity. Sculpture on public buildings can become so familiar that it is simply no longer noticed by the public. This is true of the personifications of the rivers of Ireland that are carved on the keystones of the ground-floor windows of Gandon's Custom House in Dublin. They are masterpieces of eighteenth-century Irish sculpture which have only recently received the attention they deserve.[18]

The sculptural program for the Custom House included a series of fourteen personified rivers of Ireland on the keystones of windows, the Arms of the Kingdom on each of the four corners of the building, the "Friendship of Britannia and Hibernia" in the pediment, and the personification of Commerce on the dome. The personifications of the rivers

*The River Boyne*
By Edward Smyth (1749–1812)
On the Custom House, Dublin, 1781–1791
Photo by Marilyn Stokstad

Bann and Boyne are truly monumental, conceived in terms of light and shade and yet fully sculptural, capable of dominating the high recesses into which the windows are set. Smyth created a lively personality, with sparkle and wit, in his personification of the Bann, and a meditative, tragic personality, appropriate to its role and connotations in later Irish history, in the river Boyne.

All the sculpture by Smyth survived the fire of 25–30 May 1921, except that on the south portico. Even the figure of Commerce—which rested on the intersecting diagonal arches that carried the wooden dome —though badly damaged, could be replaced on the rebuilt dome when the building was restored in 1922.

Not all Irish architecture of interest is located in Dublin. The style perpetuated by Gandon's pupils can be seen on large estates throughout Ireland. As many former absentee politicians and landlords began to spend more of their time and money in Ireland, the smaller cities and country estates, as well as the capital, prospered. Owners of estates

*The River Boyne*, Detail
By Edward Smyth (1749–1812)
On the Custom House, Dublin, 1781–1791
Photo by permission of the Commissioners of Public Works in Ireland

seemed to attempt to outdo each other in the building or rebuilding of their houses during the second half of the eighteenth and the early part of the nineteenth century. One of the most attractive aspects of Irish architecture is that the eighteenth-century standards of taste, design, and craftsmanship survived well into the nineteenth century.

Simple houses are rarely recorded, and are easily and often destroyed. Thus the study of vernacular architecture of a period is one of the most frustrating—and yet rewarding—tasks of the architectural historian. Such houses (as opposed to simple shelters which hardly deserve the term "architecture") help the cultural and social historian to visualize the life of the people more accurately than do the great mansions and civic or religious buildings which, while they may express the most advanced and brilliant conceptions of the period, are less indicative of the life of a people.

A simplified version of the pervasive Neoclassic style appears on a modest scale in Coole Glebe, county Antrim, drawings of which survive

Dwyer-McAllister Cottage
Eighteenth century; Derrynamuck, county Wicklow
Photo by permission of the Commissioners of Public Works in Ireland

in a commonplace book by "Anne," which is now in the University of Kansas Library.[19] This book contains a whimsical collection of poetry (some copies, some originals), sketches, watercolors, and essays. On leaf 34[r] Anne drew the façade of her home, Coole Glebe, parish of Coole, and below it the ground plan. Nicholas Carlisle, writing in 1810, specifically states that the church at Coole was in good repair but that there was "no glebe house,"[20] while Samuel Lewis in 1850 states: "The glebe house is a handsome building, erected by aid of a gift of £300 and a loan of £500 from the Board of First Fruits in 1814."[21]

Anne's home must be the 1814 house. Its style falls into the period of the Regency in England, a period in which the Neoclassicism of the late eighteenth century still survived in modified form. A few differences are noteworthy: for example, builders preferred brown and yellow to red brick, and they used stucco with increasing frequency as an exterior finish. (The popularity of stucco coincided with the rising costs and scarcity of building materials during the Napoleonic Wars.) Architectural decoration was also often reduced to the area around the entrance.[22]

At Coole Glebe, the eighteenth-century traditions survive in a simplified form. The watercolor rendering suggests that the house was faced with yellow brick, or perhaps stucco in accordance with Regency taste. The façade is clearly divided into five parts: a center section of two stories marked by a stringcourse, and two sides and end-sections of only one story. The central body of the house has a pitched roof and two chimneys, with three windows in the second story and two rectangular windows on either side of a door in the first story. The doorway is accented by engaged columns on either side of the door and by a fanlight above. At each side there is a single-story wing which is one-half the width of the center section and has a flat roof and one round-headed window. The end pavilions are narrower in width but deeper than the connecting wings. Although they have only one story, they are crowned by pediments; and each has one rectangular window, a chimney, and a pitched roof which runs at right angles to the façade. The windows are placed symmetrically across the façade, but the design is slightly varied by the use of round-headed windows in the wings. The windows have the usual Georgian glazing bars. The door, with its columns (as seen in the plan) and fanlight, is the focal point of the spare architectural decoration on Coole Glebe. This entry treatment was popularized by the Adam brothers, and was used widely in the eighteenth and early nineteenth centuries.

Factors other than the general simplification of the Neoclassical style may have contributed to the simplicity of design. (Anne may have omitted some details.) A utilitarian design was easier for local country craftsmen to build; it was also suitable for limited financial resources. The house cost 800 pounds at a time when in England "all country gentlemen of any note" were said to have 3,000 to 4,000 pounds a year.[23]

On the plan, Anne gives the dimensions and use of each room. The two-story center section contains the formal living rooms of the house—flanking the entrance hall, the drawing room and parlor (both 15 feet by 18 feet); behind the parlor an unidentified room that must be the dining room (10 by 18 feet); and behind the drawing room the stair hall, store room, and butler's pantry. On the second floor are four bedrooms (two of which are 15 by 18 feet; one, 10 by 18 feet; and one, 12 by 10 feet) and "Papa's closet." The wing to the left has a dairy, a scullery and a passage that leads to the kitchen (15 feet by 14 feet 6 inches), a back kitchen, and a cellar. On the right the wing is not connected to the house with a door; it has the coach house and cart house (opening to the back yard), a stable with three stalls, and behind it the cow house with an area marked off as a henhouse.

Authors of books of plans and instructions for the design of small houses extol the virtues and demonstrate the logic of a plan like that for Coole Glebe. Isaac Ware wrote in 1756:

> The plan may be so made that . . . it may appear much more considerable to the eye. The barn may now be a detached building . . . and the stables and cart house, answered by the cow-houses and calf-house, separated from the principal building only by a gate on each side, may stand as two wings; which, with very little decoration from a judicious builder, will have a very pretty effect. . . . Under the direction of a skillful architect the barns, stables and cow houses will rise like so many pavilions; and the very sheds will assist the design. In this manner every part

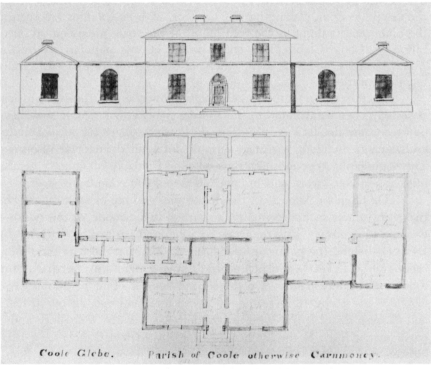

Plan and Elevation of Coole Glebe (1812)
From a commonplace book labeled *Anne*, about 1832
Coole Glebe, Carnmoney, near Belfast, county Antrim
University of Kansas Libraries, MS. C197
Photo by permission of the University of Kansas Libraries

will join; and nothing will obstruct the intention of mixing utility with great elegance.[24]

A gentleman (a Mr. Paine?) writing in Dublin in 1757 made further useful observations on the design of farmhouses in his book *Twelve Designs of Country-Houses of 2, 3, and 4 Rooms on a Floor proper for Glebes and Small Estates with Some Observations on the common Errors in Building.* Of his eighth design he wrote:

> The frugal Rule of collecting all Conveniences under one Roof may hold good in Towns where Ground for Building is set by the Foot at a high Price: But in the Country where there is Room enough, and Materials reasonable, no Inconvenience, but rather to the contrary, will attend to dispensing with that Rule. For it is impossible to have a Kitchen within a small House, without being annoyed at certain Times by offensive smells arising from thence: and the Evil is increased by the Negligence or Laziness of Servants who are apt to suffer dirty Water or other Nusance to lie some Hours longer than is needfull: but this Mischief is quite prevented by putting the Kitchen out of Doors. In this Plan [#8] there is nothing underground but two Vaults for Cellars. The Kitchen makes the right Wing, between which and the House there ought to be a Door, so contrived as to shut itself; and for Regularity a good Room is added to the other End, and makes the left Wing; so that the Whole hath the Apearance of something grand, tho' every Part is contained under a single Roof.[25]

Coole Glebe and the architectural advice of Isaac Ware and Mr. Paine give today's student a more realistic view of life in Ireland than would a study of the great estates of the landed nobility. The simple details, the harmonious proportions, and the utilitarian plans suggest the heritage of intellectual discipline and the ideal of gracious living that existed for some of the Irish in the eighteenth and early nineteenth centuries.

## NOTES

1. Eileen Harris, "The Architecture of Thomas Wright," *Country Life*, 26 August, 2 and 9 September 1971: "The Wizard of Durham," pp. 492–95; "A Flair for the Grandiose," pp. 546–50; "Architect of Rococo Landscapes," pp. 612–15.
2. Ralph Allan's biography of Wright is found in *Gentleman's Magazine*, January

1793, pp. 8–12; February 1793, pp. 126–27; March 1793, pp. 215–16. This quotation is in the February installment.

3. Thomas Wright, *Observations on Some of the most Remarkable Remains of Antiquity in Ireland. Represented in upwards of Sixty Views, & Plans, Taken in a Tour through that Kingdom, in the Year 1746*, B.M. Add MS. 33,771 (entered the British Museum as Gr. XLIX in 1847); Spencer Research Library, University of Kansas, MS. D115.

4. Wright, *Observations*, bk. 1, pl. 4, notes.

5. Ibid., bk. 2, pl. 20, notes.

6. Ibid., bks. 2 and 3, title pages.

7. Ibid., Preface.

8. University of Kansas, MS. D115, inscription on flyleaf.

9. Austin Cooper, *An Eighteenth Century Antiquary: The Sketches, Notes and Diaries of Austin Cooper (1759–1830)*, ed. Liam Price (Dublin: J. Falconer, 1942).

10. For Irish architecture and art in the eighteenth century see: Bruce Arnold, *A Concise History of Irish Art* (London: Thames & Hudson, and New York: Praeger, 1968); Maurice J. Craig, *Dublin, 1660–1860* (New York: Coward-McCann, 1952); Georgian Society, *The Georgian Society Records of Eighteenth-century Domestic Architecture and Decoration in Dublin* (5 vols.; Dublin: Dublin University Press, for the Georgian Society, 1909–1913); John H. Harvey, *Dublin: A Study in Environment* (London and New York: Batsford, 1949); John Jay Ide, *Some Examples of Irish Country Houses of the Georgian Period* (New York: n.p., 1959); Constantia E. Maxwell, *Dublin under the Georges, 1714–1830* (London: G. G. Harrap & Co., 1936), and *A History of Trinity College, Dublin, 1591–1892* (Dublin: The University Press, Trinity College, 1946); Royal Institute of British Architects, *An Introduction to Dublin Architecture* (London, 1952); John N. Summerson, *Architecture in Britain, 1530–1830* (5th ed.; Harmondworth, Eng., and Baltimore, Md.: Penguin, 1970); Denys Sutton, ed., *Apollo*, vol. 84, no. 56 (October 1966); Henry Wheeler, *Irish Architecture of the Georgian Period* (exhibition catalogue; Washington, D.C., 1960–1961); Maurice Craig and the Knight of Glin, *Irish Architectural Drawings* (exhibition catalogue; London, 1965).

11. Sir William Chambers, *A Treatise on the Decorative Part of Civil Architecture*, ed. Joseph Gwilt (London: Priestley & Weale, 1825), with a biography by T. Hardwick; H. M. Martienssen, "Sir William Chambers" (diss., London, 1949); Summerson, *Architecture in Britain*, chap. 26.

12. A. T. Bolton, *The Architecture of Robert and James Adam (1785–1794)* (2 vols.; London: Country Life, and New York: C. Scribner's Sons, 1922); John Fleming, *Robert Adam and His Circle* (London: J. Murray, 1962); James Lees-Milne, *The Age of Adam* (London and New York: Batsford, 1947); Damie Stillman, *The Decorative Work of Robert Adam* (London: Tiranti, 1966); Summerson, *Architecture in Britain*, chaps. 25 and 26.

13. Arnold, *A Concise History of Irish Art*, chap. 4; James Gandon, Jr., *The Life of James Gandon, Architect*, ed. Thomas J. Mulvany (Dublin, 1846); C. P. Curran, "Cooley, Gandon and the Four Courts," *Journal of the Royal Society of Antiquaries of Ireland* 79:20–25 (1949); Summerson, *Architecture in Britain*, chap. 27.

14. Craig, *Dublin, 1660–1860* (see note 10).

15. Maurice Craig and the Knight of Glin, *Ireland Observed* (Cork, Ire.: Mercier Press, 1970) suggest that Leinster House, 1745, inspired the design of the White House in Washington, D.C.

16. Anne Crookshank and the Knight of Glin, *Irish Portraits, 1660–1860* (London: Paul Mellon Foundation for British Art, 1969, cat. no. 96); Michael Wynne,

"Tilly Kettle's Last Painting?" *Burlington Magazine* 109:532–33 (September 1967).

17. Anne Crookshank, "Irish Sculptors from 1750 to 1860," *Apollo* 84:306–13 (October 1966), see footnote 2, p. 312.
18. See Arnold, *A Concise History of Irish Art*; Craig, *Dublin, 1660–1860*; Crookshank, *Irish Portraits*; and Harvey, *Dublin*.
19. *Anne*, MS. C 197, O'Hegarty Collection, Spencer Research Library, University of Kansas. The manuscript is a part of the O'Hegarty Collection, purchased by the University of Kansas in 1959. P. S. O'Hegarty was secretary of the Irish government post office, and manager of the Irish Book Shop in Dawson Street, and was himself a writer and editor. *Anne* has been studied by Linda Gill; the results of her investigations are published here.
20. Nicholas Carlisle, *A Topographical Dictionary of Ireland*, 1st ed., vol. 6 (London: W. Savage for W. Miller, 1810).
21. Samuel Lewis, *Topographical Dictionary of Ireland*, 2d ed., vol. 1 (A–J) (London: S. Lewis, 1849), p. 256.
22. Clifford Musgrave, *The Late Georgian Period* (London, 1959), p. 29.
23. Ibid., p. 24.
24. Isaac Ware, *A Complete Body of Architecture* (London: J. Osborne & J. Shipton, 1756), pp. 351, 353.
25. "A Gentleman" (Mr. James Paine?), *Twelve Designs of Country-houses of 2, 3, and 4 Rooms on a Floor proper for Glebes and Small Estates with Some Observations on the common Errors in Building* (Dublin, 1757), no. 8.

## SUGGESTIONS FOR FURTHER READING

Arnold, Bruce. *A Concise History of Irish Art*. London: Thames & Hudson, and New York: Praeger, 1968.
Craig, Maurice. *Dublin, 1660–1860*. New York: Coward-McCann, 1952.
Crookshank, Anne, and the Knight of Glin. *Irish Portraits, 1660–1860*. London: Paul Mellon Foundation for British Art, 1969.
Harvey, John H. *Dublin: A Study in Environment*. London and New York: Batsford, 1949.
Ide, John Jay. *Some Examples of Irish Country Houses of the Georgian Period*. New York: n.p., 1959.
Maxwell, Constantia E. *Dublin under the Georges, 1714–1830*. London: G. G. Harrap & Co., 1936.
Summerson, John N. *Architecture in Britain, 1530–1830*. 5th ed. Harmondsworth, Eng., and Baltimore, Md.: Penguin, 1970.
Sutton, Denys, ed. *Apollo*, October 1966: "The Arts in Ireland."

# THE DYNAMICS OF POPULATION

## *Kenneth C. W. Kammeyer*

$\mathcal{S}$ir William Petty, in his seventeenth-century treatise *The Political Anatomy of Ireland*, offered an unusual demographic solution for what was even then considered "the Irish problem."[1] If his proposal had been carried out, it would very likely have changed much of the history of Ireland, including the political events that are going on in that country this very day. Petty proposed to bring to Ireland an additional two hundred thousand English settlers, a number that would have increased the total number of English in Ireland to about one-half million. Then he suggested taking twenty thousand unmarried Irish women to England, where they would be married off, one in every English parish. At the same time, twenty thousand English women would be brought to Ireland, where they would be married to Irishmen. In Petty's words:

> There are among the 600 thousand above mentioned of the poor Irish, not above 20 thousand of unmarried marriagable Women; . . . Wherefore if ½ of the said Women were in one year, and ½ in the next transported into England, and disposed of one in each Parish, and as many English brought back and married to the Irish, . . . the whole Work

of natural transmutation and Union would in 4 or 5 years be accomplished.

The charge of making the exchange would not be £20,000 per Ann. which is about 6 weeks Pay of the present or late Armies in Ireland.[2]

Petty further proposed that "if the Irish must have priests," the number should be brought down to one thousand, who should be English priests:

> So that when the Priests, who govern the Conscience, and the Women, who influence other powerful Appetites, shall be English, both of Whom being in the Bosom of the Men, it must be, that no massacring of English, as heretofore, can happen again. Moreover when the language of the Children shall be English, and the whole Oeconomy of the Family English, viz. Diet, Apparel, etc. the transmutation will be very easy and quick.[3]

Petty reasoned that this human-exchange program would successfully obliterate the Irish way of life, and would substitute for it the culture, life style, and interests of the English. Apparently the logistical and human problems of this exchange were never solved, but one can imagine how great the impact of such a plan might have been had it been executed. If, with the importation of two hundred thousand English settlers, the number of English in the Irish population had reached one-half million in the seventeenth century, they would have constituted about one-fourth of the total population. While still a numerical minority, an English population that large, with its political and economic advantages, would have had important consequences for the relations between England and Ireland. But the second of Petty's prescriptions, the exchange of brides, with the great impact it would have had on communications and travel between the two countries, could have produced even greater changes. Imagine how great the consequences would have been if Petty's interisland marriage plan had been implemented—if twenty thousand English parishes had had their personal emissaries in Ireland, and each parish in return had had its resident Irish bride. Once the marital pathways between the two countries had been opened, there is no telling how many younger sisters, cousins, and nieces, or, for that matter, brothers, might have followed after. Surely the populations, the cultures, and the political relations between the two states would have evolved and developed much differently if this bold plan of Sir William's had been carried out.

But the fanciful conjectures of what might have been are indulgences that may as well be forsaken early, for the actual events and developments of the Irish population are difficult enough to sort out, verify, and explain. In this chapter we will direct our attention to an understanding of the demographic experiences of the people of Ireland. We will focus on the events and patterns in the history of the Irish family and economy that have shaped the population in modern times.

The family and the economic systems of a country always determine in large part what happens to the dynamics of its population. It is the interplay between these two primary institutional systems that will produce the births, the deaths, and the migration of people into and out of a country. This basic axiom has been validated in many societies and for many populations, but in no country is the case more vividly shown than in Ireland, especially during the last two centuries. To understand the Irish demographic experience of this period, we must examine the details of her economy and her family system. These details make a very interesting story, because the Irish demographic experience has been both dramatic and unusual. Indeed, some writers have found the population dynamics of Ireland so unusual that they have characterized them as unique. Such a characterization is too strong, for while the history of the Irish population has often been extraordinary, even extreme, it is nevertheless usually consistent with the experiences of other European and Western countries. This essay will show the unusual and extreme characteristics of Irish demography, but it will also demonstrate how the behavior of the Irish people has been quite consistent with some well established patterns found in other Western societies.

The story of the Irish population at some stages becomes very complicated, for, as is so often the case, demographic events are produced by a number of forces that operate simultaneously. Sometimes these different forces act to produce similar effects, but at other times the effects are countervailing. When the latter occurs, it is nearly impossible to comprehend all the forces and their interacting influences simultaneously. All we can do in such cases is to consider the factors serially, noting whenever possible the interrelations that exist among them.

As we examine the dynamics of the growth and decline of the Irish population through the last two centuries, we will have a number of opportunities to look at some of the distinctive and fascinating features of Irish life. We shall try to take full advantage of these opportunities to examine the lives of the people who produced the population. The study of demography need not be limited to a single-minded devotion to facts, figures, rates, graphs, and charts. While occasionally these excursions into the nondemographic features of Irish life may take us temporarily away from the central concerns of this essay, we may hope that these will be interesting, even pleasant, distractions.

It is not possible to make trustworthy estimates of the size of the population of Ireland prior to the seventeenth century. As has been described in chapter 2, the groups that peopled Ireland consisted of invaders from the European continent and the Scandinavian countries, who often came via England. They were, in order, the Celts, the Gaels (coming in the first century B.C. from Gaul), the Norse (in the ninth century A.D.), and finally the Normans (in the twelfth century). The exact numbers of people that these major invasions added to the population are lost in the mists of Irish history. As is usually the case in historiography, the chronicles of political and military events have been kept much better than the demographic facts or social conditions that characterized the lives of the people.

What we know about the Irish population of the seventeenth century we owe to the fortuitous circumstance that one of the outstanding scholars of the seventeenth century, the previously mentioned Sir William Petty, was sent to Ireland in 1652 as physician to the army of the Commonwealth. Petty, a man of many accomplishments, was one of a group of seventeenth-century scholars who labeled themselves the "political arithmeticians." The political arithmeticians were greatly influenced by the advent of the scientific age. They became the first scholars to use the scientific method to establish facts and generalizations about human behavior, especially at the demographic level.

In addition, and not without importance, the political arithmeticians saw as one of their objectives the task of measuring and reporting the resources of the state or the crown. These resources included the land, the capital, and the populations of both the home country and its provinces.

An example of the way in which people were viewed as economic resources may be seen in Petty's *The Political Anatomy of Ireland* (1691). In one section of his book, Petty was attempting to assess what had been the costs of an Irish rebellion of some years earlier. In his calculations he included the worth of the people who had been lost. His method of calculation also revealed the relative worth that he attached to Irishmen, as compared to Englishmen and members of other races:

> The value of people, Men Women and Children in England, some have computed to be £70 per Head, one with another. But if you value the people who have been destroyed in Ireland, as Slaves and Negroes are usually rated, viz. at about £15 one with another; Men being sold for

Vernacular Architecture
Gap of Dunloe, Killarney, county Kerry
Photo by Harold Orel

£25 and Children for £5 each; the value of the people lost as a result of the rebellion will be about £10,355,000.[4]

In keeping with the tasks of the political arithmeticians, Petty, when he came to his post in Ireland, made a "survey" of the country. He followed his first survey with several subsequent estimates of the Irish population in the seventeenth century.

While Petty's population estimates were accepted for many years, a recent reassessment of his figures has revealed that one of the important elements that he used in making his population calculations may have been seriously in error.[5] Since no censuses of the Irish population were taken before the nineteenth century, the population estimates that he made had to be based on other data. The so-called hearth tax provided such information. The hearth tax was introduced in Ireland in 1662. It was a tax of two shillings per year on all chimneys, stoves, and hearths.[6] Petty, as well as later scholars, typically estimated the precensus populations by multiplying the number of houses (as indicated by hearths) times the estimated average number of persons per house. While Petty's estimate of five or six people per house was probably approximately correct, there is now a good deal of evidence that he, and those who followed him, greatly underestimated the number of houses that the tax collectors missed or neglected to report. The number of houses missed was quite great, because, as we might expect, the people of Ireland were not eager to be found by the collector of the hearth tax and therefore took steps to elude him. In many rural areas, especially in western Ireland, there were often homes that could not be easily discovered by strangers, or if discovered, might not be thought of as places where people would live. These were often tiny hovels, made of sod and stone, that blended perfectly with the rocky terrain and were therefore overlooked. In some cases the tax collectors exacted the tax money from a home, but did not bother to report it, since this allowed them to keep for themselves the money they had collected. This fraudulent behavior, plus a simple lack of diligence and persistence on the part of some of the tax collectors, probably made the number of houses reported far less than the actual number. One other factor that contributed to underenumeration was the inconsistency of recording the houses that were exempt from the hearth tax. The exempt houses were those whose residents were not able to make their living by working and those occupied by widows who were living in houses that fell below certain property-value qualifications. Some collectors faithfully recorded the exempt houses, while others failed to do so, again contributing to an undercount of the total number of houses.[7]

How much this undercount of the houses led to an underestimate of the population will probably never be known, but it can be said with certainty that estimates based on the hearth tax were too low. Petty's estimate of the total population of Ireland in the late seventeenth century was from 1.1 to 1.3 million people. When adjustments have been made for the presumed undercount of houses, the revised estimate would be that the number of people exceeded two million in the late 1600s. Table 1 shows that there were an estimated 2,167,000 people in 1687.[8] While Petty's population estimates were probably wrong, they did provide the early figures and enough additional information for present-day scholars to be able to make the best possible estimates of the population size in the seventeenth century.

Table 1 goes on to present the population estimates for Ireland from the seventeenth century up to the 1841 census, the last census before the Famine of 1846. The 1841 enumeration of the Irish population recorded the largest number of people ever in the thirty-two counties of Ireland, or what is now the Republic of Ireland plus Northern Ireland.

From table 1 it can be seen that in the sixty-five years between 1777 and 1841 the Irish population more than doubled. The period between 1777 and 1791 was a time of especially rapid population growth in Ireland. The last column of table 1 presents the estimated rate of growth for this fourteen-year period as 19.4 percent per decade. (The averages have been calculated on a ten-year basis because the seven-

TABLE 1
IRELAND'S ESTIMATED POPULATION SIZE FROM THE SEVENTEENTH CENTURY TO THE
CENSUS OF 1841

| Year | Population Size, in Thousands | Growth, in Thousands | Number of Years | Percentage Growth, Total | Number of Ten-Year Intervals | Percentage Growth per Ten-Year Interval |
|------|------|------|------|------|------|------|
| 1687 | 2,167 | | | | | |
| 1712 | 2,791 | 624 | 25 | 28.8 | 2.5 | 11.5 |
| 1725 | 3,042 | 251 | 13 | 9.0 | 1.3 | 6.9 |
| 1754 | 3,191 | 149 | 29 | 4.9 | 2.9 | 1.7 |
| 1777 | 3,740 | 549 | 23 | 17.2 | 2.3 | 7.5 |
| 1791 | 4,753 | 1,013 | 14 | 27.1 | 1.4 | 19.4 |
| 1821 | 6,802 | 2,049 | 30 | 43.1 | 3.0 | 14.4 |
| 1831 | 7,767 | 965 | 10 | 14.2 | 1.0 | 14.2 |
| 1841 | 8,175 | 408 | 10 | 5.3 | 1.0 | 5.3 |

Source:  Kenneth H. Connell, *The Population of Ireland, 1750–1845* (Oxford: Clarendon Press, 1950), p. 25.

teenth- and eighteenth-century population estimates are available for irregular intervals of time. The ten-year averages allow comparisons of growth rates to be made with greater ease.)

While there was an increase of four million people in the Irish population between 1777 and 1841, even that figure does not reveal the full extent of the growth rate. During those same years there was an out-migration of one and three-quarters million people, primarily to England and to North America.[9] This latter fact is of some interest, because the assumption is sometimes made that emigration from Ireland started only in response to the Famine of 1846. In fact, a substantial emigration had begun much earlier. Even the beginnings of mass emigration date back to a partial potato failure in the fall of 1816, which led to food shortages in 1817. This, combined with a typhus epidemic, started a migration of many poor people, which increased during the food shortage of 1822.[10]

There are several possible explanations for why the Irish population grew so rapidly in the last quarter of the eighteenth century. The explanations cover a range of possibilities that are often considered in demographic analyses. But, as is often the case, individual historians have selected and supported differing and competing explanations. In order to evaluate these competing explanations we must begin by understanding that in any case of population growth, if we discount in-migration, there is only one basic demographic relationship that can produce an increase in the population: the number of births must exceed the number of deaths. Since the Irish had no substantial in-migration during the late eighteenth century, they must have had a birth rate that was higher than

*The Dynamics of Population*

their death rate. But this answer only leads to the further question of whether the birth rate or the death rate changed to bring about an excess of births over deaths. Finally there is the question of *why* one or the other of the rates, or both, changed.

The following are some of the possible reasons that have been offered to explain the high rate of growth in Ireland during the last part of the eighteenth century: (1) An earlier age at marriage, beginning in the 1780s, which presumably resulted in an increased birth rate;[11] (2) an increasing biological capacity for reproduction (called fecundity; this is a physiological explanation for increases in the birth rate or fertility);[12] (3) a decline in mortality, beginning about 1870.[13]

The first of these explanations (an earlier age at marriage) has as its major proponent the historical demographer K. H. Connell. He has argued cogently that a decline in the age at marriage during the last decades of the eighteenth century caused an increase in the birth rate. Connell used an economic argument to buttress his position that earlier marriage caused increased fertility, and thus was the reason for an increasing population in Ireland between 1777 and 1841. The principal element in his argument was built around the matter of peasants passing land on to their children. Marriage, for rural youngsters then, as now, generally had to be deferred until the young couple could find a farm, "until the couple intending to marry could find the holding on which their cabin might be put up and on which their potatoes might be grown."[14] Connell argued that such land was usually available to Irish youngsters of the late eighteenth century. That is, enough land was available so that they could raise enough potatoes for an adequate diet. The potato, as we shall see, has played a crucial role in the history of Ireland, especially in its demographic history.

It happened that in the eighteenth century both rural tenants and their landlords found it desirable and expedient to split existing farms into parts, thus making new farms available to the sons who wanted to marry. Not only were the farmers giving portions of their existing farms to their sons, but they were also often able to reclaim waste lands and hillsides to make tiny new farms. The tenant farmers were willing to do this because it allowed them to pass a piece of land on to each son (or most of their sons). With the potato as a food crop the possibility of producing adequate food on a small plot of land became feasible. Raising potatoes required very little ground, and it did not have to be particularly rich ground. As Langer has put it, "Young people rented an acre or less for a potato patch. On the strength of this they married young and had large families."[15]

The landlords, for their part, also found it desirable to split up the farms, because doing so promised to increase their rents and profits. The English population needed new food supplies at that time, so Irish corn and oats had suddenly become valuable cash crops. Especially was this the case after the passage of the Corn Laws, which allowed a special premium for Irish grain. The Irish farmers were not equipped to produce these kinds of crops on a large scale because of the preponderance of hand labor, but each farmer could produce grains on a small piece of land. The landlord therefore approved of splitting the farms into smaller and smaller units so that the profitable grains could be grown. Each peasant's farm was composed of two segments, one producing the rent crops, the other providing the potatoes for his family's subsistence.

This combination of circumstances worked to make the desires of the Irish farmers and their landlords compatible. Both were willing to divide the land into smaller and smaller units. The process of fragmentation, which was augmented by reclamation, continued to make new farms available for the young. Under these circumstances the peasant youngsters could marry very early. Without the use of any birth control within marriage, the *probable* result of these earlier marriages was an increase in the birth rate.

The two major alternative explanations for the population growth in Ireland in the late eighteenth century emphasize, first, the possible changes in Irish fecundity (the physiological capacity to reproduce) and, second, the possible decline of Irish mortality. In both arguments the potato again plays an important role. There were two surprising things about the potato diet of the Irish people: one was its quantity; the other its nutritional value. We have enough evidence to know with certainty that the average Irishman ate an extraordinary amount of potatoes when they were in abundant supply. The daily amount for an average man was from *ten to twelve pounds*. Presumably women and children ate somewhat less, but by modern-day standards these are prodigious amounts. The ten to twelve pounds consumed daily by a man, which were supplemented by a pint of milk, provided about 3,800 calories per day. But most importantly, this simple unvaried diet alone provided over 90 percent of the daily minimum protein requirement and an abundance of almost all minerals and vitamins (vitamin G is said to have been one exception, with a deficiency of 11 percent).[16]

The potato was introduced into Ireland about A.D. 1600. Salaman reports that by the end of the seventeenth century it had been generally adopted by the Irish peasantry, and by the end of the eighteenth century the common man was eating little else.[17] Since a diet of potatoes, plus a little milk, was such a healthy diet, it is possible that substantial improvements in the general health of the Irish population had been made by the end of the eighteenth century. Such improvements in health might have increased their biological capacity for reproduction, on the one hand, and their ability to resist death, on the other. Increasing fecundity would have raised the birth rate; whereas living longer would have reduced the death rate. The combined effect of these trends would have increased the size of the population.

Between these two latter possibilities, a decline in the death rate was probably the more influential factor in increasing population growth. In many countries of Western Europe during this time, the mortality rate began to move down appreciably, even with modest improvements in living conditions. Since Ireland was subjected to some of the same forces as other European countries, its population probably responded similarly.

To summarize what has been considered thus far: the Irish population started to grow very rapidly in the eighteenth century, in large part because of the introduction and acceptance of the potato as the staple of the Irish diet. The potato allowed the size of subsistence farms to be ever smaller, thus making it increasingly possible for the young rural folk of Ireland to marry. This was accomplished by splitting existing farms into ever smaller parcels, a practice that landlords condoned because it resulted in more economic profits for them. The potato was eaten in great quantities; thus the Irish population had a nutritionally adequate diet, which may have increased the reproductive capacity of the population between 1780 and 1845.

As table 1 shows, the Irish population was larger with each count through the census of 1841, at which time the Irish population exceeded eight million people. All estimates indicate that the population continued to grow until the middle of the 1840s, when it may have reached more than eight and one-half million, its greatest size either before or since that time.

But in the fall of 1845 the potato crop of Ireland was almost totally ruined by the potato blight. With the loss of this mainstay of the Irish diet, there was a winter of hunger. This was followed in the next winter by starvation, famine, and death when the potato crop of 1846 also failed. This famine, with its great loss of life and its terrible misery, produced a grim turning point in Irish history. It, more than any single event, led to a series of changes in the economic, familial, and demographic features of Irish life. Before describing and considering these changes, we shall examine what happened as Ireland approached and experienced the time of the "Great Hunger."

While the population of Ireland grew rapidly from 1780 to 1845, this population growth is not to be equated with a time of improved living conditions, or with a vital and healthy economy. The situation is much like that of present-day population growth: the countries that are experiencing the most rapid increases are often the ones in which the people are living in the most precarious conditions. Populations can, and do, grow in size, even while living conditions are wretched and poverty is nearly universal. They often grow until, it seems, they collapse from their own weight. It seems to be possible for populations to build on the most insubstantial and inadequate foundations, so that when they crumble, they do so with great destructiveness and violence. It was that way with the Irish population of the 1840s. It had grown, but on a foundation that was made of nothing more substantial than the potato bush and its edible root, both of which proved to be disastrously susceptible to rot and decay.

Accounts of the lives of most of the people of Ireland before the Famine reveal just how precarious the balance was. For example, the housing that was considered adequate for the Irish peasant family was primitive by current standards. But it had the advantage of being easy and quick to construct and almost free of cost, since the principal materials were often simply mud, stone, and sod. Frequently these one- or two-room huts of the Irish farmers were partially cut out of the hillsides. The cabins often had no windows and no chimneys. The fires, which were kept burning almost continuously, were simply placed on the dirt floor in the middle of the main room. To add to the generally dreary state of the peasant's house, it was often shared with livestock and poultry, as travelers or other observers often noted. One such description, coming even after the Famine, illustrates the conditions under which many Irish farm families lived:

> In the evening I found myself still far away from Clifden in a heavy rain, so I asked at a little cabin by the roadside for hospitality, and was welcomed cordially. There was only a kitchen and one room. In the kitchen were a cow, a calf, a dog, three or four hens and a cock fluttering noisily about, and in a corner a coop full of chickens. Here I slept on the ground near the ashes of the glowing peat fire; and in the other room slept the family—the father and mother, two girls and a boy. The silence of the night was broken from time to time by the thud and splash of dung on the mud floor, and the crowing and clatter of the fowls

woke me early. There was one chair, one bench, and several boxes to sit on, but no table; and some rude harness hanging from pegs on the wall was the only ornament. "Michael, rise up!" shouted a man's voice, about seven o'clock, and a boot, as it seemed, struck violently against the wooden partition. Michael lounged in, and rekindled the peat fire from the dying embers. In a few minutes in came his mother, and milked the cow in front of the fire into a series of dirty-looking little tin pots, that reminded me of old tomato cans. She then fed the calf on some milk and raw potatoes, and in a little time gave me a cup of excellent tea and a piece of potato bread.[18]

On a somewhat more objective basis, the census of 1841 classified houses in Ireland into four classes. The lowest class of house was the windowless mud cabin with a single room. Nearly half of the rural population lived in this class of house. In the western counties of Ireland, this fraction ranged upward toward three-fifths of the populace.[19]

Many of the Irish rural people who lived in these humble or impoverished conditions belonged to the cottier class.[20] The cottiers were farm laborers who worked on the land but had no rights to it, not even as tenants. The cottiers lived in small cottages or cabins and had plots of land only big enough for their potatoes. The potato land was obtained from a tenant farmer by means of a contract. The cottier agreed to pay a certain amount for an acre or two of land, which the farmer would till and prepare for planting potatoes. The contract was only for a period of eleven months each year, which clearly established that the cottier had no right of tenancy. This letting out of potato land was often done on an auction basis, not infrequently with middlemen bidding up the price of the rental fee. This entire procedure was known as the "conacre" system. The people in the cottier class, who obtained their food through the conacre system, lived in the most perilous economic condition of all the Irish. If the food supply of the potato failed, these people had almost no other resources to fall back on. Each potato crop was a gamble, and a failure might mean the loss of home and possessions. As we shall see, it was not safe to bet one's existence repeatedly on the potato.

Whenever rural people live at a subsistence level, they eat almost everything they produce. A subsistence-level diet that is composed primarily of a grain or cereal food (corn, wheat, oats, or rice) has one distinct advantage over one composed of a food like the potato. Grains and cereals are fairly easily stored, and surpluses from a good year can be carried over to the next. Even when the surplus grains are not retained by the peasants or farmers themselves, they are usually purchased and stored by the grain merchants, who, in times of shortage, resell them to the hungry people. By contrast, the potato generally cannot be stored over more than one year; therefore, even if surpluses are produced in a given year, these extra amounts will be of little use in the long run. Any population that relies almost totally on this single food must have a yearly crop, for there will be few unused supplies after a year, even among the merchants. Each year, the end of one potato crop must be used in planting anew to provide food for the coming year.

Among the Irish peasants in the early nineteenth century, it was not uncommon to have a supply of potatoes that only barely met the year's need. Frequently in the months of the summer, when the old potato crop was gone but the new potatoes were not yet ready, the families turned to a meal made from oats as their major source of food. These interim months were called by the Irish the "meal months," or, for some reason that is not entirely clear, the "blue months."[21] While this arrangement may have provided an existence for the Irish who had farms and produced some oat grain, it was no answer for the cottiers and those landless poor who got their supply of food through the conacre system. For them the potatoes that were produced in one summer *had* to last until the new crop became available. They had no grain in storage and no cash with which to buy any.

Because the supply of potatoes was so finely balanced with an absolute need, the Irish turned increasingly to higher-yield potato varieties in the nineteenth century. One such variety was called the "lumper." Its very name suggests that it was a bulky, but not especially desirable, food. It has been described as "an extremely ugly potato of poor quality."[22] Agriculturists recommended it primarily as an animal feed, but in fact, by the 1840s, it was the major food of nearly all the peasants and their families. The lumper, which produced a high yield under the poorest agricultural conditions, was almost universally used in the years immediately preceding the Famine. But the lumper had a shortcoming more serious than its coarseness and poor quality: it was susceptible to disease.[23]

In general, the potato, for all its good qualities, is an extremely vulnerable plant. Salaman, in his history of the potato, listed thirty-one recorded failures or partial failures of the potato crop in Ireland between 1724 and 1845. The potato sometimes failed to produce because of external factors, such as a premature frost, or an excess of rain and moisture, or a lack thereof; while on other occasions it was struck by a variety of diseases (curl, leaf roll, blight, dry rot, bacterial rot, blackleg, fungus, and infection).[24]

In sixteen of the thirty years preceding the Famine of 1846, some potato crop failure had been reported. While these were usually limited and localized, a failure of the potato crop was certainly nothing new to the people of Ireland when they entered the planting season of 1845. As that season developed, it appeared that the crop would be an extraordinarily heavy one.[25] Until the early part of July the weather was favorably warm and not too wet. But the weather changed dramatically in mid July, when it turned cold and damp. By the end of August the so-called potato blight was clearly infesting the Irish potato crop (as well as the crop in England and most countries on the Continent). This blight was a fungus infection whose scientific name is *Phytophthora infestans*; it had come to Europe from America. Within a few years, Ireland would repay this unwelcome gift from America with millions of her people, because they would no longer find enough food to survive in their home country.

When the blight struck the potato, it reduced the healthy bush to a black and withered stalk in only a few days. Then the disease caused the potato to rot in the ground. Even when the potatoes that were dug up seemed to be healthy, they soon rotted and became inedible. The stench of the rotting vines and potatoes was said to have been awful. There proved to be no satisfactory way to salvage the crop, although there were various complicated, quasi-scientific, and folk prescriptions for doing so. These varied methods had one major characteristic in common: a pathetic inability to save the inexorably rotting potatoes. Woodham-Smith reports on one such method. This particular program was prescribed by the special Scientific Commission that had been assembled by Sir Robert Peel, the British Prime Minister:

> To deal with diseased potatoes, the Irish peasant was to provide himself with a rasp or grater, a linen cloth, a hair sieve or a cloth strainer, a pail or tub or two for water, and a griddle. He was then to rasp the bad potatoes, very finely, into one of the tubs, wash the pulp, strain, repeat the process, then dry the pulp on the griddle, over a slack fire. In the water used for washing the pulp would be found a milky substance, which was starch. Good, wholesome bread could be made by mixing the starch with dried potato pulp, peas-meal, bean-meal, oatmeal or flour. "There will be of course," wrote the Commissioners, "a good deal of trouble in doing all we have recommended, and perhaps you will not succeed very well at first; but we are confident all true Irishmen will exert themselves, and never let it be said that in Ireland the inhabitants wanted courage to meet difficulties against which other nations are successfully struggling."[26]

While seventy-thousand copies of this detailed technique were distributed, the commissioners must have had some doubts about how effective the exertions of the "true Irishman" would be, for they also suggested, "If you do not understand this, ask your landlord or clergyman to explain its meaning."[27]

Like all other proposals for preserving the potatoes, this one afforded by the Scientific Commission did not work. Unfortunately, the ineptitude of this first official response to the potato failure was to be a harbinger of most governmental efforts in the disastrous years that followed. The history of the governmental response to the Famine was one of disorganization, bureaucratic paralysis, and a calculated inaction that was firmly based on the soundest principles of laissez-faire capitalism, buttressed by a firm faith that Providence works in dark and inscrutable ways.

The failure of the 1845 potato crop, while it hit almost all parts of the country, was not universal and total. It was somewhat less severe where the land was higher and drier. Also, some of the early varieties of potatoes were harvested before the blight reached its full force. The Irish who were hardest hit in the winter of 1845–1846 were, as might be expected, the people in the cottier class. Their potatoes were generally harvested just before the frost, so most of them were lost to the disease. The cottiers, in contrast to tenant farmers with some right to the land, had no other resources to fall back on. They had no livestock—though they sometimes had a pig that was used for paying rent—and they had no other crops. When their potatoes were gone in the early part of winter, they had nothing to turn to but the inadequate program of government relief work, or beggary.

But somehow most of the population made it through the winter of 1845–1846, and there was generally a faith that the new crop of potatoes would renew the food supply. In anticipation of this, the government aimed to close out its relief work by the fifteenth of August in 1846. The potato planting in the spring of that year was greater than normal, but sadly, by the month of June, the potato bushes were beginning to wither and die. The optimism and hope that had accompanied the new planting soon did the same. In 1846 the failure of the potato crop in Ireland was almost total. The distress and the misery that followed in the winter of 1846–1847 were so great that neither verbal pictures nor statistical summaries can adequately convey the condition of the people. Salaman has written: "A careful perusal of the accounts, given by different authors of the state of Ireland in the winter of 1846-7, has convinced me that it would be impossible to exaggerate the horrors of these days, or to compare them with anything which has occurred in Europe since the Black Death of 1348."[28]

If one tries to reduce this human misery to statistical terms, it is accurate to say that the Irish population was, in the literal sense, more than decimated. There were about eight and one-half million people when the famine struck, and it is estimated that one million or more of that number died during the severe famine years. The most easily identifiable killers of the people were starvation, scurvy (leading to the fatal purpura), dysentery, cholera, and typhus. The interrelatedness of all of these causes of death is obvious. The nutritional level of what the Irish had to eat was far below minimal requirements. This brought on the illnesses that reflect malnutrition; the subsequently weakened bodies were then more susceptible to the infectious diseases, which were spread more quickly by the unsanitary living conditions in which the people in their poverty existed. For example, typhus, which was the most devastating of the infectious diseases, was spread by body lice, which were endemic in the population.

Salaman also reports that two vitamin deficiencies led to additional miseries for the population, though not always to death. A deficiency of vitamin A produced ophthalmia, which led to blindness and insanity. Further, the loss of vitamin $B_7$, "which in normal times was supplied in ample quantities by the potato and the milk" in the peasant's diet, might have led to "nervous debility and even dementia."[29]

Some of the disaster that overtook Ireland during the famine years could have been reduced if the response of the government (and it must be remembered that this was essentially the English Parliament) had been more effective. This is not the place to get into an extensive review of the political, economic, and moral conditions that produced such an ineffectual response, but it is necessary to say that a substantial amount of the suffering could have been avoided if the members of Parliament had responded differently. Two attitudes held by the governing elite were responsible for the inadequacy of what was done. First, and of great importance, was the idea that commerce and profit-making had to take precedence over everything else. If there were profits to be made, the government should not interfere. Even more important, the government should engage in no action that would lead to financial losses for the commercial and business interests. The second attitude is more implicit, and must usually be inferred; but just as Sir William Petty considered an Irish life to be only about one-fifth as valuable as an English life, so, it seems, the English could not bring themselves to see the loss of Irish lives as such a serious matter. The Irish were, after all, for the most part, people who lived in a subhuman manner, as many of the travelers to Ireland had reported with a kind of perverse pleasure.[30]

After the first crop failure of 1845, the government did purchase some grain for distribution to the people, but the entire operation of that year was not very successful. In 1846 the policy on distribution was changed. It was decided, in this most severe year of the Famine, that the government would not import and supply food to the starving people. This policy was based on the assumption that the food shortages of the previous year had been "caused" by the paralysis of private enterprise. It was reasoned that no merchants would bear the cost, and take the chance, of importing grain when there was the ever-present threat that the government might undercut the market by distributing food at low prices, or for nothing. Captain Nugent, of the Royal Navy, was told when he appealed for food, "Even if it were practicable at the moment to open our [food] depots . . . it would obviously be extremely prejudicial to owners of grain, inasmuch as at present extraordinary prices can be realized."[31]

The emphasis on free trade also allowed thousands of bushels of grain to be *exported from* Ireland during the time of the Famine. By September of 1846 it was estimated that sixty thousand tons of oats had been shipped from Ireland.[32] Of course, unless the grain had been purchased by the government and distributed free, or at very low cost, it would probably not have been used, since, for the most part, the people had no money.

The famine work-relief program proposed by the government officials was built around the idea of work projects. By working at the building of roads and canals and other public projects, the impoverished people were supposed to be paid enough so that they could purchase food. But the funds provided for these work projects were totally inadequate for the task. Also, the program was administered in a cumbersome and inefficient manner, so that it fell far short of meeting the needs of the people.[33]

With the coming of the winter of 1846–1847, the people of Ireland faced starvation, disease, and death. There was no way for them to get money or food, regardless of their willingness to work. Under these circumstances, the flight from Ireland increased to such proportions that there was a permanent change in the character and the size of the Irish population. Tables 1 and 2 of chapter 16 show the numbers of Irish who went to the United States in the years between 1820 and 1860, but it must be recalled, when one looks at these figures, that while the United States was a principal destination for Irish emigrants, it was by no means the only one. From these tables it can be seen that the decade of the Famine and the one immediately thereafter were the years of highest emigration: it is estimated that at least a million and one-half people left Ireland during the years of the Famine.[34]

Many Irish also went to Canada, though relatively few chose to settle there permanently, preferring instead to go on to the United States. Great numbers of Irish also went to England in these years, usually because passage to that country was so much less expensive, but also because the trip was less hazardous and unfamiliar. While economic times in England were not particularly favorable, the English at least had a Poor Law, which gave the poverty-stricken Irish people the assurance that they would not die of hunger.[35] By contrast, to have remained in Ireland could very well have led to that result. By the second year of the Famine, many Irishmen owed their landlords rent; and under the law, debtors could not only be evicted, they could also be imprisoned. This would have left their wives and children without a place to live and with no money. To exacerbate the situation, the landowners were now being taxed for the number of people on relief in their districts, so it was distinctly to their advantage to see as many people as possible leave. Indeed, many Irish families left their homeland with the economic support and under the aegis of their landlords. In the Ireland of this time, the poverty problem was solved by sending the poor away to other lands. This action had the virtue of ameliorating the situation for the home country, at the same time that it created problems in others. Since the first emigrants began to send money back to Ireland as assistance and to help kinsmen to emigrate, it seemed to have a doubly salutary effect for an economy that was failing to provide sustenance for its people.

The hardships that the Irish suffered in the trans-Atlantic trips are sad revelations of the severity of life only a little over a century ago. The most tragic conditions occurred on ships that were headed for Quebec and Montreal, Canada, via the St. Lawrence River.[36] Many of the ships used for this traffic were in poor condition and completely lacked the resources and services needed to handle the number of people who were jammed into the holds. Water was in short supply, and it was often contaminated. Food was almost always inadequate, as were the facilities for preparing it. Legislation was passed for the purpose of protecting the emigrants from inadequate food supplies on the ships, but in fact it had almost the opposite effect. The Passenger Act provided that there should be seven pounds of provisions for each passenger per week. The shipowners could then use this barely adequate amount as a standard for meeting their legal obligations. Their moral obligation to carry some surplus food in the event that there should be spoilage or loss, or a longer than average journey, was thereby diminished. Therefore, the very laws that were designed to protect the passengers turned out instead to work to their disadvantage.

There were usually not enough facilities on the ships for the needs of the hundreds of passengers, with the result that people existed below decks in their own filfth and debris. Since the people were only casually examined before they boarded the ship, they brought typhus and other diseases into these crowded and unsanitary conditions. The result was that some of these vessels of escape were labeled "coffin ships." Thousands of Irish men and women and their children died on these ships before they reached the land where they hoped, at last, to be able to escape from poverty and disease.

For the people who did not leave Ireland in the fall of 1846 or in the spring of 1847, there was a new crop of potatoes to be planted. After two years of failure, the crop of 1847, though it was a much smaller than average planting (owing to a shortage of seed potatoes), was not struck heavily by the blight. It appeared that the worst of the famine was over, but in 1848, the infection of the potato crop was again widespread, and the somber drama continued. By some accounts, the hardships were even worse than they had been in the winter of 1846. The flow of emigration from Ireland that had built up in the earlier famine years now grew heavier as wave after wave of Irish families followed their kinsmen, especially to America.

After 1848, while there were a number of potato-crop failures, there were no times when the severity of the situation approached that of the Famine years. In large part this was due to the departure of the millions of people who continued to leave Ireland. Clearly those who departed were the ones who occupied the most marginal economic positions in the society. Those who remained were relatively better off, though the general level of living was still very low. Also the experience of the Famine did change some eating habits, with many sections of the country no longer relying solely on the potato. Now the diet was often supplemented by some vegetables (turnips and carrots), bread, milk, and sometimes fish and eggs.

Salaman believes that the potato started to relax its hold on the Irish people about 1870. While the potato is a staple of the Irish even today, it "is eaten because it is liked, not because it is necessary. . . . The potato is happily, no longer the arbiter between a bare sufficiency and starvation."[37]

In the last half of the nineteenth century the Irish people and their economy continued to react and adjust to the Famine experience. One can begin to understand the behavior of the Irish in this post-Famine period if it is viewed as a reaction to one of the most devastating traumas ever to hit a population. The memory of the Famine years was embedded in the thinking of the Irish through a telling and retelling of the events of the terrible experience of each family. The result was that the Irish people adopted a response toward family and economics that has helped to shape their basic institutions and their way of life.

The Irish, as a people, are often considered an extremely romantic group, given to believing in fairies and other mystical ways, but, as we shall see, they have become a very rational and calculating people who have carefully tailored their social and economic institutions to meet their objective needs. The economic and familial institutions in particular have been modified to meet the post-Famine life. The story of these two basic institutions, combined with the often-described history of political events of the late nineteenth and early twentieth centuries, gives a fuller picture of Ireland as it moved toward becoming an independent nation.

We may begin our consideration by examining the overall demographic pattern of Ireland since the 1870s. Table 2 shows the population of Ireland according to the censuses from 1821 to 1971.

Concentrating on the twenty-six counties that make up the Republic of Ireland (which will hereafter be referred to as Ireland), we see that the population has declined steadily from 1841 until very recently. Only since 1961 has the population of Ireland started to grow again (5.4% in the last decade), after more than a century of decline. During that period, when the population of Ireland declined from six and one-half million to less than three million, every other European country was experiencing some population growth.[38] In this respect, Ireland has been demographically unique among European countries.

The decline in the Irish population was obviously the result of the interplay among birth rates, death rates, and emigration rates. The broad outlines of these contributing factors are relatively well known to anyone who has taken even a casual interest in Ireland. It is well understood that the emigration flow, which received such a great impetus from the Famine, continued to be very high in the years that immediately followed. While the rate of emigration did slow down gradually in the latter part of the nineteenth century, it has continued to diminish the Irish population. Right up to the present time the amount of migration out of Ireland exceeds the amount of in-migration. In the ten-year period between the census of 1961 and that of 1971, emigrants from Ireland still outnumbered immigrants to Ireland by more than 140,000.[39] Since this is

TABLE 2
IRELAND'S POPULATION SIZE FROM THE CENSUS OF 1821 TO THE CENSUS OF 1971

| Year | Population of the Twenty-six Counties of the Republic of Ireland, in Thousands | Percentage of Change in Preceding Ten-Year Period | Population of All Thirty-two Counties of Ireland, in Thousands |
|---|---|---|---|
| 1821 | 5,421 |        | 6,802 |
| 1831 | 6,193 | +14.2  | 7,767 |
| 1841 | 6,529 | + 5.4  | 8,175 |
| 1851 | 5,112 | −21.7  |       |
| 1861 | 4,402 | −13.9  | 5,798 |
| 1871 | 4,053 | − 7.9  |       |
| 1881 | 3,870 | − 4.5  | 5,175 |
| 1891 | 3,469 | −10.4  |       |
| 1901 | 3,222 | − 7.1  | 4,459 |
| 1911 | 3,140 | − 2.5  |       |
| 1926 | 2,972 | − 5.4  | 4,229 |
| 1936 | 2,968 | − 0.1  |       |
| 1946 | 2,955 | − 0.4  | 4,332 |
| 1951 | 2,961 | + 0.2  |       |
| 1961 | 2,818 | − 4.8  | 4,243 |
| 1971 | 2,881 | + 2.2  |       |

Source: Robert E. Kennedy, Jr., "Irish Emigration, Marriage, and Fertility" (Ph.D. dissertation, University of California, Berkeley, 1967), p. 4; and *The Census of Population, 1971*, Preliminary Report.

the same decade in which Ireland experienced population growth, it is clear that this recent increase is due to the number of births exceeding the number of deaths.

Although the rate of fertility within Irish marriages has always been high, and continues to be so, a countervailing pattern has kept the total number of births down. This is the pattern of late marriage. In 1926 the census of Ireland revealed that the average age at first marriage for females was about twenty-nine, while for the males, it was thirty-five. In 1946 these ages were twenty-eight and thirty-three respectively.[40] By contrast, in the United States the average age at first marriage, in the 1940s, was about twenty-one for females and twenty-three for males.[41] As late as the 1930s more than half of the Irish females and three-fourths of the males between the ages of twenty-five and thirty-five were still single. By the 1960s the proportions were closer to one-third and one-half respectively.

The second unusual, but well known, feature of Ireland's marriage patterns, and also one that accounts for the failure of the Irish population to grow, is the tendency not to marry at all. Even in the 1960s roughly one-quarter of all Irish males and females forty-five years of age or older remained unmarried. While European countries generally have a higher percentage of unmarried people aged forty-five and over than does the United States (which has less than 10 percent), Ireland has a higher percentage than any country in Europe.

In addition to the comparisons between Ireland and other countries, it is also interesting to consider the patterns of Irish late marriage and permanent celibacy over a period of time. Taking the 1841 census as a starting point, we can compare the indications of late marriage and nonmarriage over the last century and a quarter. Figures 1 and 2 show these patterns.

Consider first figure 1, which shows the trend in late marriage by indicating the percentage of males and females who were still single in the age group of twenty-five to thirty-four years. Between 1841 and 1851, the decade encompassing the Famine, the number who remained single in this age group increased greatly. The percentage of the males who were still single rose from 43 to 61; for females, there was a lesser increase, from 28 to 39 percent. However, after the initial adjustment to the poverty and famine conditions, the percentage of those remaining single (between twenty-five and thirty-four years of age) dropped for the next twenty years. It was not until the census of 1881 that the figures reflected an increase in late marriage again. From that time until 1911, ever-higher percentages of the Irish married late. The final noticeable

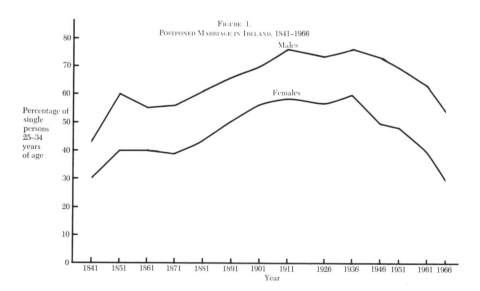

FIGURE 1.
POSTPONED MARRIAGE IN IRELAND, 1841–1966

trend in figure 1 is that since 1936 there has been a pronounced and persistent decline in the percentage of young adults who remain unmarried.

The trend line in figure 2 reflects the amount of permanent celibacy in the Irish population since the 1840s. This pattern proves to be somewhat different from the late-marriage trends. The percentage of males and females forty-five years of age and over who remained unmarried increased rather steadily from 1841 until about 1936, for males, and until 1951, for females. Thereafter, the trend has been downward, though as we have noted before, Ireland still stands at the very highest end among countries in the number of its people who remain single.

The demographic data that we have just examined provide one explanation of why the Irish population was reduced by more than one-half between 1841 and the present. The interplay between high emigration, the late age at marriage, and a high rate of permanent celibacy all worked to diminish the size of the population, even though the level of fertility among those who did marry remained high. But this demographic level of explanation is not totally satisfying. What it lacks is some insight into the workings of the economic and family systems that produced these patterns.

The nature of Ireland's agricultural order must be understood before one can deal adequately with the rest of the Irish system. We have already seen that the landlords, the farmers, and their children all col-

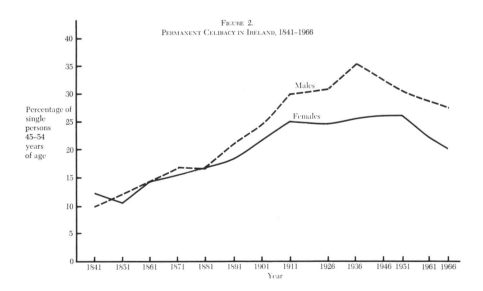

Figure 2.
Permanent Celibacy in Ireland, 1841–1966

*The Dynamics of Population*

laborated to reduce the size of the Irish farm in the eighteenth century. This process continued until approximately the time of the Famine, although some forces were already at work a few years before the Famine that encouraged the landlords to consolidate their holdings and convert small farms to pastureland. For example, in addition to the economic motive there had also been a political motivation that had earlier encouraged some landlords to split their holdings into smaller parcels. A law passed in 1793 had given a vote to the owner of any farm valued at more than £2. Under this law the landlord could increase his political power by dividing his holdings into smaller parcels, since he received a vote for every farm that met the criterion. In 1829, this law was revised so that the value of the land now had to be £10.[42] Because of this new condition, and also because the cash market for grain was not as good as it had been, the landlords were, whenever possible, evicting the tenants from some of their smaller farms and merging the released land with their neighboring farms.

In 1846 the Corn Laws were repealed by the British Parliament. When these laws were passed in the eighteenth century, they had given Irish grains a preferential treatment on the English market. As has been mentioned before, this encouraged the landlords to split their land in order to get as much grain production as possible. The elimination of this economic advantage further encouraged the landlords to reverse their earlier practice of fragmenting the farms. With the consolidation of farms and the conversion of cropland to pasture came the evictions of many Irish farmers. The story of the evictions of Irish farmers from "their" land and "their" homes was one of great bitterness and some bloodshed. Although the process of evicting tenants had started earlier, the Famine intensified it. When the potato crop failed for a second straight year, many Irish farmers could not pay their rent, because they had to sell their cash crops and livestock in order to get food. The money from these sales had normally been reserved for the landlord, but now it had to be used for survival. Since the landlords were finding it economically and politically advantageous to reduce the number of tenants and to combine the small farms, they began to make evictions on a mass scale. Often, during the Famine years, in the case of the humbler dwellings, the authorities immediately destroyed the huts of the peasants as soon as they were expelled, to preclude their return.[43]

During the last part of the nineteenth century, the Irish farmers began to organize in opposition to the abuses inherent in these evictions. Eviction was so filled with emotional impact that it served as a rallying point for the Irish peasants, and eventually, by the 1880s, their organization had produced some changes in the laws governing tenancy. This process would ultimately culminate in the right of a tenant to purchase the farm from his landlord. Although most of the changes in ownership did not take place until the twentieth century, there was an increasing tendency, even in the late nineteenth century, for the Irish farmer to feel that the farm was truly his. The Land Act of 1870 did, for example, require the landlord, if there were any change of tenure, to compensate the tenant for any improvements that the tenant had made on the farm.[44] Later laws, while not yet giving the tenants ownership, did give increasing certainty that a tenant might stay on the land and have the right to pass it on to his heir when he chose to relinquish control.

In this entire Famine and post-Famine period, the lower ranks of the agricultural population—the small plot farmers, the cottiers, and the laborers who obtained potato land by the "conacre" system—were generally the people who were forced off the land. These people constituted the majority of those who emigrated. Left in the farm population were the somewhat more substantial farmers: the ones who had farmed, by pre-Famine standards, the larger farms. They were the ones who would shape the customs and the practices of the Irish people as they moved toward the twentieth century. If we keep this in mind, it is easier to understand the inheritance system, as well as the marriage and family system, that developed in the last part of the nineteenth century. Then we can also see how late marriage and permanent celibacy emerged as such preeminent forms. Connell, who has developed and documented the ideas that follow, described the new circumstances as follows:

> The Famine dramatized the risks of improvident marriage and halted the division that made it possible. Soon the land legislation made the peasant more ambitious and calculating—more ambitious because, as proprietor, tenant-at-will no longer, he yearned, peasant fashion, to establish his name at the land; more calculating because calculation, with no landlord to annex its fruits, became a rational proceeding. But his children's reckless marrying might bedevil his calculation.[45]

When the farmer began to think in these terms, he also started to exercise special control over the marriages of his children and the selection of his heir. This led to the reemergence of a pattern of mate selection that had prevailed in earlier times, but that had all but disappeared in the early part of the nineteenth century: the arranged marriage, or the match.

By controlling the marriage of his children, the Irish peasant could be more certain that his socioeconomic status and the status of his children would be assured. Part of the problem stemmed from the fact that the Irish farm family was almost always large. As late as 1950 the average number of children in the farm family was almost six.[46] If there were to be no more increase in the number of farms, only one child could receive the land from the father. If there were sons, one of their number had to be selected as the heir. The other sons had only a few choices. They could emigrate; and many did so. A second alternative was to remain in the home, even after the chosen brother had married. But in so doing, they were relegated to a subordinate status, always beholden to the head of the household: first to their father, then to their brother.

It might be noted that unmarried sisters could choose this same alternative, and they often did so, although less often than their unmarried brothers. The sisters who could not marry in Ireland because of the lack of a suitable match were more likely to emigrate to the United States or to England. Emigration for them had two hopeful possibilities: either they could marry in the new land, or they could earn the money necessary for a dowry, and then return to Ireland to marry (more on this later).

The final choices for the siblings (especially brothers) who could not get the land were either difficult or unpalatable. Leaving the farm and taking an urban job was an alternative that was seldom chosen, because Ireland's urban employment was not growing. Indeed, manufacturing tended to decline in Ireland as the English systematically repressed emergent, and therefore competitive, industries.[47] So, it was rare that a rural male could marry and move to a city for employment. Finally, a person could marry and remain in the country as a landless farm laborer. This course was apparently very distasteful to the Irishman, because he opted for it so rarely. He preferred instead to stay in his parents' home and then later, with their passing, in the home of his brother and family. The loss of social status that came from marrying without land apparently outweighed the disadvantages of living out one's life without marrying or having children.

There are two keys to understanding the marriage system in rural Ireland.[48] First, it was a system that was controlled by the father in the patriarchal Irish family. The father determined in large measure when the son who was to be the heir would marry, and whom he would marry. There were various times in the process where the son, as well as other family members, could exert some influence, but their influence was clearly secondary to the wishes of the father.

The second key feature of Irish rural marriage was that it was based on economic considerations. Especially it involved maintaining a working unit, so that the activities of the farm could go on. The objective of a marriage (in this case, that of a son) was to bring to the farm a woman with a substantial dowry, so that the rest of the household could be taken care of and the work of the farm could be carried on efficiently.

To be run effectively, the farm required a reasonably healthy couple, so when either the husband or the wife died or became incapacitated, the family was in need of reorganization. At the time of his marriage, the son who was to receive the land replaced his father as the head of the household. Although the father and mother continued to live in the household, and were generally treated with respect, there was a distinct change in status for the principal members of the family. The marriage of the son usually signaled the time when the farm became his. The father might continue to work with and advise his son, but he was no longer the highest authority in the household. Similarly, the mother of the newly married son, while not necessarily subordinate to her daughter-in-law, did have to make room for the new woman in her kitchen.

One striking symbolic feature of this change in status was the movement of the old couple to the "west room" of the house.[49] Farm houses were typically built as rectangles on an east-west axis. The largest room, usually in the middle, was the kitchen. At the west end of the kitchen was the hearth. A door by the hearth led to the west room. The west room had a sacred and special quality. Arensberg and Kimball, who did their field work among the Irish rural folk in the 1920s, wrote:

> But in this room all the objects of sentimental value (except the shrine and the dresser in the kitchen) are always kept: the religious pictures, the ceremonial objects brought in by the bride at marriage, and the bric-a-brac associated with the past members of the household. . . . The family heirlooms are there, and, lining the walls along with religious pictures, there appear the photographs of the members of the family.[50]

After noting that the west end of the house was associated with fairies, including the spirits of the dead, Arensberg and Kimball made the obvious interpretation of the significance of the old couple being moved into the west room after the marriage of their son:

> If we remember that the old people, relinquishing their adult status and preparing for death, move into this room amid heirlooms, religious pictures, and photographs of dead members of the household, we are forced to postu-

late the sacred and semireligious nature of the attitudes surrounding the old couple and identifying them with the forces of the dead and the symbolic unity of the family, past and present.[51]

Once these facts are known, it becomes clearer why the sons who were to be the heirs of the farm married late in life. When the father allowed his son to marry, he gave up his farm and his authority, while his wife lost her sole eminence in household affairs. After that, both were relegated to the domain of things passed by. Clearly they entered the status of the dying when their son married. Under these conditions, it is not surprising that fathers delayed as long as possible before relinquishing control of their farms. The farmer's wife was a willing confederate in forestalling the marriage of the son, because her position was equally in jeopardy. So the years would pass by, the fathers withholding the land from their sons, and the mothers making their son's lives as comfortable as possible. Both members of the couple put off as long as possible the time when they would have to give up their control.

In the meantime, there was another concern for the family: accumulating a sum of money for the marriage of the daughter or daughters. This was the dowry, which by the late nineteenth century was almost always money. (In earlier days, the dowry might have included livestock or furniture, or even the labor of the girl's father on the son-in-law's farm.) The amount of money in the dowry had to be roughly equivalent to the value of the farm that the husband would be bringing to the marriage. Sometimes the relative social standings of the two families, or the differing personal qualities of the potential bride and groom, influenced the amount of the dowry, but basically the value of the land determined the amount of money. In the words of Arensberg and Kimball again, the marriage bargaining was "a matter of nice adjustment between the 'fortune' and the farm."[52]

The negotiations that surrounded the writing of the marriage contract illustrate better than anything else just how calculating the Irish could be when a marriage was to be made. As the first step in the process, an intermediary, or matchmaker, brought representatives of the two families together. If this negotiating session—which might last an entire day and involve the consumption of much stout in the backroom of a pub—led to a preliminary agreement, it would be followed by a meeting of the prospective bride and groom. Accompanied by their friends and siblings, the two might meet, often for the first time if they lived in different neighborhoods. At that time, either the man or the woman could indicate dissatisfaction with the proposed mate, and it would be reported that they were "unsuited" to each other.

The negotiations reached a crucial stage when the relatives of the bride acted as a party of "viewers" to "walk the land" of the groom.[53] "Walking the land" was done in order to see if the claims of the groom's father were accurate and if the farm was equivalent to the dowry that the girl's family was willing to offer. Preparatory to the walking of the land, the groom's family would often give the farm buildings a white-washing and the farm a general cleaning and ordering. Folklore has it that frequently the worth of the farm was enhanced in misleading ways. This kind of subterfuge often involved borrowing machinery, furniture, and stock from a neighbor or relative in order to add to the apparent wealth of the farm. Connell noted: "The commonest allegation is that the family expecting viewers 'came to a bit of an understanding' with its neighbours: gaps [in the fence] were left open, and new ones broken; cattle intermingled and machinery was borrowed. 'It's broke off,' one father told his daughter when he returned from a viewing, 'the gaps was too fresh.' "[54] If, on the other hand, these steps were completed to the satisfaction of all the principals, the marriage contract (the "writings") would be signed.

The dowry money, when it was received, was often used to pay for some of the needs of other members of the family. Brothers who had not been chosen to receive the land might be provided with an education —perhaps for the priesthood—or more commonly, they might be given part of the money so that they could emigrate. Sisters were frequently given some of the money for their own dowries, so that they would be able to marry; some, like their brothers, used the money to emigrate.

In recent years, some changes have taken place in matchmaking, though many of its fundamentals still exist in the rural counties of Ireland. When it flourished, from the 1880s until after the 1920s, it was clearly an important mechanism for keeping the Irish population within the constraints imposed by a limited land economy. In its ideal, typical form, the system provided only for the marriage of one of the sons and one of the daughters. Because the Irish farm family was generally large and because there was not likely to be enough land available, the principal choices open to the rest of the children were either to emigrate or to remain unmarried on the family farm.

As other observers have noted, the selectivity that was inherent in this process must surely have had some influence on the Irish population that remained in the home country. The basic impact of this selectivity must have been one of preserving tradition and increasing conservatism.

Since the fathers had a free choice among their sons regarding the one who would be the heir to the land, it seems plausible that they might have been inclined to pick the one who would be apt to keep the farm going in the father's way. The sons who were more innovative, creative, and restive must have seemed like poorer risks to their fathers. Since the remaining brothers had the choice of either emigrating or staying as workers on the farm, it was probably the less aggressive and progressive who stayed behind, while their opposites left home and Ireland for good. Knowing that as many as half the children in an average farm family left the country and that there is at least a prima facie case that the ones who left were different from the ones who remained behind, we must assume that the character of the Irish population was thereby changed.

Robert E. Kennedy, Jr., has argued that the persistently high fertility among Irish Catholics (as opposed to other European Catholics) can be accounted for, in part, by this process of selectivity.[55] He reasoned that the Irish males and females who stayed behind and did marry were most likely to have been the ones who were faithful and unquestioning Catholics. This was apt to be especially true of those who married young (in their twenties). Kennedy has demonstrated that in the period between 1861 and 1966, only a minority of the girls who were born in Ireland stayed there and married young: "The majority of young girls in Ireland chose to emigrate, postpone marriage until their thirties, or to remain permanently single."[56] Later he says: "Those who were most willing to go along with the conventional expectations of their church were also the ones more likely to remain in Ireland, to accept the large family ideal of Catholic teaching, and to marry early enough in life to turn the ideal into actuality."[57]

Finally, let us take a brief look at the Irish population and family today. As noted earlier, the Irish population (in the twenty-six counties) continued to decline until 1961. Only in the last two census periods has there been population growth— a 2.3 percent increase between 1961 and 1966, and a 3.0 percent increase between 1966 and 1971.[58] This recent growth has occurred in spite of a continued net loss of people from emigration. But in recent years, even the rate of out-migration seems to have slowed at last. The number of Irish youth now leaving the country yearly is estimated to be about ten thousand. Fifteen years ago the figure was as high as fifty thousand. This emigration may still represent Ireland's best young people, for it is reported that in the 1950s, two-thirds of the Irish youngsters who had completed high school were still going abroad to work.[59] Today some new economic opportunities are emerging in Ireland. This is keeping more young people in the country; but migration is also diminishing because the traditional destinations of Irish emigrants have become less attractive than earlier. One such deterrent was the possibility, in the 1960s, of males being drafted into military service if they emigrated to either the United States or Great Britain.

Most of the recent population growth has occurred in the urban areas of Ireland, with Dublin growing fastest in the early 1960s, and the regional cities of Cork, Limerick, Shannon, Waterford, and Galway making the greatest gains in the last half of the decade. The rural areas of the west and northwest are, as they have been historically, the most economically depressed; they are still losing population.[60]

Ireland today is changing because increasing numbers of her people are living in urban places and working at urban jobs. The Greater Dublin area now numbers about one million residents, more than one-quarter of the total population of Ireland.[61] More than twenty years ago Alexander Humphreys conducted field studies of Irish family life under conditions of urbanism in Dublin; even at that time he noted a great many differences from the rural families that had been described by Arensberg and Kimball some twenty years earlier.[62]

The principal change found by Humphreys was that the urban family or kin group, as a unit of the social system, had a much less pervasive influence than it had had in earlier times.[63] In rural Ireland, the family and extended kin group were all important in the conduct of everyday affairs. In Dublin, Humphreys found that much less power resided in the family groups. He attributed this loss of influence by the family unit to its loss of control over the economic unit of production. The rural family, which ran and controlled its own farm, was a distinct contrast to the urban family, in which the husband worked for a company or organization. In Humphreys's study, only the managerial and professional classes seemed to be more like the autonomous farmer with regard to controlling their own economic destiny.[64]

The interrelations between family members in the urban place had also changed greatly from what they had been in the rural areas.[65] Principal among these changes was the loss of hegemony by the urban father. No longer can the urban Irish father control every aspect of the lives of family members. More frequently than not, he works away from home; therefore he does not have the constant contact with his sons and daughters. As a consequence, his control over their lives is reduced. This is not to say that the males have lost their power and their status advantage in urban life, because males still dominate the family. But in contrast to the rural family, the urban father no longer has absolute power. He no longer controls either the economic futures of his children or their marriages.

Among the levels of occupational status it is interesting that Humphreys also found that the fathers of the professional-managerial classes retained greater control over their children's lives than did those in other occupational strata.[66]

The role of the mother in the Dublin family has also changed in the urban setting. Because the husband is away from the home more, the urban wife frequently has more domestic responsibility. Married women in Ireland are discouraged from holding jobs outside the home. Indeed, the Irish Constitution specifically expresses the ideal of the nonworking mother. In the section dealing with the family, it says that "the State recognizes that by her life within the home, woman gives to the State a support without which the common good cannot be achieved." For that reason, the Constitution goes on to say, "the State shall, therefore, endeavour to ensure that mothers shall not be obliged by economic necessity to engage in labour to the neglect of their duties in the home."[67] Under these circumstances the urban wife is not as much a producing member in the family's economy as the farm wife had been. However, there has been an increase in the responsibilities of the urban wife in the non-economic spheres of life, particularly in the control and socialization of the children. Again, these responsibilities have increased for the urban wife because her husband is gone from home much of the time. However, this change of emphasis in the wife's role—from that of being an active contributor to the economic welfare of the family to that of being the manager of the home and the children—has not particularly enhanced the status of the urban woman. Even in Ireland, in a culture that has generally venerated the mother, it seems that the mother role *alone* has not been totally satisfying. Humphreys observed, even in his field studies of 1949, that the urban woman was beginning to chafe under her "mother only" role. Long before the phrase "women's liberation" came onto the social scene, the seeds of discontent were already in the wind, even in Ireland. Urban wives who were relegated to the home were demanding more. Humphreys described the feelings of the Dublin wives in the following words:

> . . . especially among the younger wives, there is a growing demand for greater social and recreational equality with their husbands. These developments appear to spring from dissatisfaction with the general failure of the urban community to reward a wife's role sufficiently. There also seems to be an attempt by women at once to equalize family burdens and to participate more fully in those activities

upon which, according to the standards of industrial society, status is principally based.[68]

As one reads these words, with their totally contemporary sound, it becomes clear that today one can no longer speak of *the Irish family*. There are doubtless some places in rural Ireland today where a father is casting a calculating eye on his young adult sons, trying to decide which one should ultimately be his successor and take over the farm. At the same time in a Dublin suburb one can imagine a middle-class father worrying about his children's attraction to the symbols and styles of modern life. The range of family lives and family forms is probably as great in Ireland today as in any culture in the world. Many of the old traditional ways may still be found, even among the most modern urban Irish families. But urbanization and industrialization are coming to Ireland. And when the changes come, the traditional family forms and the population patterns that were the product of the rural economy will fade and leave only dim shadows of their past prominence in Irish life.

## NOTES

1. Sir William Petty, *The Political Anatomy of Ireland* (London: D. Brown & W. Rogers, 1691).
2. Ibid., p. 28.
3. Ibid., p. 31.
4. Ibid., p. 21.
5. Kenneth H. Connell, *The Population of Ireland, 1750–1845* (Oxford: Clarendon Press, 1950). The discussion that follows rests heavily on Connell's excellent demographic scholarship.
6. Ibid., p. 6.
7. Ibid.
8. Ibid., p. 25.
9. Ibid., p. 29.
10. Robert E. Kennedy, Jr., *The Irish: Emigration, Marriage, and Fertility* (Berkeley and Los Angeles: University of California Press, 1973), p. 27.
11. Connell, *The Population of Ireland*, chap. 3.
12. Michael Drake, "Marriage and Population Growth in Ireland, 1750–1845," *Economic History Review* 16:311 (1963).
13. Ibid., p. 312.
14. Kenneth H. Connell, "Land and Population in Ireland, 1780–1845," *Economic History Review*, 2d ser., 2:284 (1950); reprinted in D. V. Glass and D. E. C. Eversley, *Population in History* (Chicago: Aldine Publishing Co., 1965).
15. William L. Langer, "Europe's Initial Population Explosion," *American Historical Review* 69:12 (1963).
16. Connell, *The Population of Ireland*, pp. 151–56.
17. Redcliffe N. Salaman, *The History and Social Influence of the Potato* (Cambridge, Eng.: Cambridge University Press, 1949), chaps. 11–13.

18. Ibid., p. 328.
19. Ibid., p. 287; Cecil Woodham-Smith, *The Great Hunger: Ireland, 1845–1849* (New York: Harper & Row, 1962), p. 20.
20. Woodham-Smith, *The Great Hunger*, pp. 34–35; Salaman, *The History and Social Influence of the Potato*, pp. 247–48.
21. Salaman, *The History and Social Influence of the Potato*, 252, 278.
22. Connell, *The Population of Ireland*, p. 137.
23. Ibid.
24. Salaman, *The History and Social Influence of the Potato*, pp. 603–8.
25. The following description of the events of the Famine years is drawn primarily from Salaman, *The History and Social Influence of the Potato*, and Woodham-Smith, *The Great Hunger*.
26. Woodham-Smith, *The Great Hunger*, pp. 45–46.
27. Ibid., p. 45.
28. Salaman, *The History and Social Influence of the Potato*, p. 300.
29. Ibid., p. 305.
30. Edward MacLysaght, *Irish Life in the Seventeenth Century* (Dublin: Cork University Press, 1950), pp. 13–22.
31. Woodham-Smith, *The Great Hunger*, p. 133.
32. Ibid., p. 123.
33. Ibid., pp. 18–83, 126–56.
34. Kennedy, *The Irish*, pp. 42–43.
35. Woodham-Smith, *The Great Hunger*, p. 270.
36. Ibid., pp. 206–38.
37. Salaman, *The History and Social Influence of the Potato*, p. 331.
38. Kennedy, *The Irish*, p. 1.
39. *Irish Press* (Dublin), 22 September 1971.
40. Robert E. Kennedy, Jr., "Irish Emigration, Marriage, and Fertility" (Ph. D. dissertation, University of California, Berkeley, 1967), p. 11; John A. O'Brien, ed., *The Vanishing Irish* (London: W. H. Allen, 1954), p. 28.
41. United States Bureau of the Census, *Statistical Abstract of the United States: 1971* (Washington, D.C.: Government Printing Office, 1971), p. 60.
42. Kennedy, *The Irish*, p. 32; Thomas W. Freeman, *Ireland: A General and Regional Geography* (2d ed.; London: Methuen, 1960), p. 175.
43. Salaman, *The History and Social Influence of the Potato*, pp. 281–85.
44. Freeman, *Ireland*, p. 177.
45. Kenneth H. Connell, *Irish Peasant Society* (Oxford: Clarendon Press, 1968), p. 116.
46. Ibid., p. 118.
47. Salaman, *The History and Social Influence of the Potato*, pp. 246, 274, 275; Kennedy, *The Irish*, pp. 37–40.
48. Kenneth H. Connell, "Peasant Marriage in Ireland: Its Structure and Development since the Famine," *Economic History Review*, 2d ser., 14:502–23 (1962).
49. Conrad M. Arensberg and Solon T. Kimball, *Family and Community in Ireland* (2d ed.; Cambridge, Mass.: Harvard University Press, 1968), pp. 129–31.
50. Ibid., p. 129.
51. Ibid., p. 130.
52. Ibid., p. 106.
53. Connell, "Peasant Marriage in Ireland," p. 509.
54. Ibid.
55. Kennedy, *The Irish*, pp. 190–200.
56. Ibid., p. 192.
57. Ibid., p. 193.
58. *Census of Population, 1971*, Preliminary Report, pp. 5–6.
59. *Christian Science Monitor*, 15 November 1971, p. 8.

60. Ibid.; *Census of Population, 1971,* Preliminary Report, pp. 15–21.
61. *Christian Science Monitor,* 15 November 1971, p. 8.
62. Alexander J. Humphreys, *New Dubliners: Urbanization and the Irish Family* (New York: Fordham University Press, 1966).
63. Ibid., pp. 230, 235–36.
64. Ibid., p. 237.
65. Ibid.
66. Ibid., p. 241.
67. Constitution of Ireland, Article 41, section 2.
68. Humphreys, *New Dubliners,* p. 238.

## SUGGESTIONS FOR FURTHER READING

Arensberg, Conrad M. *The Irish Countryman.* Gloucester, Mass.: Peter Smith, 1959. (First published in 1937 in New York by The Macmillan Co.)

————, and Kimball, Solon T. *Family and Community in Ireland.* 2d ed. Cambridge, Mass.: Harvard University Press, 1968.

Connell, Kenneth H. *The Population of Ireland, 1750–1845.* Oxford: Clarendon Press, 1950.

Humphreys, Alexander J. *New Dubliners: Urbanization and the Irish Family.* New York: Fordham University Press, 1966.

Kennedy, Robert E., Jr. *The Irish: Emigration, Marriage, and Fertility.* Berkeley and Los Angeles: University of California Press, 1973.

O'Brien, John A., ed. *The Vanishing Irish.* London: W. H. Allen, 1954.

Woodham-Smith, Cecil. *The Great Hunger: Ireland, 1845–1849.* New York: Harper & Row, 1962.

# 10

# FROM THE ACT OF UNION TO THE FALL OF PARNELL

## Charles Sidman

The Act of Union took effect on 1 January 1801. With it two islands were merged into a single kingdom, the United Kingdom of Great Britain and Ireland. According to the terms of the Union, the Irish were allowed to seat one hundred persons in the House of Commons in London, a number that was fully one hundred less than they deserved by a strict proportional representation of their population. As before, Catholics were excluded by the oath from sitting in Parliament.[1] This exclusion served in general as an example of the lack of trust and the absence of equity that existed from the first between the British and the Irish under these new arrangements.

Two important offices that had vital functions before the Union—those of the Privy Council and the viceroy—were retained, but with slightly diminished authority and prestige. Ireland was left with its own treasury and its own national debt of £21 million. In addition, it was required to furnish two-fifths of the general revenue expenses of the United Kingdom, a sum that was disproportionate to its wealth and ability to pay. Moreover, while Ireland was specifically exempted from the burdens of the British debt, which stood at £446,000 in 1800, there was no practical method of keeping the two treasuries separate. Free trade was established between Ireland and Great Britain, except that the woolen industry of northern Ireland received protection. In sum, Ireland was harnessed to Great Britain, but in a position of inferiority. At no time were the rights that pertained to Englishmen intended to serve as unbreachable principles for the mass of the population living in Ireland. Grenville expounded on this fundamental inequality in 1794, six years before the Union came into being, when he observed that "Ireland must be governed in the English interest."[2] By governing Ireland in the English interest, all chances for a harmonious relationship between the two were lost.

The Union was not a carefully worked-out plan for the governance of Ireland. Still less was it designed to solve Irish problems, unless, of course, they could be solved by being ignored. It was, in its incipiency, a means of controlling Ireland during a difficult period of foreign wars and revolution—which bore directly on the British Empire and the domestic situation in Great Britain. Force was the deterrent that held Ireland to Great Britain. Furthermore, although the British admitted that there were racial and religious differences between Ireland and Great Britain, no effort was made to accommodate Gaelic or Catholic points of view.

Great Britain had posited its control over Ireland upon the reliability of the descendants of the planters. Yet, late-eighteenth-century resistance to Great Britain had emanated in large measure from Irish Protestants and Irish nationalists. The former entertained the ambition to rule Ireland *sui generis*; the latter were inspired by thoughts of liberty brought on by the American and French revolutions. Thus, by a strange anomaly, some Protestants belonged to the Protestant Ascendancy, while at the same time they led a movement against British dictation in Ireland. There were other Irish Protestants, of the Presbyterian variety, who suffered political and religious discrimination that was no less irksome for its being milder in form than that imposed upon the Catholic majority on the island. Wolfe Tone and Robert Emmet were Irish Protestant nationalists of republican persuasion. Henry Grattan, a leader of the Irish Parliament, posed no direct threat to the British connection, but he did favor an autonomous Ireland under its own leaders. He shared with Tone and Emmet a regard for Irish virtues that counted for much more than any purely confessional division between Protestant and Catholic.

The Act of Union was testimony to the failure of the local Protestant Ascendancy, which could neither please Great Britain nor pacify Ireland. It represented a vote of no confidence in the ability of the Anglo-

IRELAND AFTER THE PARTITION

*From the Act of Union to the Fall of Parnell*
227

Irish to rule Ireland with proper consideration for British imperatives. Nonetheless, the Protestant Ascendancy did not thereby lose its privileged position in Ireland. The scope of its activities was limited; the potential for mischief was nearly eliminated. The view held by the viceroy, Lord Cornwallis, by the lord chancellor, Fitzgibbon, and by Castlereagh, however, was that the Union guaranteed a perpetual place of privilege to the Protestant Ascendancy through a linking-up of the interests of the Ascendancy with those of the responsible authorities in Great Britain.

What the Union accomplished almost immediately was to make the Protestant Ascendancy irresponsible and to put the onus for every injustice perpetrated on Ireland squarely at the door of Great Britain. No matter how exaggerated its claims or fears, the Protestant Ascendancy could demand attention in the knowledge that strategic considerations, anti-Catholic prejudice, and apathy toward Ireland favored it. But this dependence on Great Britain reduced the Protestant Ascendancy to parasitic status. An earlier independent spirit was rapidly transformed into an attitude of servile assertiveness, which made the proponents of the Ascendancy more British than the British.

The so-called garrison nation in Ireland had been called to account by the Act of Union. This garrison nation had derived most of the benefits that Ireland could supply, but it existed at the expense of an underground nation of indigenous Irishmen whose religion was a bar to advancement in government service, land holding, and social position. The glories of eighteenth-century Ireland, such as they were, rested on the accomplishments of the men of the garrison nation: of Swift, Goldsmith, and Wellington. Along with the British government's chastisement of the garrison nation came the resolution of an immediate problem, the threatened disloyalty to the mother country of the implanted stock among the Irish. In the long run, however, the humiliation of the garrison nation advanced the fortunes of the underground nation. The rebellious Protestant heroes of eighteenth-century Irish history came to be celebrated in song and story by Catholic Ireland. Such tribute was paid to Wolfe Tone and Robert Emmet that what Henry Grattan said of the Irish Parliament —"Thou art not conquered yet"—might be spoken as well for the imaginative spirit of Protestant Ireland.[3] National self-esteem had in this instance overcome the heat of religious passion.

The Catholic population of Ireland accepted the Act of Union without public demur. It had been made silent through the repression that followed in the wake of the rebellion of 1798. Yet not all of the willingness on the Catholics' part to remain passive derived from the presence of one hundred thousand British troops in Ireland. The Catholic majority had no love for the Protestant Ascendancy, whose position could only be fortified by an Irish Parliament. If anything, the Catholics hoped both for relief from tithes and for Catholic Emancipation from London. Indeed, Pitt, in his fervor to win passage for the Act of Union, actually offered the latter. Thus, while the Protestant Ascendancy was bribed to relinquish its authority, the Catholic majority, by promises of reform, was lulled into accepting direct British rule. The Irish Catholic hierarchy was suspicious, in any case, of the secularism and violence inherent in the French Revolution, against which Great Britain had set her entire Empire and to which Wolfe Tone looked for succor. The hierarchy was unenthusiastic about the principle of nationalism so openly invoked by the new breed, since this principle conjured up a powerful rival to the popular allegiance shown the Catholic Church in Ireland. Cornwallis correctly reported the Irish attitude about the Union: "There was not a murmur heard in the street, nor I believe an expression of ill-humour throughout the whole city of Dublin."[4]

[This easy success in bringing about the Act of Union blinded those who had engineered the feat to the need for making a gesture of conciliation toward the majority. A period of quietude convinced the British that the Irish were contented; one of violence, that the Irish were incorrigible. In neither case was it deemed wise to concede gracefully to Irish aspirations. Pitt was an able politician, and Cornwallis was an honest man. Both were English. They meant to live by their bargain in providing for Catholic Emancipation in conjunction with the Act of Union. But Castlereagh and Fitzgibbon were Irish-born Protestants. They had no intention of making that concession. The matter was decided by the king, George III, who opposed Catholic Emancipation in principle as a violation of his coronation oath.

Pitt quickly abandoned whatever commitment he had once undertaken to work for Catholic Emancipation. Irishmen of all stripes sank into sullen lethargy as a consequence of being neglected. One member of the Protestant Ascendancy confessed: "Ireland lost all charms for me; the Parliament—source of all my pride, ambition and gratification as a public man—had been bought and sold; I felt myself nobody. I became languid, careless and indifferent to everybody."[5] The Catholic hierarchy, on its part, considered itself betrayed once again by British perfidy.]

Expressions of discontent were frequently met with resorts to coercion. Nearly sixty acts were passed—in as many years in the early nineteenth century—imposing censorship of the press, banning of public meetings, or suspension of habeas corpus. As an example of the declining importance of literate and political Ireland, Dublin was reduced to provincial rank. The architecture that mattered in Dublin was Georgian. This eighteenth-century character remained preeminent well into the twentieth century, in spite of the impressive concomitant urbanization of Great Britain.

Ireland was an overwhelmingly agricultural entity.[6] The economic condition of rural Ireland had remained stable throughout the period of the Napoleonic Wars. So long as the United Kingdom drew heavily upon the food resources and nascent industries of Ireland, there was no immediate danger. Thus, the policy of rack-renting by the Irish landlords did not bear unduly on the peasant population until after 1815. However, the numerous new small holdings that had been established proved a bane on the farm community once prices tumbled. The peasants were no longer able to pay high rents; to make matters worse, poor harvests, particularly in 1817 and again in 1822, brought famine. To compensate for their relative impoverishment, the landlords converted arable land to pasture. As suddenly as they had been invited to become tenants, many peasants were evicted from the land.

Industry in Ireland enjoyed no happier fate. With the end of protection, Irish manufacture was almost completely superseded. The Irish debt grew rapidly, while British economic development took place with agricultural and tax help from Ireland. Irish resources helped to finance British industrialization, yet Ireland remained poor. The Union, from an Irish viewpoint, was anathematized as a colossal failure within a generation of its enactment.

Out of this malaise of depression emerged a man who was singularly suited to his times. Daniel O'Connell came from a well established Irish Catholic family out of county Kerry in the west of Ireland.[7] He grew up firm in his Catholicism, opposed in principle to the revolutionary impulse of his times, whether of the Robespierre or Emmet variety. O'Connell was educated in France, one of the "wild geese" who evaded the disabilities of British educational discrimination. Taking advantage of a partial relaxation of the Penal Code, O'Connell became a barrister in his native land. He made a reputation as a fearless defender of the underdog. In debate, he was prone to rhetorical exaggeration and to denigration of his adversaries. Respected for his integrity, and beloved by those Catholic Irish clients whose cases he fought, he won success and prominence in a hostile environment. Early in his career he took up the cause of Catholic relief and Emancipation. Even more, O'Connell championed repeal of the Union by peaceful means.[8]

Lack of organization and of a base from which constant nonviolent pressure might be applied against Great Britain had long been two of

*Daniel O'Connell*
George F. Muhany
National Gallery of Ireland, Dublin
Photo by courtesy of the National Gallery of Ireland

the major shortcomings of Irish dissidents. O'Connell solved this problem in its early-nineteenth-century context by a brilliant stroke, as simple as it was effective. An act in 1796 had prohibited political associations in Ireland. The Catholic Association, founded by Daniel O'Connell in 1823, was a clever circumvention of this law. Members of the Catholic Association subscribed one penny monthly, which was popularly called the "Catholic rent." Of itself, this assessment appeared to be much too small to be useful. Yet, one penny monthly, when collected by the Catholic clergy in their individual parishes, almost as a voluntary tax on the entire Catholic population of Ireland, amounted to a considerable sum.

O'Connell worked in harmony with the Irish Catholic clergy. He spent his energy freely in giving talks about the rights of Irishmen. He explained to people throughout the island what recourse they could take against injustice. Through his Catholic Association, O'Connell brought political education to Ireland. He taught Irish Catholics how to use numbers and public opinion to further their interests. He opened the way to a democratization of Ireland. The popular tribunals that were instituted at his behest, the decisions of which were respected without complaint, were an example of O'Connel's reliance upon democratic justice. Although he spoke the Gaelic language, O'Connell never used it in a public address. Furthermore, he enjoyed a social status and an economic position that were vastly superior to those of his followers.

In addition to arousing Catholic Ireland to an awareness of its position of inferiority, O'Connell desired to pressure the government of the United Kingdom into granting long-delayed practical reforms. For some years he waged a battle of nerves with the British authorities. A master stroke involved the election of O'Connell to the House of Commons in 1828. This famous Clare election, against an opponent who was sympathetic to Catholic problems and had the forces of class and tradition behind him, caused the Tory government in Great Britain to make concessions. Even Wellington, the aged doyen of the Conservatives, used his influence in the House of Lords to prevent a veto of the Catholic Emancipation bill, which the House of Commons passed to accommodate the most vocal of Irish Catholic demands. Fear of violence should Great Britain not permit O'Connell to take his seat in the House of Commons overcame the wishes of many to test further the capacity of Ireland to meddle in British affairs. Through this impressive victory over the British, O'Connell was stamped forever in the popular mind as the Liberator.

The prospect of Irish Catholics being elected to the House of Commons from all over Ireland filled Englishmen and the Protestant Ascendancy with horror. Robert Peel, then secretary of state, persuaded Wellington, the prime minister, of the urgency of the situation. When Wellington insisted that civil war impended in Ireland, the House of Lords supinely agreed to support the Emancipation Act. The deed was done, therefore, in haste and in ill humor. It was a step that could not be retraced.

British Catholics obtained political equality along with Irish Catholics, but the Irish were punished for their efforts. The voters who elected O'Connell were effectively disenfranchised when the forty-shilling tax qualification was removed in favor of a ten-pound requirement.

O'Connell had been eminently successful in his first major confrontation with Great Britain. Operating on internal lines, with the solid support of his own people in Ireland, he had profited from the fear of violence that the organized strength of the Catholic Association inspired. Thereafter, he moved to challenge the fundamental validity of the Union itself. In this struggle he was decidedly overmatched. O'Connell had now to operate on unfamiliar terrain. As a member of the House of Commons in London, he enjoyed a forum that Catholic Irishmen had not had before. However, his audience was often antagonistic to him. At best, it was indifferent to the conditions that he complained about.

O'Connell's shortcomings were soon thrust into the foreground. He had no sympathy for violence. Once this essential commitment to the law was understood, his fulminations against the injustices of the British system lost much of their sting. What need was there to respond to additional demands if force were not to be used as a last resort to achieve them? For O'Connell, the winning of his country's freedom was "not worth the shedding of a single drop of human blood."[9]

⌐ Thus, O'Connell operated at a disadvantage when he took up the cause of repeal. Furthermore, repeal of the Union involved a concession in principle, whereas Catholic Emancipation required only a modification of policy.⌐

At home, O'Connell fell out of sympathy with younger Irish nationalists who were impatient for change. Many of the younger nationalists joined the Young Ireland movement, which evolved out of its Continental counterpart and breathed the romantic nationalist spirit of Giuseppe Mazzini. Patriotic idealism was its driving force. Its enemies were the alien occupier and the cosmopolitan dilettante. The *Nation*, the mouthpiece of Young Ireland, was a weekly edited by Thomas Davis; it had as its objective the promotion of a love of homeland. The *Nation* printed poems that exuded sentiment, much of it brought on by recollections of a great Irish culture in times past.

Itself a nonsectarian Irish movement that owed nothing directly to the Catholic tradition, Young Ireland reawakened memories of rebellions that were nearly forgotten. It praised the men of '98 and the ideals for which they had fought and died. Its members despised O'Connell, who neglected these men; they also despised the British, who would not vacate Ireland. It was to history that Davis called his readers, and to the west of Ireland that he directed their attention for inspiration concerning the future of his country.

The revolution of 1848 in Ireland, such as it was, emanated from Young Ireland. Yet, the Young Irelanders were loathe to put in with the Chartists in England. Moreover, they had no interest in the rural question in Ireland, which was a matter of deep concern among the very elements that they needed to woo if ever they were to become a truly national, not a merely nationalist, movement. That Ireland lay prostrate as a consequence of the Famine also contributed no little to the feeble response to cries for revolution in a year of revolutions. The men who had tried to rouse Ireland to revolutionary frenzy were captured, tried, and found guilty. Instead of being executed, a fate that their predecessors had suffered, they were sent into exile. Others of them emigrated in disgust. Some contemplated in print the misfortunes of Ireland, as did John Mitchel in his famous *Jail Journal*; some contributed to the improvement of another society, as did Charles Gavan Duffy, who went in disgust to Australia, where he rose to high office and was eventually knighted. One common legacy that these men left in their new homes was a hatred of Great Britain.

In the long run, there could be no common endeavor by O'Connell and the Young Irelanders. The latter did not share O'Connell's willingness to live with the religious dichotomy between Catholic Ireland and Protestant Britain. Within their ranks were Catholic and Protestant Irishmen. The two leading lights of the movement were Thomas Davis, a brilliant writer who was Protestant, and Gavan Duffy, an able administrator who was Catholic. This unconcern about religious questions per se and disregard of parliamentary expedients alienated them from O'Connell. Just as Young Ireland failed in its purpose, so, too, did O'Connell fail in his last campaign.

Father Theobald Matthew, a gentle crusader for temperance and the founder of the Pioneer movement, injected a sense of high moral purpose into the meetings that were held in conjunction with Irish reform. In turn, his movement provided O'Connell with disciplined and receptive supporters of repeal. The enthusiasm of 1828 was in the air once more. O'Connell took to the road as only he could do.[10] He spoke before large crowds all over Ireland. It was estimated that one-half million people attended the rally held among the ruins of Tara, home base of the ancient kings of Ireland. When at last O'Connell dared to schedule a meeting within sight of Dublin—at Clontarf, where Brian Boru had won an astonishing success over the Danes in 1014—the authorities intervened. The meeting was banned. As a presage of the response of the party of movement (liberals) in France in 1848, which, when confronted by government disapproval of its banquets, quietly yielded, O'Connell called off his meeting. Even the zealots of the Young Ireland movement cautioned: "People of Ireland! There is but one course. Obey the law."[11] The result of this episode was a decisive, if temporary, setback for Irish ambitions. Whether the British government knew in advance that O'Connell was only bluffing or whether it was prepared in any event for a showdown will never be known.

Daniel O'Connell's notable career had come to an end. The repeal movement faded for a time from public notice, deserted by its advocates before it had spent its considerable force. Shortly after this debacle, O'Connell was arrested and charged with high treason. Only Protestants were permitted to serve on his jury. Prejudged and found guilty, the Old Liberator, in spite of one last effective and spirited defense, was then sentenced to prison. O'Connell appealed this verdict to the House of Lords, which reversed the decision of the lower court and set him free.

It was too late, however, to reverse the tide of events. The clergy remained faithful to O'Connell and proved to be his staunchest advocates. The Catholic populace admired his courage and idolized him as a true son of Ireland. By his final defeat, O'Connell had sacrificed leadership of the pre-1848 activists. Young Ireland was committed to a different course of action from the one that had occupied his time for a generation. Lacking the energy to do battle with his myriad competitors, O'Connell decided to make his peace with God. He left Ireland in 1847, dying while on a pilgrimage to Rome.

The potato blight struck Ireland in September 1845. It lasted well into 1848. Although other parts of Europe were affected by the blight, its consequences were more immediately and disastrously felt in Ireland because of a combination of circumstances. The Irish were dependent upon the potato as no other Western people were upon a single crop. With an increase of about one hundred thousand annually, the Irish population had reached eight million by the middle of the nineteenth century. Most of the people lived in rural areas as poor tenant farmers. They were ill equipped to meet the challenge of famine, for they lacked land of their own, compassionate landlords, an understanding government, or alternate job skills and opportunities.

Since the Napoleonic Wars, when prices had been high and food ample, Ireland had suffered agrarian distress. Lawlessness in rural Ireland was not uncommon as secret societies sprang up, tenants attacked landlords, and tenants fought with each other. Commentaries on the state of misery in Ireland were numerous. The poet Percy Bysshe Shelley observed after a visit to Ireland that "the poor of Dublin are assuredly the meanest and most miserable of all."[12] John Keats commented on "the worse than nakedness, the rags, the dirt and the misery of the poor common Irish."[13] In all of the Ottoman Empire, Lord Byron related, there was not to be found the wretchedness that he saw in Ireland.

It was no better one generation later, when William Thackeray ruminated on the universal filth and dilapidation he had seen in Ireland in 1842. Unable to resist the temptation, Thackeray lectured the Irish on the deplorable weaknesses of their character, which, by implication, were largely responsible for this state of affairs. Gustave de Beaumont, a friend of de Tocqueville's, thought the Irishman worse off than the Indian in his forest or the Negro in his chains: "There is no doubt that the most miserable of English paupers is better fed and clothed than the most prosperous of Irish laborers."[14] The finest buildings in Dublin, he observed with studied sarcasm, were prisons and barracks. Nearly everything else was in ruins—and the people were walking ruins.

In Ireland there were two nations: the nation of the rich, and the nation of the poor. The rich were Protestants. They owned the land, held government offices, occupied the center of the economic and social stage, despised their Catholic inferiors, and looked to Great Britain for moral sustenance and the preservation of their privileges. The poor were Catholics. They had little respect for the law, no confidence in the courts, a long memory of injustices, and scant reason to rejoice in their condition or prospects. Count Camillo di Cavour, the unifier of Italy, commented that "such a social state has no parallel in Europe."[15]

No part of the British Empire was as thoroughly investigated as Ireland. From 1800 to the Famine, 114 royal commissions and 61 special committees concerned themselves with Ireland, while, at the same time, eighteen Coercion Acts were enacted to keep her peaceful.[16] The Devon Commission in 1843 reported on the deplorable condition of most Irishmen—how they silently endured their many privations; how their only food was the potato, and their only drink water; and how a pig and a manure heap were their only property. Yet, nothing whatever was done by the government of Prime Minister Robert Peel, who was advised by the Devon Commission to institute wide-ranging public-works projects in order to relieve poverty and reclaim wasteland.

Famine conditions evolved out of the unusually wet summers of 1845 and 1846. Ireland's social system and her dependence upon Great Britain condemned her to an even greater penalty than she deserved to pay, however. The Irish diet had become more monotonous from the eighteenth to the nineteenth centuries. Milk had almost wholly disappeared from the table, although it had been a popular drink earlier. Bread and meat were seldom eaten by the poor. The universal food was the potato. Requiring little labor and only a small patch of land, the potato was nutritious and could be stored easily. It was a symbol of the degradation of the underground nation. Three-quarters of the arable land in Ireland was planted in grain. The remaining one-quarter, which produced the potato, fed the population.

The potato crop in 1845 withered and died suddenly, just as it was ready for harvesting. Thousands upon thousands of Irishmen died of malnutrition or actually starved that winter and throughout the next year, even though grain continued to be exported to Great Britain under the protection of the Corn Laws, which ensured premium prices on the British market. Ireland produced an abundance of food, certainly enough to feed its own population, during the entire period of the Famine. Yet the population of Ireland was subjected to a period of starvation. The Irish peasantry bore with its misfortune passively. According to the Census Commission of 1851, "the forbearance of the Irish peasantry and the calm submission with which they bore the deadliest ills that can fall on man can scarcely be paralleled in the annals of any nation."[17]

Within five years, about one million human beings perished in Ireland, most of them from typhus or typhoid fever as a result of their weakened condition. Cholera, dysentery, and scurvy also took their toll. In addition, more than one million Irishmen fled the country in the first great migration of Irish Catholics from the rural west. They moved to Glasgow and Liverpool, providing these cities with a distinctive Irish immigrant culture. They crammed into small ships to cross the Atlantic, many of them dying on the way. The survivors landed as derelicts on the piers of Boston and New York. Emigration from Ireland in the early 1840s averaged 61,000 per year. That figure rose to 106,000 in 1846, and to 212,000 in 1847. The last year of mass migration was 1851, when 200,000 Irishmen left their native land.

By 1900, two and one-half million more Irish had left for the New World, thus providing an unprecedented example of the depopulation of a Western country in the modern world. Thomas Carlyle, touring Ireland in 1849, observed that the population had "gone to the workhouse, to England, to the grave."[18] If Carlyle expressed a common British view that Ireland was a country much like a beggar's coat, "not patched or patchable any longer"[19]—a view heavy with disgust and devoid of pity— the Irish experienced yet another devastating example of the incapacity of the British to do right by Ireland.

The British government treated the Famine as if it were a local and temporary problem. The canons of free trade inhibited responsible British politicians from intervening except in a desultory manner. Although the Corn Laws were finally repealed in the midst of the Famine, neither the Tory government nor the Whig government, each of which had a turn in office, made a concerted effort to ameliorate conditions in

Ireland. Less money was spent on relief for Ireland than had been allocated by Parliament in 1833 to compensate the relatively few West Indian slave owners for the loss of their slaves ( £15–20 million). Even so, more than three million Irishmen were being fed at public expense in 1847. Unnecessary road building was undertaken sporadically, but no railroad or harbor construction, which was a much more vital need (for instance, Ireland had only 164 miles of railroad in 1846, compared to 6,121 miles in Great Britain).

Evictions from the land were common during the Famine. In the twenty years between 1846 and 1866 there were no fewer than three hundred thousand evictions, involving two million persons. The British officials in Ireland, and most conspicuously the viceroy, were outspoken in their demand for effective policies of relief. Indeed, Lord Clarendon, the viceroy, a Conservative, wrote bitterly to the British prime minister, Lord John Russell, a Liberal: "I don't think there is another legislature in Europe that would disregard such suffering as now exists in the west of Ireland, or coldly persist in the policy of extermination."[20] Russell did nothing, in part at least because he was convinced that British public opinion was unsympathetic to the plight of Ireland.

More callous still was the attitude of Sir Charles Trevelyan, permanent head of the British Treasury. Trevelyan opposed spending money on Irish relief. At first he refused to concede that Ireland was in need of help. When, after two years of famine, he could no longer take refuge in ignorance, he responded: "It is hard upon the poor people that they should be deprived of knowing that they are suffering an affliction of God's providence."[21] Thus, misery and distress were allowed to run their course unabated. The legacy of bitterness that the Irish cultivated was passed on from generation to generation. It was spread across the Atlantic and Pacific oceans by those who fled Ireland. The Union had never been a success. By 1850 the magnitude of its failure was manifest.

Aside from the cultural gulf between the islands, there were four major influences that kept the Irish from becoming reconciled to their fate. These influences revolved around Thomas Drummond, the Royal Irish Constabulary, the Anglican Educational Establishment, and the Catholic Church.[22]

In his quest for justice in Ireland, Thomas Drummond gave an example of fair play, as rare as it was cherished, that long fortified some Irishmen in the belief that accommodation with Great Britain was possible. Drummond held a position of unparalleled importance at Dublin Castle for a brief period of five years, from 1835 to 1840. This upright Scots engineer and Protestant was sent to Ireland to ease the deadweight of British coercion. He was the only concession to impartiality that issued from the Melbourne ministry. Although he did not attempt to change laws in order to suit the Catholics of Ireland, he made a determined effort to administer fairly such laws as existed. In this difficult enterprise he was remarkably successful. Drummond brought Catholics into the police force and onto juries. He protected them from the pressure of the Orange lodges. He fought the Protestant Ascendancy to a standstill, and won the day; but the example he gave did not outlive his untimely death. Yet, it left Catholic Ireland with a point of reference from which it measured all subsequent British policy.

However successful Drummond was in the short run, Ireland was little improved over the long haul. But it took a concerted effort by the Royal Irish Constabulary—remodeled as it was, quite paradoxically, by Drummond himself in 1836—to hold Ireland at bay. The Royal Irish Constabulary was used to suppress Irish grievances by providing an unwholesome conjunction of law and conformity. The minds of the men in the Royal Irish Constabulary were molded, as O'Hegarty affirmed, in the way that the British wanted to mold the minds of all Irishmen. A system of informers was employed effectively to uncover disloyalty at the grass roots. The Royal Irish Constabulary was a police force; its members wore black uniforms and were armed with carbines and batons. It was a police force, but it behaved like a garrison army. The good that Drummond did by making justice accessible to the masses was nullified by the stern exactions of the Royal Irish Constabulary.

In a less direct way, and less effectively, the British tried to regulate Irish life by controlling education. The aim of British educational policy in nineteenth-century Ireland was the Anglicanization of the native Irish. The British desired to affect both the religious and the cultural life of Ireland. They deluded themselves about what was possible, and their patronizing attitude toward the Irish was transparent. Among themselves, they spoke and wrote confidently that Ireland could be proselytized and Anglicized. It was expected that through the public-school system, which was inappropriately called the National system, they would manage to separate the educated Irish from allegiance to Rome. Furthermore, by a careful censorship of textbooks, the Irish were to be instilled with proper British virtues.

The Gaelic language was most certainly in decline, and the British accepted this development as a corollary to their educational policy in Ireland. Yet, British educational policy in Ireland accomplished the opposite of what was intended. The Irish used British control over public education to maintain the cleavage that they attributed in the first place to the British presence in Ireland.

This conflict between Ireland and Great Britain was most readily apparent in the religious sphere. The British were not reconciled to a Catholic Ireland. There were many churches in Ireland, to be sure, but there was only one Irish Church—and that was the Catholic Church. The Catholic Church in Ireland had always carried within it national and universal characteristics. It had been singularly responsive to popular causes without ever losing its devotion to the Holy See. While its national traits were most easily identified, its basic attachment to the whole Church, of which Ireland was the crown jewel, remained unquestioned.

In Ireland, the Catholic Church went underground with Irish national aspirations for the duration of the Penal Laws. The priests and the people shared the same dangers and the same hopes. Both groups opposed British exploitation of Ireland. Persecution strengthened the priests in their convictions; it also solidified their popularity. The masses in Ireland were not only Catholic in religion; they were also clerical by temperament.

Mid-century Ireland fell largely under the spell of Cardinal Paul Cullen. Cullen turned to politics reluctantly, if logically, in order to defend the Catholic Church against its enemies. For him, Great Britain was the enemy because it was Protestant. This Protestantism ensured a bigoted approach to all matters of concern to Catholic Ireland. One example of the insidious influence of Great Britain in Ireland came with the founding of the famous Queens colleges at Belfast, Galway, and Cork. These were godless colleges to men like Cullen, who objected strenuously to the absence of theological faculties in them. Cullen guessed, not without some justification, that the British government hoped, through these colleges, to weaken the hold of the Catholic faith on the educated people of Ireland. What the British government intended, at the least, was to tie educated Catholic opinion to the establishment, and to make it loyal to the Union. The secularism that was furthered by this emphasis on nonsectarian schools alerted Cullen and others to another danger in the British connection. While O'Connell criticized these colleges on nationalist grounds, Cullen did so on religious grounds.

A battle then was waged between Cullen, on behalf of Catholic Ireland, and the British government, on behalf of the Union. Cullen took the clergy into the thick of the fight. He assumed leadership for the clergy in the struggle with Great Britain, which he considered a religious contest. Catholic laymen were expected to remain subordinate to the Catholic hierarchy, helping it when and as directed. This mixing of religion and politics resulted in some anticlericalism in Ireland; but the Young Ireland movement, for one, lost rather than gained because it criticized the Catholic hierarchy.

Thus, Cullen had the vast majority of Catholic Ireland behind him, in spite of his lack of tact and his clerical bias. The Young Ireland movement regressed to the extent that it restricted direction from clerics of Cullen's stamp. And Great Britain depleted its own strength continually in the effort to detach the Catholic hierarchy from Irish national causes.

Cullen was particularly incensed by the privileged position of the Church of Ireland, which owned land, obtained public revenues, and exerted influence far in excess of the actual numerical weight of its membership. The Irish population stood at 5.75 million in 1861. Of these, 4.5 million were Catholics, and fewer than 700,000 were members of the Anglican Church of Ireland. Yet, Irish Catholics were required to support the Church of Ireland through tithe payments. Disestablishment of the Church of Ireland in 1869 was meant to allay Catholic unrest. It conformed neatly to the secularist tendencies of the British Liberal party, which was in power at the time of its enactment; and disestablishment suited the desires of the Catholic hierarchy. But since it did not disturb the fundamental position of the Protestant Ascendancy, it was not able to accomplish the goals set for it. To achieve equality in such slowly measured steps, without plan or reason, led to the conviction that the system itself was at fault. The Irish majority, in short, was not satisfied with this meager evidence of British good will.

The first two significant nineteenth-century British concessions to Ireland were religious in nature. It took most of the nineteenth century for them to be realized. Indeed, having come grudgingly and after so much controversy, and not being accompanied by substantive reforms of a nonreligious type, they not only aroused the Catholics of Ireland to seek yet other remedies, they also set them more firmly on a course of Home Rule: for the Protestant Ascendancy, the goal was perceived as Rome Rule, but for most Irishmen, Home Rule was only the halfway station to independence.

Catholic Emancipation and repeal of the Union took up most of the limited energies of the Irish in the first half of the nineteenth century. Yet, since the partial displacement of the native Gaels from the land by invading Norman barons in the Middle Ages, land had been a major source of dispute between the garrison nation and the underground nation.

On the one hand, the Irish were not reconciled to the loss of their land. A basic misunderstanding existed, on the other hand, between the Irish and the British with respect to the nature of landholding. For the

British, titles to land were considered absolute, immutable, and individual. Land was a badge of social merit, a reward for successful ascendancy; it was used to make fortunes and to further careers. On this basis, Irish estates were awarded to British families, who were expected to buttress the crown in exchange for a privileged position in Ireland.

The system of landholding worked in different ways in Great Britain and in Ireland. In Great Britain the tenant rented the land, as well as everything on it—including buildings and equipment. He had security of tenure and the right to be compensated for the improvements he made. Local affairs in Great Britain were managed by a triumvirate: the lord of the manor, the constable, and the curate. The lord of the manor lived alongside his tenants. He shared with them their language, amusements, and interests. He was often the constable. The curate held his benefice from the lord of the manor, but he conducted services in English for parishioners who shared his religious views.

In Ireland no such community of interest existed. The lord of the manor was absent in Dublin or London, and his business manager wished only to extract the maximum return from the land. The constable, certainly in the western part of Ireland, spoke another language and followed customs that were foreign to those of his tenants. The curate was Church of Ireland, and therefore had little insight into what troubled the native Catholic population. From this circumstance alone, the rural situation in Ireland was vastly different from that in Great Britain.

The world of the Irish revolved around religion and land. Religion spelled the theological difference between the Irish and the British; land spelled the social difference. Ownership of land became a question of national identity with the Irish. The ultimate in Irish land reform meant a total end to alien possession of the soil. Thus, in the second half of the nineteenth century, when the British took a belated and intermittent interest in land reform, their efforts were not appreciated. The British struck at abuses, such as absentee landlordism; but the Irish wanted no landlords at all. The British diagnosed the problem with Ireland as a case of British misrule; it was British rule, however, that the Irish found intolerable.

In general, British land legislation favored the landlord over the tenant. The educated view in Great Britain—that land ownership should not be trammeled by legal restrictions—held sway until well into the nineteenth century. "The old order before the Famine had rested upon a powerful, still-confident aristocracy on the one hand and upon an impoverished and insecure peasantry on the other."[23] What the landlord did for his tenant concerned his conscience and God; it did not concern the state.

The Irish landlords owed their strong position to this legal bias—a concept of proprietorship that was dominant in Victorian England—more than to their extraordinary influence on British parliamentary life, although the latter served as a guarantee that they would not be badly used in law.[24] But the Irish landlords lost status as a result of the Famine. Many Englishmen resented paying higher taxes for the relief of Ireland, and they blamed Irish landlords for allowing an unsatisfactory situation to develop in Ireland. Closer to home, some Irishmen concluded that the root of the Irish problem was the socioeconomic condition imposed upon Ireland, and not so much the political subjection to Great Britain. Out of this view emerged various land leagues, of which the first organized post-Famine group was the Tenant League, founded in 1850. This league had the intention of sponsoring an Irish Parliamentary party to fight for land reform, but it failed in its purpose. In Great Britain the political situation was not yet ripe for such a development, and many prominent Irish Catholics—Cardinal Paul Cullen among them—feared lest the Penal Laws be reimposed.

A beginning had been made, nonetheless, if quite by accident. The Encumbered Estates Act of 1849 was conceived as a financial expedient. It worked, rather, to relieve insolvent Irish landlords of their property, and to replace them with a fresh assortment of landlords. In ten years £23 million had been spent in accordance with the provisions of this act. The new landlords were often not from the area of their recent acquisitions. Hence, they had even less sympathy for the plight of the tenants than their predecessors had had. Two classes of rural people were now being victimized by the law in Ireland: the landlords who were being dispossessed and the tenants, who, with the exception of those in Ulster, had no security of tenure.

Attempts at mid century to alleviate the conditions of Irish tenants failed because of the unwillingness of the British government to challenge the sanctity of property and because of a series of bad harvests. Unrest in rural Ireland was endemic.

Into the breach stepped Michael Davitt, whose father had been evicted from his land in western Ireland. Davitt had worked for a time in factories in England, an experience that had taught him the value of collective action. He returned to Ireland determined to teach his fellow countrymen about the advantages that he saw accrue to the English working class from trade-union organization. Davitt took the disagreements between Ireland and Great Britain out of a philosophical context and put them into a practical mold: the Irish tenant could obtain justice from his landlord by a policy of cooperative resistance. In line with this policy, Irish tenants in county Mayo refused to pay rents to their landlord—a certain Captain Boycott—or to provide him with essential services. Thus was inaugurated a system of passive opposition, a system that gained widespread popularity under the name "boycott."

The immediate objective of discontented Irish peasants was achievement of the three F's—fair rent, fixity of tenure, and free sale of land and property. In 1870 William Gladstone, the British prime minister who did the most for Ireland in the nineteenth century, regulated the relationship of the landlord and the tenant by another law that bore on Ireland. This act extended to the rest of Ireland the tenure customs that had been operative only in Ulster, where many tenants were Scots Protestants. By diminishing the exclusive property rights of the landlord through this act of Parliament, the parliamentarians further modified the control that the landlord exercised over his property.

At the end of the decade of the 1870s two events took place—one on either side of the Irish Sea—that had a profound impact on Irish affairs. Efforts in Ireland were concentrated on the establishment of the Land League. The moving force behind the Land League was a prominent Irish Protestant landowner, the indomitable Charles Stewart Parnell.[25] Parnell had recently been won over to the cause of land reform. He advocated that the state purchase land and subsequently assign it to the landless Irish, a policy that was designed to produce a country of peasant proprietors, as had been done in France.

Meanwhile, in Great Britain, Gladstone was returned to office as prime minister for the third time in 1880. If anything, his strong moral sense was more alive than ever with compassion for those who were being treated unjustly in Ireland. This time, Gladstone had the backing to do what he wanted—of liberals, whose philosophical commitment called for an end to the more flagrant inequities within the realm; of religious reformers, often Quakers or Methodists, who demanded a greater spirit of charity and toleration; and of trade unionists, whose concept of class solidarity provided Irish tenants with unexpected moral support.

Land Acts and coercion bills were passed into law together. The former were intended to mitigate rural agitation, thereby to lay to rest once and for all time the Irish problem; the latter were deemed necessary in order to put an end to the violence and disrespect for the law that were so much a part of the rural agitation. While rents were reduced by as much as 20 percent according to the Land Act of 1881, and while a special tribunal now had the power to fix rents as a countermeasure to the arbi-

*C. S. Parnell*, 1891
J. D. Reigh
Drawing
National Gallery of Ireland, Dublin
Photo by courtesy of the National Gallery of Ireland

trary will of the landlord, the law was tightened against Irish peasants who engaged in unlawful acts—whether the murder of "gombeen men" or the refusal to pay rents. By all odds, this act and its successors were political triumphs for Parnell. They brought him into national prominence in Ireland and into the mainstream of British parliamentary life.

Parnell was not for long to be remembered primarily for his contributions to the Land League. Another, and larger, issue soon came to dominate the continuing dialogue between Ireland and Great Britain under the Union. This issue was distilled as Home Rule, a renewal of that Irish effort at partial separation, at the least, from Great Britain.

Parnell had been educated in England. His family had acquired its estates in Ireland during the Cromwellian confiscations. His favorite sport was cricket. His mannerisms and speech pattern were English to the marrow. By no stretch of the imagination did he look the part of an advocate of Ireland. Indeed, Parnell's knowledge of Irish history was rudimentary, at best. A man of property, aloof and laconic of speech, Parnell enjoyed addressing himself to practical problems. He had a magnetism, in politics as well as with women, in spite of his immense reserve and his cold exterior.

There was a toughness in Parnell, a stubborn dedication to see through his commitment to obtain justice for Ireland. Parnell entered the House of Commons, at twenty-nine years of age, in 1875. He was inspired by a consummate hatred of England; it was stronger by far than his love of Ireland. Sir Charles Dilke was shocked and impressed by its vehemence: "He hated England, English ways, English modes of thought. He would have nothing to do with us. He acted like a foreigner."[26] For all of his fixity of purpose, Parnell was extraordinarily effective in Parliament. He took on the sharpest politicians in England, and repaid them lavishly in kind for the insults they hurled at him. He would not let them forget Ireland or ignore the Irish Parliamentary party, which he soon developed into a third force of no mean dimensions in the House of Commons.

British governments were forced out of office, and the British parties were split on several occasions, because of the Irish problem. It happened in 1829, with Catholic Emancipation, and again in 1846, with the repeal of the Corn Laws. While Great Britain undoubtedly controlled Ireland, the Irish in a certain sense wreaked their own special revenge on Great Britain. This was especially the case for as long as Parnell remained in the House of Commons, for the Irish vote was often needed to keep a government afloat, and Parnell bartered with skill. His policy of obstructionism infuriated the British, but it brought consideration of Home Rule for Ireland.

In its origin, Home Rule was Protestant, prosaic, and political, as O'Farrell said so well. It was also basically conservative and antipathetic to revolution. The man who conditioned Home Rule in its impact on British life was Gladstone, an English High Churchman whose religious zeal played a unique role in his own political career. The founder of Home Rule was Isaac Butt, an Irish Protestant lawyer. Its greatest advocate was Charles Stewart Parnell, a Protestant Anglo-Irish landowner.

That Home Rule was so nearly dominated in its early stages by Irish Protestants gave it a hearing and a toleration in British public life that it might not have had otherwise. That it won Irish Catholic support gave it a strength without which it could never have been influential.

The Irish Protestants who were Home Rulers thought of it as a solution to the Irish question; the Catholic Home Rulers were at best lukewarm about its potential to solve the Irish question. Most of them went along with it in the knowledge that nothing more was possible under the circumstances.

Isaac Butt was convinced that the differences between agrarian Ireland and industrial Britain were irreconcilable and that Ireland was in grave danger of moral contamination from a decadent and irreligious Great Britain. He would save Ireland from the unhealthy conditions he observed in Great Britain by providing her with a separate Parliament.

Irish Catholics shared Butt's views on British moral degradation. They were likewise enamored of the prospect of an end to Union. So warm was their support for Home Rule that they drove Irish Protestants away from the movement and into the Unionist camp, where all of those tendencies to husband privilege and to glory in servility under British patronage were reinforced.

Home Rule offered Irish Catholics a legal outlet for their aspirations in Ireland. The Catholic hierarchy in Ireland soon came to favor Home Rule agitation, although many clergymen feared lest preoccupation with Home Rule divert attention from the British need to provide for religious education in Ireland. Cardinal Cullen, for instance, did not like the idea of Home Rule, for a future Irish Parliament would probably be dominated by Protestants. In any case, it was likely to have a secular orientation, which boded ill for the Catholic Church in Ireland. To Irishmen, Home Rule meant an Irish Parliament with the broadest possible local administration; to the Irish clergy, it often meant much less. The Catholic Church in Ireland was sensitive about competition for the loyalty of Irishmen. It had benefited from the protracted struggle against Great Britain. To establish an Irish Parliament would provide competition at the same time that it diminished the tension between Ireland and Great Britain that brought such rich returns to the Catholic Church. Moreover, the Catholic hierarchy would need to establish a new relationship with the local Home Rule government, and this might jeopardize the concessions that had already been won from Great Britain.

The Catholic hierarchy finally came to support Home Rule, because the popularity of the movement allowed of no alternative. Always alert to grass-roots sentiment, the clergy fell into line once Home Rule had made its impact on the national conscience.

The success of Home Rule in Ireland was directly related to the fact that most British and Irish Protestants opposed it. The Home Rulers accused their opponents of religious discrimination: "Were the Irish all

Protestants, they [the British] would tomorrow repeal the Union, and restore to them their native Parliament."[27] In a way, every concession that the British made to Irish political pressure in the interests of Catholic equality exposed to public view the fact that Britain held Ireland by force. As Sir William Harcourt told Gladstone in December 1883: "We hold Ireland by *force and by force alone* as much as in the days of Cromwell. . . . We never have governed Ireland by the good will of its people."[28]

For those in Britain who favored it, Home Rule was an attempt at reconciliation: it was equivalent to the purchase of peace with honor. It was intended that Home Rule would end agitation and discontent in Ireland, and that thus, in a stroke, it would cement the Union and make secure the Empire. British Liberals pursued Home Rule in part because of Gladstone's impossible moral urge, and in part because they rejected the notion of government by force, even though they wished to maintain the Union.

The Conservatives were in power much longer than the Liberals during the period of intensive agitation for Home Rule. They were much less tolerant of the movement to grant Home Rule to Ireland. Nevertheless, the near balance of political power between Liberals and Conservatives, which obtained with regularity in Great Britain during the late nineteenth century, provided Parnell and the Irish Parliamentary party with an opportunity to purchase favors.

Just as O'Connell failed earlier to win repeal, so, too, Parnell failed to gain Home Rule. Yet, Parnell came nearer to success than did O'Connell. His goal was more nearly possible of realization in the existing political environment. He had a much better working relationship with political forces in Ireland and in Great Britain. Two Home Rule bills came up for a vote in Parliament. The House of Commons did not pass the first one. The House of Lords vetoed the second, which the House of Commons had passed. Gladstone had tested his considerable political leverage and had discovered the limitations of his influence. Parnell had prodded the British to the end of their patience and understanding, but he could not bring about Home Rule without the acquiescence of both houses of the British Parliament.

Although the issue of Home Rule was still very much alive, it was dealt a terrible blow by the disgrace and death of Parnell. Parnell's disgrace came about because of a divorce scandal, in which he was involved as the implicated third party. His loyalty to Kitty O'Shea, and the offense that this incident caused, ruined Parnell's career. In attempting to recover his position in Ireland, where the Catholic Church and a segment of pious opinion now turned against him, Parnell destroyed his health. His death left a void in Irish politics that was not filled for a generation. Debate about Parnell's merits and weaknesses plagued Irish public life thereafter. No amount of charity could entirely obscure the sophistry in this debate, and no amount of understanding could make acceptable any single judgment about his place in Irish history. Only one point was clear: Parnell stood as O'Connell's equal in tragedy, but not in esteem. Parnell was the better politician, but in his failure he joined a long line of men who had met their match in the British connection.

Ireland was as much transformed by the fall of Parnell as it had been by the failure of O'Connell. Both men had achieved what appeared at first glance to be improbable victories over Great Britain in the direction of freedom for Ireland. Each, in turn, was denied the ultimate triumph, and instead was discredited. Yet, just as their victories were incomplete, so in defeat they accomplished a fundamental alteration of the relationship between Ireland and Great Britain. And this was more truly the case with Parnell than with O'Connell. O'Connell worked with and through the Church to give Catholic Ireland a sense of dignity and purpose. Parnell made the Irish deputies indispensable to British parliamentary viability. He forced the Liberals to address the Irish problem. And he focused attention on the need to grant ever-widening concessions to Ireland.

## NOTES

1. On the Union, see especially James C. Beckett, *The Making of Modern Ireland, 1603–1922* (New York: Knopf, 1973), pp. 268 ff.; and Patrick S. O'Hegarty, *A History of Ireland under the Union, 1801–1922* (New York: Kraus Reprint, 1969).
2. Patrick O'Farrell, *Ireland's English Question* (London: Batsford, 1971), p. 67.
3. Giovanni Costigan, *A History of Modern Ireland* (New York: Pegasus, 1969), p. 135.
4. O'Farrell, *Ireland's English Question*, p. 73.
5. Costigan, *History of Modern Ireland*, p. 144.
6. For a brief survey of the economic situation in early-nineteenth-century Ireland, see Lawrence J. McCaffrey, *The Irish Question, 1800–1922* (Lexington: University of Kentucky Press, 1968), pp. 15 ff.
7. The best biography of Daniel O'Connell is the one by Seán O'Faoláin, *King of the Beggars* (New York: Viking Press, 1938); the most recent is Raymond Moley's *Daniel O'Connell: Nationalism without Violence* (New York: Fordham University Press, 1974).

8. On repeal, see especially Keyin B. Nowlan, *The Politics of Repeal* (London: Routledge & K. Paul, 1965), and Lawrence McCaffrey, *Daniel O'Connell and the Repeal Year* (Lexington: University of Kentucky Press, 1966).
9. Oliver MacDonagh, *Ireland* (Englewood Cliffs, N.J.: Prentice-Hall, 1968), p. 45.
10. Beckett, *Making of Modern Ireland*, p. 326.
11. O'Hegarty, *History of Ireland*, p. 166.
12. Costigan, *History of Modern Ireland*, p. 169.
13. Ibid.
14. Ibid., p. 170.
15. Ibid., p. 172.
16. For an excellent survey of economic conditions in Ireland in the mid-nineteenth century, see Francis S. L. Lyons, *Ireland since the Famine* (London: Weidenfeld & Nicolson, 1971), pp. 22 ff.
17. Costigan, *History of Modern Ireland*, p. 175.
18. Ibid., p. 178.
19. Ibid., p. 179.
20. Ibid., p. 183.
21. Ibid., p. 184.
22. On Drummond, see O'Hegarty, *History of Ireland*, pp. 75–94; on the Royal Irish Constabulary, also see O'Hegarty, *History of Ireland*, pp. 401–4; on the Anglican Establishment, see Beckett, *Making of Modern Ireland*, pp. 312–13, 329–31, 387–88; on the Catholic Church, see O'Farrell, *Ireland's English Question*, pp. 188–207.
23. Lyons, *Ireland since the Famine*, p. 37.
24. See, especially, O'Farrell, *Ireland's English Question*, pp. 114–26, 169–79, and Beckett, *Making of Modern Ireland*, pp. 351–75.
25. For an understanding of Parnell, see Richard B. O'Brien's *The Life of Charles Stewart Parnell* (2 vols.; London: Smith, Elder & Co., 1899), and Conor Cruise O'Brien's *Parnell and His Party, 1880–1890* (Oxford: Clarendon Press, 1957).
26. Costigan, *History of Modern Ireland*, pp. 231–32.
27. O'Farrell, *Ireland's English Question*, p. 164.
28. Ibid., p. 165.

See *Suggestions for Further Reading* at the end of chapter 15.

# 11

# A DRAMA FOR THE NATION

## Harold Orel

Disraeli, speaking at the Guildhall in London on 9 November 1879, admitted that the Irish were an imaginative race, then turned the dagger: "And it is said that imagination is too often accompanied by somewhat irregular logic."

This chapter chronicles a few highlights of the problems encountered by imaginative (and extraordinary) individuals in their efforts to create an Irish drama—written by Irishmen about Irish subjects, and played by Irish actors and actresses—for the nation. If occasionally the logic used by their polemics and their opponents seems wobbly, one should not be excessively surprised; an English prime minister, no less, had anticipated the possibility.

William Butler Yeats, who went to Paris in February 1894, wrote a review for the *Bookman* (April 1894) of a play that he had seen performed there.[1] (Yeats was not particularly proficient at French; his fellow playgoer, Maud Gonne, must have translated a good deal of what went on. In his autobiographical sketch *The Trembling of the Veil*, Yeats admitted that his difficulties in following the printed text gave "an exaggerated importance" to certain passages, "while all remained so obscure that I could without much effort imagine that here at last was the Sacred Book I longed for.")[2] The review afforded Yeats the

251

opportunity to denounce Ibsenism, a cultural form of "the scientific movement which has swept away so many religious and philosophical misunderstandings of ancient truth," not only because it was "busy playing ducks and drakes with the old theatrical conventions," but because its influence was bound to be "impermanent" and because its mission within the theater was "purely destructive." Yeats, who was hostile to the "photographing of life" by "the impassioned realisms of M. Zola and of Dr. Ibsen in his later style" and "the would-be realisms of Mr. Pinero or Mr. Jones," infinitely preferred traveling "by the path of symbolism to imagination and poetry, the only things which are ever permanent."

The play under consideration was Villier de l'Isle-Adam's *Axël*, and its message—"The infinite is alone worth attaining, and the infinite is the possession of the dead"—won Yeats's approval: "Seldom has utmost pessimism found a more magnificent expression." Of the importance of *Axël* it is scarcely necessary to speak—Edmund Wilson devotes a famous passage to it in a book reviewing the history of Symbolism entitled (appropriately enough) *Axel's Castle*; but of its importance to the development of a national Irish drama perhaps a few words more may be added. For Yeats, like many of his contemporaries, was dismayed by "the sordid and jangled utterance of daily life which has saddened the world," and sought to replace it with heroism, imagination, and "majestic words." What Edmund Gosse and William Archer popularized—the middle period of Ibsen's career, the plays dealing with particularized social problems: *The Pillars of Society, A Doll's House,* and *An Enemy of the People*—seemed to have become a "wave of diabolic Ibsenity." George Bernard Shaw's approval came cloaked in a transparent irony: "The Ibsen reaction, with its unloveliness, its want of faith; its hopeless, despairing creed; its worship of the ugly in art; its grim and repulsive reality, regret it as we will, is a solemn and resistless fact. . . . Society has accepted the satire, and our dramatists of the first class have one after the other broken away from the beautiful, the helpful, and the ideal, and coquetted with the distorted, the tainted, and the poisonous in life. Any appeal to them in the name of art is vain."[3] Equally triumphant—though far more straightforward in its avoidance of sarcasm—was James Joyce's essay *When We Dead Awaken,* published in the prestigious *Fortnightly Review* (1 April 1900). Writing less than a decade after Yeats's visit to the Paris production of *Axël,* Joyce reaffirmed Ibsen's hold "over the thinking world in modern times," which he rated higher than that of Rousseau, Emerson, and Carlyle. He found it specially attractive because Ibsen had "seldom, if at all, . . .

condescended to join battle with his enemies."[4] The debate over values between Yeats and Joyce had begun.

Yet it would be misleading to imply that the impetus to the formation of what was to become the Abbey Theatre derived largely, or primarily, from a distaste for problem plays written in imitation of Ibsen's middle period. Other forces were abroad in the land to remind the Irish of a cultural heritage that was waiting to be reclaimed. John V. Kelleher—in a brilliant retracing of the reasons that Matthew Arnold's *On the Study of Celtic Literature* (1867) remained immune from criticism by Irish scholars, critics, and creative writers during the entire quarter-century between 1890 and the outbreak of the Irish Rebellion— has noted that Arnold "had not predicted or desired a Celtic literary revival."[5] Although Arnold did not so much argue as assume that the Celt was inferior to the Anglo-Saxon "in any trait or talent that really counted in this world," he was not resented, because he was seen "only as one more of those perennial British reformers, kindly, innocent, and slightly foolish, who have always been ready to take a shot at solving the Anglo-Celtic question or some aspect of it without hurting anybody." After his death in 1888, he could be rewritten, reinterpreted, *used*; his admiration for the Celtic past could become the basis for a new-born romantic nationalism. Yeats's advocacy of a literature that would soar "above party"—which so exasperated Maud Gonne—was, basically, a repudiation of the theme and forms of the Young Ireland movement. His talents and respect for craftsmanship saved him from the worst aspects of the Celtic Twilight, from the overemphasis by his fellow poets of the very elements of Celticism that Arnold had praised: passion, sensuousness, style, and Titanism. "It was not successfully imitated," Kelleher writes dryly, "but it could be counterfeited—and the counter- feiting resulted in the fanciest hogwash ever manufactured in Ireland. In scores of slim green volumes the discovery of popular Celtic mysticism was celebrated. It was a great time for the feeble-minded: never before had it been so easy and practicable to be wise without wisdom, visionary without visions, acutely sensitive without feeling." But without Arnold's insights and inspirations, Yeats might never have returned to what Joyce, in a new century, was to label, scornfully, "the broken lights of Irish myth." The loss to Ireland would have been incalculable, for Yeats had already made his false starts: *The Island of Statues* ("an arcadian play in imitation of Edmund Spenser"); a number of early poems filled with "little but romantic convention, unconscious drama"; a series of playlets that might as easily have been set on the moon as in Germany or India. He had little sense of a true subject matter. As he wrote in

*Reveries,* "I had as many ideas as I have now, only I did not know how to choose from among them those that belonged to my life";[6] and, elsewhere in the same volume, "It is so many years before one can believe enough in what one feels even to know what the feeling is."[7]

There were the investigations of the antiquarians, the historians, and the linguists, and of all those who had sought to make respectable the manners of the past; and there was the artistry of the two epic cycles of Ireland—Cúchulainn and Finn. There was the electrifying presidential lecture by Douglas Hyde, delivered when he replaced the Fenian John O'Leary as chief officer of the National Literary Society in Dublin (25 November 1892), on "The Necessity for De-Anglicising Ireland," with its identification of a problem that has not wholly disappeared even in our time: "The Irish race is at present in a most anomalous position, imitating England and yet apparently hating it. . . . What we must endeavour to never forget is this, that the Ireland of to-day is the descendant of the Ireland of the seventh century, then the school of Europe and the torch of learning. . . . We can, however, insist, and we *shall* insist if Home Rule be carried, that the Irish language, which so many foreign scholars of the first calibre find so worthy of study, shall be placed on a par with—or even above—Greek, Latin, and modern languages, in all examinations held under the Irish government."[8] Yeats's polite demurrer, contained in a letter to the editor of *United Ireland* (17 December 1892), first paid respects to Hyde before stating a conviction that it was possible to build up a national tradition, a national literature, that should be "none the less Irish in spirit from being English in language";[9] but Yeats underestimated the strength of the feeling that Hyde shared with many of his countrymen, which swiftly led to the establishment of the Gaelic League and, not too many years later, to serious problems affecting the management of the Abbey Theatre.

A point needs to be scored heavily: any history of Ireland's theatrical activities at the turn of the century that concentrates on the English acting companies who toured Ireland, and on the plays that they produced, may be scholarly, but it will inevitably be limited. The developing passions of nationalistic feeling must be taken into account. Douglas Hyde in some respects was more the begetter of an Irish theater than even Lady Gregory, Yeats, Edward Martyn, or George Moore, for Hyde's eye was not limited to the confines of a playhouse within which Irish life might be dramatized. He knew, as well as the Abbey directors knew, that the repertory of any acting company was essentially English-developed. He argued a case for nationality, language, and customs with which very large numbers of Irishmen were in sympathy; the theater was only one means of communication with that public which refused to submit to "this awful idea of complete Anglicisation" (Hyde's phrase). He returned to the legends of Ireland, and others followed. His argument that "the bulk of the Irish race really lived in the closest contact with the traditions of the past and the national life of nearly eighteen hundred years, until the beginning of this century," seemed to explain and justify a great deal of what had gone wrong during the century that was then about to end (it was later to become the critical thesis of Daniel Corkery's influential *The Hidden Ireland*). Hyde refused to accept with pride Arnold's notion that Irish-feeling Irishmen were West Britons. The fact that Hyde tapped the deepest possible roots of patriotic sentiment may be documented by a brief review of what he accomplished within a half-century after his matriculation at Trinity College, Dublin: founding of the Gaelic League (which reached its peak of 550 branches by 1908); original poetry and plays, as well as translations from Gaelic in *Love Songs of Connacht* (which exerted a strong spell on both Lady Gregory and J. M. Synge), *Songs Ascribed to Raftery*, and *Religious Songs of Connacht*; a lengthy literary history of Ireland that instantly became a standard reference work; a professorship of Modern Irish at University College, Dublin; two terms as an Irish Free State senator; and nomination by both the leading political parties for the post of first president of Ireland.

Hyde wanted to live long enough to see the resurrection of a living Gaelic, but Yeats and Synge and Lady Gregory wanted a dynamic English, spoken in the country byroads, to serve as a fit medium for poetry. The founders of the Abbey wanted, from the beginning, an Irish theater to be a theater of poetry, based upon the idioms, syntax, and rhythms of men and women living in the nonindustrialized, unprofaned western counties. When Yeats wrote about popular ballad poetry in Ireland, the necessary conditions that he cited—"national traditions not hidden in libraries, but living in the minds of the populace," and no separation between populace and poets in the form of a "literary class with its own way of seeing things and its own conventions"[10]—were, he believed, already available to wordsmiths of his own age. He could afford to reject Moore, Lever, and Lover, who were "never poets of the people" and who used Ireland as a metaphor or "a merry harlequin," because there had lived within the nineteenth century so many genuine poets of the people. And even though Yeats offended some Irishmen by urging them to look abroad for the finest literary models and by arguing (in many contexts, on many platforms) that Irish writers had to learn more about European and classical traditions, he may have mollified some by characterizing English literature as aging and in decline, and by describing the Irish literature of his own age as "ballad or epic," that is to say, vigorous and young-hearted: "Alone, perhaps, among the nations of Europe we are in our ballad or epic age. . . . Our poetry is still a poetry of people in the main, for it still deals with the tales and thoughts of the people."[11]

Lady Gregory's somewhat cavalier handling of the legends adapted for her first full-length book, *Cuchulain of Muirthemne*, has been censured by George Moore (among others) for understandable reasons. She took the "best of the stories," or those parts of each that would fit best with one another, and strung them together "to give a fair account of Cuchulain's life and death." She left out a good deal that she thought readers would not care about "for one reason or another." She added nothing but linking sentences (though more of them than one might suspect from her note). But her Kiltartan—the vigorous speech patterns that so captivated President Theodore Roosevelt—received its classic formulation in the following sentence: "I have told the whole story in plain and simple words, in the same way my old nurse Mary Sheridan used to be telling stories from the Irish long ago, and I a child at Roxborough." As her "Dedication to the people of Kiltartan" made clear, she aimed at "popularisation, not scholarship,"[12] and she had no respect for the confused, pedantically reproduced versions of "the old cramped Irish, with translations into German or French or English" ("there is not much pleasure in reading them") that Trinity linguists had been churning out. She worked to add dignity to Ireland, and did so primarily through the creation of an artificial country-style language that "purified" the dross of the originals with which she worked —a language that pleased Yeats so much that he began his preface with the whooping sentence "I think this book is the best that has come out of Ireland in my time." He added a number of ecomiums about her discovery of "a fitting dialect," "a speech as beautiful as that of Morris, and a living speech into the bargain," containing "the vocabulary of the translators of the Bible, joined to an idiom which makes it tender, compassionate, and complaisant, like the Irish language itself."[13] And the excitement of John Millington Synge finally found expression in the celebrated Preface to *The Playboy of the Western World*: "In a good play every speech should be as fully flavoured as a nut or apple, and such speeches cannot be written by anyone who works among people who have shut their lips on poetry. In Ireland, for a few years more, we have a popular imagination that is fiery, and magnificent, and tender; so that those of us who wish to write start with a chance that is not given to writers in places where the spring-time of the local life has been forgotten, and the harvest is a memory only, and the straw has been turned into bricks." Synge was, in part, referring to "the modern literature of towns" that had been created by Ibsen and Zola. More important, his concept of language, a working, viable language for the Irish stage, a language of "striking and beautiful phrases" that paid due homage to its inspiration—the folk-imagination of "herds and fishermen along the coast from Kerry to Mayo," and of "beggar-women and ballad-singers nearer Dublin," that is to say, of the Irish peasantry—was directly related to the sense of excitement, shared by Yeats and Lady Gregory, over the possibilities inherent in a hitherto unexploited speech.

This is not the place to review the arguments of generations of scholars about the literary uses to which this language was adapted—whether they played fair with the original, or constituted a travesty and perversion of the language actually spoken in the Irish hinterland. (The controversy broke out anew during the Synge centenary of 1971, held in Dublin; but no consensus was reached.) World literature would certainly have been the poorer if such uses had not been made, and the Abbey would have become less distinguishable from any number of its English counterparts.

Nevertheless, it is easy to see the possibilities of mischief and a first-class row involved in the language question. In translating from the great documents of the past that antiquarians, linguists, and folklorists had been fighting to preserve, Lady Gregory made no pretense that she aimed at a literal accuracy. To those predisposed to be hostile to even the most well-meaning literary efforts of members of the Ascendancy, she was tampering with the national heritage. Yeats's comments on the relationship between nationality and literature, although informed by taste and an astonishingly wide range of reading, were never proffered with humility. Much of what he had to say about the ranting rhetoric of the Young Ireland movement—language that had gone out of control, as, in Yeats's judgment, it had in Thomas Davis's political poetry: "Suffice it to say it still goes on, whether for good or evil, serving its purpose, making opinion"[14]—raised questions about his patriotism that he finally felt obliged to answer in "To Ireland in the Coming Times":

> Nor may I less be counted one
> With Davis, Mangan, Ferguson,
> Because, to him who ponders well,
> My rhymes more than their rhyming tell
> Of things discovered in the deep,
> Where only body's laid asleep. . . .

Was he providing an adequate answer to these questions? The reader must judge. Yeats concluded his stanza with the heartfelt (but apolitical) invocation:

> Ah, faeries, dancing under the moon,
> A Druid land, a Druid tune!

As for Synge, long before the *Playboy* preface there had been hints of his willingness to provoke conservative, overly religious, or superpatriotic Irishmen; but one cannot tell even today whether a special kind of obtuseness was operating when he penned the famous sentence in his Preface to *Playboy*: "When I was writing 'The Shadow of the Glen,' some years ago, I got more aid than any learning could have given me from a chink in the floor of the old Wicklow house where I was staying, that let me hear what was being said by the servant girls in the kitchen." A Protestant (or worse, an atheist) spying on servant girls, and boasting about it! Even if Synge praised the Irish speech that he was attempting to reproduce, and even if he reproduced it with scientific accuracy,[15] his method of conducting research—at least as he himself described it—smacked of the condescension of a patron; and many took umbrage.

The problem was compounded by the natural desire of Yeats, Lady Gregory, and Synge to identify their theatrical endeavors with the spirit of the nation; in short, to create a truly national theater. Each of them said as much, and they wrote their plays with Irish coloration, Irish subject matter, and Irish characters. For example, as Lennox Robinson noted, Yeats's *The Land of Heart's Desire* (1894) "was utterly Irish in subject, it was peasant, it was faery, it was 'Celtic Twilight'—he himself coined the phrase."[16] When Yeats found the story of *The Countess Cathleen*, it was embedded in a French source;[17] he deliberately changed the scene to Ireland. Robinson, the official historian of the Abbey, interprets Yeats's behavior in joining with Lady Gregory and Edward Martyn as being motivated, not by a wish to see a particular play (*The Countess Cathleen*) enacted, but by a dream "of an Irish National Theatre, a theatre of poetry, a theatre of 'ancient idealism' and of noble Irish history." Was this not the same motivation that led Lady Gregory, in her fund-raising letter, to announce: "We propose to have performed in Dublin, in the spring of every year certain Celtic and Irish plays, which whatever be their degree of excellence will be written with a high ambition, and so to build up a Celtic and Irish school of dramatic literature. We hope to find in Ireland an uncorrupted and imaginative audience trained to listen by its passion for oratory, and believe that our desire to bring upon the stage the deeper thoughts and emotions of Ireland will ensure for us a tolerant welcome, and that freedom to experiment which is not found in theatres of England, and without which no new movement in art or literature can succeed. We will show that Ireland is not the home of buffoonery and of easy sentiment, as it has been represented, but the home of an ancient idealism. We are confident of the support of all Irish people, who are weary of misrepresentation, in carrying out a work that is outside all the political questions that divide us."[18]

The appeal for subscription money to found the Irish Literary Theatre proved remarkably successful, and members of the various professions and of the nobility cheerfully responded. The National Literary Society was the organization under whose auspices that theater began its activities in January 1899, and if we ignore one of the two first productions of that Society—Edward Martyn's play *The Heather Field*, which was not unlike many of the Ibsen dramas that Yeats had found so antithetical to his own temperament—we may see all the more clearly how controversy confounded the concept of a poetical theater untouched by contemporary problems of a social, political, or religious nature. The plot of *The Countess Cathleen* is too familiar to require more synopsizing than the following: the Countess, in a time of desperate famine, bargained with emissaries of the Devil and pledged her soul, asking only that food be given to her starving people. When she died, the "peasants" (the use of even that word set the teeth of some Irishmen grinding) lamented: "She was the great white lily of the world," and "she was more beautiful than the pale stars." Everything, Yeats wrote in his stage-direction, was "lost in darkness," but then the darkness was broken by a visionary light; the peasants seemed to be kneeling upon the rocky slope of a mountain, "and vapour full of storm and ever-changing light" swept above and behind them. "Half in the light, half in the shadow," stood armed angels, and "the Peasants cast themselves on the ground." An Angel spoke to them:

> The light beats down; the gates of pearl are wide;
> And she is passing to the floor of peace,
> And Mary of the seven times wounded heart
> Has kissed her lips, and the long blessed hair
> Has fallen on her face; The Light of Lights
> Looks always on the motive, not the deed,
> The Shadow of Shadows on the deed alone.

The publication and wide-spread distribution of Frank Hugh O'Donnell's free pamphlet *Souls for Gold* led to rumors that unorthodox opinions were expressed in the play. A cardinal, who was innocent of the sin of having actually read the play or witnessed a performance,[19] wrote a letter to the *Daily Nation* ( 1899):

> You invite my opinion on the play of Mr. Yeats "The Countess Cathleen." All I know of this play is what I could gather from the extracts given in Mr. O'Donnell's pamphlet and your paper. Judging by these extracts, I have no hesitation in saying that an Irish Catholic audience which could patiently sit out such a play must have sadly degenerated, both in religion and patriotism.
>
> As to the opinions said to have been given by Catholic Divines, no doubt the authors of these opinions will undertake to justify them, but I should not like the task were mine.

In the flurry that followed, Yeats asked Martyn to delete anything that he thought might give offense to any Catholic; he also requested Dr. Barry, an English critic of some reputation, "to alter or omit any passages that a theologian of so much literary culture as yourself might object to." Although Dr. Barry was more enthusiastic about the play's orthodoxy than was Martyn (whose "conventional" religious opinions were later cruelly savaged by George Moore's *Hail and Farewell*), the fact remains that both Dr. Barry and Martyn stood by Yeats, and the play finally prospered. Most worthy of note, however, is the surprise that overtook Yeats when he discovered that an imaginative play dealing with the relationship between human and divine beings might raise concern about offenses to established religion. In all fairness to Yeats, he was completely sincere in saying to Dr. Barry that the last thing he wanted to do was to give legitimate offense to any of his countrymen; but that he should be so unprepared for the possibility of some Irishmen taking offense (whether legitimately or not) was surely a mark of surprising ingenuousness in a man who was widely recognized as his nation's most distinguished poet: for 1899 was also the year of the publication of *The Wind Among the Reeds*.

*The Countess Cathleen* was but the first of a series of controversial productions that made Dublin the center of more literary brouhaha than any other capital in Europe. When a selection from Joseph Holloway's journal "Impressions of a Dublin Playgoer" was published in 1967, its editors, Robert Hogan and Michael H. O'Neill, commented on the life of the architect who had been hired to renovate the old Mechanics Theatre for the Irish Players and who later became the most extensive, gossipy historian of the Abbey Theatre, in the following terms: "In many, many ways Holloway's journal is a very faulty book, but any book through whose pages stride the violent and combative figures of Shaw, Yeats, O'Casey, and scores of their opinionated contemporaries has some claim to greatness. If one might choose to relive any fifty years of literary history, one would probably first consider the Athens of Pericles or the London of Shakespeare, but the Dublin of Holloway would not be such a bad choice either."[20]

Why? Because the theater was up and doing what had only been dreamed before. In 1901 George Moore recommended working with a stock company of English-trained actors, and when Yeats, who was impressed by the amateur productions of William and Frank Fay, passed on to them his new play, *Cathleen ni Houlihan*, Moore decided to withdraw (Martyn had already done so). Rehearsals began in a little hall in Camden Street. The name changed, in the early months of 1902, from the Irish Literary Theatre to the Irish National Theatre Society. Yeats became its president. From a series of farces, written in collaboration with Lady Gregory, to money-earning, genuinely popular productions, the Society flourished. It underwent its most critical metamorphosis in 1904, when the Abbey Theatre, under the triple-headed directorship of Yeats, Synge, and Lady Gregory—all members of the Anglo-Irish Ascendancy class and all attempting to create a national Irish theater in an overwhelmingly Catholic land that was ridden by taboos, hostile prejudices, memories of betrayal, and violent political aspirations—emerged as the liveliest cultural force from what Joyce, writing that very year in a letter that explained the intention underlying *Dubliners*, described as a "paralysis," a living death "which many consider a city."

The word "national" meant different things to different groups, obviously. In an age of growing faith that Sinn Fein might provide solutions to otherwise insoluble problems, Yeats was being more provocative than he may have wanted to be when, lecturing on "The Reform of the Theatre," he said: "We must learn that beauty and truth are always justified of themselves, and that their creation is a greater service to our country than writing that compromises either in the seeming service of a cause. We will, doubtless, come more easily to truth and beauty because we love some cause with all but all our heart; but we must remember when truth and beauty open their mouths to speak, that all other mouths should be as silent as Finn bade the son of Lugaidh be in the houses of the great. Truth and beauty judge and are above judgment. They justify and have no need of justification."[21] Was impartial meditation impossible in Ireland? For a long time Yeats thought that the plays he and his colleagues were producing provided an affirmative answer. In the stirring polemics of *Samhain* and *The Arrow*, Yeats pressed his argument against journalists and editors of the *Leader*, the *United Irishman*, and the *Independent*; he refused to concede that "the rough-and-ready conscience of the newspaper and the pulpit" had any claim "in a matter so delicate and so difficult as literature," or that *Cathleen ni Houlihan* had been written "with an obviously patriotic intention" (rather it had been written on the basis of "a very vivid dream"); he defined a national theater as one in which Literature—"the great teaching power of the world, the ultimate creator of all values"—might find a welcome home; he defended the right to translate and produce foreign masterpieces; and he argued up hill and down dale against other Dublin theaters (the Gaiety, the Theatre Royal, and the Queen's), the solicitor general, and the propagandist plays that were being spawned by "the Gaelic revival" as being apt to "drive out everything else." For Yeats, morals were less than literature; and changes in government, language, religion, or manufacturing and export patterns had nothing to do with the imaginative faculty. Some of the issues stirred up by Abbey productions hardly seemed worth debating: should a policeman be portrayed favorably in *The Rising of the Moon*? Would not the English misunderstand the behavior of the heroine of *In the Shadow of the Glen*? Did marital infidelity really take place in Ireland? If it did, was it proper to put it on the stage? Nevertheless, one could not leave the field to the enemy.

Viewed from a necessary distance, a theater that called itself national was asking for trouble when it limited itself, from the beginning, to two kinds of plays: those dealing with peasant life, and those dealing with "a romantic and heroic life, such as one finds in the folk-tales." Two observations seem inescapable: the first is that Yeats's attempts to create "a drama of energy, of extravagance, of fantasy, of musical and noble speech" were continually being distracted and interfered with by no inconsiderable number of his countrymen who preferred the middle-class sentimentalities of Gerald Griffin and of Charles Kickham to "a hard old man like Cosgar, or a rapacious old man like Shan, or a faithless wife like Nora Burke, or . . . treacherous Gormleith for a theme";[22] the second is that Synge, more than any of his fellow workers, was able to write both types of drama that Yeats wanted to have as the enduring stock-in-trade of the Abbey.

As a consequence, the rage of Arthur Griffith, editor of the *United Irishman*, very soon began to concentrate on Synge's contributions to the Abbey repertory. If Griffith's intemperateness today offends readers much as it offended Yeats and Synge during the first decade of this century, one must recall that, indeed, Synge was the most important playwright of the Abbey during that period, and that Griffith's target was well chosen. "Europe," as Herbert Howarth has written, "accepted Synge with extraordinary speed. . . . While Ireland was bickering over its new playwright, there were Czech performances of *In the Shadow of the Glen*, German of *The Well of the Saints*, and performances in a number of British cities."[23] Synge was, in short, an international force. His awareness of the wider world—wider than Irish tastes could easily accommodate—will surprise only those who think of him as Yeats's disciple because of a lazy interpretation of Yeats's famous advice: "You will never create anything by reading Racine. . . . Go to the Aran Islands. Live there as if you were one of the people themselves; express a life that has never found expression." Synge was nobody else's man. Yeats, in "The Death of Synge," emphasized his integrity; John Masefield, in a comparable memoir, emphasized his inscrutability. The Nationalists and Unionists knew that Synge was a worthy antagonist. He epitomized everything that Yeats had proclaimed; he was a veritable John the Baptist. He selected for his subjects any number of controversial matters: the loveless, arranged marriage (an Irish institution, as John Butler Yeats dryly observed in an article praising *In the Shadow of the Glen*); unpleasant priests; sexually attractive young women; and hypocritical representatives of the middle class. When one considers that Synge's candor about his Irish countrymen added insult to the injury of a theater without sixpenny seats for the "common people" of Ireland or to the injury of Kiltartan travesties on sacred myths and folklore, one is not surprised at the inevitable consequence: an argument that was pursued with increasing hoarseness by Griffith and like-minded Irishmen. They claimed that Irishwomen were the most virtuous in the world, that Synge's dramatizations of women were a libel on Irish womanhood, and that a theater that would produce good art but not propaganda for the Great Cause had not the right to call itself either Irish or National. The climax came in 1907, with what has been called the most notorious single event in modern theatrical history: the production of Synge's *The Playboy of the Western World*.

Synge's position should be stated first. "An Irish drama that is written in Ireland about Irish people, and not on a foreign model, will and must be national in so far as it exists at all. . . . If you do not like a work that is passing itself off as national art, you had better show that it is not art. If it is good art it is vain for you to try and show that it is not national." This is not conciliatory language. Whatever others might think of him, Synge was not frightened by the Griffiths of Ireland. He believed deeply that English was "likely to remain the language of Ireland," and he did not regret the likelihood. The best possible function of the Gaelic League might be to keep "the cruder powers of the Irish mind occupied" until—as his biographers note—"the influence of an Irish literature written in English" had defined itself more clearly.[24]

The ironies implicit in the relationship of a theater that called itself national in order to win wide acceptance, accepted subsidies from an English patroness (Miss Horniman), and refused to stage political plays that might offend England simply in order to placate patriotic members of the audience would inevitably have fostered crises; but Synge's partiality for using violent language in oaths "rammed with life"—to adapt his favorite saying from Ben Jonson—led directly to Lady Gregory's request that these oaths be toned down or deleted. Many were. One that has since been restored in the printed text was not spoken on opening night: Pegeen's accusation that the Widow Quin had reared a black lamb at her breast, so that "the Lord Bishop of Connaught felt the elements of a Christian, and he eating it after in a kidney stew." But Synge violently objected to excision of another line, which was spoken by Willie Fay on the fateful night (26 January 1907): "It's Pegeen I'm seeking only, and what'd I care if you brought me a drift of chosen females, standing in their shifts itself, maybe, from this place to the eastern world?" (Fay substituted the more brutal-sounding "Mayo girls" for "chosen females." The reason for doing so has never been clear.)

There is no need to recapitulate the history of the *Playboy* riots, but it is essential to give a few statements illustrating the irreconcilability of attitudes. Beyond Holloway's dislike of Synge's play—"What did Synge mean by such filth? Was there no one to supervise the plays?"— lurked his long-time distrust of Yeats: "Synge is the evil genius of the Abbey and Yeats his able lieutenant. Both dabble in the unhealthy."[25] The playwright William Boyle blamed Miss Horniman as being at the back of it: "Her hatred of the Irish people almost amounts to lunacy. She wouldn't allow a word of patriotic sentiment to be brought out in what she calls her theatre!"[26] Lady Gregory, who had been "almost bewildered by its abundance and fantasy" during the first reading of *Playboy*, never overcame her sneaking sympathy for those who thought the play "a libel on the Irish countryman, who has not put parricide upon his list of virtues." Nevertheless, she would not allow the Nationalists to blow and brandish the tin trumpets. Her courage in defending Synge was basically what it would have been for "a far inferior play . . .

written by some young writer who had never been heard of."[27] Plays were not to be cut and rearranged by local committees of shopkeepers. To her the principle was far more sacred than *Playboy* itself: "It was a definite fight for freedom from mob censorship." In an interview with a reporter from the *Freeman's Journal* (printed the next day, 30 January 1907), Yeats expressed his outrage by saying that "the people who formed the opposition had no books in their houses," adding: "We will go on until the play has been heard sufficiently to be judged on its merits. We had only announced its production for one week. We have now decided to play all next week as well, if the opposition continue, with the exception of one night, when I shall lecture on the freedom of the theatre, and invite our opponents to speak on its slavery to the mob if they have a mind to." One hardly has to do more than identify Griffith's paper *Sinn Fein* or the Gaelic League's *An Claidheamh Soluis* (edited by Padraic Pearse) to suspect that both would editorialize, with ill-disguised pleasure, on the death of the Anglo-Irish dramatic movement and on the need for a true Irish national theater.

"It is hard to understand the ferocity of the Catholic reaction to Synge," Michael O'Donovan (Frank O'Connor) wrote many years later, "so much fiercer than the reaction to Joyce. Though it is doubtful if Yeats himself understood it, instinct seems to have warned him that his theories stood or fell by Synge's work. It must have been instinct too that warned Arthur Griffith what to attack."[28] Central to any assessment of the achievement of the Abbey is an understanding of why Synge's contribution counted for so much. Lady Gregory thought, with justifiable pride, that his working with dialect "set free his style," and that he had learned the trick from her *Cuchulain of Muirthemne*; but her appreciation of Synge was to some extent circumscribed by patrician tastes. She thought, mistakenly, that Synge looked on politics and reform "with a sort of intolerant indifference," in the same way that Yeats once said, in a notorious formulation, that "Nature had made him [Synge] incapable of a political idea." (Synge, in fact, had strong political convictions.) When Yeats summarized the good and the bad elements of Synge's life in his essays "Celebrations" and "Detractions," he emphasized Synge's independence: "In the arts he knew no language but his own." But whether we emphasize his language or his subject matter, his work or his life, he was *sui generis,* and he could not be made to serve political ends. The victory of the Abbey—for the opponents of *Playboy* were unable to cancel a single performance in Dublin —was a victory for an apolitical, imaginative, and innovative play, for

Literature, just as Yeats had promised only a decade before, after witnessing a performance of *Axël*.

Fundamentally serious issues had been at stake, despite the tendencies of some historians to think of Yeats's rhetoric and the *Playboy* imbroglio as a typical Irish bash in a tunnel. In terms of theatrical history, the stage Irishman, "the vulgar and unnatural butt" of the English stage, had been destroyed, or at least shown up clearly for what he was; the poetic drama had successfully presented an alternative to Ibsen's social-problem play; and for plays written in both English and Gaelic, the directors had managed, with incredibly hard work, to provide their audiences with a tradition of acting, a repertory of plays about Irish themes and characters written by a very large number of native Irishmen, and an aesthetic theory on which most of them could agree for at least a decade. In even larger terms, the Abbey justified the faith of its founders in the possibilities of a national theater that would encourage artists to write out of their deep life, to record and dramatize "the emotions and experiences that have been most important to themselves," as Yeats once put it in *Samhain* (1904).

For fully half a century now the Abbey has not been primarily the home of poetic drama, nor have its productions been dominated by men of theory. Satire is considered important, and realism runs riotously with the ketchup that signifies blood on actors' clothing. Naturalism, which perhaps has been exhausted in most other national literatures as a movement, still stresses the dual influences of heredity and environment in Irish behavior. But this is not the same as saying that the Abbey has surrendered to the trolls, as Joyce thought (prematurely) that it had in 1901, when he wrote "The Day of the Rabblement," a denunciation of the Irish Literary Theatre for producing Hyde's *Casad-an-Súgán* in Gaelic and Yeats and Moore's *Diarmuid and Grania*: "The Irish Literary Theatre must now be considered the property of the rabblement of the most belated race in Europe."[29] Like any active theater, the Abbey has known changing fashions. The secession in 1905 of seven valuable players—Maire Nic Shiublaigh among them—for the sake both of political ideals and of a more active prosecution of the work of the Gaelic League; the decision of Miss Horniman to stop her subsidy (as retribution for the Abbey's refusal, in 1910, to shut down on the day of King Edward VII's funeral); an increasing number of mediocre plays during the second decade; Yeats's startled self-discovery, after the Easter Rebellion, that he was capable of impassioned patriotic feelings after all (and his return to lyric poetry after a long, dry period of failed inspirations); and the nationalist quarrels roused by the last of Sean

O'Casey's three great plays of the 1920's—*The Shadow of a Gunman* (1923), *Juno and the "Paycock"* (1924), and *The Plough and the Stars* (1926)—all provided evidence, if it were needed, of a growing dissatisfaction with the original impulse that had led to the establishment of a poetic and heroic drama. The triumph of realism was accompanied by some bittersweet moments. Men still alive can recall the opposition and hostile reviews encountered by the three Cork dramatists T. C. Murray, R. J. Ray, and Lennox Robinson. Nevertheless, the creation of the Republic finally resolved the old quarrel between the poets and the Nationalists. Other problems, after all, replaced the issue of independence as soon as Ireland took its place in the congress of nations. With the deaths of Lady Gregory (1932) and Yeats (1939), the last links with the old feeling for an essentially literary rendering of "peasant dialect" went; but the recognition of the Abbey's importance to Ireland (a belated recognition, inasmuch as American audiences had long since stopped throwing potatoes and watches at touring companies of Abbey players) had antedated their passing. In 1924 the Irish government voted an annual subsidy of £850 to the Abbey, making it "the first State-subsidised Theatre in the English-speaking world."[30] If any lingering doubts remained that the government was taking a direct and personal interest in the health of the Abbey or that the subsidy was simply *pro forma*, they were surely removed by the replacement of the fire-destroyed Abbey with a handsome, modern, and technically sophisticated structure for both the Abbey and the Experimental Theatre (the Peacock Theatre). The subsidy has grown enormously. Actors and directors may still complain in the Green Room about the niggardliness of the state's contributions to a theater that will never fully pay its own way, even though it is more often realistic than poetic and often is as concerned with "hits" as the crassest of Broadway producers. Yet the Abbey, for all its faults and despite the fact that several other theaters within the country rival its productions and perhaps surpass them for innovativeness and even skill, is today recognized, not only abroad but at home, as Ireland's national theater.

## NOTES

1. William Butler Yeats, *Uncollected Prose by W. B. Yeats: First Reviews and Articles, 1886–1896*, ed. John P. Frayne (vol. 1; New York: Columbia University Press, 1970), pp. 320–25.

2. William Butler Yeats, *The Autobiography of William Butler Yeats* (New York: Doubleday Anchor Books, 1958), p. 213.
3. Quoted by Una Ellis-Fermor in *The Irish Dramatic Movement* (2d ed.; London: Methuen, 1954), pp. 28–29.
4. James Joyce, *The Critical Writings of James Joyce*, ed. Ellsworth Mason and Richard Ellmann (New York: Viking Press, 1959), p. 48.
5. John V. Kelleher, "Matthew Arnold and the Celtic Revival," in *Perspectives of Criticism*, ed. Harry Levin, Harvard Studies in Comparative Literature, vol. 20 (Cambridge, Mass.: Harvard University Press, 1950), p. 217.
6. Yeats, *Autobiography*, p. 55.
7. Ibid., p. 69.
8. Douglas Hyde, "The Necessity for De-Anglicising Ireland," reprinted in *1000 Years of Irish Prose*, ed. Vivian Mercier and David H. Greene (pt. 1; New York: Devin-Adair Co., 1952), pp. 79–89.
9. Yeats, *Uncollected Prose*, p. 255.
10. Ibid., p. 147.
11. Ibid., pp. 273–74.
12. Elizabeth Coxhead, *Lady Gregory: A Literary Portrait* (New York: Harcourt, Brace & World, 1961), p. 61.
13. Reprinted in William Butler Yeats, *Explorations*, selected by Mrs. W. B. Yeats (New York and London: Macmillan, 1962), pp. 3–13.
14. Yeats, *Uncollected Prose*, p. 159.
15. Synge "did not exaggerate when he wrote in the preface to *The Playboy* that he had used only one or two words that he had not actually heard spoken, and it must have angered him when his Dublin critics accused him of foisting an outlandish vocabulary upon the peasants of the west of Ireland." David H. Greene and Edward M. Stephens, *J. M. Synge, 1871–1909* (New York: Macmillan, 1959), p. 139.
16. Lennox Robinson, *Ireland's Abbey Theatre: A History, 1899–1951* (London: Sidgwick & Jackson, 1951), p. 3.
17. William Butler Yeats, *Letters*, ed. Allan Wade (London: Rupert Hart-Davis, 1954), p. 346.
18. Lady Gregory, *Our Irish Theatre* (New York: Capricorn Books, 1965), pp. 8–9.
19. The practice of condemning artistic works sight unseen is, unfortunately, not dead. The Most Reverend Paul F. Leibold, Roman Catholic Archbishop of Cincinnati, vigorously denounced Leonard Bernstein's Mass as "offensive to our Catholic sense and belief" in a letter sent to the priests of his archdiocese. He added that he had not seen the production and that his observations were based "on reports of those who have seen it and on words and actions as described in the libretto." Invited to attend a performance of the production, "he said that his scheduled commitments made that impossible." *New York Times*, 20 May 1972.
20. Robert Hogan and Michael J. O'Neill, eds., *Joseph Holloway's Abbey Theatre: A Selection from His Unpublished Journal "Impressions of a Dublin Playgoer"* (Carbondale and Edwardsville: Southern Illinois University Press, 1967), p. xx.
21. Yeats, *Explorations*, p. 107.
22. Ibid., p. 190.
23. Herbert Howarth, *The Irish Writers, 1880–1940* (New York: Hill & Wang, 1959), p. 233.
24. Greene and Stephens, *J. M. Synge*, p. 130.
25. Greene and Stephens, *J. M. Synge*, p. 238; Hogan and O'Neill, *Joseph Holloway's Abbey Theatre*, p. 81; cf. Hogan and O'Neill, *Joseph Holloway's Abbey Theatre*, p. 86: "Yeats, Synge, and Gregory are all degenerates of the worst type; the former pair indulge in sensuality in their later work, and the latter condones with them."

26. Hogan and O'Neill, *Joseph Holloway's Abbey Theatre*, p. 87.
27. Lady Gregory, *Our Irish Theatre*, p. 117.
28. Michael O'Donovan (pseud. Frank O'Connor), *A Short History of Irish Literature: A Backward Look* (New York: G. P. Putnam's Sons, 1967), p. 186.
29. Joyce, *Critical Writings*, p. 70.
30. Robinson, *Ireland's Abbey Theatre*, p. 126.

## SUGGESTIONS FOR FURTHER READING

Coxhead, Elizabeth. *Lady Gregory: A Literary Portrait*. New York: Harcourt, Brace & World, 1961.
Ellis-Fermor, Una. *The Irish Dramatic Movement*. 2d ed. London: Methuen, 1954.
Fay, Gerard. *The Abbey Theatre: Cradle of Genius*. New York: Macmillan, 1958.
Fay, William G., and Carswell, Catherine. *The Fays of the Abbey Theatre*. New York: Harcourt, Brace & Co., 1935.
Greene, David H., and Stephens, Edward M. *J. M. Synge, 1871–1909*. New York: Macmillan, 1959.
Gwynn, Denis. *Edward Martyn and the Irish Revival*. London: J. Cape, 1930.
MacBride, Maud Gonne. *A Servant of the Queen*. London: V. Gollancz, 1938.
Moore, George. *Ave*. New York: D. Appleton & Co., 1914.
———. *Vale*. New York: D. Appleton & Co., 1914.
Robinson, Lennox. *Ireland's Abbey Theatre: A History, 1899–1951*. London: Sidgwick & Jackson, 1951.

# 12

# THE ARTS IN TWENTIETH-CENTURY IRELAND

*Marilyn Stokstad and Mary Jean Nelson*

The Irish cultural revival during the Georgian Period proved to be short-lived. The terrible famines of the 1840s destroyed the economic base for the patronage of the arts; stately homes could not be supported by blighted fields.[1] The reality of economic failures and divisive, futile political maneuvering and strife drove artists and writers to escape into romantic fantasies about their country's heroic past. But even historical painting was not entirely dedicated to glorious moments. In the most famous Irish painting of the nineteenth century, *The Marriage of Eva and Strongbow* (1854), Daniel Maclise represented the triumph of the Normans in Ireland and the end of Celtic power and civilization.[2] The angry pride and the despair that pervade this painting characterize modern Ireland better than the image of the comic or sentimental figures depicted by the popular writer and watercolorist Edith Oenone Somerville or the genre painter William Mulready. In the twentieth century, Samuel Beckett established a philosophy of art that was singularly appropriate for his countrymen. Perhaps Beckett's "aesthetic of failure" could only have been so poignantly and brilliantly realized and so elegantly stated by a person

*Marriage of Strongbow and Eva* (1854)
Daniel Maclise (1806–1870)
Oil on canvas, 121½″ x 199″
National Gallery of Ireland, Dublin
Photo by courtesy of the National Gallery of Ireland

who had been formed by both the Irish and the French experience. Beckett lays the burden of responsibility for creative failure entirely on the artist. The artist is compelled to create; and because he is an artist, he is, in Beckett's view, bound to fail. Beckett wrote: "To be an artist, is to fail, as no other dare fail, that failure is his world and to shrink from it desertion, art and craft, good housekeeping, living."[3] At times it must have seemed that not only painters and poets were doomed to failure in Ireland but that all cultural enterprises were in jeopardy.

Although scholarly societies survived and artists and craftsmen continued to find some employment during the nineteenth century, a great new Irish art did not emerge until the end of the century; and even then literature—poetry and drama—rather than visual arts dominated the cultural scene. Folklorists took their place beside the antiquaries and archeologists; among the artists, the painters and poets, because they were less dependent on lavish patronage, could still flourish, but the architects and sculptors could not. The Gaelic League, whose members were dedicated to the study of language, music, dance, and folklore, was founded in 1893 by Douglas Hyde. In 1899 William Butler

Yeats, Lady Gregory, and Edward Martyn founded the National Theatre in Dublin, a company that became the Irish National Theatre Society. Irish art came of age in 1904 with this company's production of Yeats's *Cathleen ni Houlihan* as one of the four plays (two by Yeats and one each by Synge and Lady Gregory) to inaugurate their new theater. The Abbey Theatre was to become one of the most influential centers of twentieth-century drama.[4] Politicians who dismissed these activities as harmless recreation learned to their sorrow that the arts in Ireland served to promote the ideal of a free and resplendent country.

The study of Irish history and literature is enriched by a study of the work of the elder Yeats, John Butler Yeats. His portraits—whether finished paintings or casual drawings—tell the student more about the Irish leaders than do most photographs. His drawing of Synge and his painting of his son William must be counted among the finest examples of modern realistic portraiture. Yeats is at his best with sensitive, slightly melancholy, or introspective subjects. He was a writer and

*John Millington Synge*, 1905
John Butler Yeats
1839–1922
Crayon on paper
12½″ x 10″
National Gallery of Ireland, Dublin
Photo by courtesy of the
National Gallery of Ireland

*William Butler Yeats as a Very Young Man*, 1900
John Butler Yeats
1839–1922
Oil on canvas
30⅛″ x 25¼″
National Gallery of Ireland, Dublin
Photo by courtesy of the
National Gallery of Ireland

philosopher himself, and thus he was emotionally as well as technically equipped to interpret the contemplative, though hardly passive, side of some of the leaders of the Irish cultural revival.

An influential contemporary of Yeats's was Sarah Purser. She lived and studied in France during the last quarter of the nineteenth century; and when she returned to Ireland, she remained an exponent of contemporary Parisian painting and continued to be a strong-willed supporter of modern art. Her portrait of Douglas Hyde is a sensitive and sympathetic characterization, while her study of Maud Gonne emphasizes the remarkable strength of the woman. In 1903 Purser effectively began the revival of the art of making stained glass in Ireland by founding the Tower of Glass (An Túr Gloine). She designed some glass herself; but more importantly, she provided opportunities in her studio for many fine designers. One of the Tower of Glass group who soon developed an independent style and international reputation was Evie Hone, who joined the group in 1932. Evie Hone is best known for **her Last Supper and Crucifixion windows in the chapel of Eton College.**

*Douglas Hyde*
Sarah Purser
1849–1943
Oil on canvas, 30″ x 25″
National Gallery of Ireland, Dublin
Photo by courtesy of the
National Gallery of Ireland

*Maud Gonne*
Sarah Purser
1849–1943
National Gallery of Ireland, Dublin
Photo by courtesy of the
National Gallery of Ireland

In spite of the activities of such eminent artists as John Butler Yeats and Sarah Purser, the state of the visual arts in Ireland could not have been called propitious at the beginning of the twentieth century. The irony of Sir Hugh Lane's struggles to establish a museum of modern art in Dublin illuminates the narrow base of Irish culture at the time. His efforts, like those of William Butler Yeats and Lady Gregory at the Abbey Theatre, dramatize the conflict between the ideals of the few and the conservatism of the many. The uproar over "the Lane pictures" was almost as loud as, and certainly longer than, the outcry over *Cathleen ni Houlihan* or *The Playboy of the Western World*.[5]

Hugh Lane was already a successful London art dealer when, while visiting his aunt Lady Gregory in Dublin, he saw an exhibition of paintings by John Butler Yeats and Nathaniel Hone. He commissioned the elder Yeats to do a series of portraits of Irish leaders (Yeats and Lane later quarreled, and Sir William Orpen and Sarah Purser finished the series). Once his interest was engaged, Lane began skillfully to promote the arts in Dublin. He organized an exhibition, "Old Masters from Irish Collections," in 1902–1903; in the next year, a show of contemporary Irish artists; and finally, a large exhibition of modern Continental art in the Royal Hibernian Academy. By including paintings from private collections and from dealers, he assembled a group of works from which he hoped to form a gallery of modern art for Dublin. To increase public interest in and appreciation of modern painting, he sponsored a series of evening lectures by Yeats, George Russell (Æ), and George Moore. He also initiated discussions on the possibility of acquiring paintings as well as permanent exhibition space. Lane and his friends offered to give Dublin some one hundred paintings and drawings; they also raised money for acquisitions. By 1905 Lane had assembled 127 works of art for the proposed museum.

At this point, opposition to a museum of modern art began to develop. Older painters were opposed to "modern art," including such "objectionable" modern paintings as works by Courbet, Corot, and Manet, which were hardly radical departures even in 1905. They were joined in their protest by some citizens of Dublin who feared that a museum might cause their taxes to be increased. In spite of the arguments of this coalition, members of the City Corporation finally agreed to the project. In 1908 Lane announced the gift to Dublin of his collection of British paintings, his portraits of contemporary Irishmen, and Rodin's *Age of Bronze*; he also loaned the city his collection of modern Continental paintings, with the understanding that a museum building be erected to house them. Lane was knighted in 1909 in recognition of his generosity and his service to the arts.

Lane's collection illustrates the taste of a careful collector in the opening years of the twentieth century. Among the finest paintings are Renoir's *Les Parapluies,* Corot's *The Palace of the Popes at Avignon,* Daumier's *Don Quixote,* and Manet's *Eva Gonzales* and *Tuileries Concert,* as well as works by Courbet, Degas, Ingres, Monet, Pissaro, Vuillard, and Berthe Morisot. Predictably, Lane also acquired Puvis de Chavannes's *Martyrdom of St. John the Baptist,* late Corot landscapes, and popular works by Daubigny, Diaz de la Pena, Fantin Latour, Gerome, Jongkind, Madrazo, and Monticelli. Lane's conservative side is indicated by his inclusion of paintings by Jacob Maris, Antonio Mancini, and Alfred Stevens, artists who inspire enthusiasm primarily among admirers of Victorian painting, and by John Lewes Brown (1829–1890), an Irishman who was born in Bourdeaux and lived all his life in France.

No sooner was the Dublin Municipal Museum of Modern Art about to become a reality than a new argument began, this time over the site of the building. Four years later, when no progress had been made in even selecting a site, Lane threatened to withdraw his collection. The architect Sir Edwin Lutyens wittily suggested that the museum be built on a bridge over the river Liffey in order to avoid the problem of selecting and purchasing a site. Lutyens actually produced five elegant designs for such a museum-bridge. Public protest mounted; charges of "humbug," "waste of money," and "profiteering" were hurled at the promoters of the museum. In disgust and dismay, Lane withdrew his collection and deposited the paintings, on loan, in the National Gallery of London. He bequeathed the Continental paintings to London and other paintings to the National Gallery of Ireland—not to the city of Dublin. Relations with the National Gallery in London were not entirely happy either: most of the Lane collection, including Renoir's masterpiece *Les Parapluies,* was placed in storage.

In 1914 Lane became Director of the National Gallery of Ireland, and he began to build that collection. His friends all agreed that he still intended to return his modern paintings to Dublin eventually. Æ said, in testimony taken during the controversy over the ownership of the paintings:

> I met Sir Hugh Lane on the day previous to his departure from Dublin for the last journey to the United States. I asked Lane . . . , "Are we to lose the pictures?" He replied: "Oh, Dublin will get the pictures all right. I made threats to frighten people here to get them to move."

*Lady Gregory,* 1903
John Butler Yeats
Oil on canvas, 24½″ x 20½″
National Gallery of Ireland, Dublin
Photo by courtesy of the National Gallery of Ireland

I believe these to be actually the words he used. I remember them precisely, because I was most anxious that those pictures should be in some Dublin Gallery.[6]

Lane, in fact, wrote a codicil to his will just before he left for America in 1915. In the codicil he left the paintings to Dublin if a museum building had been erected to house them within five years after his death. His sole trustee was his aunt, Lady Gregory. The will had been witnessed by his sister, not by two people, as required by law; and the codicil was not witnessed at all. Ironically and tragically, Lane elected to return to Ireland on the *Lusitania,* and thus lost his life when the ship sank on its maiden voyage in 1915.

After Lane's death a heated debate over the ownership of his collection began. William Butler Yeats became a leading champion of Lane and the Irish claim. His bitter poems "To a Shade" and "To a Friend Whose Work Has Come to Nothing" express his sorrow and his disgust with the people of Dublin. Lady Gregory also campaigned vigorously for the return of the paintings from England and for the establishment of a museum. She wrote a pamphlet in 1911, a book on the subject in 1921, and another pamphlet in 1926. Finally, in 1928, at the suggestion of Sarah Purser, Charlemont House on Parnell Square (built by Sir William Chambers for James Caulfeild, first earl of Charlemont) was selected to house the collection. The project was agreed upon in 1929, and modern galleries were added in the garden behind the Georgian house. Dublin finally had its Museum of Modern Art. The Lane paintings, however, are exchanged between London and Dublin every three years, an agreement that was reached only in the last decade.[7]

Sir Hugh Lane's determination to bring the best in contemporary art to Dublin was revived on a grand scale in 1967 with the institution of a quadrennial exhibition of contemporary art.[8] Few opportunities had existed for either students or the public—or, for that matter, for professional artists—to see contemporary painting in Ireland. In 1943 the Irish Exhibition of Living Art, where both native and foreign work was shown, was established by Evie Hone and Mainie Jelett. Other gallery owners, such as Victor Waddington, began to hold small exhibitions of foreign work and to develop collectors' interest in modern art. The Municipal Gallery, however, was usually too poor to mount successful shows; and the Royal Hibernian Academy and the National College of Art had become "pleasant" but "splendidly irrelevant."[9] An exhibition, Rosc '67 (Rosc is an Old Irish word meaning "the poetry of vision"), was organized to reintroduce the Dublin public to contemporary art of high quality. Works of fifty artists were selected for exhibition at the Royal Dublin Society, and at the same time an exhibition of early Celtic art provided a sense of the greatness of the Irish past. Four years later a second group of fifty artists exhibited at Rosc '71, and on this occasion the art of the Viking Age formed the historical foil to contemporary art. The "Poetry of Vision" exhibitions have helped to establish Dublin as an important art center in Europe.

The Irish government has done as much as international exhibition committees have done to further the image of Ireland as a center of the creative arts by making the country a financial haven for artists. In the Irish budget for 1969–1970 the finance minister, Charles Haughey,

*The Post Car*
Jack B. Yeats (1871–1957)
Hand-colored woodcut; Cuala Press, n.d. (1912?)
Photo by permission of the University of Kansas Libraries

introduced a tax-free status for writers, composers, painters, and sculptors.[10] To qualify for the exemption, an artist has to reside six months of the year in Ireland or maintain a furnished house there for his or her use, but he does not have to be an Irish citizen. The artist has only to submit a form to the revenue commissioners, and if the application is approved, from then on the artist reports his or her yearly earnings for the record but pays no Irish income taxes. Within the first two years of the program, 207 people had been accepted, and today many more enjoy these financial benefits. Such a policy is one of the most ingenious and enlightened forms of art patronage to be devised by any government in recent years. In a sense the concept reflects the heritage of the ancient Celtic kingdoms in which the poets enjoyed a privileged status.

Turning from the politics of art to art itself means returning to the Yeats family. John Yeats's son Jack gained international recognition during the first half of the twentieth century, although he never attained the stature in the arts that was achieved by his brother William. Nevertheless, Jack Yeats, in the words of Thomas Mac Greevy, director of the

*The Country Shop*
Jack B. Yeats (1871–1957)
From *Life in the West of Ireland* (Dublin & London:  Maunsel & Co., 1912)
Photo by permission of the University of Kansas Libraries

*St. Columcille*
Jack B. Yeats and Lily Yeats
Wool and silk
Designed by Jack Yeats; embroidered by Lily Yeats
National Museum of Ireland, Dublin
Photo by permission of the National Museum of Ireland

National Gallery of Ireland, "paints the Ireland that matters."[11] For Samuel Beckett, he was Ireland's greatest painter.

Jack Yeats first came to public attention as an illustrator who, in his drawings, effectively captured the spirit and tragedy of Ireland. He played a part in the Gaelic Revival by illustrating the *Irish Readers* for children (1902–1906), turning the otherwise dreary school books into a stimulating visual experience with his lively drawings. He also wrote and illustrated fanciful books and puppet plays, and he illustrated the broadsheets printed at the Cuala Press, where his brother William, Lady Gregory, Æ, and others published their poetry; he even made drawings for his sister's embroidery.

In the 1920s Jack Yeats began to develop a very personal style, and he eventually gave up illustration altogether in order to turn his attention entirely to painting.

Thomas Mac Greevy wrote:

> In the life of Ireland fact and poetry had parted company. Jack Yeats's work became a passionate recall to poetry—to the splendour of essential truth. . . . In the treatment of objective reality, a drastic selective sense comes into play and form is deferred to only in so far as it is congenial to a much more self-consciously fastidious artistic temperament than of old. The balance between observation and imagination has, in fact, altered. The artist particularizes less, generalizes more. At times he will make some quite humble scene look positively apocalyptic.[12]

Samuel Beckett, reviewing Mac Greevy's book on Yeats, defined the role of the artist and described Jack Yeats's contribution in terms that have been applied to his own work as well as to Yeats's:

> He is with the great of our time . . . because he brings light, as only the great dare bring light, to the issueless predicament of existence, reduces the dark where there might have been, mathematically at least, a door. The being in the street when it happens in the room, the being in the room when it happens in the street, the turning to gaze from land to sea, from sea to land, the backs to one another and the eyes abandoning, the man alone trudging in sand, the man alone thinking (thinking!) in his box —these are characteristic notations having reference, I imagine, to processes less simple, and less delicious, than those to which the plastic *vis* is commonly reduced, and to a world where Tir-na-nOgue makes no more sense than Bachelor's Walk, nor Helen than the apple-woman, nor asses than men, nor Abel's blood than Useful's, nor morning than night, nor the inward than the outward search.[13]

In spite of the growing abstraction of his painting, Jack Yeats remained a great draftsman. In 1940 he returned briefly to work as an illustrator, producing six drawings for the poem *A Lament for Art O'Leary*. Art O'Leary, an eighteenth-century rebel, became a twentieth-

*Art's Wife Carrying His Coffin*
Jack B. Yeats (1871–1957)
From *A Lament for Art O'Leary*
Cuala Press, 1940
Photo by permission of the University of Kansas Libraries

century folk hero. He was an Irish Catholic officer in the Austrian army who, on his return to Ireland, struck a Protestant who had tried to force him to sell his fine horse for the legal limit of five pounds. He was outlawed, and later was captured and shot (1773). The lament, or keen, of his wife, Eileen O'Connell, translated into modern verse by Frank O'Connor (Michael O'Donovan), recalls traditional Celtic poetry in its emphasis on intense personal emotion in its rhythms and its imagery. The poem —and Yeats's illustrations, such as Art's bloodied horse or Eileen carrying his coffin—epitomize the troubled Ireland of the past and the present:

> My love and my treasure,
> Though I bring with me
> No throng of mourners
> 'Tis no shame for me,
> For my kinsmen are wrapped in

A sleep beyond waking
In narrow coffins
Walled up in stone.[14]

As he grew older, Yeats's painting became increasingly personal, intense, and mysterious. Forms dissolve into color patterns, yet the sure eyes and hands of the draftsman continue to undergird the images. As he explored an illusive inner world, Yeats began to approach Beckett's ideal of the artist as a solitary, frustrated being, stripping away the layers of reality or meaning to arrive finally at a complete identification—or at nothing at all.

In *Les Lettres Nouvelles*, Beckett wrote an "Homage to Jack B. Yeats":

High solitary art uniquely self-pervaded, one with its wellhead in a hiddenmost of spirit, not to be clarified in any other light.

Strangeness so entire as even to withstand the stock assimilations to holy patrimony, national and other.

What less celt than this incomparable hand shaken by the aim it sets itself or by its own urgency?

As for the sureties kindly unearthed in his favour, Ensor and Munch to the fore, the least one can say is that they are no great help.

The artist who stakes his being is from nowhere, has no kith.

Gloss? In images of such breathless immediacy as these there is no occasion, no time given, no room left, for the lenitive of comment. None in this impetus of need that scatters them loose to the beyonds of vision. None in this great inner real where phantoms quick and dead, nature and void, all that ever and that never will be, join in a single evidence for a single testimony. None in this final mastery which submits in trembling to the unmasterable.

No.

Merely bow in wonder.[15]

Art criticism by Samuel Beckett often surpasses in quality the material he is analyzing and becomes a work of art in itself. But he disliked the role of critic, writing: "The chartered recountants take the thing to pieces and put it together again. They enjoy it. The artist takes it to pieces and makes a new thing, new things. He must."[16] Nevertheless, Beckett accepted art criticism as a social necessity. He saw that a responsible and sensitive critic could introduce the public

*Queen Maeve Walked upon This Strand*
Jack B. Yeats (1871–1957)
1950; oil on canvas, 36″ x 48″
National Gallery of Scotland, Edinburgh
Photo by courtesy of the National Gallery of Scotland (by Annan, Glasgow)

to the work of art by interpreting it for them. As he wrote in his review of Mac Greevy on Yeats:

> It is difficult to formulate what it is one likes in Mr. Yeats's painting, or indeed what it is one likes in anything, but it is a labour not easily lost, and a relationship once stated not likely to fail, between such a knower and such an unknown.
>     There is at least this to be said for mind, that it can dispel mind. And at least this for art criticism, that it can lift from the eyes, before rigor vitae sets in, some of the weight of congenital prejudice.[17]

Beckett dealt with the visual arts as aesthetic problems rather than as tangible objects. His sensitivity to the word rather than to the object is evident, for he can write superbly about works of dubious quality and in flights of fancy forget the painting that was his point of departure. For example, in a tribute to a friend (Bram van Velde),

Beckett developed a brilliant image far more applicable to Irish art than to the painting he was supposedly discussing:

> In the immovable masses of a being shut away and shut off and turned inward forever, pathless, airless, cyclopean, lit with flares and torches, coloured with the colours of the spectrum of blackness. An endless unveiling, veil behind veil, plane after plane of imperfect transparencies, light and space themselves veils, and unveiling towards the unveilable, the nothing, the thing again. And burial in the unique in a place of impenetrable nearnesses, cell painted on the stone of cell, art of confinement.[18]

Beckett captures in words the special quality of the Irish vision. If to his image one adds the ferocious energy of the poets of *The Táin* and the involved subtleties of the *Book of Kells*, one may, as Giraldus Cambiensis said, "penetrate to the secrets of the artistry," and catch a glimpse of the essence of Irish art—be it Celtic, Christian, or Contemporary.

## NOTES

1. Kenneth Kammeyer, "The Dynamics of Population," chap. 9 of this book.
2. Daniel Maclise, 1806–1870. The painting hangs in the National Gallery of Ireland.
3. Samuel Beckett, "Three Dialogues," *Transition Forty-nine*, no. 5, pp. 97–103 (December 1949); *Peintres de l'empêchement* (Galerie Maeght, Paris, 1948). I would like to thank John Erickson, editor of *L'Esprit créateur*, for directing me to a study of Beckett as a critic.
4. Harold Orel, "A Drama for the Nation," chap. 11 of this book.
5. For a full discussion of Sir Hugh Lane and the controversy over his collection of paintings see Thomas Bodkin, *Hugh Lane and His Pictures* (Dublin: Brown & Nolan, 1932); John J. Reynolds, *Statement of the Claim for the Return to Dublin of the 39 Lane Bequest Pictures Now at the Tate Gallery, London* (Dublin, 1932); Reynolds, ed., *Proposed Gallery of Modern Art for Dublin: Report of Proceedings at the Public Meeting Held on the 9th of Feb., 1906, with Reprint of Leading Articles in the Dublin Daily Press* (Dublin, 1906); and the many statements by Lady Gregory.
6. Bodkin, *Hugh Lane*, p. 48.
7. A curious footnote to the Lane controversy (and admittedly a digression of interest primarily to collectors of esoterica) was found by Mary Jean Nelson in the Johnson papers at the University of Kansas. The following summary is provided by Ms. Nelson and Ms. Ann Hyde, manuscript librarian. In 1925, at the height of the controversy over the Lane bequest, when most of the intellectual leaders of Dublin seemed to be embroiled in the argument, William Savage Johnson (chairman of the Department of English at the University of Kansas)

and his wife, Claudia, made a "pilgrimage" to the British Isles. They wanted to meet poets; to them, controversies over paintings were distractions. Nevertheless, through George Russell they met Thomas Bodkin, Yeats, and others; they even bought a painting by Russell. The painting remained in their home until 1972, when many of the Johnson papers were given to the University of Kansas by the family. Professor Johnson's notebook was privately printed by his nephew, Foster Johnson, in 1972: *An Account of a Summer's Pilgrimage . . . 1925.* Claudia Johnson's papers have not been published. William Savage Johnson wrote, 10 August 1925, of his visit with Yeats, accompanied by Æ:

> As soon as we were seated, Yeats continued the subject he was already discussing. Ireland's possession of certain pictures. A controversy going on as to whether England or Ireland should possess them. Unfortunately two or three busybodies (one was our friend Bodkin) had written to the *Irish Times* as if the matter had already been settled in favor of England. This was a great mistake. Yeats wanted a vigorous article to be written putting the matter right. [*Pilgrimage*, p. 53.]

Johnson later wrote:

> Yeats . . . [took] Æ out of the room to discuss the picture business in private. "Matters of State," he said. When they left we said we thought we must be going, were afraid we were intruding. The others laughed and said they were glad to get rid of the picture business, which evidently bored them. [*Pilgrimage*, p. 54.]

The "others," according to Johnson, were Oliver Gogarty, Lennox Robinson, Walter Starkie, and an unidentified man. Claudia Johnson wrote:

> After a hurried greeting Yeats immediately began discussing with A.E. the matter at hand—Namely that Bodkin and several others had given out false news concerning the purchase of paintings by Ireland from England. The Irish T— had published that the pictures were unattainable when the matter had not been decided—England had not given her answer. Yeats said there must be a statement in the paper saying that they were procurable. All the while Yeats was very intense, and quite wrought up. A.E. sat back in his chair very calm. In a few moments the two men asked to be excused to discuss the matter. It was then we had a chance to talk with Lennox Robinson and the others. [Mrs. Johnson's diary, manuscript collection, Spencer Library, University of Kansas.]

Of all the people they met in Dublin, the Johnsons preferred George Russell. His poetry and personality embodied Ireland for the Johnsons and many other Americans. Claudia Johnson wrote:

> From time to time this striking man softly quoted poetry. His voice was mellow and when quoting poetry, which he does constantly, becomes very unusual indeed. He was steeped in it and in fact he had seemed the most poetic of all the poets I have met. All the while we were with him, I thought to myself how he embodied all the charm I had connected with Ireland. His idealism, his love of beauty, his constant lapsing into poetry and last of all his striking personality. Never have I met any one like him. His appearance seemed somewhat between a sea captain and an artist and yet his poetic nature isn't all. Russell was full of the beauty of Ireland. [From Mrs. Johnson's diary.]

The Johnsons found the Yeats family, on the other hand, somewhat less attractive. Claudia Johnson's description of the Cuala Press and the Misses Yeats is amusing, when one considers that the lady fancied herself a literary amateur:

In the afternoon we visited the Cuala Press where one Miss Yeats has charge of embroidery and another Miss Yeats of prints etc. . . . The embroidery was frightfully expensive, some things were lovely such as the shawl—a baby cover with Blake's lines & a mantle piece with Yeats verse. Other pieces were not very difficult work. . . . The prints we found very interesting. Many were printed from drawings by the poet's brother Jack Yeats and then hand colored in the shop. We found both Miss Yates [sic] fine looking gray haired ladies well groomed & gowned—the one in charge of prints talked to us quite a bit. She said that they had never really lived in Sligo but their grandparents did & they went there for six months or more on visits. In England they had lived in Chiswick. . . . Always lived in Dublin off & on. Yeats went to Trinity College. . . . The Misses Yeats were after the almighty dollar and spoke of referring our millionaire friends to them etc. But they are a talented family the one brother is an artist as is his wife. We purchased pictures but no books. [Diary.]

8. See catalogues *Rosc '67, Rosc '71.*
9. For a summary of the state of the arts in Ireland at mid century see Brian O'Doherty's introduction to the exhibition *The Irish Imagination, 1959–71,* pp. 15–16; also Bruce Arnold, *A Concise History of Irish Art* (New York: Praeger, 1968).
10. For further information: Revenue Commissioners, Dublin Castle, Dublin. See also Dorothy Walker, "Artists and Irish Taxes," *Art in America,* May 1971, p. 23.
11. Thomas McGreevy, *Jack B. Yeats: An Appreciation and an Interpretation* (Dublin: Waddington, 1945), p. 5; see also Hilary Pyle, *Jack B. Yeats* (London: Routledge & K. Paul, 1970). For additional material on Jack Yeats, recent exhibition catalogues are useful: *Jack B. Yeats, 1871–1957: A Centenary Exhibition,* Dublin, Belfast, and New York, forward and introduction by James White (London: M. Secker & Warburg, 1971); *Jack B. Yeats, 1871–1957,* exhibition at the University of Wisconsin-Milwaukee, 1972, introduction by Jack Wasserman (including reprint of the excellent essay on Yeats by Ernie O'Malley [Dublin, 1945]).
12. McGreevy, *Jack B. Yeats,* pp. 27–28.
13. Samuel Beckett, "MacGreevy on Yeats," *Irish Times,* 4 August 1945.
14. Eileen O'Connell, *A Lament for Art O'Leary,* translated by Frank O'Connor (pseud. of Michael O'Donovan) (Dublin: The Cuala Press, 1940).
15. Samuel Beckett, "Homage to Jack B. Yeats," *Les Lettres Nouvelles* 2:10 (April 1954), trans. James White; in Yeats centenary exhibition catalogue, p. 10.
16. Samuel Beckett, "An Imaginative Work!" *Dublin Magazine,* vol. 11, no. 3, p. 80 (July-September 1936). This is a review of Jack B. Yeats's *The Amaranthers* (London: Heinemann, 1936).
17. Beckett, "MacGreevy on Yeats." Attempting to "lift some of the weight of congenital prejudice," Brian O'Doherty has become the spokesman for contemporary Irish art in the United States. In the catalogue to an exhibition that he organized and called *The Irish Imagination, 1959–71* (Corcoran Gallery, Washington, D.C., October–November, 1972), O'Doherty tried to define the special quality of Irish painting:

Its atmosphere is characterized by a mythical rather than historical sense, an uneasy and restless fix on the unimportant, and a reluctance to disclose anything about what is painted, let alone make a positive statement about it. . . . This atmosphere dominated the "look" of Irish painting well into the sixties. It caused the rejection of everything that didn't apply—not to Irish art but to the Irish experience [e.g., Pop art, Op art, and Technological art]. . . . The atmospheric mode was breached in the mid-sixties by Michael Farrell whose work, while it indulges some romantic feeling, is aggressive and intellectually hard. . . . This second generation of painters [O'Doherty also includes Brian King, Robert Ballagh, and Brian Henderson] gives to painting in Dublin a diversity and energy it did not have before, and most of them show an acute political awareness.

18. Samuel Beckett, "Three Dialogues," quoted in *Bram Van Velde* (New York: Grove Press, 1960).

## SUGGESTIONS FOR FURTHER READING

*Apollo*, ed. Denis Sutton. Volume dedicated to the arts in Ireland, October 1966.

Arnold, Bruce. *A Concise History of Irish Art*. New York: Praeger, 1968.

Beckett, Samuel. *Peintres de l'empêchement*. Galerie Maeght, Paris, June 1948.

———. "Three Dialogues." *Transition Forty-nine*, no. 5, pp. 97–103 (December 1949).

McGreevy, Thomas. *Jack B. Yeats: An Appreciation and an Interpretation*. Dublin: Waddington, 1945.

O'Doherty, Brian. *The Irish Imagination, 1959–71*. Washington, D.C.: Corcoran Gallery, 1972.

Pyle, Hilary. *Jack B. Yeats*. London: Routledge & K. Paul, 1970.

# 13

## THE IRISHRY OF
## WILLIAM BUTLER YEATS

### *Harold Orel*

To summarize Yeats's attitudes toward Ireland and Irish culture demands a broad canvas. Most swift surveys of Yeats's career settle for one of two images: that of the romanticizing poet of the 1890s who coined the phrase "Celtic Twilight" and experimented trickily with masks and esoteric doctrines, or that of the extraordinarily difficult "modern" poet who died on the eve of World War II. His career was lengthy and eventful. He was deeply involved in a great many matters that were peripherally related to literature. He met everyone from the Pre-Raphaelites and Whistler on. He moved restlessly between England and Ireland, publishing an endless stream of books, pamphlets, and anthologies. He left behind him a mass of manuscript material that testifies to much more meticulous and painstaking rewriting than is generally believed to have taken place. He was an idealist who well understood the need for pragmatic adjustments, but even those who disliked him personally never claimed that his writings contained *less* than met the eye, or that he betrayed his own youth to become the protagonist of "Among School Children"—"a sixty-year-old smiling public man." He was, as David Daiches wrote, "without doubt the most remarkable poetic genius in English of his time, and one of the great English poets. He absorbed all his age had to offer him. Yet he did so wholly in his own way." T. S. Eliot, who was well aware that Americans considered him the greatest American poet of the century, conceded not once but several times that Yeats was the best poet writing in the English language. And, however sketchily we block in the reasons why others have shared Eliot's opinion, there seems to be no controversy today over the judgment that Yeats must be the central figure in any assessment of the achievement of Irish culture during the last century.

Let us begin with his middle years, when he served proudly as a member of the first Senate of the Irish Free State (1922–1928). Learning the syntax of public speech (he had given his life to the syntax of "passionate speech") at the same time that he gave advice to the government on matters concerning education, literature, and the arts, he concentrated his activities on three major Senate committees: the Irish Manuscript Committee, which concerned itself with the Gaelic language, music, folklore, ancient poetry, and the compilation of a dictionary; the Coinage Committee, which sponsored and approved the necessary designs for the remarkably beautiful coins of a new nation; and the Committee for the Federation of the Arts, which somehow or other was unable to implement its scheme for a College of the Arts, along the lines of the Royal Swedish Academy.[1]

The fact that Yeats found congenial the conservative members of the Senate is explainable in terms of his eighteenth-century affinities, his admiration of Swift and Burke, and his recognition of the contributions made by the "Big Houses" to a sense of community in many parts of Ireland. His objective—worth defining, since it is easier to understand why politicians want a figurehead poet than why a poet should consent to serve as figurehead—was to unify Ireland through cultural activities. He failed at it. His final frustration was the failure of the College of the Arts scheme writ large. He ascribed his difficulties to the triumph of political democracy, to the systematic passing of power and leadership "from the mediocre to the imcompetent."

Nevertheless, it would be a mistake to think of his disillusionment as total or permanent, or to think of this actively political period as a distraction from the more important work of poetry. For example, he was speaking in characteristic fashion for himself as well as for a Protestant constituency when he delivered his comments on the significance of any measure that might deny divorce permanently to the Irish. He noted that the North would gradually turn to England if the

South became oppressive, denying rights that had been won "by the labours of John Milton and other great men, and won after strife." Not only would a wedge between the two nations be introduced, but indissoluble marriages would lead inevitably to separation and to irregular sexual relations. He cited O'Connell, Parnell, and Nelson as "three very salutary objects of meditations which may, perhaps, make us a little more tolerant," and he concluded with a moving, powerful, and proud peroration:

> I wish to close more seriously; this is a matter of very great seriousness. I think it is tragic that within three years of this country gaining its independence we should be discussing a measure which a minority of this nation considers to be grossly oppressive. I am proud to consider myself a typical man of that minority. We against whom you have done this thing are no petty people. We are one of the great stocks of Europe. We are the people of Burke; we are the people of Grattan; we are the people of Swift, the people of Emmet, the people of Parnell. We have created the most of the modern literature of this country. We have created the best of its political intelligence. Yet I do not altogether regret what has happened. I shall be able to find out, if not I, my children will be able to find out whether we have lost our stamina or not. You have defined our position and given us a popular following. If we have not lost our stamina then your victory will be brief, and your defeat final, and when it comes this nation may be transformed.[2]

"We are the people of Burke. . . ." Yeats was neither deliberately nor continually seeking to be "modern." When he referred to the great folk literature of Ireland, in his speech to the Irish Literary Society (30 November 1925), he, perhaps more than any man in that room, knew how important it had been to the Irish literary renaissance which he had helped to lead. He urged his listeners to "feed the immature imagination upon that old folk life," and he added: "and the mature intellect upon Berkeley and the great modern idealist philosophy created by his influence, upon Burke who restored to political thought its sense of history, and Ireland is reborn, potent, armed and wise. Berkeley proved that the world was a vision, and Burke that the State was a tree, no mechanism to be pulled in pieces and put up again, but an oak tree that had grown through centuries."[3] An appreciation of the continuity of centuries was crucial if children were to develop their sense of duty to community and neighbor; nor was Yeats thinking in terms of a dryly abstract lesson in Civic Duty. He had in mind intelligent, unified teaching of religion, civic duty, and history "as all but inseparable," as "one lesson and not a mass of unrelated topics." "Every child in growing from infancy to maturity [he may have been thinking of his own childhood in Sligo] should pass in imagination through the history of its own race and through something of the history of the world, and the most powerful part in that history is played by religion."[4] The cadence of that sentence has an inevitability of practiced rhetoric, but the final word, *religion*, is still capable of surprising us, particularly when we recall the famous, better-remembered sentence from *The Trembling of the Veil*: "I am very religious, and deprived by Huxley and Tyndall, whom I detested, of the simple-minded religion of my childhood, I had made a new religion, almost an infallible church of poetic tradition, of a fardel of stories, and of personages, and of emotions, inseparable from their first expression, passed on from generation to generation by poets and painters with some help from philosophers and theologians."[5] Yet we should not be surprised. Yeats is still talking about the poetry, grace, and mystery that are inseparable from genuine religious feeling. The truly unexpected feature of Yeats's approach to education is that he saw the efficiency of education as ultimately measurable in terms of nationalist feeling: "If your education therefore is efficient in the modern sense, it will be more national than the dreams of politicians." His father had advocated similar principles in teaching art. Everything came back to Ireland ultimately. If the state is truly a tree, individuals must learn about and recognize their cultural heritage, respect it, add to it, and transmit it from one generation to the next.

To say this is to say no more than that Yeats, from the beginning, defined his problem as discovering a satisfactory means of defining his relationship to Ireland. His father once portrayed him as a king gone mad (a picture to accompany his poem about King Goll in the wilderness, who "sat and mused and drank sweet wine"), as one who wandered while in his ears beat the sounds made by mysterious Presences: "They will not hush, the leaves a-flutter round me, the beech leaves old." The pose proved satisfactory neither to his father nor to himself, so other poses replaced them. Yeats with a beard? A mustache? He tried both toward the end of the century. Like a poet—the *image* of one—rather than *as* a poet, he cultivated colorful over-sized neckties, and draped over his shoulders a heavy Inverness cape; everyone commented on the appropriateness of his appearance to the role that he had chosen and of the manner that he adopted toward those who wanted to meet the historian, genealogist, and taxonomist of faery lore. Long before he worked out the elaborate schema of *A Vision*, he wore a mask, or (more precisely) a succession of masks. Doing so did not commit him to the attitude expressed by any of the masks. It was hard to get beyond or behind the masks if one had not known him over a long period of time. Many who worked for the Abbey regarded him as an awesome apparition rather than as a real human being. Sean O'Casey, in his autobiography, could not bring Yeats to life, perhaps because of a suspicion that a man who could reject *The Silver Tassie* on abstract grounds was more than a little abstract himself. Even George Moore, at one time a collaborator with Yeats (who was then a younger man than when O'Casey knew him), expressed bafflement, perhaps mixed with a little envy, at some of the rhetoric that his coauthor slipped in and out of so easily.

A mask, despite its attraction to many *fin-de-siècle* artists, has serious limitations as a technique for distancing oneself from the coarseness, the thickness of life. Its rigidity cannot adjust to change, whether in the artist's personality or in the external realities that the artist observes. Even if there be no change, the same mask will not do for the variety of situations, personal and social, through which we must move in time periods as brief as a single day. And a mask may be objected to as essentially passive, as being incapable of expressing any lively, active emotion.

At the same time, Richard Ellmann's elaborate discussion of why masks so appealed to Yeats is worth recapitulating: a mask can be used to express one's social self (we face with a mask both the world and the beloved); the mask includes all the differences between one's own and other people's conception of one's personality (we can look at ourselves as if we are somebody else); the mask is defensive armor, and wearing it prevents one from being hurt by love that goes awry; and the mask can be a weapon of attack, which one puts on to sustain a noble conception of oneself.[6] A good deal of this talk goes on in *The Player Queen* (a poetic drama that may possess greater interest for Yeats scholars than for most playgoers). Ellmann quotes one of the play's characters: "To be great we must seem so. Seeming that goes on for a lifetime is no different from reality."

The view of some critics—that Yeats wore masks as some kind of compensation or replacement for religious traditions in which he could no longer believe—minimizes, perhaps unduly, an element of fun. The joy of playacting was there, too, even when the donning of a mask became a plausible occasion for lofty talk about the differences between appearance and reality. Nor can a biographer speak too positively as he traces stages in Yeats's movement from one intellectual interest to another—from (let us say) his interest in romantic literature as exemplified by Shelley to his interest in the theosophical literature that so fascinated him in the early 1890s. Yeats added chambers to his mind; he never seemed to subtract any. The heavy emphasis placed by recent critics on single aspects of Yeats's readings or personal relationships—on the *Upanishads* and *Vedas*, or S. L. MacGregor Mathers, or spiritualism, or Arthur Symons—is inevitably misleading. No one key will unlock more than a single doorway to Yeats's thinking. If there is any constant, it does not lie in cultural relativism—that is, all ideas have equal value in a world bereft of absolute religious truths—but rather in the concept of an Ireland worthy of men's most heroic and self-sacrificial deeds.

Yeats, who needs no praise to assure his place in world literature, often seems to need a rescue operation from those who would identify him too readily with the arcane movements he participated in, and from those who, having taken the trouble to steep themselves in many a quaint and curious volume of forgotten lore, believe that such volumes define the scope of Yeats's genius. Yeats has not become his admirers—yet. We are fortunate that Yeats's greatness transcends both his sources and his explicators.

"All poetry," wrote Yeats, "should have a local habitation when at all possible." When he studied Oriental philosophy, admired elements in the thought of the Indian missionary Mohini Chatterji, and became excited by Druidism, he did so because, in the same "intuitive" way that led him to discover Irish ancestors for William Blake, he was convinced that Irishmen had been living in Asia until the Battle of the Boyne, and that, as a consequence, borrowings from the East were legitimate: "Tradition is always the same. The earliest poet of India and the Irish peasant in his hovel nod to each other across the ages, and are in perfect agreement."

If *The Wanderings of Oisin* (1889) is to be regarded as the turning point in Yeats's attitude toward an appropriate subject matter —it was resolutely, consistently Irish thereafter—a few words on the kind of Ireland that he created for his imaginative art become essential. In the roughest of time divisions, his first period may be said to extend from 1885 (the publication of *Mosada*) to 1899, and the printing of *The Wind Among the Reeds*. Ireland, which Yeats was seeking to define in a number of anthologies of folklore and fairy tales undertaken during this period, was seen as a land of two historical ages: the first, ancient and heroic; the second, modern but sadly diminished in stature.

Oisin, the hero of Yeats's long poem, had spent several centuries in an enchanted world with a woman from a "fairy state"; when he returned to modern Ireland, he had become "blind and hoary," used up. The basic framework of *The Wanderings of Oisin* is a dialogue between Oisin and St. Patrick, between, in other words, an unrepentant pagan and an intolerant representative of the Christianity that has secured its grip on modern life. We are not meant to love Oisin, but to admire his willingness to stake all for beauty. (This kind of simple, passionate nature is what Yeats had in mind when, in *The Celtic Twilight*, he wrote that we too shall be among the fairies and divine people if we purify ourselves.) The "man of crosiers" invokes a God of wrath to threaten Oisin, and he describes the Fenians as lost souls:

> Where the flesh of the footsole clingeth on the burning
>     stones is their place;
> Where the demons whip them with wires on the burning
>     stones of wide hell,
> Watching the blessed ones move far off, and the smile on
>     God's face,
> Between them a gateway of brass, and the howl of the
>     angels who fell.

But Oisin, undaunted, will not give up the singing of war chants. He promises, at the end of the poem, to go to the Fenians, "be they in flames or at feast," and to make converse with them "of Eri, of wars, and of old wounds and rest."

In later years Yeats extensively revised *The Wanderings of Oisin*. But, as A. Norman Jeffares and others have noted, Yeats "departed from the spirit of the Gaelic originals,"[7] *Oisin i dTir na nOg* and *Agallamh na Senorach*, precisely because he believed in the existence of strong resemblances between Irish and Eastern legends. What concerns us at the moment is the portrait of Ireland that emerges from Yeats's tinkerings with the texts he was using, and this portrait did not change substantially in any later version. Ireland is a fanatical, intolerant, unforgiving, and joyless land. St. Patrick, cursed by his vision of rightness and hostile to the stranger, no matter what vision he summons up, informs Oisin that the gods of the Fenians are dead, that "the sacred cairn and the rath" are no longer guarded; "bell-mounted churches" have replaced them. The men of modern Ireland have become "a small and a feeble populace stooping with mattock and spade"; their chieftains, Oisin sees, have "bodies unglorious" and await "in patience the straw-death." In such a land, two men, "stumbling apart," "sweating," "staggering," cannot carry a sack full of sand. Oisin is scornful of them. He knows that men who wear horsehair shirts and who cringe before the wrath of their God ("Trembling, on the flags we fall, / Fearful of the thunder-ball, / Yet do with us whate'er thou wilt, / For great our error, great our guilt") can accomplish nothing great.

The praise that attended the publication of *The Wanderings of Oisin* was sincere, enthusiastic, and widespread. The grounds for dissatisfaction in an occasional review—"One critic saw in the poem the English romantic movement in process of decomposition"[8]—were more literary, more concerned with changes that had been made from the sources and with technique, than with the ideas expressed within the poem. Yet, looking back on the poems that Yeats wrote between 1889 and 1899, we can only wonder that so little was said about the cheerlessness of this reading of Ireland's present condition. The very poem that opens the Definitive Edition, "The Song of the Happy Shepherd," states unequivocally (and did when it was originally written) that "the woods of Arcady are dead." Even if the lyric is torn from its dramatic context in *The Island of Statues*, the sentiment was Yeats's, and he found an astonishingly large number of ways to restate it. The Happy Shepherd, originally a satyr who carried a sea shell, was lamenting a world that had turned away from "dreaming" to "Grey Truth" as her "painted toy," to "words" taken as "certain good"—the only certain good at that—to "entangled" stories of the past that will never come again, to misplaced faith in "the starry men" who watch the skies "with the optic glass":

> . . . the cold star-bane
> Has cloven and rent their hearts in twain,
> And dead is all their human truth.

Since no poet rewrote his youth with greater care than Yeats and since Yeats had ample cause to regret the softness and the overluxuriance of his earliest productions, the kind of world that was no longer fit for Oisin or Cúchulainn may be inferred from a number of poems that he wrote during the 1890s. "A Legend" (not included in the Definitive Edition) describes a city beneath the waters of Lough Gill that has been drowned by the tears of God. Who would not lose patience with the speeches of passing men who are neither patient nor good; of "a grey professor" and a mayor who fear talk of the poor; and of a bishop who worships "his god of stupor and of wrath"? When Fergus, king of the "proud Red Branch kings," speaks despairingly (in another poem) of the age that has overcome him, he laments the "great webs of sorrow" that lie "hidden in the small slate-coloured thing!" The whole point of "The Lake Isle of Innisfree," Yeats's unexpectedly popular lyric, is that one can retreat from "the roadway" and "the pavements grey," far from men and modern civilization.

Yeats's defense against those who censured his writings for not serving the cause of nationalism is discussed in chapter 11, on the Abbey Theatre. The vulnerability of lyrical poetry to precisely this kind of charge from Nationalists and Unionists is obvious enough, and Yeats's fascination with the hypothesis that fairies and divine people were once human beings is no more satisfactory as a rebuttal merely because these are *Irish* fairies and divine people. Yeats wrote a great deal about what it meant to be Irish in his lectures, letters to the "new island" (journalism for the *Providence Sunday Journal* and *Boston Pilot*), and in his books: *Fairy and Folk Tales of the Irish Peasantry* (1888), *Stories from Carleton* (1889), *Representative Irish Tales* (1891), *The Countess Kathleen and Various Legends and Lyrics* and *Irish Fairy Tales* (1892), and *The Celtic Twilight* (1893). Even so, what he wrote to Katharine Tynan in June 1888 has a nervous ring of truth: "I must write in this letter no more bookish news as I know you think me too little interested in other things. The real fact of the matter is that the other things at present for many reasons make me anxious and I bury my head in books as the ostrich does in the sand. I am a much more human person than you think."[9]

Ireland's numbed shock after Parnell's death could not last forever. The response of the audience to the performance of Yeats's *Cathleen ni Houlihan*, however familiar an anecdote, should be recalled. "She was Ireland herself," Yeats wrote about his heroine, who had appeared to him in "a dream almost as distinct as a vision of a cottage"; and in the hands of Frank and William Fay, and with the lead played by Maud Gonne, the play was "most enthusiastically received." Crowds were turned away from the doors every night in April 1902. At the end of his life, many years later, a troubled Yeats asked, in "The Man and the Echo":

> All that I have said and done,
> Now that I am old and ill,
> Turns into a question till
> I lie awake night after night
> And never get the answers right.
> Did that play of mine send out
> Certain men the English shot?
> Did words of mine put too great strain

On that woman's reeling brain?
Could my spoken words have checked
That whereby a house lay wrecked?
And all seems evil until I
Sleepless would lie down and die.

Working in his own way for Ireland, Yeats sometimes touched to the quick those who responded more energetically to dreams than to political incantations. Some have claimed that a poet should not be given credit for influencing the development of Ireland's political history. We remember how Oliver Gogarty responded to a member of the nominating committee of the Irish Senate, who had inquired why a poet should be given a political office in the Irish Free State: "If it had not been for W. B. Yeats there would be no Irish Free State!"[10]

Yet the stereotyped view of Yeats's poetry of the 1890s as being essentially passive is a hard one to overturn, despite Walter Starkie's praise of *The Celtic Twilight* as "full of freshness and early-morning sunshine," a book that "might have been written in the open air,"[11] and despite recent elaborate analyses of the balance struck between dynamically active and introspective lyrics in *The Wind Among the Reeds*. The reason (as suggested earlier) is that Yeats preferred what he thought he knew about the remote, and only partially retrievable, past to what he hated in Ireland's present realities. Indeed, he knew more than most of his contemporaries about that past, because of his eclectic reading in libraries of materials on Ireland, including obscure chapbooks "brown with turf smoke on cottage shelves." His footnotes to his own poems and to stories and legends in his anthologies testify to an extraordinarily wide—if not always accurate—range of information. Yeats several times fantasied himself as a man of action, but he could not have continued indefinitely as a writer of Celtic Twilight poetry without repeating themes based on a very limited number of emotions. His years as one of the directors of the Abbey were, at least partially, a self-conscious effort to change and revitalize his art. The irony of his middle period lay in the relative sterility of his poetic production, the thinness of his output, and his dissatisfaction with almost everything he published. He admired Synge greatly, but knew that he could not go to the Aran Islands himself. He joined the Irish Republican Brotherhood, but it was a well-kept secret (his wife knew nothing about it until after his senatorship had been confirmed), and he was never one of its more active members. Moreover, he underestimated the potential effectiveness of violence. This double decade may be arbitrarily opened or closed several years in either direction; its extent is not agreed on by Yeats scholars; and yet something so important to Yeats's career took place that T. R. Henn's descriptive tag for it—"Recognition and Reversal"—has never been improved upon.[12] The world Yeats knew was collapsing, just as the Great War was causing the collapse of the values of the larger world. It was apparent to all save a generation of Chekhovian dreamers that the Ascendancy class was no longer directing the struggle for independence. The Big Houses were obsolete; many of them would be burned during the Troubles. Personal tragedies—those of Hugh Lane and Robert Gregory, among others—marked moments of consternated recognition that the poet was growing, inevitably, older.

Yeats did not move swiftly to embrace his new identity. Less than a year before Easter, 1916—the moment when his acquaintances who worked at "counter or desk" in "eighteenth-century houses" doffed their motley, when everything "changed utterly" and "a terrible beauty was born"—Yeats refused a request made by Edith Wharton, through Henry James, that he write a "war poem": "I think it better that at times like these / We poets keep our mouths shut; for in truth / We have no gift to set a statesman right. . . ." And, as he added in a note to James, "It is the only thing I have written of the war or will write, so I hope it may not seem unfitting. I shall keep the neighbourhood of the seven sleepers of Ephesus, hoping to catch their comfortable snores till bloody frivolity is over."[13]

A poet may ignore Armageddon in favor of personal concerns, but at the cost of having his fellow countrymen ignore his plea to follow his advice on how best to achieve Unity of Culture. A phrase like "bloody frivolity" suggests an attitude of thin feeling. Yeats was self-consciously seeking a worthy cause; his feelings were, of course, far from those of a dim, drained poet. In 1919, when he published "If I Were Four-and-Twenty," he confessed that for much of his life his three interests—in a form of literature, in a form of philosophy, and in a belief in nationality—seemed to have nothing to do with one another; that his love of literature and his belief in nationality came together first; and that he learned later how his "whole character" conjoined all three. He had had to hammer his thoughts into unity. He may have been over-optimistic about the hammering process having reached that final stage before the warfare of the Black and Tans had concluded, but it was essential that he complete it before he could recommend to the nation "a new doctrine, that of unity of being."[14]

Yeats took very seriously the charge that he laid upon younger poets, and if what he considered "well made" changed from decade to decade, writing craftsmanlike poetry in an important sense always transcended his concern with subject matter. Take a trivial example: Yeats's concern with punctuation dominates a surprising fraction of his correspondence with publishers. Or a more serious observation: the feeling that one derives from reading the original printed version of almost any poem is often significantly different from the reader's response to the final version in the Definitive Edition. As the editors of the *Variorum Edition of the Poems* have said:

> Sometimes the revisions were of entire poems; sometimes of but single lines or single words; and sometimes they were merely of punctuation or of spelling. He continued to revise until the end; he was never content. "It is myself that I remake," he wrote in 1908 to friends who objected to his constant reworking of his verse; and in the preface written in 1927 for the thirteenth reprinting and revision of his *Poems* (1895) he said: "This volume contains what is, I hope, the final text of the poems of my youth; and yet it may not be, . . . One is always cutting out the dead wood."[15]

In an important study by Jon Stallworthy, *Between the Lines: Yeats's Poetry in the Making* (Oxford: Clarendon Press of Oxford University Press, 1963), that process is further defined. Yeats apparently had a strong structural sense; he knew what shape a poem would have before he began. His rhetoric, partly learned from Spenser, Shelley, and Donne, was vertebrate with recurring figures. He selected his rhyme scheme before he began his stanza, and with increasing skill he varied his pace, rhythm, and rhymes. The revisions made the lines sing more freely and enabled them to move from a subjective beginning to a larger, more universal meaning: "Although many poems spring from a subjective seed, they open out into an objective flower."[16] He cut and pared away; he seldom added: "He works inwards toward a centre, rather than outwards and away from it."[17] Other studies by Curtis Bradford, Joseph Hone, A. Norman Jeffares, Richard Ellmann, and Thomas Parkinson have showed how these revisions converted relatively simple poems into collections of drafts, into the daw's nest described in Yeats's "The Tower."

Nor was Yeats's interest in revising his plays any less intense. Several scholars have already written about the problems of considering the texts of plays that have been massively rewritten. S. B. Bushrui's comment on the revisions made within a single decade—"When we come to study the texts we find that the process of continuous revision makes it extremely difficult to assign to any play a fixed place in a chronological order"[18]—must be seen as tacit approval of Ernest Boyd's exasperated comment that "a new edition often means a new play." Russell K. Alspach, in his Introduction to the *Variorum Edition of the Plays*, notes that a large part of his problems as an editor began with the fact that there was no final revised text available for the plays as there had been for the poems (a two-volume edition published in 1949). Alspach's rather dry-toned description of all the problems created by Yeats's constant revisions must be read to be fully appreciated ("intelligible collation was virtually impossible" for *The Countess Cathleen*, for example).[19] Hennessy Vendler once remarked that she was continually confronted by the need to choose between two texts of Yeats's *A Vision*. The distance between the *A* and *B* texts was not one of thought so much as of language that had been worked away at, whittled, and not always happily refined: "His ideas changed, but not drastically. The second edition moves toward greater precision and, at the same time, greater sophistication. Sometimes, however, precision becomes verbiage and sophistication becomes mystification; at those times I resort to the more primitive version."[20] It is not surprising that a man who would willingly undertake to revise and publish his *Collected Works* in eight volumes in his mid forties would provoke A.E. to tell George Moore that Yeats intended to spend the rest of his life revising his poems, and had expressed to him the desire to do so. There is something of the grand manner in Yeats's request to Katharine Tynan that, the next time she planned to publish any of his letters, she should send them on to him: "I may even, in defiance of all right conduct, improve them."[21] Need one add that he subjected his prose essays to countless revisions as well?[22]

A diary kept in 1930 provided Yeats with an opportunity to compare two great representatives of Yeats's favorite century: Burke and Swift. Yeats unhesitatingly preferred Swift. "Burke is only tolerable in his impassioned moments, but no matter what Swift talks of, one delights in his animation and clarity."[23] Partly, as a reason for Yeats's preference, Swift thought in English rather than French or Latin; partly, too, Burke's choice of audience—"men in an assembly"—made for a stiffness and formality that was circumvented by Swift's choice—"men sitting at table or fireside." Yeats called Swift's age "that one Irish century that escaped from darkness and confusion."[24] He had no faith in democracy, Rousseau, or the French Revolution—the successors to Swift's lifetime. *The Words upon the Window-pane* (1930) gave Yeats's interpretation of the reason for Swift's celibacy, which is one of the most puzzling, and perhaps ultimately insoluble, questions of literary history. Yeats knew all the theories that had been propounded: Sir

Walter Scott's notion that a physical defect might have been operant; the view that Swift entertained a pathological dread of sexual temptation; Lecky's notion that Swift feared the onset of madness; the possibility of syphilis; or even the discovery of ties of consanguinity, after a possible marriage between Swift and Stella. If Yeats modified Lecky's theory, it was to make a larger point about the movement of Irish history. John Corbet (Yeats's spokesman within the play) is a rationalist and a student at Cambridge who is working on his doctoral dissertation, "an essay on Swift and Stella." He is erudite, humorless, and not wholly convinced that powers beyond his ken are at work during the fateful seance of the Dublin Spiritualists' Association; yet he is not intended to be unattractively priggish. Twice he proffers an explanation for Swift's crack-up.

On the first occasion, he rejects Dr. Trench's oversimplification of Swift's tragedy as being in essence the tragedy of "Bolingbroke, Harley, Ormonde, all those great Ministers that were his friends, banished and broken." "I do not think you can explain him in that way," Corbet responds quickly, "—his tragedy had deeper foundations. His ideal order was the Roman Senate, his ideal men Brutus and Cato. Such an order and such men had seemed possible once more, but the movement passed and he foresaw the ruin to come." The common run of men coming into their own meant that Swift would be disinherited, and Swift's epitaph would speak—with relief—of his passing to "where fierce indignation can lacerate his heart no more."

On the second occasion, Mrs. Henderson, the medium who has transmitted Swift's voice—"I have something in my blood that no child must inherit," that is to say, a madness that might be transmitted to a new generation—has unwittingly fallen in with a theory that Corbet regards as "the only plausible one." Corbet asks Mrs. Henderson a final series of questions: "Swift was the chief representative of the intellect of his epoch, that arrogant intellect free at last from superstition. He foresaw its collapse. He foresaw Democracy, he must have dreaded the future. Did he refuse to beget children because of that dread? Was Swift mad? Or was it the intellect itself that was mad?"

Mrs. Henderson, who knows nothing of Swift, is unable to answer the questions satisfactorily, because she is now conscious and no longer acting as a medium; but Yeats had his own conviction. Swift's madness came at the end of an era, the last when Unity of Culture might be presumed to have been both possible and a fact.

For Yeats there were other great periods of history: Greece, when civilization "rose to its high-tide mark"; Byzantium (Yeats's famous note in *A Vision* should be quoted: "I think that in early Byzantium, maybe never before or since in recorded history, religious, aesthetic and practical life were one, that architect and artificers . . . spoke to the multitude and the few alike"); and the Renaissance; but the eighteenth century had a mind so clear "that it changed the world." After the light, the dark; the possibility of the second coming: "And what rough beast, its hour come round at last, / Slouches towards Bethlehem to be born?" When Yeats, writing in July 1931 about Bishop Berkeley, came to his concluding paragraph, he remembered how men of the 1890s had turned from the political poetry of Young Ireland as a foundation of Irish politics and had "substituted an interest in old stories and modern peasants." He was thinking partly of his own youth. Since then the Irish Free State had come into existence, and sacrifice no longer seemed necessary. The young men "have begun to ask if their country has anything to give." Everything was upside down.[25]

Yet this summary of Yeats's attitude toward the indomitable "Irishry" (a word that he borrowed from Toynbee and constantly used with great relish) does not conclude with a too-ready assumption that his final two decades were deeply and darkly embittered by the civil war that the Free State Constitution precipitated, by the passing of power from his own class to the Catholic majority, by his shock at the death of one old friend after another, or even by his readings in Spengler and other disenchanted philosophers or by his rage at turning into "a wild old man in the light." Despite his sharp and telling judgments on others, he never considered himself to be a mere spectator at the play. With deep feeling he wrote, in "The Municipal Gallery Revisited" (1937), an invitation to subsequent generations of critics:

> You that would judge me, do not judge alone
> This book or that, come to this hallowed place
> Where my friends' portraits hang and look thereon;
> Ireland's history in their lineaments trace;
> Think where man's glory most begins and ends,
> And say my glory was I had such friends.

More needs to be written about Yeats's generosity to younger poets and to even the most casual strangers who requested aid and advice, as well as about his willingness to acknowledge intellectual and personal debts to his contemporaries in age ("And say my glory was I had such friends"). He saw the depths of the abyss ahead. Like Swift, he refused to entertain sanguine hopes about the future. But even in the characteristically self-deprecatory "The Apparations" (1938), where he refers to himself as "a coat upon a coat-hanger," the note of affirmation is strong: "When a man grows old his joy / Grows more deep day after day." Even if as an old man he finds himself increasingly given over to the enumeration of "old themes," as in "The Circus Animals' Desertion" (1939), he remembers that the best of his works—*The Wanderings of Oisin, The Countess Cathleen, On Baile's Strand*—began in "a mound of refuse or the sweepings of a street." Art gave them form. They grew to life under Irish skies. They had been appreciated by Irish friends. A faith in cyclic theories of history means—if it means anything at all—that Georgian Ireland may be out of favor now, as in the fifth and most biting stanza of "Under Ben Bulben":

> Irish poets, learn your trade,
> Sing whatever is well made,
> Scorn the sort now growing up
> All out of shape from toe to top,
> Their unremembering hearts and heads
> Base-born products of base beds. . . .

But if poets and sculptors continue to do their work, to "bring the soul of man to God," to remember the lessons of "seven heroic centuries," the better age will come again. Yeats was prepared for a new generation of Irish poets to take over from him; and justified by a lifetime of hard work and artistic achievement, he knew, even in his most arrogant moments, that others could do as well if they would only keep the faith:

> Cast your mind on other days
> That we in coming days may be
> Still the indomitable Irishry.

## NOTES

1. Donald R. Pearce, ed., *The Senate Speeches of W. B. Yeats* (Bloomington: Indiana University Press, 1960), pp. 11–26.
2. Ibid., pp. 98–99. These remarks were made on 11 June 1925.
3. Ibid., p. 172.
4. Ibid., pp. 173–74.
5. William Butler Yeats, *The Autobiography of William Butler Yeats* (New York: Doubleday Anchor Books, 1958), p. 77.
6. Richard Ellmann, *Yeats: The Man and the Masks* (New York: E. P. Dutton, 1948), pp. 172–73.
7. A. Norman Jeffares, *A Commentary on the Collected Poems of W. B. Yeats* (Stanford, Calif.: Stanford University Press, 1968), p. 521.

8. Joseph Hone, *W. B. Yeats, 1865–1939* (2d ed.; London: Macmillan, 1962), p. 62.
9. *The Letters of W. B. Yeats*, ed. Allan Wade (London: Rupert Hart-Davis, 1954), p. 75.
10. Pearce, *The Senate Speeches of W. B. Yeats*, p. 15.
11. Walter Starkie's Introduction in Yeats's *The Celtic Twilight and a Selection of Early Poems* (New York: New American Library, 1962), p. xviii.
12. Thomas R. Henn, *The Lonely Tower: Studies in the Poetry of W. B. Yeats* (2d ed., rev. and enl.; London: Methuen, 1965), p. 5.
13. *The Letters of W. B. Yeats*, pp. 599–600.
14. William Butler Yeats, *Explorations*, selected by Mrs. W. B. Yeats (London: Macmillan, 1962), p. 280.
15. Introduction to *The Variorum Edition of the Poems of W. B. Yeats*, ed. Peter Allt and Russell K. Alspach (New York: Macmillan, 1957), p. xv.
16. Jon Stallworthy, *Between the Lines: Yeats's Poetry in the Making* (Oxford: Clarendon Press, 1963), p. 246.
17. Ibid., p. 252.
18. Suheil B. Bushrui, *Yeats's Verse Plays: The Revisions, 1900–1910* (Oxford: Clarendon Press, 1965), p. xiv.
19. *The Variorum Edition of the Plays of W. B. Yeats*, ed. Russell K. Alspach (London: Macmillan, 1966), p. xii.
20. Helen Hennessy Vendler, *Yeats's Vision and the Later Plays* (Cambridge, Mass.: Harvard University Press, 1963), p. 262.
21. Bushrui, *Yeats's Verse Plays*, p. xiv.
22. Curtis B. Bradford, *Yeats at Work* (Carbondale: Southern Illinois University Press, 1965), pp. 305–85 passim.
23. Yeats, *Explorations*, p. 293.
24. Ibid., p. 345.
25. Yeats, *Essays and Introductions* (London: Macmillan, 1961), p. 411.

## SUGGESTIONS FOR FURTHER READING

Donoghue, Denis. *William Butler Yeats.* New York: Viking, 1971.
Ellmann, Richard. *Eminent Domain: Yeats among Wilde, Joyce, Pound, Eliot, and Auden.* New York: Oxford University Press, 1967.
———. *Yeats: The Man and the Masks.* New York: E. P. Dutton, 1948.
Hall, James, and Steinmann, Martin, eds. *The Permanence of Yeats.* New York: Macmillan, 1950.
Hone, Joseph. *W. B. Yeats, 1865–1939.* New York: Macmillan, 1943.
Jeffares, A. Norman. *A Commentary on the Collected Poems of W. B. Yeats.* London: Macmillan, 1968.
———. *W. B. Yeats: Man and Poet.* London: Routledge & K. Paul, 1949.
Loftus, Richard J. *Nationalism in Modern Anglo-Irish Poetry.* Madison: University of Wisconsin Press, 1964.
Unterecker, John E. *A Reader's Guide to William Butler Yeats.* New York: Noonday Press, 1959.
Ure, Peter. *Yeats, the Playwright.* London: Routledge & K. Paul, 1963.

# THE TWO ATTITUDES OF
# JAMES JOYCE

## *Harold Orel*

When James Joyce described his style in *Dubliners* as being a deliberately cultivated "scrupulous meanness," he provided not merely the title for a scholar's recent book but also a meaningful paradox for all his readers. Any analysis of Joyce's attitude toward Ireland must begin and end in paradox. For Joyce, Ireland was an object of both love and hatred, and his art was deeply affected by the ambiguities of his response to the land from which he deliberately exiled himself while still a young man. Although the Irish have been more conscious of Joyce's scorn than of his affection—to the point where *Ulysses* has only recently been made available for book buyers in Ireland, and sites associated with Joyce remain for the most part unmarked in the vague hope that tourists will be unable to locate them—the fact of that affection can hardly be denied. Nevertheless, the scorn implicit in the characterization of the old milkwoman in the opening chapter of *Ulysses*, of the emaciated symbol of what Kathleen ni Houlihan had become as "a wandering crone, lowly form of an immortal serving her conqueror and her gay betrayer, their common cuckquean, a messenger from the secret morning," is everywhere, too, and that scorn must not be minimized.

Joyce did not underestimate the likelihood that his lukewarm attitude toward the cause of Irish nationalism would evoke appropriate feelings of hostility from the Irishmen he had left behind to fight the battle in the only place where it could be fought. The supposed objectivity of his three lectures given at the Università Popolare in Trieste in 1907 provided only the thinnest of layers between his subject matter and his true feelings. Joyce's interest was basically not in the historical review of evidence identifying the linguistic family to which Gaelic belonged or in praising "the three great heresiarchs John Duns Scotus, Macarius, and Vergilius Solivagus," but in characterizing his native land as a country destined to be the everlasting caricature of the serious world. No longer, Joyce argued, could an Irishman be said to live in the Island of Saints and Sages. "The economic and intellectual conditions that prevail in his own country do not permit the development of individuality," he argued. "The soul of the country is weakened by centuries of useless struggle and broken treaties, and individual initiative is paralysed by the influence and admonitions of the church, while its body is manacled by the police, the tax office, and the garrison. No one who has any self-respect stays in Ireland, but flees afar as though from a country that has undergone the visitation of an angered Jove."[1] Both priest and king would have to be shaken off, and the process would take forever: "In time, perhaps there will be a gradual reawakening of the Irish conscience, and perhaps four or five centuries after the Diet of Worms, we will see an Irish monk throw away his frock, run off with some nun, and proclaim in a loud voice the end of the coherent absurdity that was Catholicism and the beginning of the incoherent absurdity that is Protestantism."[2] As for supplanting the king, "Ireland has already had enough equivocations and misunderstandings. If she wants to put on the play that we have waited for so long, this time let it be whole, and complete, and definitive. But our advice to the Irish producers is the same as that our fathers gave them not so long ago—hurry up! I am sure that I, at least, will never see that curtain go up, because I will have already gone home on the last train."[3]

It was, perhaps, inevitable that the first decade of the century, with his rootless wanderings through Pola, Rome, and Trieste, should have led Joyce to his most explicit remarks about the values of Irish culture. The series of articles that he wrote for *Il Piccolo della Sera* (1907–1909) on the evils of Empire as found in Ireland were drawn from a bottomless well of bitter memories. The attack was mounted simultaneously against the British Empire, Ireland, and the Vatican, particularly in his opening essays on Fenianism, Home Rule, and the Irish Nationalists who were pressing the cause of independence. His first subject was

*James Joyce,* 1935
Sean O'Sullivan (1906–1964)
Drawing
National Gallery of Ireland, Dublin
Photo by courtesy of the National Gallery of Ireland

*The Two Attitudes of James Joyce*

John O'Leary, who had died in Dublin on St. Patrick's Day, 1907, only a week earlier. Like Yeats, Joyce saw the old man's death as the end of an era of heroic, though abortive, violence. But Yeats's lines—"Romantic Ireland's dead and gone; / It's with O'Leary in the grave"—memorialized O'Leary as hero, while Joyce's review of the development of Fenianism deliberately underplayed the heroism of O'Leary's fellow insurrectionists. Rather, as Joyce put it, the Fenians were always betraying each other, even if they had organized in small cells—a plan "eminently fitted to the Irish character because it reduces to a minimum the possibility of betrayal." In Ireland, as Joyce wrote, an informer would always appear. Joyce predicted that O'Leary's funeral would be marked with great pomp, because the Irish, even though they broke "the hearts of those who sacrifice their lives for their native land," never failed to show "great respect for the dead."[4]

The despair of those who could not feed their families and of those who perceived the intellectual futility of the Irishman's plight led to a mass emigration. Later the emigrants would sentimentalize Ireland in song and poem. The reasons for Joyce's violent reaction against Rome, which had shaped Ireland's concepts of right and wrong, may be briefly summarized:[5] the city reminded him of "a man who lives by exhibiting to travellers his grandmother's corpse,"[6] and it was also the city of the papacy. He shocked his pupils in Trieste by saying, "I like Papal Rome because it makes me think of that pig of a pope, Alexander VI, in the arms of his mistress and daughter Lucrezia Borgia, and of Julius II, who built his tomb during his lifetime, and of Leo X and Clement VI, two popes who besides being great rakes were great friends of Martin Luther. I can easily understand why Ibsen felt uncomfortable in that city."[7] But if the wealth in Rome, to which he himself had no access, offended him, that of the Church in Ireland offended him more:

> And almost as if to set in relief this depopulation there is
> a long parade of churches, cathedrals, convents, monas-
> teries, and seminaries to tend to the spiritual needs of those
> who have been unable to find courage or money enough to
> undertake the voyage from Queenstown to New York. Ire-
> land, weighed down by multiple duties, has fulfilled what
> has hitherto been considered an impossible task—serving
> both God and Mammon, letting herself be milked by Eng-
> land and yet increasing Peter's pence.[8]

The true sovereign of Ireland, Joyce believed, was the pope, who continued the tradition of misconceived rights that Adrian IV had believed in when, in a burst of generosity, he donated Ireland to Henry II of England. In other words, both the medieval and the modern papacies were deaf to Irish cries of help. Why did papal policy prefer, in its devious way, to conciliate Edward VII rather than to take care of a people of proven Catholic loyalty?

Joyce was well informed on Home Rule legislation. His anger at the emasculated bill being considered by the House of Lords in 1907 derived from his feeling that Gladstone, as a hypocrite, pretended an interest in the problem only because he knew that the Lords would reject the bill sent up by the House of Commons. Joyce's brush tarred a large canvas: neither the Liberal party nor the English Catholics could be trusted, for they were as unreliable as the Irish Parliamentarians. The real hope of the future lay (he believed) with the Sinn Fein movement, with its policy of economic resistance and passive disloyalty to British rule. The boycott was the one weapon that he thoroughly approved of, especially since it was of Irish manufacture.

In the midst of this brief flurry of journalistic paper Joyce could not refrain from an occasional patriotic outburst. For example, knowing (as any Irishman necessarily knew) the extent to which Englishmen deceived themselves about the nature of English oppression in Ireland, he discovered within himself a welling outrage at the denunciations printed in English newspapers of some acts of agrarian terrorism committed in Ireland. Partly, of course, the Irish were inarticulate and could not defend themselves. In 1882, the year of Joyce's birth, there had been a murder trial of Myles Joyce, an old man who spoke nothing but Gaelic. Desperately attempting to defend his innocence in that language before a judge and jury who could not follow his statements, cursed by having to speak to an interpreter who made no effort to render his story fairly, Myles Joyce was found guilty and was executed by a brutal hangman. "The figure of this dumbfounded old man, a remnant of a civilization not ours, deaf and dumb before his judge, is a symbol of the Irish nation at the bar of public opinion. Like him," Joyce wrote in mounting anger, "she is unable to appeal to the modern conscience of England and other countries. The English journalists act as interpreters between Ireland and the English electorate, which gives them ear from time to time and ends up being vexed by the endless complaints of the Nationalist representatives who have entered her House, as she believes, to disrupt its order and extort money."[9] The agrarian crimes that had made the telegraph office "hop" were, after all, not only rare, but they should have been seen as genuine acts of desperation. Ireland, no matter what British journalists might say, was not a country of louts and savages. To find "brutality" (Joyce's conclusion would have pleased the Fenians), one should look not to Irish terrorism but to British mistreatment of Ireland.

Moving between denunciations of England for not caring and of Ireland for not protecting its own interests more effectively, Joyce was particularly distressed by the Irish willingness to betray her heroes "always in the hour of need and always without gaining recompense."[10] The prime example of a great man torn apart by the wolves—Irish wolves, not English—was, of course, Parnell. The reasons for Joyce's admiration are considered in still another essay written for *Il Piccolo della Sera* (16 May 1912), and they are even more impressive when we note the number of limitations in Parnell's kind of leadership that Joyce enumerated: "without forensic gifts or any original political talent," "a speech defect and a delicate physique," ignorance of the history of his native land, separation from his own colleagues by a "cold and formal bearing," and "a distinct English accent." Nor, at first glance, do his virtues (as listed by Joyce) suggest the inevitability of success on the battlefield of Parliament: an unwillingness to acknowledge the applause of his supporters no more than the howls of his avowed enemies, his indifference to the amenities of political relationships, and his melancholy at the knowledge that he would ultimately be betrayed. But these are elements in the make-up of an uncrowned king who could bargain with his captors in his cell at Kilmainham, who refused to defend himself when persecuted by the ministers Gladstone and Morley (a moral issue was the ostensible issue, but "a veto over the political affairs of Ireland" was the real prize), and whose extraordinary personality impressed all who saw him in action. Joyce quoted, in more than one context, Gladstone's characterization of Parnell as "an intellectual phenomenon."

The literary uses to which Parnell's life might be put were so numerous that one may watch the process, in Joyce's writings alone, whereby history is reshaped into myth with theological overtones. At the age of nine, Joyce wrote "Et Tu, Healy," in which Parnell towered over all other Irish politicians as an eagle, surveying the land from his "quaint-perched aerie." "Ivy Day in the Committee Room," a dramatization of the ancient and seldom-honorable craft of ward heeling, is a story that takes place on Parnell's anniversary (it was Joyce's favorite of all the tales in *Dubliners*). Henchy's fierce speech to Crofton bore Joyce's stamp of approval: "He was the only man that could keep that bag of cats in order. 'Down, ye dogs! Lie down, ye curs!' That's the way he treated them." Betrayal, as a theme, comes into its own in the poem recited by Mr. Hynes that concludes the story, for here Parnell is first equated with Christ:

Shame on the coward, caitiff hands
   That smote their Lord or with a kiss
Betrayed him to the rabble-rout
   Of fawning priests—no friends of his.

Joyce could never forget that the citizens of Castlecomer had thrown quicklime into Parnell's face, and the image turns up in "Gas from a Burner," written as protest at censorship of topical and place-name allusions in *Dubliners*, the sheets of which had been burned by Messrs. Maunsel ("publishers-in-ordinary to the Irish revival"): " 'Twas Irish humour, wet and dry,/Flung quicklime into Parnell's eye."[11] The great set piece of *Portrait*, the argument over Parnell at the Christmas dinner in the third part of chapter 1, should prepare us, through its invective over who has betrayed whom, for the rumbling series of betrayals that ultimately lead Stephen to flee from the entangling nets of Irish life: by the Jesuits (Father Conmee and Father Dolan laugh together at the injustice of a beating administered to Stephen), by the Dean of Studies (an unworthy disciple of Loyola), by the Catholic Church of Ireland ("the scullerymaid of christendom"), by his father (unworthy of respect after the trip to Cork), by Heron (who urged him to "Admit!" as he struck him with the cane across the calf of the leg), and by Cranly ("the child of exhausted loins"). In brief, Joyce's identification of himself with Parnell—the Caesar of "Et Tu, Healy" who became the Christ of Mr. Hynes's poem—is well-nigh complete by the end of *Portrait*. Betrayal is to remain a motif capable of all kinds of variation in Joyce's single play, *Exiles* (Richard Rowan is essentially Stephen all over again), and in *Ulysses* (the milk-woman, or Ireland, betrayed, as we have seen, by both Haines and Mulligan). Stephen believes that he must always be wary lest he be betrayed; he carries his wariness to such an extreme that finally he veers away from his long-lost father, who, however briefly, reclaims him in Beaver Street, after the flight from Bella Cohen's whorehouse; nor should we forget the fact that Leopold has once again been cuckolded by Molly. In *Finnegans Wake* the national pastime seems to be peeping and telling.

Much of this information about Joyce's views on Irish history; the relationship of the Catholic Church to its communicants, to Rome, and to the English throne; emigration patterns; one proposed Home Rule bill after another; and the significance of Parnell's downfall—all must be kept in mind if we are to say some sensible things about Joyce's contribution to Irish culture and about the reasons why the Irish have never cheerily become reconciled to Joyce the man. The magnifying glass of an ordinary storyteller had turned into a scanning electron microscope: no wart, blemish, or imperfection could escape. And there is no question that

Joyce began his career with the grimmest possible view of the possibilities inherent in Irish life. *Dubliners*, completed in 1907, did not appear in 1910, as originally planned, but four months after *Portrait* had begun to appear serially in the *Egoist*. By June 1914, when *Dubliners* came out, Ezra Pound might be excused for regarding the collection as a minor production (minor, that is, when measured against *Portrait*). The early reviewers, too, might well have been depressed by the unpleasantness of the incidents, the slice-of-life technique (however skillful), the unrelenting pessimism, and the possibility that Joyce had recounted a series of sketches and anecdotes without any definite structure in mind.

Although in the last quarter-century, critics have stressed the symbols of *Dubliners* and have read meanings out of the stories that Joyce never had put in, and although Joyce's realism has increasingly been played down in favor of an enthusiastic hunt for motifs linking the fifteen case histories—these "annals of frustration"—it may be that Joyce's original intention has been gradually lost sight of.

What was that intention? The Irish recognized enough of the surface of life to suspect that, so far as Joyce was concerned, the depths were murky too. The publication of Joyce's letters over the decades in increasingly reliable texts has confirmed the suspicions of many that Joyce's quarrel with his native land, even if regarded as a lover's quarrel, was unnecessarily and excessively sour on Joyce's part. The Joyce who identified himself in "The Holy Office" as "unfellowed, friendless and alone"—a stag flashing his antlers on the air (again the Parnell image), while a "motley crew" "crouched and crawled and prayed" below him—believed sincerely that he was writing a chapter in the moral history of his country and that Dublin might be chosen for the scene because that city seemed to him to be the center of paralysis (so Joyce wrote his publisher). When Joyce wrote to his wife that he, like other Irish writers, was trying to create a conscience for his race, he was stating as a personal goal what he gave to Stephen as the journal entry for 26 April: "Welcome, O life! I go to encounter for the millionth time the reality of experience and to forge in the smithy of my soul the uncreated conscience of my race." Why—as Robert Scholes has asked—should people need to have a conscience created for them, especially a people so conspicuously religious as the Irish?[12] Scholes went on to answer his own question:

> Joyce felt—and his letters support the evidence of the works themselves—that it was precisely their religious orthodoxy, combined with other sorts of "belatedness," that made the Irish so conscienceless. They had turned over the moral responsibility for their lives to their confessors and

religious leaders. Thus their ability to react sensitively to moral problems, to make ethical discriminations—to use their consciences—had atrophied. In Dubliners he offered his countrymen his own counterpart to St. Ignatius's *Spiritual Exercises*. The evaluation of motive and responsibility in these stories—the histories of "painful" cases for the most part—must inevitably lead the reader beyond any easy orthodoxy. These case histories encourage us to exercise our spirits, develop our consciences: to accept the view that morality is a matter of individual responses to particular situations rather than an automatic invocation of religious or ethical rules of thumb.

The stories of *Dubliners* were, of course, written out of a didactic impulse. Why should anybody, including Joyce, be surprised if the class for whom the lesson was intended rebelled against being told that they lived in a city of "hemiplegia or paralysis"; that they should be willing to pay "for the special odour of corruption" that (Joyce hoped) floated over his stories; that Joyce had "very little intention of prostituting whatever talent" he might have "to the public"; and that *Dubliners* represented "the first step towards the spiritual liberation" of Ireland? These scraps of bravura, extracted from a number of letters to his cautious publisher, Grant Richards, bespeak a wonderful self-assurance. Some have characterized it as an artist's impassioned defense of freedom of the press. Others see it as a series of calculated affronts to a nervous-Nellie temperament that Joyce found personally repellent. "Even if Dublin rejected *Dubliners*," writes one critic, "he would still be able to conquer Ireland, in the artist's traditional way, by setting up the criteria by which it must judge and be judged."[13]

*Dubliners*, even so, is not quite what Joyce says it is. Granted, he deliberately avoids anything like an event, he merely watches in story after story, he "reveals" his characters, and his emphasis is on the technique of exposure.[14] Things almost happen. None of the protagonists is able to escape from Dublin by traveling eastward across the seas, and physical or spiritual paralysis (sometimes both) overwhelms most impulses for action. But the key story, "The Dead," which Allen Tate said "brings to the highest pitch of perfection in English the naturalism of Flaubert,"[15] may well be about Joyce's vision of himself (Gabriel Conroy) if he had not left Ireland. The attitude toward the land from which Conroy can never disengage himself is deeply ambiguous. The history of differing critical interpretations of what Joyce intended to say in the ending of the story is fairly complicated.[16] It may be recalled, however, that

Gabriel, having become aware that his wife still cherishes her memory of a younger lover who died for her, finds that his eyes fill with "generous tears" and that he knows instinctively that "such a feeling must be love." He turns to the window to see the snow falling "all over Ireland." It is falling "on every part of the dark central plain, on the treeless hills, falling softly upon the Bog of Allen and, farther westward, softly falling into the dark mutinous Shannon waves." The critical question that has arisen (and is still not resolved) has to do with whether Gabriel's stance in the final moment that we see him—"His soul swooned slowly as he heard the snow falling faintly through the universe and faintly falling, like the descent of their last end, upon all the living and the dead"—represents still one more, and perhaps the most crushing, example of the paralysis that Joyce intended to demonstrate was either characteristic of Irish life (nay, was the essence of Irish life) or afforded grounds for hope of a re-birth as Gabriel escapes from his own ego (Tate's interpretation) "into the larger world of humanity, including 'all the living and the dead.' "[17] Is snow symbolic of sterility (the cemetery in which the lover of Gabriel's wife lies buried is filled with "crooked crosses and headstones," the little gate has "spears," the thorns are "barren") or of the promise that life inevitably renews itself (Gabriel's name speaks of annunciation; Christ's passion is a pledge of rebirth; the Liffey in one sense is to be taken as the waters of life; the memory of love has inspired tears)? The critics who seek to define Joyce's attitude do so on the basis of whether they read "The Dead" as the fifteenth "case history" (i.e., as the final fictional em-bodiment of a claustrophobic, embittered view of Ireland's condition) or as a short story to be considered in its own right, out of sequence, as an afterthought on Joyce's part. He had not intended to include "The Dead" as one of the original case histories. Kenneth Burke's view (which is representative of a very large body of critical opinion) is that the phrase "upon all the living and the dead" stands, in Joyce's mind, for an "ideal sociality" that has moved beyond "material divisiveness."[18]

Joyce found it difficult to stick to one view of Ireland even before he began the writing of "The Dead." At the age of twenty-four (September 1906), he was writing to his brother Stanislaus, "Sometimes thinking of Ireland it seems to me that I have been unnecessarily harsh. I have reproduced (in *Dubliners* at least) none of the attraction of the city for I have never felt at my ease in any city since I left it except in Paris. I have not reproduced its ingenuous insularity and its hospitality. The latter 'virtue' so far as I can see does not exist elsewhere in Europe. I have not been just to its beauty: for it is more beautiful naturally in my opin-ion than what I have seen of England, Switzerland, France, Austria or

Italy." He knew that it was too late to rewrite *Dubliners*; he knew that if he tried, he would find again what Stanislaus called "the Holy Ghost sitting in the ink-bottle" and the "perverse devil" of his literary conscience sitting on the hump of his pen.[19] In many ways Rome, Pola, and Trieste had not compensated for the loss of Ireland. The hypothesis of Walzl—"that the ambiguity of this conclusion [to 'The Dead'] was deliberate on Joyce's part and that it arose from the history and development of *Dubliners* as a collection"—is completely convincing to more than one reader.[20]

*A Portrait of the Artist as a Young Man*—the novel that is often read by adolescents as Joyce's clear-cut, unequivocal advocacy of an artist's right to defy the inhibiting forces of family, church, and nation (the entangling nets from which he must escape)—turns out, on closer inspection, to be equally troubled and ambiguous in its point of view. Stephen may tell his friend Davin that "Ireland is the old sow that eats her farrow," but Stephen is not necessarily Joyce. The irony with which he is presented at a few identifiable critical moments seriously undermines an argument of William York Tindall, a life-long admirer of Joyce, to the effect that Stephen "is shown sublimating personal anger into impersonal vision."[21] Tindall concedes that Joyce may be holding the Irish up to scorn, but he believes that Joyce is comparatively free from savage laughter or moral indignation; that his vision is far less satiric than contemplative, less destructive or edifying than creative; that he is less concerned with what is wrong with man than with the nature of man and the power of creation. This view, essentially one that emphasizes Joyce's word "artist" rather than the phrase "as a young man," which carefully qualifies the reader's understanding of the kind of artist Stephen is, makes good sense; but the question of whether Joyce's technique was essentially satirical is not to be answered so easily by the proposition that his satire is non-Swiftian. The process of disentanglement—the three "severings" that take place rapidly one after the other close to the end of the book—can hardly be reckoned as complete if we remember that the man who left his native land in 1904 with Nora Barnacle to teach English at the Berlitz School in Trieste, who traveled on the Continent from then on, and who died at the age of fifty-nine in Zurich in 1941, always dealt, basically, with the information that he had on hand when he became a self-imposed exile at the age of twenty-two. It is worth saying again, because the implications of the statement bear reexamination: he never wrote about anything except Ireland. As Ellmann suggests, "The writer's mature attitude is that of the boy in 'Araby,' a mixture of 'anguish and anger,' mitigated by his obvious pleasure in Dublin talk."[22] In "The Dead" a legitimate reading sees the possibility of redemption looming up not only for Gabriel Conroy but for Dublin and for Ireland. In *Portrait* a reader, as he assents to the strength of Stephen's final position, forgets, at his peril, the limitations of Stephen's character.

Books have been written about Joyce's characterization of Stephen, and we have time for only a few highlights. There is—if we begin with Stephen's university days—his disdain for classmates who meekly bend their heads as they write in their notebooks "the points they were bidden to note, nominal definitions, essential definitions and examples or dates of birth or death, chief works, a favourable and an unfavourable criticism side by side" (the thundering platitudes that in Ireland passed for higher education, as John V. Kelleher once noted). As Stephen fingered "the pages of his timeworn Horace," he knew that modern Ireland could not appreciate the "dusky verses"; but "it wounded him to think that he would never be but a shy guest at the feast of the world's culture and that the monkish learning, in terms of which he was striving to forge out an esthetic philosophy, was held no higher by the age he lived in than the subtle and curious jargons of heraldry and falconry." His soul fretted in the shadow of the language of the conqueror. Hence, his uneasiness over the dean's reaction to the Irish word "tundish" (which later turns out to be English, "and good old blunt English too"). "His language," thinks Stephen, "so familiar and so foreign, will always be for me an acquired speech. I have not made or accepted its words." When Davin urges him to be "one of us" because in his heart Stephen was Irish, even if his pride was "too powerful," Stephen responds that he has no responsibility for paying the debts incurred by his ancestors, who "threw off their language and took another," who submitted to foreigners, who betrayed their leaders (Tone and Parnell). When Stephen propounds the riddle of the man who was "hacking in fury" the image of a cow from a block of wood, Lynch ridicules him: "That has the true scholastic stink," and he ignores the questions that Stephen has posed about the nature of art. Stephen scorns his family, and glibly enumerates his father's attributes. He knows that he has failed in his efforts to unite his will with the will of God, to love God. He will not serve. His way of life henceforward will use for its defense three strategies—silence, exile, and cunning.

Thus Stephen in his pride has come to believe that no man can be a lover of the true and the good unless he abhors the multitude. He is, in significant respects, not very different from the Joyce who despised the rabble who had taken over the Irish Literary Theatre, that mob with its sodden enthusiasm and clever insinuation and every flattering influence of vanity and low ambition; from the twenty-year-old Joyce who told the famous Yeats, "I have met you too late. You are too old," thus momentarily disturbing Yeat's self-composure ("the younger generation is knocking at my door"); or from the image that Joyce sought to create for himself, aptly described by one critic as that of "an idealistic perfectionist whose unfulfillable hunger is for God" (as if, somehow, God has failed Stephen by not satisfying the hunger).

Generations of young men have regarded Stephens' cause as theirs, similarly denouncing what they can no longer believe in ("whether it call itself my home, my fatherland, or my church"). They may not have noted the humorlessness and the arrogance of Stephen. At the turn of the century (Joyce was telling his countrymen), Dubliners were all deeply entangled in the nets. Fifteen years later the situation had not perceptibly improved. Stephen was to be commended for escaping. Even so, Stephen had not proved himself as an artist, nor had he demonstrated to anybody who knew him that he owned the ability to forge in the smithy of his soul the uncreated conscience of his race. An aesthete would have great difficulty in clarifying the muddled stream of even his own personal life.

We do not have to go so far as Hugh Kenner, who once wrote, with asperity, "It is high time, in short, to point out once and for all that Stephen's flight into adolescent 'freedom' is not meant to be the 'message' of the book." But the evidence of Stephen's inadequacies as a human being and as an artist does add up to a substantial total. He is an undeniable prig when he engages in what Kenner calls "cold-blooded" dialogues with Cranly on mother-love. He writes Frenchified verses in bed "in an erotic swoon." The villanelle (our only tangible evidence that Stephen has literary talent) is filled with stale images. Stephen identifies the origin of aesthetic beauty with the soul of an artist almost independently of external realities; the supreme quality of *quidditas*, or the "whatness" of a thing, is felt by the artist when the aesthetic image is first "conceived in his imagination." When Joyce describes white pudding, eggs, sausages, and cups of tea as "simple and beautiful" (and thus characterizes Stephen's state of mind as repentant after his retreat), it is difficult to avoid the suspicion that the artist as a young man is being mocked. Kenner writes:

> The insufferable Stephen of the final chapter is explicable on the assumption that Joyce is preparing his bridge into *Ulysses*; but the moral difficulty of accepting the *Portrait* as satisfactorily finished off in its own right imposes an intolerable strain on the reader. It is painful to be invited to close the book with an indigestibly Byronic hero stuck in our throats. We are compelled to take Stephen seriously so that *Ulysses* may have its desired tragic effect (also, one may

whisper, because Joyce had known a time, to which he here does homage, when he himself had been wrapped in an identical pride), but to take him seriously is very hard indeed.[23]

The ending of *Portrait* is the fifth chapter—which is twice as long as any other, fully one-third of the entire book—but that portion of the ending to which Kenner directs our attention is made up largely of a series of diary entries, twenty-two of them in fact, which cover twenty days, between March 20 and April 27. Ellmann has described them as a style shift of "savage abruptness."[24] They have no earlier counterpart in the novel. Their strategic placement indicates that Joyce believed his book would end most satisfactorily with a series of statements made directly by his protagonist. Unfortunately, debate over the appropriateness of the device has been confused for some time. The consensus is not clear as to whether these entries are lyrical or impersonal;[25] whether they constitute a satisfactory ending, or belong to a chapter that attempts "to finish off temporarily a book that on its own terms cannot be finished";[26] or whether, indeed, diary fragments are "a form for disorder and despair."[27]

What do they tell us about Stephen's attitude toward Ireland? On April 6 Stephen denies any affiliation with Yeats's Celtic Twilight and a literary movement that proclaims nostalgia for the past. Michael Robartes may delight in pressing in his arms "the loveliness which has long faded from the world," but Stephen turns impatiently from Yeat's image ("Not this. Not at all."), and announces, "I desire to press in my arms the loveliness which has not yet come into the world," a loveliness which some readers may see as a "new beauty" or "surd."

Yet, shortly afterward, Stephen, talking about his current activities and future plans with Emma, must consider the wisdom of his renunciation of Ireland. His farewell to her is uneasy: how much does he like her, a little or much? "Don't know." And he must tell himself, "O, give it up, old chap! Sleep it off!" The diary entries record Stephen's repudiation of Cranly (the Judas-betrayer image again) and of the irony and sarcasm with which Stephen responds to the fumbling efforts of parents to guide the prodigal son, and all in such a splintery way that we can sympathize with the reader's report (sent on 26 June 1916, from the publisher, Duckworth and Company, to James B. Pinker, Joyce's agent), which alludes to the way in which the novel makes its final statement: "And at the end of the book there is a complete falling to bits; the pieces of writing and the thoughts are all in pieces and they fall like damp, ineffective rockets." (Edward Garnett may have been the reader, but the evidence for attribution is equivocal.)[28]

The conclusion of *Portrait* is personalized because it follows the convention of a dramatic soliloquy: complete candor. Hamlet, for example, does not equivocate with his audience when he debates the question of the value of existence. He is saying what he thinks. The diary is intended to be a candid confession of the soul. In Harry Levin's piquant phrase, drama has retired before soliloquy.[29] The diary form is a fictional counterpart for Joyce's alphabetical notebook and the bits and pieces of paper on which he wrote his epiphanies (none of the extant epiphanies was used in *Dubliners*). We recall that Stephen brooded about the insubstantiality of epiphanies in *Ulysses*: ". . . epiphanies on green oval leaves, deeply deep, copies to be sent if you died to all the great libraries of the world, including Alexandria? Someone was to read them there after a few thousand years." Further confirmation of the lyrical quality of the diary entries lies in our knowledge that several epiphanies are incorporated therein. One of them records the troubled moment "between boyhood (*pueritia*) and adolescence (*adulescentia*)—17 years." Stephen recognizes the impossibility of continued fealty to family, faith, and Ireland; and the tone of the entries is self-consciously elegiac. Stephen hoped to become the artist-hero of his generation and of "the *faubourg Saint Patrice* called Ireland for short"; but he was leaving behind much that he loved, much that he could never fully, permanently renounce. An image as strongly drawn as any in the concluding pages of *Portrait* is that of John Alphonsus Mulrennan's Irish-speaking, smoking, spitting, ancient man in a mountain cabin, about whom Stephen writes: "I fear him. . . . It is with him I must struggle all through this night till day come, till he or I lie dead, gripping him by the sinewy throat till . . . Till what? Till he yield to me? No, I mean him no harm." Stephen, given to dreams (as in the entries for March 25, "a troubled night," and April 10), knows how difficult it is to wake from history, and the antecedent of "him" is surely as much Simon Dedalus as it is Mulrennan's red-eyed peasant.

Joyce's Trieste Notebook, recorded between 1907 and 1909, has Joyce's mordant jotting, "Irish art is the cracked looking-glass of a servant."[30] (The statement was later incorporated in *Ulysses*.) But by now the suspicion has probably arisen, on the basis of this review of Joyce's vacillation between the poles of affection and bitterness, that a writer who so continually rationalizes the reasons for his repudiation of Ireland, who insists on putting all kinds of justifications into print and on the record, cannot have been completely convinced about the unworthiness of Ireland.

Neither *Ulysses* nor *Finnegans Wake* introduces a novel attitude toward Joyce's "fatherland" that *Dubliners* and *Portrait* had not in some way adumbrated, though both of the later works use a much greater quantity of accurate information about the physical appearance of Ireland, particularly of Dublin. Shane Leslie, writing in the *Quarterly Review* (October 1922, p. 226), pointed out immediately that *Ulysses* was "a book which, owing to accidents of circumstance, probably only Dubliners can really understand in detail. Certainly, it takes a Dubliner to pick out the familiar names and allusions of twenty years ago." The difficulties involved in identifying the full particularities of Joyce's Dublin have been partially solved by generations of scholars—who frequently have had to "work up" their knowledge of the *Evening Telegraph, Thom's Dublin Directory*, Sacher-Masoch's book *Venus im Pelz*, Joyce's minor acquaintances, and the significance of 16 June 1904—in order to make sense of important passages in *Ulysses*. Keys, guides, and concordances abound. But even the most dedicated Joyceans concede that the Irish allusions in the *Wake* are far too numerous, and far too deeply buried, to be completely retrievable.

In the nineteen scenes of "The Wandering Rocks" episode of *Ulysses*, Joyce shows us most fully the looks of Dublin. The method, as he informed us, is labyrinthine, and is designed to remind us of the maze constructed by Daedalus for the fabulous bull. "The Wandering Rocks" is the central chapter of the structure of *Ulysses*, but the only plan or order one may see in the comings and goings of the various characters is what one may trace elaborately on a map of Dublin. The most important people do not meet each other: the earl of Dudley and Father Conmee, as the governors of the city; Stephen and Bloom. Perhaps an infinite number of movements, striking off at tangents to one another, is the only movement that Joyce thought made sense in his busy but nondirected metropolis. It is a fact that "The Wandering Rocks" episode does not advance the action.

Joyce offers no new opinion about Dublin as a microcosm and as the seventh city of Christendom in this, his fullest treatment of Dublin. *Ulysses*, as a whole, shows us how the personification of the city (Leopold Bloom) can be set alongside the portrait of the artist. They are "isolated together," in Levin's formulation. "Neither is complete without the other, he [Joyce] knew very well, but he also knew that both are usually incomplete. He succeeded in uniting them by a literary *tour de force*, by crossing the two keys of topography and mythology. Bloom, however, is unaware of his symbolic role, just as Stephen is out of touch with his municipal environment."[31]

Joyce pointed out to Budgen (10 December 1920) that the Ulysses

(Bloom) who romanced about Ithaca would find, when he got back, that it gave him "the pip."[32] Joyce was simply being honest with himself. He stressed the political, social, and intellectual shortcomings of Ireland at the turn of the century because he knew he would be cruelly disappointed in his memories if he went home again, because he had to fight the continuing temptation to sentimentalize, because he was an emigrant like all other emigrants and could not cut his ties. The total recall of his memories of Ireland may be accounted a curse if one wants to stress only the "special odour of corruption" that permeates many, but not all, of the short stories of *Dubliners*; but it must be considered a blessing, too, since it made possible his subject matter and his art. As Vivian Mercier has pointed out, Joyce developed his fantastically detailed knowledge of Ireland through a combination of very special circumstances: his family's inexorable descent through several social strata, moving from one house and neighborhood to another, the manageable size of Dublin in 1904, and his own love of long walks.[33] Stanislaus was undoubtedly correct in believing that his brother regarded patriotism as the last refuge of a scoundrel,[34] particularly when Irish poets like William Rooney presumed upon national feelings to betray readers into reacting favorably to shoddy verses; but Joyce's quarrel with the island of saints and sages was also a quarrel within himself, between two attitudes. His first public lecture in Italian, which was delivered at the Università Popolare on 27 April 1907, concluded with the heartfelt cry, "It is well past time for Ireland to have done once and for all with failure."[35] It is difficult to imagine an Irishman who was indifferent to Ireland, or an Irishman who hated Ireland, saying that.


# NOTES

1. James Joyce, *The Critical Writings of James Joyce*, ed. Ellsworth Mason and Richard Ellmann (New York: Viking Press, 1959), p. 171.
2. Ibid., p. 169.
3. Ibid., p. 174.
4. Ibid., p. 192.
5. Richard Ellmann, *James Joyce* (New York: Oxford University Press, 1959), pp. 231–51.
6. Ibid., p. 233.
7. Ibid., p. 266.
8. Joyce, *Critical Writings*, p. 190.
9. Ibid., p. 198.
10. Ibid., p. 213.
11. Harry Levin, *James Joyce* (Norfolk, Conn.: New Directions Books, 1941), p. 14.

The entire edition of a thousand copies was destroyed: whether by burning, as Joyce believed, or guillotining and pulping, as George Roberts insisted, is a moot point.

12. Robert Scholes, " 'Counterparts' and the Method of *Dubliners*," in *Dubliners*, ed. Robert Scholes and A. Walton Litz (New York: Viking Press, 1969), p. 382.
13. Ellmann, *James Joyce*, p. 344.
14. Levin, *James Joyce*, p. 30.
15. Allen Tate, "The Dead," in James Joyce's *Dubliners*, p. 404.
16. For a startlingly long, but still incomplete, bibliography, see Florence L. Walzl, "Gabriel and Michael: The Conclusion of 'The Dead,' " in *Dubliners*, pp. 424–26.
17. Tate, "The Dead," p. 409.
18. Kenneth Burke, "Stages in 'The Dead,' " in *Dubliners*, p. 416.
19. James Joyce, *Letters of James Joyce*, ed. Richard Ellmann (New York: Viking Press, 1966), 2:166.
20. Walzl, "Gabriel and Michael," p. 423.
21. William York Tindall, *James Joyce: His Way of Interpreting the Modern World* (New York: Charles Scribner's Sons, 1950), p. 7.
22. Ellmann, *James Joyce*, p. 218.
23. Hugh Kenner, "The *Portrait* in Perspective," in *James Joyce: Two Decades of Criticism*, ed. Seon Givens (New York: Vanguard Press, 1948), pp. 153, 172–73.
24. Ellmann, *James Joyce*, p. 307.
25. Marvin Magalaner and Richard M. Kain, *Joyce: The Man, the Work, the Reputation* (New York: New York University Press, 1956), p. 124. Harry Levin interprets the whole of *Portrait* as a lyrical statement. For another view, see Grant H. Redford, "The Role of Structure in Joyce's *Portrait*," *Modern Fiction Studies* 4:21–30 (Spring 1958). Redford argues that the diary entries are in the main impersonal. Ellsworth Mason, however, believes that Joyce is *always* dramatic: "The dramatic form of art is the result of complete conscious control in the creative process and complete depersonalization of the artist's emotion." "Joyce's Categories," *Sewanee Review* 61:427–32 (Summer 1953).
26. Kenner, "The *Portrait* in Perspective," p. 172.
27. William York Tindall, *A Reader's Guide to James Joyce* (New York: Noonday Press, 1959), p. 68.
28. James Joyce, *A Portrait of the Artist as a Young Man: Text, Criticism, and Notes*, ed. Chester G. Anderson (New York: Viking Press, 1968), pp. 319, 320.
29. Levin, *James Joyce*, p. 48.
30. Robert Scholes and Richard M. Kain, *The Workshop of Daedalus: James Joyce and the Raw Materials for* A Portrait of the Artist as a Young Man (Evanston, Ill.: Northwestern University Press, 1965), p. 100.
31. Levin, *James Joyce*, p. 85.
32. James Joyce, *Letters of James Joyce*, ed. Stuart Gilbert (London: Faber & Faber, 1957), 1:152.
33. Vivian Mercier, "Dublin under the Joyces," in *James Joyce: Two Decades of Criticism*, pp. 291–94.
34. Stanislaus Joyce, *My Brother's Keeper: James Joyce's Early Years* (New York: Viking Press, 1958), p. 201.
35. Joyce, *Critical Writings*, p. 174.

## SUGGESTIONS FOR FURTHER READING

Brandabur, Edward. *A Scrupulous Meanness: A Study of Joyce's Early Work.* Urbana: University of Illinois Press, 1971.

Ellmann, Richard. *James Joyce.* New York: Oxford University Press, 1959.
Givens, Seon, ed. *James Joyce: Two Decades of Criticism.* New York: Vanguard Press, 1948.
Gorman, Herbert S. *James Joyce.* New York and Toronto: Farrar & Rinehart, 1939.
Joyce, James. *Dubliners.* Edited by Robert Scholes and A. Walton Litz. New York: Viking Press, 1969.
Levin, Harry. *James Joyce.* Norfolk, Conn.: New Directions Books, 1941.
Magalaner, Marvin. *Time of Apprenticeship: The Fiction of Young James Joyce.* New York: Abelard-Schuman, 1959.
————, and Kain, Richard M. *Joyce: The Man, the Work, the Reputation.* New York: New York University Press, 1956.
Scholes, Robert, and Kain, Richard M. *The Workshop of Daedalus: James Joyce and the Raw Materials for* A Portrait of the Artist as a Young Man. Evanston, Ill.: Northwestern University Press, 1965.
Tindall, William York. *James Joyce: His Way of Interpreting the Modern World.* New York: Charles Scribner's Sons, 1950.
————. *A Reader's Guide to James Joyce.* New York: Noonday Press, 1959.

Ourselves
thru

# 15

## FROM THE FALL OF PARNELL TO MODERN IRELAND

### Charles Sidman

Three new forces were at work in Ireland during Parnell's time. The one had a historical and nationalist orientation; it was typified by the Gaelic League, an organization founded by Douglas Hyde for the purpose of preserving the Irish language.[1] The Gaelic League was nonsectarian and apolitical, but its purpose fit nicely into the newer nationalism. Basically, Hyde and his followers looked backwards to a time when the Irish language was predominant and pure. They could not visualize a free Ireland without a Gaelic-speaking Ireland; they aspired to unity through cultural immersion. To ensure the continuous existence of a national identity, they counted on emphasizing the differences between the Irish and the British.

A second major force in Ireland drew the Irish away from their ancient traditions: this was the force of modernization. However slowly or imperfectly modernization manifested itself, Ireland could no more resist modernization than it could deny the hold that Great Britain had on the country. Obviously, the modernization of Ireland worked at cross purposes to the aspirations of the men of the Gaelic League. The paradox was that these two forces could grow and prosper simultaneously. Horace

Plunkett began the cooperative movement in 1889.[2] Through technical improvements and the conference method, he sought to make Ireland a second Denmark. The Gaels were urged to "Buy Irish"; they were also encouraged to take the leap economically into the modern world.

Indeed, a trade-union movement with Marxist overtones pervaded a segment of the working class. James Connolly, the leading light of the Irish trade unionists, saw the conflict between capital and labor as the fundamental one confronting Irish society. For him, Great Britain signified everything about the modern economic system to which he was opposed.[3] Yet he would have had Ireland forswear nationalism for internationalism so as to bring to reality the ultimate utopia of the secularists. Likewise, Thomas Kettle aimed past Ireland, to that wider Christian Europe whose singular heritage he wished to preserve through unity.

The socialism of Connolly and the Christian Democracy of Kettle, though both were potentially powerful movements, did not capture the imagination of the Irish in the way that the third of the major forces of the late nineteenth century did. That third force went by the name of Sinn Fein, and it was clearly the most powerful movement in Ireland between the fall of Parnell in 1890 and the Easter Rising in 1916.[4]

The inspiration for Sinn Fein came from a Dublin journalist, Arthur Griffith. Griffith had launched the newspaper the *United Irishman* in 1899. Although this newspaper drew upon the Fenians for its title, it relied upon the Gaelic League and slogans such as "Buy Irish" for its strength. More so by far than the Gaelic League, however, Sinn Fein stressed the importance of patriotism.

Sinn Fein may be translated from the Gaelic as "Ourselves Alone." The movement most certainly emphasized the overriding need of Ireland to strike out on a course that was independent of Great Britain, particularly in the economic and cultural spheres. As John O'Hagan wrote in his ballad, "Too long our Irish hearts we schooled in patient hope to bide, / By dreams of English justice fooled and English tongues that lied. . . . / Our hope and strength we find at last is in *Ourselves Alone*."[5]

Griffith was a man who was dedicated to nonviolent reform and to a broader accommodation within the British Empire. His model was the Dual Monarchy of the Habsburgs, about which he wrote in 1904 in his "The Resurrection of Hungary." In brief, he wished for Ireland to become the Hungary of the British Empire, and he saw himself as the Francis Deak of Ireland.

With the help of money from the United States, the men of Sinn Fein hoped to build up native Irish industries so that they could compete with those of Great Britain. They wanted high tariffs for Ireland, to give their country a chance to develop viable industries. By the weaving of tweeds in county Donegal and by boycotting British goods they attracted the attention of persons who, like Jawaharlal Nehru, were disenchanted with the British colonial system.

The object of Sinn Fein was to achieve the separation of Ireland from the United Kingdom except for the bonds of crown and Parliament. In 1910, when Griffith at long last succeeded to the presidency of Sinn Fein, the organization had one hundred and thirty branches, some of them in northern Ireland. But that was the limit of Sinn Fein expansion. Quite rapidly the organization became unhinged. The Home Rule movement diverted attention from Sinn Fein, since the final initiative of the British Liberal party on behalf of Home Rule made it seem to be well on its way to success by 1912–1913. Moreover, Sinn Fein was tarnished with the brush of anticlericalism, much as Fenianism had been before it. Every effort by Griffith to repudiate clerical interference in the national movement brought a rebuff and alienated the countryside from Sinn Fein. The Catholic clergy in Ireland may have had no appreciable influence over Sinn Fein, but it had the respect of the vast majority of its flock. It was sufficiently national in outlook to command the center stage, and no amount of intellectual ridicule could force it to one side.

Sinn Fein ran counter to the prevailing attitude of Catholic Ireland. It won the support of only a few members of the erstwhile Protestant Ascendancy. By contesting for seats in Parliament, but failing to win even one in several electoral attempts, Sinn Fein revealed its weakness as a popular movement. Its quarrel with the Catholic Church was further evidence of this isolation from public opinion. Few men would deny the spirit of self-sacrifice and honesty in Sinn Fein; but most critics of Sinn Fein were struck by its mediocre literary accomplishments, by its lack of a sense of humor, and by its political naïveté. At the outbreak of war in 1914, Sinn Fein was a quiescent force. To all intents and purposes, it had spent its brief moment in history.

Home Rule was not passed into law during the lifetime of either Gladstone or Parnell. Indeed, the Liberals, who had risked so much on the urgings of Gladstone, seemed well rid of the sticky embarrassment of having Irish parliamentarians as allies. Once again Ireland was forgotten by Great Britain, this time for more than twenty years.

The two British parliamentary elections in 1910 produced a political stalemate. For the first time since the days of Parnell, the Irish deputies were needed by the Liberals, the more so in view of the extensive social reforms that the Liberals counted upon so heavily.

The Irish Parliamentary party had come under the leadership of

John Redmond, a moderate Home Ruler who was quite respectable and honest personally but was given to circumspection and deference. Redmond managed to trade Irish votes for a reconsideration of Home Rule. In the course of this wave of Liberal reform, the House of Lords lost its absolute veto over legislation. Home Rule had failed the last time that Gladstone brought it before Parliament because of the veto of the House of Lords. The way now seemed clear to the final passage of Home Rule.

A third Home Rule bill for Ireland was introduced in 1912. It passed the House of Commons three times in the next two years, only to be rejected each time by the House of Lords. Since the House of Lords now had only a suspensive veto, the Home Rule bill ultimately came to the king for his signature. The bill became law on 15 September 1914.

This twentieth-century debate over Home Rule produced a frenzy of opposition. Home Rule was labeled a first step in the dismemberment of the British Empire, a betrayal of the Constitution, an act of ingratitude toward the Unionists in northern and southern Ireland, and a fatal concession to the evils of popery. The Conservatives had long prided themselves on being defenders of British law and order. They now took the lead in advocating defiance of the law in order to frustrate the effectiveness of Home Rule.

Defiance of the law was preached in London and Oxford, but in Belfast a movement soon gained support which challenged the integrity of British parliamentary government. Over one-half million Ulster Irishmen signed a "Solemn League and Covenant" in which they pledged to defeat all efforts to establish a Home Rule Parliament. A private army was recruited—the Ulster Volunteers. A large proportion of the leading generals of the United Kingdom had come from Ireland. Indeed, the fighting qualities of the Protestant Irish had been justly praised from the days of Marlborough. Thus, when Lord Roberts, "the most distinguished soldier in England," was selected as commander in chief of the Ulster Volunteers, the threat of treason became a living reality.

The driving force behind this Ulster rebellion was Sir Edward Carson, one of the most famous barristers in Irish history. Carson was not an Ulsterman by birth. He was born in southern Ireland, had graduated from Trinity College, Dublin, and had made his home and his career in Dublin. In religion, Carson had not progressed beyond the seventeenth century. His convictions were pronounced; his prejudices blatant. Just as he had no use for democracy or for any of the myriad reforms of the British Liberal party, so, too, did he trumpet the virtues of the Cromwellian settlement. Carson was a man without humor. He was aggressive and unyielding. And the Orangemen of northern Ireland took him to their hearts.

The physical violence that was fomented in Belfast resulted in the killing of several Catholics and the injuring of more than one hundred. The bitter legacy of British domination over Ireland produced a superiority complex among the Protestants of Ulster, who looked down upon Irish Catholics. Southern Ireland was denigrated because it was Catholic and because it was poor. Among the Protestants in northern Ireland, the work ethic was deified, and providence was always found on the one side.

Edward Carson did not just intend that Home Rule be limited to southern Ireland; he did not want any portion of Ireland to have it, whatever the size of the majority in its favor. This was precisely the view of the Conservatives of Great Britain. Between them, the Orangemen and the Conservatives bid fare to destroy the proper working of British parliamentarianism.

While Redmond allowed his native supineness to be reinforced by confidence in the Liberal government, which, having passed Home Rule, was expected to enforce its provisions on northern Ireland, the National Volunteers were formed in Dublin as Catholic Ireland's answer to the Ulster Volunteers. The National Volunteers drew heavily upon the membership of the Gaelic League and the Irish Republican Brotherhood. Redmond's Home Rulers wavered indecisively as outsiders. Two armed camps stood counterpoised: the Ulster Volunteers, numbering some 110,000 men; and the National Volunteers, numbering some 180,000 men. An Irish civil war impended.

All the while, the British government of Henry Asquith stood by passively. The only member of the British cabinet to speak out on behalf of obedience to the law was Winston Churchill, the future British prime minister, but he was very nearly torn apart by a Belfast mob when, with quite different intentions, he repeated his father's famous visit to that city.

The British government's failure to control the army resulted in a fatal paralysis of leadership. British Liberals and Conservatives could preach to the world about respect for law; but when it suited their purposes, they allowed the principle to be modified at home. In the Curragh incident, the threat of a mass resignation of officers from the British army was enough to prevent any attempt at curbing the militarization of Orange Ireland. Then, on 24–25 April 1914, thirty thousand rifles and three million rounds of ammunition from Germany were smuggled into northern Ireland for the Ulster Volunteers. The National Volunteers obtained a much smaller cache of weapons in the same way on 26 July 1914. While British troops interfered with the transfer of weapons to the

National Volunteers in the south, no moves whatsoever were made to impede the activity of the Ulster Volunteers.

The outbreak of the First World War in August 1914 took the British government out of an embarrassing dilemma. For the time being, at least, it did not need to implement Home Rule. Yet, a fatal miscalculation was to cost Great Britain that integral arrangement upon which the rule of an Empire depended for security. The British government used the occasion of a foreign war to reconsider its pledge, which had now become law, to provide Ireland with Home Rule. It tampered again with Irish expectations; this time it was to pay the price.

On behalf of the Irish Parliamentary party and in the name of an Ireland that he did not consult, Redmond, after hesitating for seven weeks, cast the lot of Ireland with that of Great Britain, much to Germany's astonishment. His magnanimity was misplaced; for while Carson was quickly added to the British cabinet, Redmond was not. At first, Catholic Ireland accepted its obligation to fight with Great Britain against Germany. But the British government could not overcome in a crisis the suspicion that it had fostered for centuries. The Ulster Volunteers were treated as natural allies in wartime, but the National Volunteers were regarded as potential mutineers. Catholics found it difficult to obtain commissions. Ireland, unlike Scotland, was not given its own regiment. Even Redmond ultimately complained that "from the very first our efforts [at cooperation] were thwarted, ignored and snubbed."[6]

Within Ireland, Redmond was condemned by Sinn Fein and the Fenians. Enlistments from the National Volunteers were about equal to enlistments from the ranks of the Ulster Volunteers. But as wartime casualties increased and war weariness set in, a greater resistance to Ireland's commitment to Great Britain developed in Ireland. Support for Redmond's Irish Parliamentary party had slipped perceptively by the second year of the war, but it took a catastrophe of the first magnitude to destroy altogether its hold on Catholic Ireland.

Sinn Fein lay dormant; the mainline Fenians were resolved to act only in defense. A small group of dissident Fenian conspirators, however, was determined to strike a blow for the freedom of Ireland.[7] The men of the Easter Rising harbored no illusions about the risks they ran. They offered themselves up as martyrs for Ireland in the confident expectation that Great Britain would oblige by making them pay for their convictions with their lives. They kept the National Volunteers ignorant of their plans; they deceived Dublin Castle; they won the support of James Connolly, whose labor following was a necessary auxiliary to their plans; and they negotiated for German arms.

On Easter Monday, 1916, the rising took place. It was not a farce in the way that Robert Emmet's uprising was. Nor was it a mere street demonstration. As usual, the Irish plans came off badly. German arms were not forthcoming; the countryside was not properly aroused. Dublin fought virtually alone.

Despite vacillation and inept execution, the insurrectionists put up a valiant struggle. They controlled the General Post Office, and narrowly missed capturing Dublin Castle. A proclamation signed by, among others, Patrick Pearse, James Connolly, and Joseph Plunkett, proclaimed Ireland a republic. Over three hundred and fifty persons were killed, and damage ran to £3 million in the one week of fighting, before reinforcements from Great Britain brought the rebellion under control.

At first consideration, the Irish had been horrified by the casualties and the damage. And the British took swift revenge by interning three thousand rebels in Great Britain and by executing the leaders of the Easter Rising, including Connolly and Pearse. In northern Ireland the Orangemen rejoiced in the stringent steps taken against the rebels, whose resort to arms confirmed in the Orangemen's minds the utter impossibility of an arrangement that would leave Ireland intact and autonomous.

But Patrick Pearse had wagered correctly: defeat meant victory for Ireland.[8] After the initial shock wore off, Catholic Ireland rallied to the defense of its would-be leaders. A new nationalism had been born in Dublin. It was Perfidious Albion exerting its will on Ireland without respect for the sentiments of the local population. Overnight, Britain again became the foreign occupier, and Ireland became the exploited land. Sinn Fein had regained its lost vitality.

The Irish War of Independence began with the Easter Rising. This time, no amount of British tact or deceit would suffice to thwart it. Almost from the first, the British government attempted to recover the initiative. In May 1916, for instance, Carson was given to understand that the six northern counties would not be included in a Home Rule settlement, while Redmond was assured that a final disposition of Ireland would be made at an imperial conference after the war. When the palpable contradiction in these promises was made public, Carson and Redmond claimed "foul" as if with one voice.

At a meeting in 1917 under the leadership of David Lloyd George, the successor to Asquith as prime minister, additional time was gained by a British government that was desperate to win its war against Germany. A solution to the Irish problem was not found, and no call for reconciliation and reasonableness was likely to bring it about. The best that David Lloyd George could do momentarily was to shift blame for the impasse onto the most extreme of the contending factions—the Ulster Unionists and the Irish Republicans.

Redmond died in March 1918. His Irish Parliamentary party had lost credibility at home, as three successive by-election losses to Sinn Fein in early 1918 made clear. When Great Britain enforced conscription on Ireland, a final insult was added to the many that preceded it. In deep pessimism, Redmond had once claimed that the British did everything to Ireland that he enjoined them not to do, and failed to act in every instance in which he counseled action.

The Irish Parliamentary party at long last did what Sinn Fein advocated: it withdrew from the House of Commons in protest against conscription for Ireland. But the move came too late; Sinn Fein had already replaced it as the foremost nationalist political body in Catholic Ireland. The British government, on its part, had also forfeited its last remaining credits in Ireland. Winston Churchill put it well when he said: "We had the worst of both worlds, all the resentment against compulsion and in the end no law and no men."[9]

Sinn Fein dominated Ireland in the immediate postwar years, but not because of an overwhelming popular mandate. While seventy-three Sinn Fein politicians were elected to the House of Commons in the famous khaki elections in December 1918, they received less than one-half of the votes in every one of the constituencies where they put up candidates. The electoral law helped them to set Ireland on a course from which there could be no retreat.

Instead of going to Westminster, the Sinn Fein members of the House of Commons met in Dublin on 21 January 1919, for the purpose of forming an independent Irish Republic. An Irish legislature, the Dáil, was organized; an Irish President, Eamon De Valera, was elected by the Dáil as head of state.

The Irish were not able to win international recognition for this republic from the statesmen negotiating an end to the First World War in Paris. Nonetheless, they pressed forward with plans that invited repudiation. In early 1920, David Lloyd George supported a government of Ireland bill that recognized the legitimacy of two Irish parliaments— one for the southern twenty-six counties, and one for the northern six. From that time on, two Irish governments were in existence, with the approval of Great Britain. The British government then moved to end its struggle with southern Ireland, which had resulted in so much adverse publicity for the government.

The men of Sinn Fein were called upon to come to terms with Great Britain. For over two years the Irish Republican Army and the

*Eamon de Valera,* 1931
Sean O'Sullivan (1906–1964)
Drawing
National Gallery of Ireland, Dublin
Photo by courtesy of the National Gallery of Ireland

*From the Fall of Parnell to Modern Ireland*
337

British force in Ireland, augmented to fifty thousand men with the aid of the notorious Black and Tans, had engaged in a war of reprisals. For success the Irish depended on the unwillingness of Great Britain to utilize its obvious superiority in manpower and equipment.

With their material resources nearly exhausted, the men of Sinn Fein decided to meet in conference with David Lloyd George. Arthur Griffith and Michael Collins represented Sinn Fein in London. They did surprisingly well against a team of able British politicians, obtaining a status for the twenty-six counties that was every bit as favorable as the one enjoyed by Canada within the Empire. The agreement that they brought back to Dublin kept the twenty-six counties in the Empire; it also affirmed a separation of northern Ireland from southern Ireland. It was opposed vehemently by Eamon De Valera's group, which was outraged more by the maintenance of an imperial tie than by acknowledgment of a political division of the island. No amount of reasoning would conciliate the De Valera group. In De Valera this group possessed one of the most compelling leaders in modern Irish history, a man who could be compared to O'Connell and Parnell.[10]

Eamon De Valera's long public life gave him a continuous influence over Irish affairs that has not been matched by any other modern leader of that people. Incongruously enough, De Valera was born in New York City, the child of a Spanish father and an Irish mother. He moved to Ireland as a youth, was educated there, and eventually went on to become a teacher of mathematics. His devotion to national self-interest, though incomparably strong, always took second place to his firm loyalty to the Catholic Church. De Valera joined Sinn Fein. He participated in the Easter Rising, and the unit he commanded at Boland's Mill was the last to surrender. His United States citizenship saved him from being executed along with the other leaders of the rising. After a period of imprisonment, De Valera resumed his activities on behalf of independence for Ireland. After a brief hesitation, he turned his back on the accomplishments of Griffith and Collins, thereby precipitating a fierce internal struggle that cost the lives of many more Irishmen, including Collins, who was ambushed by followers of De Valera. De Valera was not able to prevent the work of Griffith and Collins from coming to fruition, and their work produced the Irish Free State.

The Irish Free State was established as a self-governing dominion within the British Empire in accordance with the Anglo-Irish Treaty, which was signed on 6 December 1921. Numerous issues arose along with partition. The Irish in the Free State had a responsibility for thei. own affairs that they had not enjoyed for many centuries. They now had to grapple with and resolve their own problems. Yet, Sinn Fein, which had precipitated the events that led to the Free State, was very much at cross-purposes over its acceptability. The two-party system in Ireland emerged from a cabinet meeting at which the treaty was accepted, four votes to three. Unable to carry his cabinet, De Valera went into the streets. His campaign of obstructionism led to an Irish civil war, which seriously jeopardized the significant gains won in battle and in conference.

The Anglo-Irish Treaty was signed in an atmosphere of extreme uncertainty. There was the British government's threat to impose by force whatever conditions it wanted, should the Irish not accept what had been negotiated; there was a strong reaction among Irish nationalists around De Valera against the treaty because of its alleged shortcomings —partition in the large, the oath of allegiance to the Crown in the small. Yet, the treaty was signed, and a commitment was made to abide by its terms. It was the will of the majority in Ireland, who were tired of war. It was considered a maximum concession by those Irish nationalists who accepted it and who feared the consequences of Fenian rejection.

In the short run, Great Britain had certainly achieved her objectives in Ireland. Northern Ireland was saved for the United Kingdom, and southern Ireland for the Empire. A domestic preoccupation of over one century's standing had been put to rest. The unwholesome example of Great Britain as an insensitive colonial power was muted.

The Catholic Irish were relieved to be done with the fighting. As in so many of their confrontations with the British, they considered, almost immediately after the fact, that they had again been treated badly. And yet, had they? The British were denied the opportunity, so often provided in times past, to crush the Irish by force of arms. "If hostilities do recommence," General Macready wrote from Ireland, "we must be in a position in which the onus must be entirely on Sinn Fein."[11] This the British were not able to claim. Hence, they were not able to impose their conditions entirely on the Irish. Furthermore, as the Irish themselves realized shortly, the blow struck to the United Kingdom by the Irish presaged dismemberment of the Empire. By their continued presence in Ireland, the British retained most of the blame for what went wrong in Ireland, both in the North and in the South. This blame, however, was not compensated for by any redeeming advantage, either social or strategic.

The antitreaty men in Ireland fought a civil war because they accepted the same interpretation of the treaty that the British government did. The treaty kept Ireland within the Empire, and it maintained British power on the island, at least enough so that the British could control what it was necessary to control.

The protreaty men were much more realistic. They counted on movement with the times. From the outset they were willing to allow the antitreaty men to take the most perfunctory of oaths to the crown, or none at all. While this concession was rejected at first, the Free State did in fact develop independently. The British had not realized that few people in the Free State regarded the treaty as fixed or permanent. Tact was required, but the Free State Irish proceeded in stages to establish a republic; and the British were not given enough provocation again to single the Irish out for punitive action.

Griffith and Collins were with the sixty-four in the Dáil who favored the treaty; De Valera was with the fifty-seven who opposed it. But an overwhelming number of Irishmen were unwilling to support De Valera's dangerous game of rejection. The basic conservatism of the Irish proved a stronger attraction than did distrust of British intentions. Besides, the Catholic Church condemned the violence and the excessive nationalism of the antitreaty men. With the threat of excommunication hanging over them, the antitreaty men met their match. Although they died in the struggle, Griffith and Collins won out over De Valera in a brief civil war that cost Ireland in energy and manpower.

The successor to Griffith and Collins as leader of the protreaty forces in Ireland was William Cosgrave. Slowly but firmly Cosgrave built his strength. He was aided by the extreme positions taken by De Valera, who, between 1919 and 1923, made one mistake after another. First, De Valera remained in the United States instead of returning to Ireland; then, he stayed in Dublin instead of journeying to London; next, he would not allow his negotiators in London to negotiate; and finally, he refused to accept a majority decision by the Dáil in favor of the treaty.

Meanwhile, Cosgrave set about proving that the treaty could be used to serve Irish ambitions, that it was malleable, not inflexible. Once set on a course of independence, the Irish leaders of the Free State adopted British practices with an alacrity that would have pleased the most critical Unionist during the life of the Union. Only somewhat less remarkable than this irony was the ability of the Free State Irish to establish efficiency in government. The Irish Republican Army was rendered largely innocuous. Most impressive of all, the Cosgrave government made every effort, in spite of its own dislike of the antitreaty group and in the face of a political disservice to itself, to bring the De Valera group into the legitimate political process.

By 1927 De Valera had managed to disengage himself from his

previous associates. He had broken with the Irish Republican Army. He even explained away the noxious oath to the crown, which was finally taken by him and his followers "without becoming involved, or without involving their nation, in obligations of loyalty to the English Crown."[12]

The Free State had a one-party government until 1927, because De Valera's Fianna Fáil party refused to participate in Parliament as a loyal opposition. From 1927 on, Fianna Fáil entered the Dáil to contest for power with Cosgrave's Fine Gael, and by 1932 it became the government party. For all but six years in the next generation, De Valera was *taisoach* (head of the government), and his party utterly dominated Free State (and Eire) politics.

Once De Valera had been reconciled to Free State Ireland, it remained for the Free State to be made into a functioning democracy. William Cosgrave obliged in a first step by permitting De Valera to assume power legally; De Valera returned the favor by refraining from a purge of the Irish Civil Service and by a general policy of equal application of the law.

As *taisoach*, De Valera conducted a costly economic war against Great Britain from 1932 until 1938, as a result of his refusal to pay annuities due on land purchases of property owned in the South by absentee, mostly English, landowners. When that matter was settled in 1938, Great Britain turned over to the South the port cities that she had controlled since the treaty. By then, De Valera had promulgated a new constitution (1937), one that effectively established the republic. Eire, as the republic was called, remained neutral throughout the Second World War. Perhaps it was the partition (which gave Great Britain a foothold in Ireland), perhaps it was concern over the disapproval that would come from a blatant application of force against Ireland (such as Winston Churchill actually suggested in 1939—an idea endorsed by Franklin Delano Roosevelt in 1941), or perhaps it was the absence of fear about a German invasion by way of Ireland—in any case, for the first time in modern memory, Great Britain, when faced with a crisis, kept its hands off Ireland.

The Constitution of Eire, incidentally, reconciled any differences that had existed between the antitreaty men and the Catholic Church in Ireland. "The State recognizes the special position of the Holy Catholic Apostolic and Roman Church as the guardian of the faith professed by the great majority of the citizens"—as the Constitution read, or, according to De Valera: "The Ireland we dreamed of would be the home of a people who valued material wealth only as the basis of a right living. . . . It would, in a word, be the home of a people living the life that God desires men to live."[13]

While the larger part of a divided Ireland made its own way in the world as an independent republic, officially from 1947, the six northern counties, which had a Catholic minority of over 33 percent, remained united to Great Britain, but with the advantages of its own Home Rule Parliament at Stormont.

Virtual independence for the twenty-six counties of the South did not solve the Irish problem, despite assertions to that effect, especially from British historians. The British had yet to deal with the six northern counties, which were allowed to remain inside the truncated United Kingdom; and the dull compliance of the new Irish minority in that area was deceptive of contentment only to those who were self-satisfied and unsuspecting.

"Partition petrified Northern Ireland as a historical fossil," according to O'Farrell.[14] With respect to Northern Ireland, Great Britain answered the Irish question by reducing the problem from the scope of thirty-two counties to that of six. The Protestant Ascendancy, once a hopeless minority on the island, was converted into a majority in a contrived unit, rump Ulster. Sir James Craig, the first prime minister of Northern Ireland, called its political instrument "a Protestant Parliament for a Protestant people."[15] Northern Ireland became a successor to Unionist Ireland; it was a society based upon "Protestant Unionist ascendancy and anti-Catholic discrimination."[16]

Justification for the existence of Northern Ireland depended on the link with the mother country, a dramatic contrast with the usual relationship between colony and mother country. Loyalty to Great Britain was preached as a virtue in Northern Ireland. The privileges of the Protestant Ascendancy, as before, were guaranteed by the implied threat of British force.

The refusal of the Protestant Ascendancy in Northern Ireland to stand on its own feet—to take ultimate responsibility for its actions—bred an unhealthy dependence upon Great Britain. It produced an incurable frustration in Northern Ireland whenever Great Britain threatened to end its passive role, which would have been to the detriment of the privileged order.

The most important single consideration in Northern Ireland after 1920 was the maintenance of the Union. All other issues were seen in that perspective or were subordinated to it. The consequences of this overriding concern were predictable: a one-party government, the stunting of the labor movement, seeing opposition as treason, the total absence of social reform, and the viewing of economic prosperity as an indication of stability.

Between 1921 and 1959 the rate of economic growth in southern Ireland averaged one percent each year. The assets of the Free State (and Eire) were invested largely in Great Britain. The Irish were fully absorbed in defining the nature of their political independence. In 1959 Eire launched an enlightened program of economic expansion, which was brought on primarily by the wish to mitigate emigration. The transformation of Eire into a modern state economically ran counter to De Valera's long standing *idée fixe*, which was to promote both the family ownership of small plots of lands and a society at peace with its modest inheritance. It was no coincidence that De Valera moved into the ceremonial post of the presidency in the same year that Eire began its assault on modernity.

The question of the unity of Ireland, of the North with the South, was raised again once Eire demonstrated its ability to compete in the markets of the world. Religion continued to play an important role in the politics of the island. Indeed, the Unionists blamed the Catholic Church for all of the difficulties that precluded an indefinite prolongation of the special situation in Northern Ireland. The Reverend Ian Paisley's passionate crusade exuded the spirit of religious fervor. For the Protestans, Catholicism was the "Greatest of All Heresies," and the pope was the Antichrist. Paisley was as wrong about the reasons for the troubled situation in Northern Ireland as was Bernadette Devlin. For Paisley, Catholics were the cause of trouble; for Devlin, economic and social injustices were. But the problems were religious more than economic— Protestant in origin rather than Catholic.

Paisley was not an anachronism in Northern Ireland. He stood squarely in the center of the tradition of the Protestant Ascendancy. It was he who proclaimed that "the Unionist Party cannot barter our heritage,"[17] just as Captain Terrence O'Neill a few years before (in 1965) had said, "Let no one in Ireland, North or South, no one in Great Britain, no one anywhere make the mistake of thinking that, because there is talk of a new Ulster, the Ulster of Carson and Craig is dead."[18]

Devlin, on her part, was much less realistic. The economic injustices that she would have liked to make the primary concern took second place to deeper-seated religious animosities—and, in any case, her position was compromised irretrievably by a confused personal life and an inconsistent effort.

Whatever the force of these emotions, membership in the European Economic Community has blunted the edge of the debate. Northern Ireland has come grudgingly to accept dictation from Great Britain; the Irish of the South have become more tolerant of their continuing

English connection. The British, on their part, belong to the wider community of the Common Market, as also does Eire. Thus, the Irish question can no longer be considered in its singular context. It will no longer revolve around differences of race or religion. It has become a question of adjustment to modern Western society, of which Great Britain and Ireland are both essential parts. Time and circumstances have become the great healers. More so than ever before in history, Great Britain and Ireland are likely to cooperate against the strange ways of the Continent in order to preserve some of their common legacies.

# NOTES

1. Patrick S. O'Hegarty, *A History of Ireland under the Union, 1801–1922* (New York: Kraus Reprint, 1969), pp. 613–19; and Francis S. L. Lyons, *Ireland since the Famine* (London: Weidenfeld & Nicolson, 1971), pp. 222–32.
2. O'Hegarty, *History of Ireland*, pp. 620–22.
3. James C. Beckett, *The Making of Modern Ireland, 1603–1923* (rev. ed.; London: Faber & Faber, 1969), p. 416.
4. Lyons, *Ireland since the Famine*, pp. 243 ff.
5. Giovanni Costigan, *A History of Modern Ireland* (New York: Pegasus, 1969), p. 273.
6. Ibid., p. 305.
7. See, especially, *1916: The Easter Rising*, ed. Owen Dudley Edwards and Fergus Pyle (London: MacGibbon & Kee, 1968).
8. These events may be followed in *The Irish Struggle, 1916–1926*, ed. Desmond Williams (London: Routledge & K. Paul, 1966), and in Dorothy McCardle, *The Irish Republic* (London: V. Gollancz, 1937).
9. Oliver MacDonagh, *Ireland* (Englewood Cliffs, N.J.: Prentice-Hall, 1968), p. 83.
10. For a treatment of the Irish problem involving De Valera from the time of the civil war, see Denis Gwynn, *The History of Partition* (Dublin: Browne & Nolan, 1950).
11. Patrick O'Farrell, *Ireland's English Question* (London: Batsford, 1971), p. 294.
12. Lyons, *Ireland since the Famine*, p. 493.
13. O'Farrell, *Ireland's English Question*, pp. 298–99.
14. Ibid., p. 300.
15. Ibid.
16. Ibid.
17. Ibid., p. 304.
18. Ibid., p. 305.

# SUGGESTIONS FOR FURTHER READING

## I. BASIC BACKGROUND

Beckett, James C. *The Making of Modern Ireland, 1603–1923.* Rev. ed. London: Faber & Faber, 1969.
Costigan, Giovanni. *A History of Modern Ireland.* New York: Pegasus, 1970.

Curtis, Edmund. *History of Ireland*. 6th ed., reprinted. London: Methuen, 1968.
Lyons, Francis S. L. *Ireland since the Famine*. London: Weidenfeld & Nicolson, 1971.
MacDonagh, Oliver. *Ireland*. Englewood Cliffs, N.J.: Prentice-Hall, 1968.
O'Farrell, Patrick. *Ireland's English Question*. London: Batsford, 1971.

## II. NINETEENTH CENTURY

Black, R. D. Collison. *Economic Thought and the Irish Question, 1817–1870*. Cambridge, Eng.: Cambridge University Press, 1960.
Connell, Kenneth H. *The Population of Ireland, 1750–1845*. Oxford: Clarendon Press, 1950.
Curtis, Lewis P. *Coercion and Conciliation in Ireland, 1880–1892*. Princeton, N.J.: Princeton University Press, 1963.
Edwards, R. Dudley, and Williams, T. Desmond, eds. *The Great Famine: Studies in Irish History, 1845–1852*. Dublin: Browne & Nolan, 1956.
Freeman, Thomas W. *Pre-Famine Ireland: A Study in Historical Geography*. Manchester, Eng., and New York: Manchester University Press, 1957.
Gash, Norman. *Mr. Secretary Peel*. Cambridge, Mass.: Harvard University Press, 1961.
Gwynn, Denis R. *Young Ireland and 1848*. Cork, Ire.: Cork University Press, 1949.
Hurst, Michael. *Parnell and Irish Nationalism*. London: Routledge & K. Paul, 1968.
Kee, Robert. *The Green Flag: A History of Irish Nationalism*. London: Weidenfeld & Nicolson, 1972.
Lee, Joseph. *The Modernization of Irish Society, 1848–1918*. Dublin: Gill & Macmillan, 1973.
Lyons, Francis S. L. *The Fall of Parnell, 1890–91*. London: Routledge & K. Paul, 1960.
––––––. *Ireland since the Famine*. London: Weidenfeld & Nicolson, 1971.
––––––. *The Irish Parliamentary Party, 1890–1910*. London: Faber & Faber, 1951.
––––––. *John Dillon*. London: Routledge & K. Paul, 1968.
McCaffrey, Lawrence. *Daniel O'Connell and the Repeal Year*. Lexington: University of Kentucky Press, 1966.
––––––. *The Irish Question, 1800–1922*. Lexington: University of Kentucky Press, 1968.
McDowell, Robert B. *The Irish Administration, 1801–1914*. London: Routledge & K. Paul, 1964.
––––––. *Social Life in Ireland, 1800–1845*. Dublin: Lochlainn, 1957.
MacIntyre, Angus. *The Liberator: Daniel O'Connell and the Irish Party, 1830–1847*. London: H. Hamilton, 1965.
Mansergh, Nicholas. *The Irish Question, 1840–1921*. New and rev. ed. London: Allen & Unwin, 1965.
Moley, Raymond. *Nationalism without Violence*. New York: Fordham University Press, 1974.
Moody, Thomas. *The Fenian Movement*. Cork, Ire.: Mercier Press, 1968.
Norman, Edward R. *The Catholic Church and Ireland in the Age of Rebellion, 1859–1873*. London: Longmans, 1964.
Nowlan, Kevin B. *The Politics of Repeal*. London: Routledge & K. Paul, 1965.
O'Brien, Conor Cruise. *Parnell and His Party, 1880–1890*. Oxford: Clarendon Press, 1957.
––––––. *States of Ireland*. London: Hutchinson, 1972.
O'Brien, Richard B. *The Life of Charles Stewart Parnell*. 2 vols. London: Smith, Elder & Co., 1899.
O'Faolain, Seán. *King of the Beggars*. London: T. Nelson & Sons, 1938.
O'Hegarty, Patrick S. *A History of Ireland under the Union, 1801–1922*. London: Methuen, 1952; New York: Kraus Reprint, 1969.

Statistical and Social Inquiry Society of Ireland. *Centenary Volume, 1847–1947*, with a history of the Society by R. D. Collison Black. Dublin: Eason, 1947.

Thornley, David. *Isaac Butt and Home Rule*. London: MacGibbon & Kee, 1964.

Whyte, John H. *The Independent Irish Party, 1850–9*. London: Oxford University Press, 1958.

Woodham-Smith, Cecil. *The Great Hunger: Ireland, 1845–1849*. London: H. Hamilton, 1962.

## III. TWENTIETH CENTURY

Bell, J. Bowyer. *The Secret Army: The I. R. A., 1916–1970*. New York: John Day Co., 1971.

Brown, Malcolm J. *The Politics of Irish Literature: From Thomas Davis to W. B. Yeats*. Seattle: University of Washington Press, 1972.

Chubb, Basil. *The Government and Politics of Ireland*. London: Oxford University Press, 1970.

Colum, Padraic. *Arthur Griffith*. Dublin: Browne & Nolan, 1959.

Coxhead, Elizabeth. *Daughters of Erin: Five Women of the Irish Renascence*. London: Secker & Warburg, 1965.

De Paor, Liam. *Divided Ulster*. Harmondsworth, Eng.: Penguin, 1970.

Digby, Margaret. *Horace Plunkett: An Anglo-American Irishman*. Oxford, Eng.: Blackwell, 1949.

Edwards, O. Dudley, and Pyle, Fergus, eds. *1916: The Easter Rising*. London: MacGibbon & Kee, 1968.

Farrell, Brian. *The Founding of Dail Eireann*. Dublin: Gill & Macmillan, 1971.

Gallagher, Frank. *The Anglo-Irish Treaty*. London: Hutchinson, 1965.

Gwynn, Denis R. *The History of Partition*. Dublin: Browne & Nolan, 1950.

Jones, Thomas. *Whitehall Diary*. Vol. 3: *Ireland, 1918–1925*. Edited by Robert Keith Middlemas. London: Oxford University Press, 1971.

Larkin, Emmet. *James Larkin: Irish Labour Leader*. London: Routledge & K. Paul, 1965.

Levenson, Samuel. *James Connolly*. London: Martin Brian & O'Keeffe, 1973.

Longford, Frank Pakenham, and O'Neill, Thomas P. *Eamon De Valera*. Houghton Mifflin, 1971.

———. *Peace by Ordeal*. 3d ed. London: G. Chapman, 1962.

McCardle, Dorothy. *The Irish Republic*. London: V. Gollancz, 1937.

Martin, F. X., and Byrne, F. J., eds. *The Scholar Revolutionary: Eoin MacNeill*. Shannon: Irish University Press, 1973.

Meenan, James F. *The Irish Economy since 1922*. Liverpool, Eng.: Liverpool University Press, 1970.

Miller, David W. *Church, State and Nation in Ireland, 1898–1921*. Dublin: Gill & Macmillan, 1973.

Nowlan, Kevin B., ed. *The Making of 1916*. Dublin: Stationery Office, 1969.

O'Tuama, Sean, ed. *The Gaelic League Idea*. Cork, Ire.: Mercier Press, 1972.

Stewart, Anthony T. Q. *The Ulster Crisis*. London: Faber, 1967.

Wallace, Martin. *Drums and Guns: Revolution in Ulster*. London: G. Chapman, 1970.

Williams, Desmond, ed. *The Irish Struggle, 1916–1926*. London: Routledge & K. Paul, 1966.

Younger, Calton. *Ireland's Civil War*. London: Muller, 1968.

———. *A State of Disunion*. London: Muller, 1972.

# 16

# THE IRISH EXPERIENCE IN AMERICA

## *Norman R. Yetman*

$I$t would be presumptuous to attempt to describe the experience of the nearly five million Irish immigrants and their descendants in a single brief chapter. Rather, I have sought to delineate and to interpret aspects of that experience that appear to have most greatly influenced, and been influenced by, American life. As I surveyed the diversity and drama that have characterized more than a century and a half of Irish-American life, what struck me most forcefully was the crucial role of the social institutions that the Irish created, maintained, and dominated. Indeed, as I examined Irish-American institutions more closely, it became increasingly apparent that it was here that Irish creativity had been most fully manifested; it is through an examination of the role of these institutions that the Irish experience in America becomes most intelligible. Therefore, in this essay I have focused primarily upon the changing character of several social institutions—the religious, the educational, and the political—that have informed and, in turn, been informed by the Irish-American experience.*

Irish migration to the United States was part of the general movement of European peoples, the greatest in the history of man, that

---

* Without holding them accountable for any of its deficiencies, I would like to thank Stephen Fox, Kenneth Kammeyer, David Katzman, Timothy Smith, Hoy Steele, and Ronald Walters for their criticisms of an earlier version of this chapter.

spanned the seventeenth through the twentieth centuries. Since the beginning of the seventeenth century, more than seventy million people have emigrated from Europe; the United States has been the primary destination of more than half. The factors that impelled the Irish to leave their homeland represented a microcosm of changes that were transforming Europe during this period: increases in population, displacement of traditional handcraft industries by the industrial revolution, an upheaval in agriculture, and migration of substantial numbers from rural to urban areas. The reasons for migration to the United States—primarily the lure of American economic opportunity—were also similar to the attractions that this country held for other immigrants. There were, of course, always idiosyncratic factors, but these should not obscure the common grounds that Irish immigration shared with the immigration of other ethnic groups.

As Kenneth Kammeyer has noted in chapter 9, the nineteenth-century Irish diaspora was one of the salient features of Irish history. The United States was the primary destination of the hundreds of thousands of Irish who emigrated from their homeland. Although the Irish also migrated to Great Britain, Canada, Australia, and to several Latin American countries, it has been estimated that 80 to 85 percent of those who left Ireland in the nineteenth century came to the United States. Although the peak of Irish emigration did not occur until the mid nineteenth century (See tables 1 and 2), Ireland had been producing population for the United States from the early seventeenth century. Earliest of these emigrants were the Ulster Irish, who constituted better than one-sixth of the infant nation's population in 1776. United States Census Bureau figures do not distinguish between those from northern Ireland and those from the southern twenty-six counties, but there is general agreement among historians that the Protestant Scotch-Irish migration had slowed to a trickle by the 1820s and that figures on subsequent Irish immigration overwhelmingly represent Catholic migrants, primarily individuals from the southern twenty-six counties.[1]

The Irish constituted a substantial portion of the total immigration to the United States before the Great Famine of 1846–1851 (see table 1). Although the absolute number of Irish entering the United States increased markedly during the years of the Famine, and immediately thereafter, the percentage of Irish among the total number of immigrants remained relatively stable for more than four decades after 1820. In other words, at the time that the Irish were fleeing the Famine's devastating effects, the number of persons who were entering the United States from other European countries—though in many instances for different reasons

—was also increasing. Except for 1846, in every year from 1820 to 1853 the number of immigrants from Ireland exceeded that from any other country. Moreover, a substantial Irish immigration continued after the Great Famine, about half of the nineteenth-century Irish immigrants arriving after 1860. From 1820 to 1900 nearly four million Irish entered this country, a total that is second only to the more than five million German immigrants.

A more distinctive feature of Irish migration to the United States was their pattern of settlement: they were the first immigrant group to settle primarily in American cities. Consequently, one of the most important features of the Irish experience is the manner in which they adapted to urban conditions. In a sense the Irish presaged many developments in the late nineteenth and early twentieth centuries when immigration to the United States, greatly augmented by the "new" immigrants from southern and eastern Europe, reached its zenith. Dennis Clark has argued that the Irish, as the first large mass immigrant group and the first to be urbanized, "were in many ways prototypes in testing how immigrants would adjust to the industrial city and how the city would react to

TABLE 1
IRISH IMMIGRATION TO THE UNITED STATES BY DECADE, 1820–1970

| Decade | Number of Immigrants | Percentage of Total Immigration to United States during Decade |
|---|---|---|
| 1820–1830 | 54,338 | 35.8 |
| 1831–1840 | 207,381 | 34.6 |
| 1841–1850 | 780,719 | 45.6 |
| 1851–1860 | 914,109 | 35.2 |
| 1861–1870 | 435,998 | 18.6 |
| 1871–1880 | 436,971 | 15.5 |
| 1881–1890 | 655,482 | 12.5 |
| 1891–1900 | 388,416 | 10.5 |
| 1901–1910 | 388,977 | 4.4 |
| 1911–1920 | 146,131 | 2.5 |
| 1921–1930 | 220,591 | 5.4 |
| 1931–1940 | 13,167 | 2.5 |
| 1941–1950 | 27,503 | 2.6 |
| 1951–1960 | 57,332 | 2.3 |
| 1961–1970 | 37,461 | 1.1 |
| Total, 1820–1970 | 4,764,476 | 10.4 |

Source:  U.S. Department of Commerce, Bureau of the Census, *Historical Statistics of the United States: Colonial Times to 1957* (Washington, D.C.: Government Printing Office, 1960), pp. 56–57, and *Statistical Abstract of the United States: 1971* (Washington, D.C.: Government Printing Office, 1971), p. 92.

them."[2] Irish immigration to the developing urban areas coincided with and facilitated the mid-nineteenth-century period of economic and industrial "takeoff" in the United States.

Moreover, Irish settlement has not only been an urban phenomenon; it has occurred overwhelmingly in the largest urban centers of the nation, particularly in those in the Northeast. In the mid nineteenth century the Irish were found almost exclusively in eastern seaboard cities, where they constituted the largest foreign-born population. In 1870 three-fourths of the Irish were concentrated in urban centers in Massachusetts, Connecticut, New York, New Jersey, Pennsylvania, Ohio, and Illinois. By 1910 more than 80 percent of the Ireland-born immigrants in the U.S. lived in urban areas, and by 1940 better than nine of ten of

TABLE 2
ANNUAL IRISH IMMIGRATION TO THE UNITED STATES, 1831–1860

| Year | Number of Immigrants |
|------|---------------------|
| 1831 | 5,772 |
| 1832 | 12,436 |
| 1833 | 8,648 |
| 1834 | 24,474 |
| 1835 | 20,927 |
| 1836 | 30,578 |
| 1837 | 28,508 |
| 1838 | 12,645 |
| 1839 | 23,963 |
| 1840 | 39,430 |
| 1841 | 37,772 |
| 1842 | 51,342 |
| 1843 | 19,670 |
| 1844 | 33,490 |
| 1845 | 44,821 |
| 1846 | 51,752 |
| 1847 | 105,536 |
| 1848 | 112,934 |
| 1849 | 159,398 |
| 1850 | 164,004 |
| 1851 | 221,253 |
| 1852 | 159,548 |
| 1853 | 162,649 |
| 1854 | 101,606 |
| 1855 | 49,627 |
| 1856 | 54,349 |
| 1857 | 54,361 |
| 1858 | 26,873 |
| 1859 | 35,216 |

Source: U.S. Department of Commerce, Bureau of the Census, *Historical Statistics of the United States: Colonial Times to 1957*, p. 57.

those Americans who had been born in Ireland were urban residents, more than half of them living in New York, Chicago, Philadelphia, Boston, and San Francisco alone. And the urban cast of Irish-Americans continues to the present.[3]

The urbanism of Irish immigrants contrasted to the experience of other mid-nineteenth-century immigrant groups—most notably the Germans, fewer than 20 percent of whom settled in urban areas. Two primary factors account for this affinity for the city on the part of the Irish, who in their native land had been predominantly a rural people.[4] First, an overwhelming number of Irish immigrants were extremely poor; most of them lacked the substantial financial resources that were needed to meet the costs of land and equipment with which to establish a viable farming operation.[5] Any additional money that the Irish immigrant might have retained after paying his passage, or that he might possibly have accumulated, was returned to Ireland to help family members survive or emigrate.[6]

Secondly, few Irish immigrants actually appear to have been farmers. In the mid nineteenth century only 14 percent of Irish male immigrants declared to immigration officials that they were farmers, as compared to 82 percent of Swedish, and 64 percent of German, immigrants.[7] And in 1890, when the number of Irish-born in the United States was at its apex, less than 15 percent of the males had previously been engaged in agriculture.[8] Edward M. Levine has argued that few, if any, of the immigrant Irish ever really farmed:

> They were generally cotters or squatters who had never truly belonged to an agricultural class. Subsisting on the produce from small plots that required little skill in planting or harvesting, they had been essentially field laborers and, as such, were completely without experience in transforming expanses of fertile land into fields of grain. Nor had they ever had the opportunity to own, raise, or care for herds of cattle. Consequently, they had little thought of beginning anew in the farmlands of the Midwest.[9]

Once initiated, the Irish urban concentration was perpetuated by the sense of community that their countrymen's presence in the major metropolitan areas afforded. Incoming immigrants sought the security of familiar values, attitudes, life styles, kinsmen, and acquaintances. The social patterns of an essentially rural Irish proletariat were reconstituted in an urban setting in the United States.

In chapter 9 Kammeyer has described the intimate relationship between demographic, social, and cultural factors in Ireland. The same factors that produced the high rates of celibacy and deferred marriage also brought high rates of emigration from Ireland, beginning even before the pressures of the Great Famine. As a consequence, Irish emigration had some distinctive characteristics. First, it was made up overwhelmingly of the young and unmarried. Between 1850 and 1887 more than two-thirds of the Irish entering the United States were between fifteen and thirty-five years of age, and the number who were married before entering rarely exceeded 16 percent, or about one-sixth, of the immigrants. Second, in contrast to the overwhelming preponderance of males in the immigrant populations of most other ethnic groups, the Irish had the greatest percentage of female immigrants. Indeed, the Irish were the only nineteenth-century immigrant group in which the annual number of immigrant females frequently outnumbered the males.[10]

The implications of these demographic factors have not been adequately explored by historians, and assessment of them would substantially contribute to an understanding of the impact of American society and culture upon the basic characteristics of the Irish community. Historical analysis of Irish-American family structure would provide a fruitful index of Irish acculturation, yet many pertinent questions still need to be examined in a systematic manner. For instance, did the extremely high rates of celibacy, postponed marriage, and fertility that prevailed in Ireland occur in this new environment as well? What were the effects of transplantation to the United States upon traditional Irish inheritance patterns? Many Irish females who emigrated served as domestics in middle- and upper-class Protestant households, and thus had greater opportunities than Irish males for contact with majority-group culture. What effects did this have upon Irish values, socialization patterns, and family relations? Finally, it has been alleged that at the time of large-scale Irish immigration, America was the most liberal of nations in regard to the equality of women. If this was the case, what effect did the new environment have upon the typical Irish pattern of male dominance?

While these questions remain to be answered, I would suggest that one effect of the relatively balanced sex ratio was a high rate of ethnic endogamy, or in-marriage, among the Irish. Handlin, in his analysis of the Famine-generation immigration to Boston, noted that Irish endogamy was higher than that of any other ethnic group, including blacks.[11] As a consequence, assimilation with the larger society was retarded. The Irish, upon their entrance into American society, were already an English-speaking group. Although cultural and religious differences separated them from the mainstream of American society, if the sex ratio had been similar to that of other ethnic groups (all of whom had a preponderance of males), it is plausible to assume that there might have been a greater degree of intermarriage with native Americans and with members of other ethnic groups. Instead, the equality of the sex ratio and the consequent high degree of endogamy reinforced the insularity and separatism that was to become the hallmark of the Irish community.

Elsewhere I have argued that the nature of an ethnic group's adjustment to the dominant society is contingent upon three interrelated but distinct factors, one of which is shaped and conditioned by the majority group, the remaining two emanating from the characteristics of the minority group.[12] The first factor is the intensity of external disabilities experienced by the group—the degree of discrimination imposed by the majority group; this sets limits within which the subordinate group may function. A second factor is the nature of the minority group's "cultural inventory"—its own values, attitudes, and/or world view—and the extent to which it conforms to or diverges from that of the dominant

*St. Patrick's Day in New York, Parade at Union Square, Early 1870's*
Lithograph
J. Clarence Davies Collection, Museum of the City of New York
Photo by courtesy of the Museum of the City of New York

*The Irish Experience in America*
353

group. Finally, factors of social structure—the organizations and social institutions that the minority group has transplanted or developed—influence the nature and extent of the minority group's interaction with the dominant society. As I will argue, examination of Irish-American social institutions is especially crucial to an understanding of their experience in America. In the ensuing discussion the mutual interrelation of discrimination, values, and social institutions will be examined.

The Irish of the Famine generation composed less than one-third of the Irish immigration in the nineteenth century, yet their experience was a formative one in determining Irish response to America and the response of native Americans to them. The peasants who fled the potato blight that ravaged Ireland personified the "tired," "poor," "huddled masses" that Emma Lazarus described in her famous celebration of America's ability to assimilate and transform a diversity of ethnic groups. However, most native Americans perceived the Irish, as Lazarus ambivalently characterized all American immigrants, as "wretched refuse." The Famine-generation Irish were caught in the nineteenth-century equivalent of what Daniel P. Moynihan has termed a "tangle of pathology." Basically unskilled, the Irish were relegated to the most menial jobs—as longshoremen, teamsters, boatmen, and miners or unskilled laborers in a multiplicity of jobs that required strong, untiring backs. They quickly became an urban proletariat, one whose impoverished state and character traits were often invidiously compared to those of black slaves in the South.

The Famine-generation Irish suffered from the most severe ills that afflicted the rapidly expanding urban areas. The slums and tenement quarters in which they lived were among the most congested and squalid in the cities. Because of the crowding, the unsanitary conditions, and the inadequate diet that was available to them, they suffered mortality, morbidity, and insanity rates that were disproportionately higher than those of any other group, whether native or foreign-born. In New York City, arrests of the Irish exceeded those of any other group, and the rate of convictions for Irish criminals was six times that for native Americans.[13] Given these conditions, the Irish became disproportionately dependent upon nineteenth-century welfare—public and private charity—to survive. Poor, illiterate, and prone to high consumption of alcohol, the turbulent Irish "acquired a fearful reputation for ignorance, drunkenness, vice, and violence."[14]

The conflict between native Americans and Irish-Americans was exacerbated by the fact that the two groups differed not only in terms of social class but ethnically and religiously as well. The antipathy of native

Americans for the Irish heightened an already deeply embedded opposition to the Catholic faith. The Church, in turn, became identified with the hated Irish, and was perceived as alien to and incompatible with American democratic institutions and values. As they had been the object of tyranny by Anglo-Saxon Protestants in Ireland, so the Irish found themselves the object of persistent discrimination by Anglo-Saxon Protestants in the United States. The forms of derogation were many, ranging from stereotypes and epithets through social, educational, and economic discrimination to physical attack and violence. Their social status was bleakly reflected in the notorious addendum to "help wanted" notices: "No Irish Need Apply."

The most dramatic depredations against the Irish—the 1831 burning of the Ursuline Convent in Charlestown, Massachusetts, and the Philadelphia riots in which thirteen people were killed and two Roman Catholic churches were destroyed—antedated the great exodus generated by the Famine. They symbolized, however, the tension and hostility toward the increasingly Irish-oriented Roman Catholic Church that were exacerbated by the influx from famine-plagued Ireland. Although overt mass physical violence would not recur on a comparable scale thereafter, distrust, suspicion, and enmity between Roman Catholics and Protestants persisted and were reflected in the rise of the nativist Know-Nothing party of the 1850s. Later the xenophobic American Protective Association of the 1890s, the Ku Klux Klan of the 1920s, and the religio-ethnic opposition to the presidential candidacy of Al Smith in 1928 were recurring reminders of the "Protestant Ascendancy's" antagonism for the Irish that for over a century simmered just below the surface.[15] Even the candidacy of John F. Kennedy in 1960 revived latent Protestant suspicions. For many, to have a Catholic president would be bad enough; to have an *Irish* Catholic would be unthinkable.

As the Roman Catholic Church became increasingly identified with the Irish, the antagonism between Irish-Americans and native Americans became drawn along religious lines. The Irish perceived, not incorrectly, that a major Protestant concern was the elimination of the Catholic Church from their midst, a stance that merely increased their defensiveness and insularity. John Tracy Ellis has remarked: "Inevitably, the campaign of bigotry [that was most marked in the Know-Nothing campaign of the 1850s] tended to make the Catholics [by then predominantly Irish] draw in upon themselves more than ever before. It enhanced their feeling of inferiority as a minority group and increased their sensitiveness concerning the attitudes of outsiders toward their affairs."[16]

Although Irish perceptions of Protestant antipathy were justified,

Protestant perceptions of Roman Catholic intolerance were not unfounded. Irish Catholic priests viewed Protestants with suspicion and hostility, and often with a missionary zeal they denounced the "errors" of Protestant beliefs and practices.[17] This strong anti-Protestant strain among Irish-Americans still persists. Bruce Biever, in his superb analysis of differences between the values of contemporary residents of Ireland and second-generation American-Irish, found that the latter were more defensive, militant, and intolerant of Protestantism. Less likely to accept the idea that one church is as good as another, or the idea of intermarriage, they tended to be less tolerant of non-Catholic religious views and more defensive and hostile towards those who did not agree with their own religious convictions.[18] Biever concluded:

> The religious intolerance and tension which we had projected might be the case in Ireland is in fact not verified there but in the United States where the American Irish are most antagonistic towards those whom they consider to be their enemies, militant in their convictions that Catholicism has a right and a responsibility to be the moral pace-setter of the nation, and disenchanted to the point of being almost scornful of Protestant claims to be either true Christians or capable of perpetuating their historical role as the "religion of the American people."[19]

In addition to the inevitable social and religious friction, Irish cultural norms conflicted with the dominant cultural values. The conservatism of the Irish was early reflected in their resistance to abolitionist, temperance, and woman-suffrage reform movements of' the mid nineteenth century. The temperance and woman-suffrage movements conflicted with deeply held Irish social patterns, and the Irish perceived the abolitionist campaign as inimical to their own economic interests, since emancipation would probably bring black laborers into competition with them. But these movements also failed to gain support from among the Irish simply because they reflected a Protestant ethos and had been initiated by Protestants, who stood diametrically opposed to and critical of everything Irish and Catholic. The Irish were also apprehensive of reform in America because they felt it would ultimately undermine clerical authority, since, especially in Europe, radicalism and reform were frequently militantly anticlerical.[20]

The Irish aversion to social reform, which they shared with a substantial portion of the mid-nineteenth-century American population, emanated from a deep-rooted social conservatism that has historically been one of the hallmarks of the American-Irish subculture. Levine has described the Irish Catholic conception of the nature of man:

> The belief underlying the Irish Catholic view of the cause of social evils is that man, due to original sin, is fallen; as a result, he has many frailties and suffers grave hardships not susceptible of great transformation by mere mortal efforts. The assertion of will power and the exercise of reason, therefore, will not relieve the individual or society of serious problems and distress except with Divine assistance. Even then, the imperfect nature of man is such that he must inevitably suffer. Consequently, reliance upon human effort guided almost entirely, if not exclusively, by reason (upon which Protestant reformers based their efforts) to achieve such profound social changes has decidedly limited possibilities.
>
> From the Irish point of view, the most effective prescription for ameliorating the difficulties and dilemmas inherent in the human condition was acknowledgment and repentance of sin, of error, and the hope that Divine intervention would be forthcoming in response to the prayer of the penitent seeking relief from the lot meted out by Providential design.[21]

The disjunction of Irish and native-American values and life styles contributed to pressures—from Catholic "liberals," as well as from Protestant nativist groups—for the Irish to divest themselves of their ethnic identity and become more fully Americanized. Such suggestions, however, merely strengthened the resolve of the Irish to maintain their distinctiveness. As other immigrant groups had done and would continue to do, they stubbornly resisted majority-group pressures for social and cultural integration.

The Irish, like other ethnic groups, viewed ethnic pluralism, not complete assimilation with Protestant America, as the appropriate means of adjusting to American society. "Unable to participate in the normal associational affairs of the community, the Irish felt obliged to erect a society within a society, to act together in their own way. In every contact therefore the group, acting apart from other sections of the community, became intensely aware of its peculiar and exclusive identity."[22] The most salient feature of the Irish experience in America was the separate institutional system they fashioned, a separatism as comprehensive as that of any other European ethnic group. This separate system was instrumental in reinforcing and perpetuating Irish-American identity, which proved remarkably durable for over a century. The persistence of Irish identity was even more striking because, unlike most other American ethnic groups, the Irish lacked what sociologists have termed the boundary-maintaining mechanism or the unifying force of a distinct, non-English language.[23]

The impetus toward separatism was both ethnic and religious in character, with the consequence that ethnic and religious identities became indistinguishable for most Irish. Emmet Larkin has argued that because of the spiritually bankrupt condition of the Irish Church during and preceding the Great Famine, the Church was relatively remote from the Irish masses, and consequently few Irish closely identified with or derived identity from it. As among other ethnic groups, migration heightened religiosity for many of the Irish, and their faith assumed meaning only *after* their initial confrontation with a hostile America. The "devotional revolution" that creatively reformed and transformed the mid-nineteenth-century Irish Church was the consequence of an Irish crisis of identity. Larkin has said: "Irishmen who were aware of being Irish were losing their identity [under pressures of English and American institutions], and this accounts in large part for their becoming practicing Catholics. The devotional revolution . . . provided the Irish with a substitute symbolic language and formed them a new cultural heritage with which they could identify and be identified and through which they could identify with one another."[24] Biever has pointed out that these functions of ethnic identity were explicitly recognized and advanced by the Irish clergy who migrated to minister to their countrymen in America: "The central theory of the Irish clergy was that of maintaining a strong organizational complex for the preservation of national identity as well as religious orthodoxy."[25]

Thus, for the nineteenth-century Irish, the Irish-controlled Church served as an "institutional bulwark in a Protestant society."[26] The Church was a comprehensive institution, only one of whose functions happened to be religious: it incorporated social, educational, political, and welfare functions as well. It stood as the most visible symbol of the Irish community and as the center around which that community was organized. The institutional system that the Church developed—schools, hospitals, orphanages, asylums, homes for the aged, and charitable and athletic organizations, as well as informal social groups—integrated the Irish community and served to maintain Irish solidarity and identity for generations.

The effects of this separatism upon the Irish were paradoxical. It isolated the Irish from the rest of society, while at the same time it served as an agency of acculturation. Milton M. Gordon's distinction between "behavioral" and "structural" assimilation is useful at this juncture. The former refers to the acquisition by a minority group of the values, attitudes, and life styles of the majority—what has usually been referred to as "acculturation." "Structural assimilation," on the other hand, occurs when social equality and interaction has occurred—in voluntary associations, informal cliques, institutional activities, and intermarriage—between majority and minority group.[27] While the church-centered institutional system impeded structural assimilation for the Irish, it facilitated behavioral assimilation; though many Irish ultimately became fully culturally integrated into the mainstream of American culture, their patterns of social interaction long remained intratribal.

In his article "The Devotional Revolution in Ireland, 1850–75," Emmet Larkin has argued that, as a consequence of what he has termed the "devotional revolution" in the Irish Church, the character of the Irish community was transformed in nineteenth-century America. The valiant efforts on the part of Church leaders to improve the quality of Church leadership and the lack of other occupational opportunities in Ireland resulted in increased recruitment of clergymen. This, coupled with the population decline of the Famine years, led to an increased ratio of clergy to laymen, which enabled the clergy to deal much more intimately and effectively with the spiritual, moral, and secular needs of their flocks. The secular consequences of these reforms within the Irish Catholic Church, which were felt in both America and Ireland, was an improvement in the stability of and respect for the clergy itself, a decline in family disorganization, and an increased concern for education, which produced a remarkable decline in Irish illiteracy, to the point that it was virtually eliminated by 1900. Deeply affected by the devotional revolution, the late-nineteenth-century Irish migration to the United States was, according to Larkin, culturally and socially distinct from the earlier "culture of poverty" immigration of the Famine exodus. The consequence was greater congruity of values and thus decreased friction between Irish immigrants and native Americans.[28] Whether the transition from the impoverished "shanty" Irish of the Famine generation to the more respectable "lace curtain" Irish of the late nineteenth century can be attributed to the "devotional revolution" alone is problematic. Improvement of their economic status was also instrumental in effecting changes, so that by the late nineteenth century the stereotype of the turbulent Irishman had waned. But the Church and its agencies did facilitate acculturation, emphasizing to immigrant and second-generation Irish a sense of propriety and sobriety that was congruent with Victorian sensibilities.

Thus, paradoxically, while the Church perpetuated Irish identity, the values it emphasized imparted to Irish-Americans a distinctively American stamp.[29]

The advent of the Irish into American society closely paralleled the growth of the Catholic Church in the United States. Between 1850 and 1900 the membership of the Church increased from one and one-half million to over twelve million. Simultaneously, the Catholic institutional system of churches, schools, hospitals, and charities was developing. The Irish were instrumental in the phenomenal growth of the Church during this period. Few would disagree with Biever's assessment that historically "the greatest single influence on American Catholicism has been that of Ireland," whose priests and nuns fashioned the Catholic institutional system.[30] It was largely through Irish energies that the Catholic Church in America was transformed into the largest religious denomination in the country, and "the wealthiest, most stable branch of world Catholicism."[31]

During the colonial period and until the beginnings of substantial Irish immigration to the United States, Roman Catholicism had not been identified in the minds of Protestant Americans with the Irish. However, as the Irish constituency of the Catholic Church increased, so also did the vehemence of nativist opposition to the Church, with its alleged "foreign entanglements." By the outbreak of the Civil War more than 80 percent of American Catholics were Irish, and the Church derived its identity from the Irish laity that provided its primary financial support as well as from the Irish clergy that gradually assumed its leadership. Although today fewer than 20 percent of American Catholics are of Irish descent, still the Irish wield a power and an influence in the affairs and conduct of the Church in the United States that greatly exceed their percentage of the total Catholic population.[32] Demonstrating the same kind of political acumen and organizational skill that have characterized their role in partisan politics, the Irish have long dominated the hierarchy of the American Catholic Church. Although other ethnic groups quickly organized their own parishes, they found it extremely difficult to penetrate the Irish-dominated hierarchy. Of 464 bishops appointed in the American Catholic Church from 1789 to 1935, 268, or 58 percent, were the sons of Irish fathers, a figure that may underestimate the actual number of Irish bishops, since many others may have had Irish mothers.[33] In addition, for many years there was strongly Irish leadership in Catholic lay organizations such as the Knights of Columbus, the Catholic Daughters of America, and the National Catholic Welfare Conference.

The prominence of the Irish in the affairs of American Catholicism has contributed immeasurably to its distinctive cast. This was painfully apparent to later ethnic groups (such as the Poles and Italians), who found Catholicism in the United States to be of a Celtic, not an American, variety.[34] Despite vigorous opposition from those supporting a more liberal, accommodating stance (spearheaded by Irish prelates such as James Cardinal Gibbons and John Ireland), a conservative, isolationist, and fundamentalist strain has characterized American Catholicism, in general, and Irish-American priests and prelates, in particular. Irish-American Catholic thought has been highly sectarian, defensive, and characterized by what Duff has termed a "siege mentality."[35] Innovation, change, and accommodation with secular culture were suspect, which accounts for the paucity of Irish support for programs of social reform that extended into the twentieth century. This has placed the Roman Catholic Church as one of the staunchest institutional defenders of the status quo on many issues, a stance that prompted William Howard Taft to praise it as "one of the bulwarks against socialism and anarchy in this country."[36]

Biever found that the overwhelming majority of Irish-Americans in the early 1960s still denied the legitimacy of Church involvement in social concerns and social reforms. He argued that Irish-American social conservativism was a function of the strong individualistic and fundamentalist orientation of the Irish—clergy and laity alike—toward the role of their Church; the Irish firmly believed that social reform and the transformation of the world were not legitimate functions of the Church. Instead the Church and its representatives should stand as arbiters of the personal morality of its constituency.[37] This conservative stance permeated not only the Church but also the Irish-dominated system of Catholic parochial schools.

In addition to their role in organizing parishes and in building churches throughout the United States, the Irish were instrumental in the creation and development of the Catholic parochial-school system. There had been some separate parochial schools prior to the Famine exodus to the United States, but it was not until after the Civil War that Catholic leaders set themselves the task of systematically creating the elaborate Catholic educational system, the objective of which was to isolate its adherents from the Protestant-dominated public schools. It was an impressive undertaking; it was unparalleled in scale in any other Catholic national community. The considerable expense of developing the entire separate Catholic institutional system was borne substantially by working-class Irish. It is plausible to assume that the financial commitment of the Irish to establishing the system diverted monies that might have been invested in other ways; consequently the achievement of personal and family monetary "success" and movement into the middle class were slowed for the Irish.[38]

Catholic education ultimately extended to all levels, from the parish nursery and primary schools to the system of primarily urban colleges and professional schools that for years provided a substantial portion of Irish higher education. Irish clergy were intimately involved in the design and control of the system's organization, curriculum, and staffing.[39] The rationale for its establishment emanated from the hostility toward Catholic (and ethnic) values that pervaded the secular (but in reality strongly Protestant) orientation of the public-school system during the nineteenth century, which was perceived as a threat to the faith and morals of the Catholic minority. The parochial school was conceived as having two primary functions—to educate Catholic children and to preserve their faith; of these, the latter was deemed the more important.

The dual impulses for assimilation and for separation, noted above, were nowhere more apparent than in the Catholic educational system. On the one hand, the acquisition of skills—both cognitive (e.g., literacy) and moral (e.g., the values of "sobriety" and "respectability")—that were necessary for effective participation in the mainstream of an increasingly complex urban environment was facilitated by the education received in these schools. On the other hand, the consequences of these priorities was isolation and insularity—what John Tracy Ellis has termed a "self-imposed ghetto mentality."[40] If the separate school system provided an effective defense against subversion of the Catholic faith,[41] it also produced a truly parochial—i.e., narrowly sectarian—education. The strong emphasis on authority, obedience, and discipline that long prevailed in Catholic schools was frequently criticized as being inimical to genuine intellectual inquiry; and it led to charges that the quality of education that Catholic students received was notably inferior to that received by their secular counterparts. Studies such as those of Robert H. Knapp and his associates, which demonstrated that Catholic institutions of higher learning ranked lowest in the nation in the production of scientists and humanistic scholars, were instrumental in generating self-examination and debate within the Catholic community about the quality of its intellectual life.[42] Thomas F. O'Dea was among the Catholic intellectuals who themselves criticized the aridity of Catholic intellectual life:

> The American Catholic group has failed to produce —both qualitatively and quantitatively—an appropriate intellectual life. It has failed to evolve in this country a vital intellectual tradition displaying vigor and creativity in pro-

portion to the numerical strength of American Catholics. It has also failed to produce intellectual and other national leaders in numbers appropriate to its size and resources.[43]

The sources of this indifference to intellectual concerns and pursuits were both ethnic- and class-related. Richard Hofstadter has pointed out that because of Irish domination, "the American Church absorbed little of the impressive scholarship of German Catholicism or the questioning intellectualism of the French Church, and much more of the harsh Puritanism and fierce militancy of the Irish clergy."[44] Moreover, because the Catholic constituency in America was for many years largely working-class in composition, the dogmas and authority of the Church were rarely challenged, and the Church and its educational institutions could remain —as liberal Catholic reformers and strident anti-Catholic alike charged— unintellectual. Church leadership, moreover, historically was derived predominantly from working-class origins. The social and cultural backgrounds of Catholic Church officials was reflected in the late Cardinal Cushing's proud claim that "in all the American hierarchy, resident in the United States, there is not known to me one Bishop, Archbishop or Cardinal whose father or mother was a college graduate. Every one of our Bishops and Archbishops is the son of a working man and a working man's wife."[45] Although the members of the hierarchy were themselves educated, such backgrounds were scarcely conducive to the development of an intellectual tradition.

Most important, however, in accounting for the alleged lack of scholarly productivity among American Catholics was the social-class backgrounds of Catholic immigrants. Steinberg has demonstrated that, in comparison with Jewish immigrants, whose descendants have been proportionately overrepresented in American academic life, Catholic immigrants entered American society with greater disabilities. Although both Jewish and Catholic immigrants arrived in America with meager financial resources, Jews possessed the prerequisites for mobility in the form of higher literacy rates and occupational skills, which, in turn, facilitated their children's adaptation to the American educational system. Jewish academicians have been disproportionately drawn from middle-class backgrounds.

A greater proportion of Catholics, on the other hand, entered American society illiterate and unskilled, and remained among the working classes. Thus, lack of Catholic representation in academia was not so much a function of differences in the value attributed to education and learning—the alleged absence of an intellectual tradition—per se, as it was a consequence of the lower socioeconomic position of Catholics as a group. As Catholics have become upwardly mobile this situation has changed. Especially since World War II, Catholic representation in all academic fields has increased markedly, and present trends indicate that soon the proportion of Catholics among university and college faculty will equal or exceed their distribution in the general population. Therefore, Catholic "anti-intellectualism" was not inherent in a Catholic value system, but was more a consequence of the lower social-class standing of the Catholic population.[46]

While Irish group consciousness and solidarity were enhanced by the Catholic institutional system, a parallel and competing source of ethnic identification and leadership was Irish-American nationalism, which was in large measure a response to Irish-American poverty, to the pressures of American nativism, and to the sense of alienation and inferiority they fostered.[47] From the Famine migration to Irish independence in 1921, nationalism proved to be a powerful emotional force integrating the Irish-American community. Irish-Americans found no difficulty in reconciling loyalty to Ireland with loyalty to Amercia, since they conceived that the democratic ideals and aspirations of both societies coincided, especially since both American and Celt had resisted British tyranny. Consequently, they felt no contradiction in manifesting a fierce patriotism to both.

In contrast to the thrust of the Church, the thrust of nationalism was secular and radical. The primary agency promoting nationalism was the Irish immigrant press, which flourished in urban areas that had large Irish populations. The press dramatized the inequities of British exploitation. The intensity of their agitation prompted the London *Times* in 1885 to assert that "the Irish question is mainly an Irish-American question."[48] Nationalism was manifested in an intense identification with and concern for the "auld sod" (with a corollary Anglophobia), in substantial financial support for the independence movement in Ireland, and in the establishment of numerous Irish nationalist organizations. Most prominent of these was the separatist Irish Revolutionary Brotherhood, or Fenians, which was conceived as "a distinct Republic within the American Republic," replete with its own flag, its own armed forces, and a governmental structure patterned after the American federal system. The Fenians gained permanent mention in American history by their ill-conceived and ill-fated attempts in 1866 and 1870 to invade and conquer Canada, which was then to be held hostage until Great Britain had freed

Ireland. This dramatic, but abortive, effort enjoyed widespread popular sympathy among working-class Irish.[49]

But the most important effects of Irish-American nationalism were felt in the United States, not in Ireland. Although the movement appeared to isolate the Irish from American society, Thomas N. Brown has argued that its most important function was, ironically, to act as an agency of assimilation and to erode the cultural isolation that separated Irish immigrants from the mainstream of American society:

> Irish nationalism was the cement, not the purpose of Irish American organizations. Essentially they were pressure groups designed to defend and advance the American interests of the immigrant. Nationalism gave dignity to this effort, it offered a system of apologetics that explained their lowly state, and its emotional appeal was powerful enough to hold together the divergent sectional and class interests of the American Irish. This nationalism was not an alternative to American nationalism, but a variety of it. Its function was not to alienate the Irish immigrant but to accommodate him to an often hostile environment.[50]

Although the institutional system that the Irish created isolated them from the mainstream of American society, politics provided their primary institutional linkage with it. For the Irish, politics was the secular equivalent of religion. Both reflected the Irish flair for organization; both served to unite and solidify the Irish community and to provide institutional avenues to success. It has been in these two institutional spheres that the Irish presence in American society has been most keenly felt. As Moynihan and Glazer have pointed out, "apart from building their church, [the creation of an Irish-controlled Democratic party organization] was the one singular achievement of the nineteenth-century Irish. 'The Irish role in politics was creative, not imitative.' "[51] The Irish were able to fashion the American political system to their own ends, and it was through their preeminence in politics, more than in any other avenue of American social life, that the Irish rose to power.[52]

Dennis Clark has written that "the advent of the Irish immigrant political organization coincided with the reshaping of urban political life."[53] Whether the municipal political machine was an innovation of the Irish is problematic; however, it is indisputable that they developed it most efficiently. Through the machine the Irish rationalized modern American urban political life. By centralizing power, machine bosses responded to the new needs and realities of the industrial city and provided a sense of order to cities fragmented by their rapid growth in the latter half of the nineteenth century.[54] Machine politics, which appeared hopelessly corrupt to reformers, was based upon self-interest and reciprocity; one supported politically those who had demonstrated their personal utility and fidelity. The machine was based upon personal ties and allegiances; it involved a community welfare system that cut through the increasing isolation and impersonality of urban existence; it also provided assistance, jobs, and conspicuous community facilities. The rationality of the machine was even more explicitly manifested in its operation, since it efficiently embodied in its massive bureaucracy the organizational principles of division of labor and chain of command. In the machine, power was hierarchical; and the functioning of the machine was reinforced by the traditional Irish respect for order, rank, and duly constituted authority.[55] Thus the emergence of the Irish to prominence in American politics was related to their isolation from the dominant society in other spheres; the social solidarity of the Church, the school, and the neighborhood facilitated the social interaction and personal ties that are so essential to the creation of cohesive voting blocs. The reliance upon personal relations and upon Irish age-graded social patterns so strongly reflected Irish tradition that Glazer and Moynihan have characterized the political system that the Irish established as "the social system of the Irish village writ large."[56]

The Irish were one of the earliest of a succession of American ethnic and racial groups to organize and effectively mobilize their collective power in order to enhance the status of their group and to advance their own interests. Their rise to political power was facilitated by the fact that they, unlike most other immigrant groups, were familiar with the Anglo-Saxon system of government and with the English language. But their view of politics was heavily conditioned by the experience of corruption and exploitation in Ireland under British domination. It was personalistic, pragmatic, and nonideological. In politics, as in religion, the Irish tended to be conservative and to be suspicious of "reformers" and idealists.[57] As Brown has written, "political office was not valued by the Irish as a way of fulfilling civic obligations but as a means of acquiring wealth, social status, and, of course, power."[58] This instrumental view of politics helps to explain the apparent paradox between the political conservativism of Irish-Americans and their allegiance to the Democratic party, which historically has been the more reform-minded of the two major American political parties.

William V. Shannon, an Irish-American who has provided one of the most able and engaging interpretations of the experience of his countrymen in America, has written that

> Irish machine politics was carried on in an intellectual void. It was the intuitive response to practical necessities and unrelated to any comprehensive theory of politics and society. Until the emergence of Finley Peter Dunne's "Mr. Dooley" in the late 1890s and the realistic investigations of politics by Lincoln Steffens and other muckraking magazine writers early in this century, the code by which the Irish politicians and their mass of supporters lived and governed remained unarticulated and undefended. As a result, the larger society outside the Irish community looked upon the party bosses as grotesque; politics seemed a morality play in which, despite frequent scandals and exposures, vice always triumphed; and the gloomier observers despaired of democracy. But for the Irish, politics was a functioning system of power and not an exercise in moral judgment. While E. L. Godkin and Henry Adams despaired of the American experiment, the Irish took over City Hall.[59]

But power was an end in itself. The nonideological nature of the quest of the Irish for power precluded the possibility that their contribution to governmental theory or to a vision of societal change would be enduring. With notable exceptions, such as Al Smith, "the very parochialism and bureaucracy that enabled them to succeed in politics prevented them from doing much with government. . . . In a sense, the Irish did not know what to do with power once they got it."[60]

The political power of the Irish was enhanced by the fact that they preceded other immigrant groups into the major urban areas. As the number of "new" immigrants from southern and eastern Europe increased near the end of the nineteenth century, the Irish assumed what Milton Barron has termed an "intermediary" role, both politically and economically. Although the Irish had not yet achieved a social status equal to that of native Americans, the facts that they spoke English and that they had arrived earlier had enabled them to occupy median status jobs—as labor organizers, labor leaders, foremen, firemen, policemen, and contractors—and it had enabled them to achieve political power, especially within the Democratic party.[61] But the Irish did not restrict participation in the machine to themselves; the machine that they were instrumental in creating was remarkably resilient, embracing representatives of other ethnic groups and extending its services to them as well. Even though the system came to include members of other ethnic groups, the Irish established patterns of political power, as they had done in the Church, that later immigrant groups found difficult to break. The Irish retained power long after their percentage of the population had declined in the face of the influx of "new" immigrants and, later, of black Americans—as in Richard J. Daley's Chicago of today.[62]

In the process the Irish "politicized" the social structure so that all activity—work as well as leisure—had political overtones. The economic structure of the Irish community became heavily dependent upon its retention of political power. Municipal jobs that were necessary to city functioning—most prominently in the police and fire departments, but in a multiplicity of other services, including utilities, sanitation, and transportation—were obtained through the machine. As the city expanded, public works provided a continuing source of opportunity for enterprising builders, and the contracting business became closely intertwined with the politics of urban development. Since the late nineteenth century the Irish have been more prominent in the building trades and construction than any other ethnic group, and the role of the "contractor boss," "the builder-developer with strong political ties and influence," has been central to the dynamics of Irish power.[63]

Since nativist eruptions against the Irish were identified primarily with the Federalist, Whig, Know-Nothing, and, later, Republican parties, it is not surprising that the Irish were, by and large, attracted to the Democratic party. In addition, the more egalitarian stance of the Democratic party appealed to the strong antiaristocratic, populist Irish tradition. The Democratic party was, as Levine noted, "the one social institution of consequence that did not spurn or derogate them."[64] Even before the Famine generation appeared, the Irish were solidly identified with the Democratic party, having cast an estimated 95 percent of their vote for the Democratic candidate in 1844.[65] And with some local deviations (e.g., Philadelphia),[66] the Irish remained the mainstay of the Democratic party in the North for well over a century.

Despite their success and power within the Democratic party and in municipal politics in urban areas throughout the North and East, it was not until the election of John Kennedy as president of the United States that the Irish could feel themselves to have been granted full equality in the political process. Paradoxically, however, if Kennedy's election marked the triumph of the Irish political tradition in America, it also symbolized its culmination. Glazer and Moynihan have nostalgically recalled the significance of John F. Kennedy to the entire experience of the Irish in America:

[John F. Kennedy] is gone, and there is none like him. Although he may yet emerge as the first of a new breed, all that is certain is that he was the last of an old one. The era of the Irish politician culminated in Kennedy. He was born to the work and was at every stage of his life a "pro." He rose on the willing backs of three generations of district leaders and county chairmen who, like Barabbas himself, may in the end have been saved for their one moment of recognition that something special had appeared among them. . . .

It was the last hurrah. He, the youngest and newest, served in a final moment of ascendancy. On the day he died, the President of the United States, the Speaker of the House of Representatives, the Majority Leader of the United States Senate, the Chairman of the National Committee were all Irish, all Catholic, all Democrats. It will not come again.[67]

The significance of John F. Kennedy's election transcends the Irish role in politics, however, for it symbolically occurred just as consciousness of Irish ethnicity—by Irish and non-Irish alike—was waning in American life. Having achieved "success" and "respectability" in America, the Irish-Americans' sense of their own ethnic identity has declined, if not vanished. (Even traditional Irish symbols, such as St. Patrick's Day, no longer evoke a distinctive ethnic identity but have become "Americanized.") And this has occurred at precisely the time in American life when it has become fashionable to be conscious of and to proclaim one's ethnicity. The Irish, whose comprehensive plural institutional system was designed to maintain their ethnic identity, have become fully culturally "integrated" into American society at the moment in American life when there has arisen an awareness that in the process of "integration" much of the value and integrity of one's ethnic heritage is lost. As Andrew Greeley has lamented, "the legitimation of ethnicity came too late for the American Irish."[68]

The decline of precisely those factors that had initially separated them from the larger society was what contributed to the decline of Irish ethnicity. Today the Irish have become fully respectable and virtually indistinguishable from their non-ethnic American counterparts. Their Catholic faith is generally no longer a hindrance but has become accepted as a legitimate manifestation of the "American way of life." Economically the Irish have been absorbed into the vast, amorphous American middle class, and the stereotype of the drunken, illiterate, ill-mannered, wild

Irishman has virtually vanished. Under the impact of these forces the class structure of the Irish community has become variegated, and their traditional loyalty to the Democratic party has been substantially eroded.[69]

Most importantly, the factors that most fully contributed to Irish identity and cohesion—the institutions of the Church and the school—have been substantially altered in the lives of the American Irish. The Church is no longer a primary integrating force for the Irish community, nor are the educational functions of the Church supported by that community. Whereas in nineteenth-century America the parish was the "focal point of the community or neighborhood, the social as well as religious center for its people," the contemporary American parish "stands only as a religious haven."[70] The contemporary Irish-Americans derive no sense of identity from the parish; they do not feel that they are part of the parish community, and few are active in its activities. The providing of social relations and a sense of community are functions that are now performed by secular voluntary association (such as business associations, country clubs, etc.). The Church has essentially ceased to perform these functions, and Biever has found that the Irish are not much inclined toward having the Church revive them. Although Irish-Americans remain strongly committed to Catholicism, they view their Church as essentially a religious organization, not as a social or community institution.[71]

Biever also found that a striking amount of criticism is directed toward the parochial-school system. The Irish today increasingly question the efficacy (let alone the financial wisdom) of maintaining separate schools when they appear to differ little from their public-school counterparts. In addition, Irish-Americans question the wisdom of retaining religious indoctrination. Most of them do not perceive that the parochial schools are essential to the maintenance of the Catholic faith, which is today no longer under direct attack from competing religious faiths. Indeed, many Irish-Americans agree that the needs of the nineteenth century justified the existence of parochial schools, but they are skeptical about whether these needs persisted in the America of the 1960s, where the Irish had entered into the mainstream of American society.[72] Thus the identity functions that the separate Catholic school system previously performed have declined.

This criticism of the parochial-school system reflects an increasing refusal of Irish-American laymen to accept traditional Catholic views uncritically. Since nowadays their educational attainments frequently equal or exceed those of the clergy, Irish Catholic laymen have increasingly demonstrated reluctance to base their respect for the Church or its representatives on traditional values or appeals to authority. The Irish-American community has produced many vigorous and devout Catholic laymen who, while not anticlerical, are skeptical, even cynical, of the traditional, legalistic stance of the Church on many issues and who seek far greater personal involvement in the determination of Church policy. According to Biever, such a critical stance is in marked contrast to the unquestioning acceptance in Ireland of the Church's claims to authority; thus, it would appear to serve as an excellent index of Irish acculturation.[73]

This emerging Irish-American intellectual vigor, as well as the decline of Irish political homogeneity, is unquestionably a consequence of increased educational attainments. Research at the National Opinion Research Center has revealed that the Irish had the highest level of educational attainment among Catholics, who, as noted above, have increased their representation in the academic world substantially since World War II. Moreover, it was found that Irish Catholics were now nearly twice as likely as the general American population to graduate from college. In addition, a 1968 survey of people who had graduated from college in 1961 showed that Irish-Americans were overrepresented in the physical and biological sciences. And despite the fact that their undergraduate training had been taken at less prestigious colleges and universities, the Irish who were pursuing scientific careers were more likely than members of any other ethnic or religious group to have attained a Ph.D. or to be working in an academic or research setting.[74] These data suggest that the commitment of Irish-Americans to scholarly endeavors has equaled, if not surpassed, that of other ethnic groups in the United States. Since these data are based upon very recent trends, it will be several decades before it will be possible to assess fully the effects that these changes will have upon Irish-American contributions to American intellectual life. But they do indicate very important changes in Irish-American society and culture.

A further index of the decline of Irish identity can be found in the indifference with which the American Irish have reacted to the Catholic-Protestant turmoil in Northern Ireland. Although the conflict has generated a resurgence of Irish-American organizations, the principal function of which is to raise funds to support the Catholic cause in Northern Ireland, leaders of these organizations have agreed that the response to their efforts among Irish-Americans has been meager.[75] The lack of enthusiasm for this cause is in distinct contrast to the intense identification with and support (both financial and emotional) for Irish nationalist causes that the American Irish have displayed in the past. To the American Irish, disruptions of established order have always been suspect.

*The Irish Experience in America*
371

Today, more affluent and more secure in their own identity as Americans, they appear to be even less sympathetic to the Ulster campaign, which has been characterized by violence and terrorism and which has adopted much of the revolutionary rhetoric of the black-liberation movement in the United States. Moreover, the establishment of an independent Ireland, despite the lingering question of Northern Ireland, appears to have undermined the issue of Irish nationalism, which for years provided a source of Irish identity in America.

Thus, despite the effort to preserve traditional Irish culture and values, which is manifested in the establishment of the separate Catholic institutional system, the immense changes that have transformed American life during the last century have left the American Irish increasingly remote from their ancestral roots in Ireland. Contemporary Irish-American character is derived not so much from the heritage of the past in Ireland as from the dynamics of the experience of the Irish in America. The final product is markedly different from the original. Bruce Biever's impressions of John F. Kennedy's visit to Ireland reflect the distance between the worlds of the contemporary native Irish and Irish-Americans:

> The overwhelming impression of the visitor . . . , as he watched the great outpouring of public veneration for John Kennedy by the throngs of Irish who lined the streets to welcome him, was that while they loved the man, gloried in his accomplishment and shared it with fierce Celtic pride, yet vast areas of this man's personality eluded their understanding. He was Irish and he was a Catholic,, but his understanding of these two realities and their own involved differences so momentous that they almost surpassed even token understanding. A typical comment offered by an Irish gentleman standing next to the author that day underlined this confusion: "It was nice of him to come, you know. It means a lot to our people, but you can't get around the impression that he is much more of you [American] than he is of us."[76]

# NOTES

1. William Forbes Adams, *Ireland and Irish Emigration to the New World from 1815 to the Famine* (New Haven, Conn.: Yale University Press, 1932); Arnold Schrier, *Ireland and the American Emigration, 1850–1900* (Minneapolis: Uni-

and the Italians: Politics in a Chicago Ward, 1896–1921," *Journal of American History* 57:67–84 (1970).

63. See Clark, "The Philadelphia Irish," in Davis and Haller, *The Peoples of Philadelphia*, p. 143; Glazer and Moynihan, *Beyond the Melting Pot*, p. 255.
64. Levine, *The Irish and Irish Politicians*, p. 7.
65. Duff, *The Irish in the United States*, p. 50.
66. Clark, "The Philadelphia Irish," in Davis and Haller, *The Peoples of Philadelphia*, pp. 141–42.
67. Glazer and Moynihan, *Beyond the Melting Pot*, p. 287.
68. Andrew H. Greeley, "The Last of the American Irish Fade Away," *New York Times Magazine*, 14 March 1971, p. 33.
69. Despite Irish defections from the more liberal Democratic party, a 1970 national survey of ethnic groups, including white Protestants, which was conducted by Andrew Greeley and his associates, found that the Irish were surpassed in their political liberalism only by the Jews. In contrast to the stereotype of the conservative, racist, hawkish Irish, it was found that support of both black and student militancy was stronger among the Irish than among any other white ethnic group except the Jews. The Irish also demonstrated strong opposition to the war in Southeast Asia, a finding that contradicts stereotypes of Irish-American superpatriotism. See Andrew M. Greeley, "Political Attitudes among American White Ethnics," *Public Opinion Quarterly* 36:213–20 (1972).
70. Biever, "Religion, Culture, and Values," p. 589.
71. Ibid., pp. 543–50.
72. Ibid., pp. 636–49.
73. Ibid., pp. 536, 551, 574.
74. Andrew M. Greeley, *Why Can't They Be Like Us?* (New York: E. P. Dutton, 1971), p. 71; and Greeley, "The Ethnic and Religious Origins of Young American Scientists and Engineers: A Research Note," *International Migration Review* 6:282–89 (1972).
75. Cf. "Backers of Ulster Minority Getting up Their Irish Here," *New York Times*, 2 December 1971, p. 49.
76. Biever, "Religion, Culture, and Values," p. 534.

## SUGGESTIONS FOR FURTHER READING

Adams, William Forbes. *Ireland and Irish Emigration to the New World from 1815 to the Famine.* New Haven, Conn.: Yale University Press, 1932.
Brown, Thomas N. *Irish-American Nationalism.* Philadelphia: Lippincott, 1966.
Clark, Dennis J. *The Irish in Philadelphia.* Philadelphia: Temple University Press, 1973.
Glazer, Nathan, and Moynihan, Daniel P., *Beyond the Melting Pot: The Negroes, Puerto Ricans, Jews, Italians, and Irish of New York City.* Cambridge, Mass.: M.I.T. Press, 1963.
Greeley, Andrew M. *Why Can't They Be Like Us?* New York: E. P. Dutton, 1971.
Handlin, Oscar. *Boston's Immigrants: A Study in Acculturation.* Rev. ed. New York: Atheneum, 1970.
Levine, Edward M. *The Irish and Irish Politicians.* Notre Dame, Ind.: University of Notre Dame Press, 1966.
Shannon, William V. *The American Irish.* Rev. ed. New York: Macmillan, 1966.
Thernstrom, Stephan. *Poverty and Progress: Social Mobility in a Nineteenth Century City.* New York: Atheneum, 1969.
Wittke, Carl F. *The Irish in America.* Baton Rouge: Louisiana State University Press, 1956.

versity of Minnesota Press, 1958); Robert E. Kennedy, Jr., *The Irish: Emigration, Marriage, and Fertility* (Berkeley: University of California Press, 1973).

2. Dennis J. Clark, "The Philadelphia Irish: A Persistent Presence" (paper presented at a conference on the History of Peoples of Philadelphia, Temple University, April 1–2, 1971), p. 2. See also Dennis J. Clark, "The Philadelphia Irish: Persistent Presence," in *The Peoples of Philadelphia*, ed. Allen F. Davis and Mark H. Haller (Philadelphia: Temple University Press, 1973), pp. 135–54, and Dennis J. Clark, *The Irish in Philadelphia* (Philadelphia: Temple University Press, 1973).
3. Kennedy, *The Irish*, p. 75.
4. For a study of efforts to settle the Irish in the rural Midwest see James P. Shannon, *Catholic Colonization on the Western Frontier* (New Haven, Conn.: Yale University Press, 1957).
5. Oscar Handlin, *Boston's Immigrants: A Study in Acculturation* (rev. ed.; New York: Atheneum, 1970), p. 37; Robert Ernst, *Immigrant Life in New York City, 1825–1863* (New York: King's Crown Press, 1949), p. 62. Fred Shannon estimated that in 1860 at least $1,000 was needed for the transportation and equipment that was necessary to begin an agricultural enterprise and that later in the nineteenth century this amount increased. See Fred A. Shannon, "A Post Mortem on the Labor-Safety-Valve Theory," *Agricultural History* 19:31–37 (1945).
6. William Forbes Adams argued that the expenses of migration during the Famine were borne primarily by the American Irish, who returned more than £20 million to Ireland in 1863 alone. Adams, *Ireland and Irish Immigration*, p. 392. Kennedy estimated that three-fourths of the money supporting Irish immigration between 1848 and 1900 came from Irish-Americans. See Kennedy, *The Irish*, p. 22. This pattern of monetary support for families (and nationalist causes) continued well into the twentieth century. Without this strong demonstration of communal support, the scale of Irish migration to America would have been substantially diminished. See also Clark, "The Philadelphia Irish," p. 31.
7. Kennedy, *The Irish*, p. 75.
8. Thomas N. Brown, "The Origins and Character of Irish-American Nationalism," *Review of Politics* 18:328–29 (1956).
9. Edward M. Levine, *The Irish and Irish Politicians* (Notre Dame, Ind.: University of Notre Dame Press, 1966), p. 58. See also Brown, "The Origins and Character of Irish-American Nationalism," p. 328; and James P. Shannon, *Catholic Colonization.*
10. U.S. Congress, Senate, *Documents*, 61st Cong., 3d sess., 1910–1911, U.S. Immigration Commission, *Reports of the Immigration Commission: Statistical Review of Immigration, 1820–1910*, 20:7, 20–48. The sexual identity of immigrants was recorded only after 1868. During the period 1869 to 1910 there were twenty years during which the number of female Irish immigrants exceeded that of males, and in the remainder, the sex ratio was nearly balanced. Among *all* other national groups there were only two years during this period when females outnumbered males: in 1897 and 1898 a slight preponderance of Swedish immigrants was female.
11. Handlin, *Boston's Immigrants*, p. 177.
12. Norman R. Yetman and C. Hoy Steele, eds., *Majority and Minority: The Dynamics of Racial and Ethnic Relations* (2d ed.; Boston: Allyn & Bacon, 1975), pp. 233–35.
13. Ernst, *Immigrant Life*, pp. 54–55; Stephan Thernstrom, *Poverty and Progress: Social Mobility in a Nineteenth Century City* (New York: Atheneum, 1969), p. 172.

14. Emmet Larkin, "The Devotional Revolution in Ireland, 1850–75," *American Historical Review* 77:651 (1972). See also Ernst, *Immigrant Life*; Handlin, *Boston's Immigrants*; and Clark, "The Philadelphia Irish," in Davis and Haller, *The Peoples of Philadelphia*.
15. Brown, "The Origins and Character of Irish-American Nationalism," p. 332. The term was coined by the Irish themselves.
16. John Tracy Ellis, *American Catholicism* (2d ed., rev.; Chicago: University of Chicago Press, 1969), p. 68.
17. For a discussion of Irish Catholic militancy see Handlin, *Boston's Immigrants*, pp. 185–87; and Bruce F. Biever, "Religion, Culture, and Values: A Cross-Cultural Analysis of Motivational Factors in Native Irish and American Irish Catholicism" (Ph.D. diss., University of Pennsylvania, 1965), pp. 564–717.
18. Biever, "Religion, Culture, and Values," pp. 717–23.
19. Ibid., p. 723.
20. Aaron I. Abell, *American Catholic Thought on Social Questions* (Indianapolis, Ind.: Bobbs-Merrill, 1968), p. xxi.
21. Levine, *The Irish and Irish Politicians*, pp. 91–92.
22. Handlin, *Boston's Immigrants*, p. 176.
23. See note 39 below.
24. Larkin, "The Devotional Revolution in Ireland," p. 649.
25. Biever, "Religion, Culture, and Values," p. 716. See also Thernstrom, *Poverty and Progress*, p. 179.
26. Levine, *The Irish and Irish Politicians*, p. 78.
27. Milton M. Gordon, "Assimilation in America: Theory and Reality," *Daedalus* 90:263–85 (1961).
28. Larkin, "The Devotional Revolution in Ireland." Thomas N. Brown has similarly argued that the experience of the Irish in the United States was heavily and continually conditioned by events in Ireland. See his *Irish-American Nationalism, 1870–1890* (Philadelphia: Lippincott, 1966).
29. Larkin, "The Devotional Revolution in Ireland"; Clark, "The Philadelphia Irish," in Davis and Haller, *The Peoples of Philadelphia*.
30. Biever, "Religion, Culture, and Values," p. 533.
31. John B. Duff, *The Irish in the United States* (Belmont, Calif.: Wadsworth Pub. Co., 1971), p. 73.
32. Biever, "Religion, Culture, and Values," p. 533.
33. Carl F. Wittke, *The Irish in America* (Baton Rouge: Louisiana State University Press, 1956), pp. 91–92.
34. See Rudolph J. Vecoli, "Prelates and Peasants: Italian Immigrants and the Catholic Church," *Journal of Social History* 2:217–68 (1969).
35. Duff, *The Irish in the United States*, p. 76; Biever, "Religion, Culture, and Values."
36. Quoted in Robert D. Cross, *The Emergence of Liberal Catholicism in America* (Cambridge, Mass.: Harvard University Press, 1958), p. 35.
37. Biever, "Religion, Culture, and Values," pp. 540–90.
38. Nathan Glazer and Daniel P. Moynihan, *Beyond the Melting Pot: The Negroes, Puerto Ricans, Jews, Italians, and Irish of New York City* (Cambridge, Mass.: M.I.T. Press, 1963), p. 230; Clark, "The Philadelphia Irish," in Davis and Haller, *The Peoples of Philadelphia*, pp. 139–40; Thernstrom, *Poverty and Progress*, pp. 176–77. See also Levine, *The Irish and Irish Politicians*, pp. 77–78.
39. Although the Irish were prominent in the parochial-school movement, their support was not so enthusiastic as that of German Catholics, who felt that separate schools were needed in order to preserve their language. Robert D. Cross, "Origins of the Catholic Parochial Schools in America," *American Benedictine Review* 16:194–209 (1965).
40. Ellis, *American Catholicism*, p. 137.
41. Andrew M. Greeley and Peter H. Rossi, *The Education of Catholic Americans* (Chicago: Aldine, 1966), pp. 53–76. For the effects of Catholic education upon fertility values see Charles F. Westoff and Raymond H. Potvin, *College Women and Fertility Values* (Princeton, N.J.: Princeton University Press, 1967), pp. 39–49.
42. Robert H. Knapp and H. B. Goodrich, *Origins of American Scientists* (Chicago: University of Chicago Press, 1952); Robert H. Knapp, *The Origins of American Humanistic Scholars* (Englewood Cliffs, N.J.: Prentice-Hall, 1964). In contrast to the relatively small number of scholars, Catholic institutions were characterized by an extremely high productivity of lawyers. This situation was congruent with Irish prominence in, and their pragmatic attitude toward, political affairs.
43. Thomas F. O'Dea, *The American Catholic Dilemma* (New York: Sheed & Ward, 1958), p. 152. See also John Tracy Ellis, "American Catholics and the Intellectual Life," *Thought* 30:351–88 (1955).
44. Richard Hofstadter, *Anti-Intellectualism in American Life* (New York: Knopf, 1963), p. 138.
45. Quoted in Glazer and Moynihan, *Beyond the Melting Pot*, p. 238.
46. Stephen Steinberg, *The Academic Melting Pot: Catholics and Jews in American Higher Education* (New York: McGraw-Hill, 1974).
47. Brown, *Irish-American Nationalism*, pp. 20–23.
48. Quoted in Brown, "The Origins and Character of Irish-American Nationalism," p. 327.
49. Ibid., and Thomas N. Brown, "Social Discrimination against the Irish in the United States" (unpublished paper, American Jewish Committee, 1958).
50. Brown, "Social Discrimination," p. 23.
51. Glazer and Moynihan, *Beyond the Melting Pot*, p. 223.
52. Levine, *The Irish and Irish Politicians*.
53. Clark, "The Philadelphia Irish," in Davis and Haller, *The Peoples of Philadelphia*, p. 141.
54. See, for example, Seymour Mandelbaum, *Boss Tweed's New York* (New York: J. Wiley, 1965), and Zane L. Miller, "Boss Cox's Cincinnati: A Study of Urbanization and Politics, 1880–1914," *Journal of American History* 54:8[23]–38 (1968).
55. Glazer and Moynihan, *Beyond the Melting Pot*, pp. 227–28.
56. Ibid., p. 226.
57. Although the Irish have been generally distrustful of radical—even refo[rm] political movements, there has been a persistent radical strain among [Irish] Americans, one that is not unrelated to British exploitation and the Irish [inde]pendence movement. Among the more prominent Irish-American radicals [were] the Populists Ignatius Donnelly and Mary Ellen Lease, who gained fa[me] allegedly urging Kansas farmers to "raise less corn and more hell," and Co[mmu]nist leaders William Z. Foster and Elizabeth Gurley Flynn. Irishmen [were] prominent in the radical IWW, as well as in the Irish secret society [the] Molly Maguires, which sought to obtain social justice in the anthraci[te] mines of nineteenth-century Pennsylvania.
58. Brown, "Social Discrimination," p. 30.
59. William V. Shannon, *The American Irish* (rev. ed.; New York: Ma[cmillan,] 1966), p. 67.
60. Glazer and Moynihan, *Beyond the Melting Pot*, p. 229.
61. Milton L. Barron, "Intermediacy: Conceptualization of Irish Status in A[merica," *Social Forces* 27:256–63 (1949).
62. For an interesting case study of the capacity of Irish politicians to reta[in power] despite ethnic changes in their constituency see Humbert S. Nelli, "Joh[n

# INDEX

Bishop Cormac MacCarthy (*see* Mac-Carthy, Cormac)
Bishops' War, 122
Black and Tans, 338
Black Death (1348), 204
Blake, William, 296
Boland's Mill, 338
*Book of Armagh*, 172
*Book of Durrow*, 62, 64, 72–73, 172
*Book of Kells*, 46, 56, 58, 61, 64, 69, 71–73, 76, 106, 172, 286
Boorde, Dr. Andrew, *The Fyrst Boke of the Introduction of Knowledge*, 133
*Boston Pilot*, 299
Boycott, Captain, 244
Boyd, Ernest, 303
Boyle Abbey, 102
Boyle, William, 264
Boyne, Battle of the, 127, 296
Boyne River, 29, 179–80
Bradford, Curtis, 302
Bres, 130
Bretons, 28
Brian Boru, 33, 34, 87, 94, 99, 234; Harp of, 106
Britain, 26, 29, 30, 32
Brittany, 26
Brogan, 22
Broghill, 124
Bronze Age, 49
Brown, Thomas N., 365–66
Budgen, Frank, 324
Builg, 28
Burgh, Colonel Thomas, 171
Burgh, Lord, 116
Burghs, De, 37
Burke, Edmund, 156, 292, 303
Burke, Kenneth, 318
Burlington, Lord, 172
Bushrui, S. B., 302
Butler family, 38, 105, 110, 113, 123
Butler, James, 105
Butler, Sir Piers, 104
Butt, Isaac, 246–47
Byron, Lord, 235
Byzantium, 73, 304–5

Cailte, 18
Cambrensis, Giraldus, 286; *Topography of Ireland*, 69, 71
Camden, earl of, 161
Campbell, Colin, *Vitruvius Britannicus*, 173
Candlemas, 131
Canterbury, 31, 32

Carlisle, Nicolas, 182
Carlow, 37, 109
Carlyle, Thomas, 237, 252
Carolingian ivories and manuscripts, 82
Carson, E. H. C., 332–33, 334, 335
Carteret, 155
Cashel, Rock of, 99
Cassel, Richard, 172
Castlereagh, 228, 229
Cathach of St. Columba, 62
Catholic, 115, 117, 119, 120, 121, 122, 125–27, 135, 138, 143, 147, 150, 154, 157–58, 161, 162, 218, 226, 233, 236, 241, 247, 249, 313, 331, 333, 339, 340, 341, 342, 343, 348, 355, 356, 357, 361, 362, 363, 364, 369–71, 372; Home Rulers, 246, 247; restrictions on, 148; restrictions removed, 160; persecution of, 162; Relief Bill, 161
Catholic Association, 231–32
Catholic Church, 118, 238, 240, 360, 370
Catholic Committee, 161
Catholic Daughters of America, 360
Catholic Emancipation, 161, 162, 163, 229, 233, 241, 246
Cattle Acts (1663), 152
Cattle Raid of Cooley, 51
Caulfeild, James, 172
Celts, 6, 9, 25, 26, 28, 29, 30, 34, 43, 44, 52, 58, 59, 62, 114, 135, 136, 137, 138, 192, 253, 271, 279, 283, 361, 364; art of, 104, 278; language of, 165; La Tène, 49, 51; P-, 28; period of, 76; Q-, 28; tribes of, 5
Chambers, William, 172, 173
Charlemont House, 172, 278
Charles I, 105, 120, 123–24
Charles II, 72, 105, 125, 126, 147
Chartists, 233
Chatterji, Mohini, 296
Chesterfield, 155
Chichester, Sir Arthur, 118, 119, 120
Chi-Rho, 59
Christ, 59, 60, 81, 82
Christian Democracy, 330
Christianity, 25, 26, 84; conversion of Vikings to, 34; era of, 50; rise of, 30, 31, 138
Churchill, Winston, 333, 336
Cistercian, 102; abbey, 104
Civil War, 360–61
Clann Baiscne, 20, 21
Clann Morna, 20, 21

Rocks, The," 324; MISCELLANE-
OUS: "Et Tu, Healy," 314–15;
"Holy Office, The," 316; "Trieste
Notebook," 323
Joyce, Myles, 313
Joyce, Stanislaus, 318, 319, 325

Kammeyer, Kenneth, 348, 351
Keane, 89
Keats, John, 235
Kelleher, John V., 253
Kells, Abbot of, 139; church at, 100
*Kells, Book of* (see *Book of Kells*)
Kennedy, John F., 355, 368–69
Kennedy, Robert E., Jr., 218
Kenner, Hugh, 321–22
Keppel, 149 (*see* Albermarle, Arnold)
Kerry, 110, 230
Kettle, Thomas, 330
Kettle, Tilly, 175–76
Kickham, Charles, 262
Kildare, 31; earl of, 38, 104, 109, 112
Kilkenny, 37, 156
Killaloe, 168
Kilmainham, 314
Kilmalkedar, 58
Kiltartan, 256
Kimball, 215, 219
King Goll, poem about, 294
King's County, 120
Kluckhohn, Clyde, 130
Knapp, Robert H., 362
Knights of Columbus, 360
Know-Nothing party, 355, 368
Ku Klux Klan, 355

*Labor Gabala*, 25
Lacy, Hugh de, 94–95
Lacy, Hugo de, 35
Lacy, Walter de, 95, 97; daughter, Ma-
tilda, 97
Lancastrian, 110, 113
Land Act (1870), 213; (1881), 244
Land League, 244–45
Lane, Sir Hugh, 275–78, 301; collection
of paintings, "Old Masters from
Irish Exhibitions," 275–78
Larkin, Emmet, 358; "The Devotional
Revolution in Ireland, 1850–75," 359
Last Judgment, 81
La Tène, 28
Latin Culture, 31
Laugier, Abbé Marc-Antoine, 172
Lazarus, Emma, 354
*Leader*, 262

Lecky, W. E. H., 304
Leinster, 5, 17, 28, 33, 35, 115, 138; king
of, 35, 94
Leix, 114
Lent, 135
Leslie, Shane, 324
Lever, Charles, 255
Levin, Harry, 323, 324
Levine, Edward, 357, 368
Lewis, Samuel, 182
Lhuyd, Edward, 165
Liberal, 249, 313, 332–33
Liberal party, 149, 238, 241, 248, 331
Liberator (*see* O'Connell, Daniel)
Limerick, 33, 110, 127, 168
Lindesfarne, 31–32; Northumbrian mon-
astery of, 79
Lisburn, 152
Lismore Castle, 90
Lismore Crosier, 90
Little Bell of Gold (*see* Bell of Saint
Senan)
Liverpool, 237
Londonderry, 119
Longford, 120
Longinus, 81
Louis XIV, 147
Louis XV, 172
Lover, Samuel, 255
Lug, 9, 12
Lughnasa (*see* Assumption)
*Lusitania*, 277
Lutyens, Sir Edward, 276
Lyons (France), 9

MacCarthy, Cormac, 99
MacCumail, Finn (*see* Finn MacCumail)
MacDurthacht, Eogan, 7
MacGreevy, Thomas, 279, 282, 285
Macha, 7
Maclise, Daniel, *The Marriage of Eva
and Strongbow*, 271
MacManus, Reverend Henry, 140
MacMorna, Goll (*see* Goll MacMorna)
Macready, General, 339
MacRoth, 16
Malachy, 33
Malton, James, 173
Manet, Edouard, 275
Marino, casino at, 172
Marsh, Archbishop Narcissus, 171; library
of, 169
Martyn, Edward, 254, 258, 260, 261,
273; *The Heather Field*, 258

Wilson, Edmund, *Axel's Castle*, 252
Winchester, 31
Wolsey, Cardinal, 113
Wood, Robert, 172
Woodham-Smith, Cecil, 202
Woolfe, John, 173
World War I, 334, 336
World War II, 341, 364, 371
Wren, Sir Christopher, 173
Wright, Thomas, 165–69; *Observations on Some of the most Remarkable Remains of Antiquity in Ireland*, 168–69

Yeats, Jack, 279, 281; ILLUSTRATIONS: *Irish Readers*, 281–82; *Lament for Art O'Leary, A*, 284
Yeats, John Butler, 263, 273, 274, 275, 279
Yeats, William Butler, 106, 251–53, 254, 255, 257–59, 260–62, 263, 264, 265, 266–67, 272–73, 279, 282, 291–308, 312, 320, 321, 322; BOOKS: *Celtic Twilight, The*, 297, 299, 300, 322; *Collected Poems, Definitive Edition*, 298, 302; *Collected Works*, 303; *Fairy and Folk Tales of the Irish Peasantry*, 299; *Irish Fairy Tales*, 299; *Representative Irish Tales*, 299; *Stories from Carleton*, 299; *Variorum Edition of the Poems*, 302; *Vision, A*, 295, 303; *Wind Among the Reeds, The*, 260, 296, 300; PLAYS: *Cathleen ni Houlihan*, 261, 262, 273, 275, 299; *Countess Cathleen, The*, 258–60, 306; *Countess Kathleen and Various Legends and Lyrics, The*, 299; *Diarmuid and Grania*, 266; *Island of Statues, The*, 253, 298; *Land of Heart's Desire, The*, 258; *Mosada*, 296; *On Baile's Strand*, 306; *Player Queen, The*, 295; *Words upon the Windowpane, The*, 303; SHORTER WORKS: "Apparitions, The," 305–6; "Celebrations," 265; "Circus Animals' Desertion, The," 306; "Death of Synge, The," 263; "Detractions," 265; "Easter 1916," 301; "Lake Isle of Innisfree, The," 299; "Legend, A," 298; "Man and the Echo, The," 299; "Municipal Gallery Revisited, The," 305; "Reveries," 254; "Song of the Happy Shepherd, The," 298; "To a Friend Whose Work Has Come to Nothing," 278; "To a Shade," 278; "To Ireland in the Coming Times," 257–58; "Trembling of the Veil, The," 251, 294; "Under Ben Bulben," 306; "Wanderings of Oisin, The," 296–98, 306
York, 31, 109
Young Ireland movement, 233, 234, 241, 253

Zola, Émile, 252, 257